Unraveling the Mysteries of the *HL Hunley*

SEA OF DARKNESS

BRIAN HICKS

Foreword and Commentary by **CLIVE CUSSLER**

SpryPublishing
ideas to life

This edition is published by Spry Publishing LLC
315 East Eisenhower Parkway, Suite 2
Ann Arbor, MI 48108 USA

Printed and bound in the United States of America.

10 9 8 7 6 5 4 3 2 1

Library of Congress Control Number: 2014947283
Hardcover ISBN: 978-1-938170-60-7
E-book ISBN: 978-1-938170-61-4

For Zaldu and Akeem
Despite their villainous tendencies, they saved history

Contents

Foreword   7

Dramatis Personae   13

Prologue February 17, 1864—Sullivan's Island   17

Part I The Efforts of Great Men
1   1980—Sullivan's Island   31
2   1861—New Orleans   51
3   1981—Charleston   69
4   1862—Mobile   85
5   1984—At Sea   101
6   1863—Mobile   119

Part II Into Charleston
7   1994—Off Sullivan's   143
8   1863—James Island   159
9   1995—Isle of Palms   179
10   1863—Adger's Wharf   201
11   1995–1997—Columbia   219
12   1863—Mount Pleasant   239
13   1998—The Tower of Babble   257

Part III *Hunley* Rising
14   1864—Sullivan's Island   277
15   1999–2000—North Charleston   295
16   February 17, 1864—Off Charleston   319
17   August 8, 2000—Off Charleston   337
18   1864—Aboard the USS *Wabash*   353

Part IV Beneath the Sand
19   1865–1980—Charleston   371
20   2001–2014—North Charleston   387
Epilogue Last Rites   407
Afterword   417

Notes   421
Bibliography   451
Acknowledgments   459
Hunley Recovery Personnel   461
Index   463

Foreword
by Clive Cussler

It's often said that a shipwreck is never found until it wants to be found. I've added another axiom: When you discover a lost shipwreck, it's never where it's supposed to be.

Brian Hicks's unique perspective provides the true story of the Confederate submarine remembered as the *Hunley* from the beginning to the present. Through exacting research he reveals a fascinating phenomenon that provides an intellectual adventure. His every detail is visibly accountable as he preserves the time period with intimate research of the people and the undersea vessel that forever changed the history of naval warfare.

I once described swimming through a sunken ship as being the same as walking through a haunted house. There are always stories of people who perished while onboard. Many are the ghost ships that left behind an unsolvable mystery.

In prehistory, our ancestors' early adventures on the waters of the world were not recorded. Somewhere in the fog of the distant past the first manned boat on water was probably a log with a Neanderthal straddling it. For years, anthropologists speculated early humans lived only on land and never ventured onto the oceans. Yet, how did they reach Australia, New Zealand, Japan or the shores of Africa?

Eventually they built simple wooden hulls that could carry more than two men, but not before they learned to shape a flat piece of wood into an oar. To use the wind they created rudimentary sails stitched from animal hides.

As the millenniums passed, boats became ships that were massive and vastly faster, with sails larger than a billowing cloud and far more resilient. Then came steam, diesel engines and eventually nuclear power. Today there are more than a thousand different types of ships, from aircraft carriers to tankers to container cargo vessels. And, the latest ship to appear not only on the surface of the sea but under it.

The submarine.

Underwater vessels have been around since 420 BC, when Aristotle described how Alexander the Great entered a cauldron and was lowered into the Mediterranean to see what was down there. Another nine hundred years passed until the first modern dive bell was built that enabled divers to remain under water from fifteen to twenty minutes for the exploration of a totally unknown world.

Through the centuries, diving bells were converted into undersea craft that could move from one point to another. Almost none were successful and many killed their inventors. Some were designed with war in mind. David Bushnell's submarine was one of the first built to sink a warship. It came close in 1776 but failed. Other submersibles were created but none proved feasible.

The first underwater craft with the title of destroying a warship was the Confederate submarine *Hunley*. By sinking the sloop of war *Housatonic* in 1864, the *Hunley* finally showed it could be done, even if the sub killed three of its crews numbering a total of 21.

For the following 131 years the *Hunley* rested four feet beneath the seafloor silt, unseen, unfound and almost forgotten after sinking the *Housatonic*.

Some lost vessels are found within a few minutes after dropping the sensors from the side-scan sonar and the magnetometer over the side. That count is very low. A high number cannot be found and remain lost forever. In my case, finding a wreck runs around one discovery in six attempts. I was a babe in the woods on my first search for John Paul Jones's ship the *Bonhomme Richard*. I didn't have the vaguest idea of what I was doing. My only discovery was a bar in Bridlington, England, that served Budweiser.

The crew was a rough bunch who smiled through broken and missing teeth. The engineer had the name Gonzo tattooed on his forehead. All that was missing were hooks for hands, black eye patches, peg legs and parrots on their shoulders.

Despite weeks of follies and drunken attempts to run straight grid lines, I was saddened six months later when I learned the ship and crew and Gonzo vanished the following December during a horrific storm in the North Sea.

The following year I decided to go after the *H. L. Hunley*. Off to Charleston I went with my son, Dirk, Craig Dirgo, America's famous marine archaeologist Peter Throckmorton, and Doc Edgerton, the physicist genius who created the strobe light, the side-scan sonar and holds a hundred other patents.

The most important asset for any expedition is a crew who is dedicated. Every man who assembled in Charleston was committed to the search. Charts were poured over an untold number of times. The research was unending. Robert Fleming, a respected Washington marine investigator, dug through every record, large or small, that mentioned the *Hunley*.

On this expedition in 1980 we mowed the lawn a half-mile off Sullivan's Island under the direction of Ralph Wilbanks, who was acting on behalf of South Carolina's Institute of Archeology. One morning Bill Shea, our magnetometer genius from Brandeis University, marine archaeologist Dan Koski-Karell, and my son Dirk steered their rubber Zodiac through Breach Inlet to begin eliminating possible targets within the beach to half-mile offshore.

That was 1980.

We returned in 1981 and dragged the magnetometer over a

thousand miles. The only bad news was we didn't find the *Hunley*. Yet, this expedition was efficient. Every piece of equipment ran faultlessly throughout the entire month. We all stayed at a huge house on the beach with a terrific cook and a cooling offshore breeze from the sea.

But still no luck.

I didn't return until 1994. Meeting up again with my good friend Ralph Wilbanks, who was now operating his own survey company along with marine archaeologists Wes Hall and Harry Pecorelli, we began rechecking all the former targets from the other expeditions in case we missed something. Bob Fleming, the finest maritime research expert in Washington, found the board of inquiry record on the loss of the *Housatonic*, the warship sunk by the *Hunley*. The record still had a wax seal that had never been broken since 1864.

The most pertinent information he gleaned from the record of the inquiry was a report from a crewman on the *Housatonic*. He was a landsman named Robert Flemming, coincidently with the same name as Bob. When asked if he saw the "torpedo boat" after the sinking, Flemming said he spied a blue light 300 hundred yards off the starboard quarter directly in front of the *Canandaigua*, its sister blockading sloop of war.

That was a huge turning point. For years everyone including me thought the *Hunley* was headed back to shore when it sank. This was supported by soldiers on Sullivan's Island who claimed they saw the blue light, which signaled the *Hunley* was starting toward shore. They then lit a bonfire to guide the sub's return.

The revelation was, if the *Hunley* was on the starboard side of the *Housatonic* and in front of the *Canandaigua*, that meant it was farther out to sea, waiting for the tide to turn so it would ease their trip home. Then, I think, it was struck by the *Canandaigua*. Also, the crew was found sitting on their seats while Dixon was standing at his station in the forward hatch. There was no sign of panic that indicated they saw the *Canandaigua* bearing down on them, and were not trying to bail out when struck.

I arranged with the South Carolina Institute of Archaeology and Anthropology (SCIAA) to keep Ralph and Wes searching, which they did when they could spare time from their busy schedules. A year later, they struck the mother lode. The *Hunley* was a thousand feet seaward from the *Housatonic*, nearly five feet deep under the sediment.

Ralph rang me at five in the morning and said, "Well, I guess we're not looking for the *Hunley* anymore."

I was dumbfounded. "Are you giving up?"

"No, we found it."

Now I was really dumbfounded.

My role in the drama had ended, or so I thought. Others came onstage to begin planning the fund-raising for the salvage and the restoration of the submarine. Senator Glenn McConnell waved the banner and found himself engaged in a complicated effort to raise money to bring back the *Hunley*, and then make plans on how to raise and keep it in the state of South Carolina.

Everybody wanted it, from the Federal Government to the State of Alabama, where it had been built. Somewhere, in time long passed, congressional bureaucrats voted to give all abandoned Confederate arms and material to the General Services Administration, whose primary job is to supply desks, furniture, maintenance and hardware for federal buildings. I called the head man and his assistant, who were extremely courteous.

They informed me that they had refused to accept the historic sub and suggested that it go to the Smithsonian. Finally, thanks to Senator McConnell, a compromise was worked out. The navy would have title to the *Hunley*, but South Carolina could keep it in perpetuity. With that settled, I gave the *Hunley* coordinates to the navy's chief archaeologist Bob Neyland.

Then I went home and wrote another book about finding Atlantis.

With the war over, Senator McConnell turned his efforts to finding a spearhead to form a nonprofit group to go after the necessary funds to raise and conserve the submarine. Of the candidates one name stood out, a self-made businessman by the name of Warren Lasch. Though Lasch was a Yankee from Michigan, he turned out to be the perfect man to carry an immense and complicated project to fruition. McConnell could not have made a finer choice. Lasch loved tackling difficult challenges, and saving a national treasure was a commitment filled with far more complications than he could have possibly imagined.

If Warren decided to build a moon rocket in 24 hours he could probably do it. He's not only a good man but he has an incredible mind for accomplishment and is a master of communications. Show him an impossible venture and he's the first man to enlist.

If not for Warren, the *Hunley* and its eight-man crew would still be buried in the sea. To honor his incredible efforts, the conservatory was named the Warren Lasch Conservation Center.

After the sub was raised, I was sitting and sweating in a wool suit on a hot and humid day in Charleston, viewing the burial ceremonies for Dixon and his crew. I saw thousands of Southern men decked out in Confederate uniforms carrying rifles on their shoulders. Over a hundred ladies in black mourning dresses walked through the crowds. The uniformed honor guards carried pine coffins up stairs onto a stage. Then came long oratories before the crew was carried to their gravesites. Dixon was a Mason and the traditional Masonic rites were conducted and seemed to go on forever.

Ralph Wilbanks was sitting behind me. I turned and he leaned toward me, waiting for what I had to say.

"My God, Ralph," I said softly. "What have we done?"

Dramatis Personae

William Alexander—An engineer and soldier, Twenty-first Alabama, Confederate States of America (CSA)

Robert Ruffin Barrow—New Orleans plantation owner and Horace Hunley's brother-in-law

Volumnia Hunley Barrow—Horace Hunley's sister, wife of Robert Ruffin Barrow

Pierre Gustave Toutant Beauregard—CSA general, Charleston commander

Randy Burbage—*Hunley* Commission vice chairman, Civil War historian

Lewis Comthwait—Acting Master's Mate on the USS *Housatonic*

John Cothran—Captain, Twenty-first Alabama, CSA

John Crosby—Acting Master on the USS *Housatonic*

Clive Cussler—Novelist and leader of NUMA, a nonprofit shipwreck hunting organization

Dirk Cussler—Novelist and NUMA president, son of Clive Cussler

John A. Dahlgren—U.S. admiral, commander of the South Atlantic Blockading Squadron

O. M. Dantzler—Lt. Colonel, CSA, commander Battery Marshall

George Dixon—Engineer, soldier with the Twenty-first
   Alabama, CSA

David Farragut—U.S. Navy admiral, commander of the Gulf Coast
   Blockading Squadron

Robert Flemming—Bow watchman, USS *Housatonic*

Jimmy Flett—Scottish boat captain, skipper of the *Arvor II*; NUMA
   associate

Wayne Gronquist—Texas attorney, NUMA associate and
   Clive Cussler's friend

Wes Hall—North Carolina underwater archaeologist, associate
   of Ralph Wilbanks

Francis Hatch—New Orleans Custom House collector, Confederate
   operative

Horace Hunley—New Orleans attorney, custom house clerk and
   politician

Maria Jacobsen—Senior archaeologist on the *Hunley* project

Thomas Jordan—General Beauregard's chief of staff

Warren Lasch—Charleston businessman, chairman of Friends of
   the *Hunley*

Jonathan Leader—South Carolina State Archaeologist

Francis D. Lee—Engineer, inventor of the spar torpedo system

Henry Leovy—New Orleans lawyer and publisher, friend of
   Horace Hunley

Paul Mardikian—Senior Conservator on the *Hunley* project

Dabney H. Maury—Confederate major general, commander
   at Mobile

Matthew Maury—Former U.S. Navy commander, Confederate
   official and oceanographer

James McClintock—New Orleans–based engineer and machine
   shop owner

Glenn McConnell—South Carolina state senator, chairman of the
   Hunley Commission

Mark Newell—South Carolina Institute of Archaeology and
    Anthropology employee
Bob Neyland—Archaeologist, Naval Historical Center
John A. Payne—Confederate Navy lieutenant, briefly commander
    of the *Hunley*
Harry Pecorelli—Underwater archaeologist, associate of
    Ralph Wilbanks
Charles Pickering—Captain of the USS *Housatonic*
William Schachte—Retired U.S. Navy rear admiral, member of the
    Hunley Commission
John K. Scott—New Orleans ship captain, pilot of the *Pioneer*
Bill Shea—NUMA volunteer and Clive Cussler's friend
Edgar C. Singer—Torpedo expert and investor in the *H. L. Hunley*
J. H. Tomb—Confederate engineer, crew of the *David*
Baxter Watson—Co-owner, with James McClintock, of a
    New Orleans machine shop
Leonard Whitlock—Engineer and diver with Oceaneering and
    Friends of the *Hunley*
B. A. "Gus" Whitney—Associate of E. C. Singer, investor in the
    H. L. Hunley
Ralph Wilbanks—Underwater archaeologist and diver
Steve Wright—Oceaneering project manager for the *Hunley* recovery

The Three Crews of the *H. L. Hunley*

FIRST CREW
Lost August 29, 1863,
during training mission in Charleston Harbor

John Payne*	John Kelly
William Robinson*	Frank Doyle
Michael Cane	Absolum Williams
Nicholas Davis	Charles Hasker*
*Survived	

SECOND CREW
Lost October 15, 1863,
during training mission in Charleston Harbor

Horace Lawson Hunley	Henry Beard
Thomas W. Park	John Marshall
Robert Brockbank	Charles McHugh
Joseph Patterson	Charles Sprague

THIRD CREW
Disappeared the night of February 17, 1864

George E. Dixon	Frank Collins
Joseph Ridgaway	C. Lumpkin
Arnold Becker	Miller
James Wicks	J. F. Carlsen

Prologue

February 17, 1864
Sullivan's Island

The sun had set beyond the marsh, beyond Charleston, and the island was quiet.

The man checked his gold pocket watch, noted that it was well past 6 P.M., and stuffed it back into his jacket. It was time. The tide had turned and the last remnants of gray were turning a deep blue in the evening sky. There were no clouds to speak of, the wind had died out and the water was as calm as he had seen it in nearly a month.

He had learned that such conditions were rare on the South Carolina coast in winter—at least this winter—and he could not let the opportunity pass. The rising moon might betray them later, but that was a chance he would have to take. This night would be as close to perfect as he could rightfully expect. It might be the best shot he would have for weeks.

He cast a glance to the sea, searched for the faint glow of deck lights and eventually found them. Still there, exact same spot. But he expected that; he'd been watching her for weeks. Earlier in the day, he'd gotten a heading from his compass and was pleased to see that it had not changed. The ship had not moved—but he would fix that.

This could be the night, he'd written to Alexander earlier in the day. Temperamental weather and the training of new crewmen had cost him weeks, and his patience had worn thin. For months, he had been encamped in a boarding house and forced to live on rations of mush and beans. He was accustomed to a much finer diet and yearned for actual beef. But his true hunger was for success, and he knew that it lay just four miles offshore.

The man, whose name was George Dixon, was tired of setbacks and delays, just as Beauregard had grown weary of his excuses. The general had given him everything he'd requested, had been most courteous and generous. But then, he was desperate. Gen. Pierre Gustave Toutant Beauregard and the city's military leaders needed Dixon much more than he needed them. That became evident when President Davis had boasted publicly that the Confederacy had "other means" of breaking the blockade. That careless remark, which left Beauregard livid, had given Dixon some power over the situation. The general did not want to look foolish, especially not in Davis's eyes.

Dixon knew Beauregard had strong misgivings about the machine, and that was understandable. But the general had little other choice. Beauregard was encouraged that Dixon had waited for the right conditions and hoped that such attention to detail might avoid further loss of life. Still, Dixon had told one of his friends that he knew the general and his men looked at him accusingly, wondering "Why don't he do something," while the city of Charleston fell deeper into despair each day.

Some people openly told Dixon he was on a fool's errand. His commanding officer in Alabama had urged him to give up this folly and return to Mobile. Capt. John Cothran held Dixon in high regard and told his friends that "there never was a braver man in the service of any army." But Cothran held no sway over Dixon. He was stubborn, would not give up. Dixon knew that he could do this. He had been aboard the machine when it sank that barge Mobile Bay. He had piloted it to the very edge of the harbor on countless nights. He knew the boat would work, that his plan would succeed, and he intended to prove that on this night.

"You stated that my presence was very much needed on your little island," Dixon had written to Cothran. "I have no doubt it is, but when I will get there is far more than I am able to tell at present, for beyond a doubt I am fastened to Charleston and its approaches until I am able to blow up some of their Yankee ships."

Dixon realized that he was the last chance. All of the others who understood the fish-boat were gone. McClintock had left town in a rage; Alexander had been recalled to Mobile. Park and Hunley were dead. Dixon knew that without him the *H. L. Hunley* would be written off as just another failed experiment, a lost cause. And if he did not make it work soon, he would never get the opportunity. His leave had been extended twice at least; he could not count on the luxury of another.

And then what? A return to Alabama, far from the front lines, hundreds of miles from the action? He could not abide that. Dixon felt that he could make a difference right now, right here. He would push the situation, make his own luck. If conditions were not ideal tonight, so be it. This would be good enough.

Dixon had complete faith in the machine. Despite the accidents— all the deaths—he had proven that, when operated correctly, the boat was seaworthy. His crew had been offshore a dozen times, had gotten so close to blockaders that they actually heard Yankee sailors singing on deck. Only bad luck and poor timing had prevented them from attacking. But now everything was falling into place. Finally.

The crew loitered near the docks, awaiting his order. He briefly looked them over. They were a good bunch, took to the training well. They did not seem nervous, and that was good—they had every reason to be, given the machine's history. Dixon was pleased to have so many veteran seamen working for him. Ridgaway and Wicks had been sailors since long before the war began; Becker, like Dixon, had worked the riverboat circuit. Even Carlsen, who had replaced Alexander just two weeks earlier, had served aboard the notorious privateer *Jefferson Davis*. Dixon had made them all submariners in his likeness.

"I have got a splendid crew of men," Dixon had written to his friend Henry Willey, "the best I think I ever seen."

This crew had followed him for months now, trusted him with their lives. The men rose late, had breakfast and walked from their boarding house to the ferry landing. They crossed the creek to Sullivan's in a borrowed boat and then marched the length of the island to the dock at Battery Marshall—a five-mile trek that worked out the stiffness of the previous day.

Once they arrived at the dock, they climbed into a strange craft that had killed more than a dozen men. They did not question the machine or the perceived lunacy of their actions. They simply practiced two hours each day and then toiled through the night, in the darkness, without complaint. Perhaps they felt the same connection to the sub that Dixon did, or maybe they just enjoyed the fringe benefits of the assignment. If they were successful, they would share in the reward money. Even if they never became wealthy, they at least enjoyed a lifestyle far better than the typical Confederate. And, the truth was, their chance of death was not really all that much greater.

At times, Dixon had to wonder about the serpentine path that had led him to this beach, this moment.

Before the war he'd been riding the rivers, working on steamboats in the Midwest. He was an engineer by trade and a successful one. When the fighting began, he found himself stuck in Mobile. On a lark—perhaps out of boredom—he'd joined the Mobile Grays, an auxiliary police force. Shortly after the fighting began, the Grays enlisted en masse. Dixon simply followed them in a fit of patriotism. He had little tie to the cause, but had made it his. Then six months later, Shiloh.

It was one of the bloodiest battles of the war to that point, and Dixon had nearly died in the damned Tennessee countryside. He was shot early on the first day of fighting, which may have been a blessing—it spared him the worst of the carnage. It was nothing less than a miracle that he had survived. The bullet meant for his leg struck a sturdy $20 gold piece in his pocket, warping the coin and shredding his leg. The injury had been severe, but he had lived. Dixon may have considered it some sort of divine intervention.

Perhaps he had been spared for a reason, he thought; maybe he had another purpose in this war.

The injury left Dixon with a pronounced limp, limiting his use on the battlefield, but he had gained a good luck piece in trade. The coin, his life preserver—he could feel its weight in his pocket even now—had become his talisman. The odds of that shot were beyond Dixon's ability to comprehend, and his survival could not help but give him faith that he had unusual luck. Even though he wasn't particularly superstitious, Dixon never went into the fish-boat—or anywhere else—without the coin. And he wouldn't for the rest of his life.

It was during his convalescence in Mobile that he first became acquainted with James McClintock and the *Hunley* project. Because he'd shown an aptitude for the boat's engineering, he had been allowed to sail on her first test runs. He'd been there when the submarine first dove under that barge in the bay, sinking the hulk with a contact mine tethered at the end of a long rope. That had been a good day, the best he could remember. The boat had since proven dangerous to many men, but she had never failed to return him to shore.

When they'd taken the boat from Mobile, he had been disappointed. But Charleston needed such a weapon much more than the Alabama port, which was so far inland that it rarely heard the report of guns. Denied a chance to serve on its crew at first, Dixon did not linger when offered the opportunity to join Horace Hunley in Charleston.

The city where the war began surprised Dixon. By the end of 1863, everyone who could afford to leave the city had already done so. Union troops had begun shelling Charleston on a weekly basis, and the Yankees who had taken over the abandoned Battery Wagner were bombarding Fort Sumter so regularly that he became accustomed to the noise, finding that he could sleep through blasts that rattled the windows of his Mount Pleasant boarding room.

Dixon had told Cothran that "a more uncomfortable place could not be found in the Confederacy." Charleston was miserable and broken, so much so that locals were left with little choice but to put an inordinate amount of faith in a machine that thus far no one had proven actually worked. They had seen it fail, and buried its victims. Still, they hoped.

The *Hunley* was a delicate piece of machinery, to be sure—Dixon was under no illusions. The fish-boat was unforgiving, as poor Hunley had learned. The boat was a much more complicated craft than most people realized. McClintock was a genius, but even he had not mastered its operation. Dixon had. But to make matters more complicated, they had recently changed the method by which it attacked—and that added a dangerous variable to Dixon's mission.

Towing a contact mine was too dangerous, they'd learned, so they had chosen to attack as a ram. The boat had been fitted with a spar, which the semi-submersible torpedo boat *David* had proven was an effective weapon. The *New Ironsides* had limped off for repairs months earlier, a testament to that fact. But there was a trade-off. When the torpedo detonated, he and his men would be scarcely twenty feet from the blast, and no one was sure what impact it might have on them. He was confident they could survive it. But then, he had to believe that, and in his unusual luck, as there was no way to test the theory.

Dixon, like Charleston, was running on faith.

He had spent the afternoon adjusting the sub's spar and torpedo system—getting it just right was a constant chore. Every time the *Hunley* went out, the sea knocked something out of alignment. Dixon had used some soldiers from Battery Marshall, where the submarine was docked, to assist him with the work—he would not ask his own men to do any more.

The Battery Marshall troops were understandably curious about the strange contraption, with its slender hull and protruding hatches. Dixon knew most of these officers considered him a dead man walking, and perhaps he had even heard them call his boat the "Little Devil." Dantzler was at least gracious. The Battery Marshall commander did everything he could to accommodate Dixon and his crew, and he gave them something the *Hunley* had never before had: a shore crew.

Dixon had explained his plans to Dantzler earlier that afternoon. This night they would target the USS *Housatonic*, a 207-foot sloop that held the northernmost point in the blockade of Charleston. The *Housatonic* guarded the flank against blockade runners using a northern route to gain entry to the city. It was not a significant ship, and almost never participated in the attacks on Fort Sumter, but it would have to do.

Originally, Dixon and Alexander had their sights set on the USS *Wabash*, one of the more feared blockaders. It carried a higher bounty, which was enticement enough. But the *Wabash* moved constantly and sometimes lingered nearly 12 miles offshore. The *Housatonic* anchored far from the rest of the fleet, closer to shore, minimizing Dixon's chance of running afoul of other enemy ships.

The *Housatonic*'s proximity was important for several reasons. First, the *Hunley* carried only one torpedo, which would leave it defenseless after a single attack. And secondly, the Yankees knew he was coming. Word of the torpedo-boat project had leaked to the blockading squadron—such was the porous nature of both Confederate and Union intelligence. Dixon was not sure exactly what they knew, only that they realized such a craft existed.

"The Fleet offshore have drawings of the sub-marine and of course they have taken all precautions that it is possible for Yankee ingenuity to invent," Dixon had admitted in his letter to Willey, "but I hope to Flank them yet."

His only remaining element of surprise was timing.

Ultimately, the *Housatonic* was an attractive victim because it was the closest ship to Breach Inlet, the narrow stream between Sullivan's and Long Island. From there, it would take them only about two hours to reach the blockader once they hit open water. That would leave the crew with a couple hours of idle time before the tide turned and they could begin the journey back. Perhaps they would set down on the bottom to wait on inbound currents, or inch themselves homeward on the adrenaline that would surely come with success. That was the only aspect of the plan Dixon did not have mapped out to the minute. He would have to improvise that part.

Finally, Dixon walked down to the dock where his men were gathered and gave the order to load up. Once more, they got into the *Hunley*. They climbed aboard two at a time, one man through each hatch, in the order in which they had to sit—there was no room to move around inside. Carlsen, the newest member of the crew, had to go first. The old man, Wicks, had to take off his navy peacoat to climb inside, but carried it with him anyway. Wicks did not want to leave anything of value behind—a sentiment Dixon understood all too well. He carried several trinkets that were too valuable to leave at their boardinghouse. Desperate times forced men to do desperate things. Dixon himself was proof of that.

Ridgaway—who had proven an able replacement for Alexander—climbed inside last, as Dixon passed a few final words with Dantzler. Afterward, he said, he would give two signals of blue light to alert the fort they were headed back. Dantzler assured him that his troops would light a fire on the point to guide the fish-boat into the inlet. That in itself was a considerable risk, as any light from shore was likely to draw fire from the blockade.

Dixon took his leave of Dantzler just before 7 P.M. He made his way to the boat and stepped onto the hull. There were no grand pronouncements; they had been through this before, all too many times. But tonight felt different. He cast one final glance toward the marsh, toward Charleston.

Dixon quietly climbed through the impossibly tight hatch and situated himself in the cramped captain's station. He lit a candle, its light dancing on the painted white iron walls, and closed the hatch. The Battery Marshall troops removed the gangplanks, cast off the lines and pushed the boat off. Dixon watched this with his head in the conning tower, one hand on the rudder stick, and then gave the order. They were underway.

The *Hunley* sailed into the treacherous currents of Breach Inlet, allowing the tide to help it on its way. The progress was slow at first, it always was. The crew said little, responding automatically to the occasional order that Dixon called out. They would ride along the surface for a while, finally diving to avoid surface drag—even though he had told Beauregard he would not do that. The general didn't understand the boat, though. Dixon knew the *Hunley* was perfectly safe so long as he was at the helm. He had all the luck they would need, right there in his pocket.

Although he did not realize it, George Dixon was sailing into immortality. The events of the night would be remembered for years, its repercussions reverberating well into the twenty-first century. He would become legend, and his efforts would lead future generations of men on other grand adventures. Dixon would not change the course of the war, but he would change history.

For the moment, none of that mattered. Dixon thought only of his mission—of the *Housatonic*—as his submarine sliced through cold saltwater. Soon, the men fell into their usual choreography and the boat moved slowly and smoothly. The rhythmic sound of the turning crank lulled the men into a sense of familiarity and security as they felt the *H. L. Hunley* cut into the cold, black Atlantic.

Once again, into the sea of darkness.

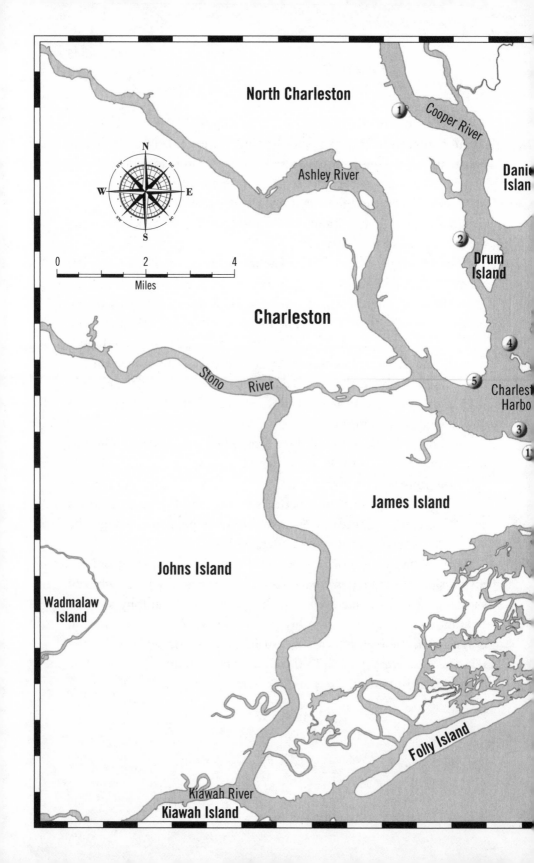

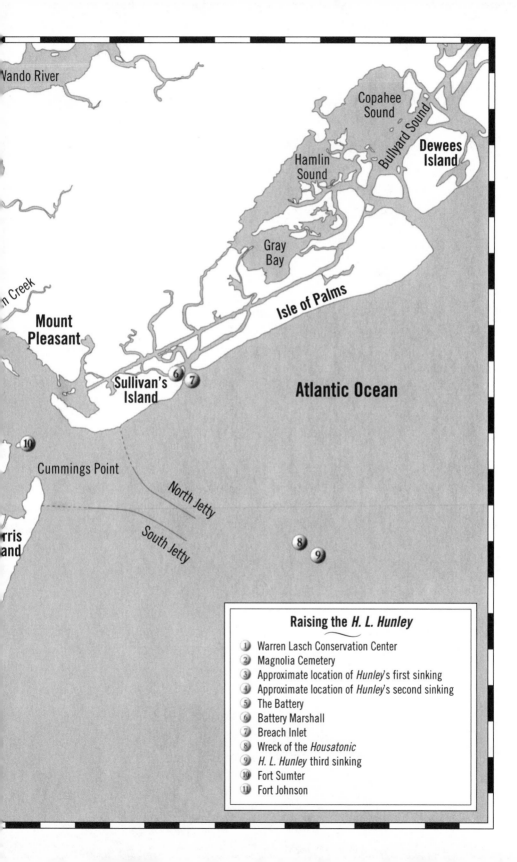

Vando River

Copahee Sound

Hamlin Sound

Bullyard Sound

Dewees Island

Gray Bay

n Creek

Mount Pleasant

Isle of Palms

Atlantic Ocean

Sullivan's Island

⑥ ⑦

⑩

Cummings Point

North Jetty

South Jetty

rris and

⑧
⑨

Raising the *H. L. Hunley*

① Warren Lasch Conservation Center
② Magnolia Cemetery
③ Approximate location of *Hunley*'s first sinking
④ Approximate location of *Hunley*'s second sinking
⑤ The Battery
⑥ Battery Marshall
⑦ Breach Inlet
⑧ Wreck of the *Housatonic*
⑨ *H. L. Hunley* third sinking
⑩ Fort Sumter
⑪ Fort Johnson

Part One

The Efforts of Great Men

CHAPTER 1

1980
Sullivan's Island

The little boat rode the ebb tide out of Breach Inlet, fighting manic currents, dodging sandbars and oyster beds, pushing for the open water just ahead. The narrow cut between the Isle of Palms and Sullivan's Island had only gotten more treacherous in the past century and few boats dared to use the route anymore. The Zodiac handled the tricky channel with relative ease, but it was slow going.

The three men aboard the rubber boat had to be careful. People had died in this water, some more than two centuries earlier when the British tried to march 3,000 troops through the mile-wide inlet in the early days of the Revolutionary War. The attempt to take Fort Sullivan had not gone well for the Redcoats in 1776, and the changing topography of the South Carolina coast was even less forgiving in the twentieth century. In recent years, the Isle of Palms had posted a sign warning swimmers away from Breach Inlet. To make the point abundantly clear, islanders had painted the Grim Reaper on the sign. The ghastly image loomed large over the inlet, and in the minds of local swimmers.

From their base on the island, Breach Inlet was not only the crew's quickest route into the Atlantic, it held symbolic significance as well. A little more than a century ago, the *H. L. Hunley* had sailed from the same inlet on its appointment with history. It had slipped out of Breach Inlet, into the Atlantic Ocean and engaged the U.S. Navy's blockading squadron on a winter's night in the waning days of the Civil War. But the sub never came back, and its story had passed into legend. More than 116 years later, so little evidence of the *Hunley*'s story remained that some wondered if the tale was even true. The men in the Zodiac were part of the first serious effort in more than a century to find the lost privateer, the first submarine to sink an enemy ship in combat.

They would scan the ocean floor just offshore, covering the shallow water along the barrier islands to test their theory that the *Hunley* had actually made it back close to the coast that night. Meanwhile, a cabin cruiser would search points farther offshore and serve as a platform for divers. It was a big ocean, but they felt they could narrow the search to a relatively small area.

That morning the Zodiac carried archaeologist Dan Koski-Karell, magnetometer miracle worker Bill Shea and Dirk Cussler, the 19-year-old son of the expedition's leader. As Cussler steered and Koski-Karell navigated, Shea would use his mag to detect errant iron on the ocean floor just beyond the breakers. They were minutes away from starting the day's search when they heard the screams.

The two women onshore were frantic, waving their arms, yelling and pointing toward the swirling water just off the beach. The men in the Zodiac soon saw what had caught their attention: three tiny heads in the water, bobbing up and down, quickly being pulled out to sea. The riptide was working overtime, the Grim Reaper watching from his sign with satisfaction. But the Zodiac crew would deny Death his morning take.

Cussler whipped the Zodiac around, charging toward the three boys as fast as the outboard would push them. The black raft—with "TIMEOUT BOATS" printed on the side—jumped the breakers and hit the water with a crash. Cussler spun the wheel and, as soon as they were close to the kids, Shea and Koski-Karell jumped overboard.

With a few strokes, the two scientists reached the boys. The children—none more than nine years old—were already blue and in the early stages of shock. They didn't have much time.

Cussler steered in close, and the two scientists passed the children up to him one at a time. Luckily, the boys were light and didn't take up much room in the overcrowded launch. As soon as they were secure, and the scientists pulled themselves aboard, Cussler aimed the Zodiac for the beach. They took the breakers at teeth-rattling speed.

The beached Zodiac was met by the children's mother and an aunt. The women were so traumatized they did not say a word to the rescuers—all their attention was focused on the blue boys. Dirk Cussler, Shea and Koski-Karell watched as the women hustled the three kids into a car and drove off. The three men were left to fight their way back through the breakers in the Zodiac—a proposition more harrowing than navigating Breach Inlet.

It was the most excitement they would see all day.

Aboard the 27-foot cabin cruiser *Coastal Explorer*, Clive Cussler heard about the rescue over the radio, shook his head and laughed. Truth, he thought, really is stranger than adventure fiction. What were the odds that, at the very moment the riptide took those kids, there would be a boat in the area that could not only spot them but actually reach them? Those were not odds he'd take in any bet. At least something good would come of this expedition.

Cussler's arrival in Charleston in July 1980 marked his third major expedition as shipwreck hunter. He had spent the previous two summers in the North Sea searching for the *Bonhomme Richard* and now wanted to try his hand in American—and shallower—waters. First he would look for the famous lost Civil War submarine, and then head north to Virginia to seek out other relics of the War Between the States. Already, he was finding that underwater exploration—even within sight of land—was not particularly easy.

By the summer of 1980, Clive Cussler was a famous man. He had published four adventure novels, all of them best sellers—that is, after his *Raise the Titanic!* became a literary sensation. His name was suddenly everywhere. Before the beach season ended, a major motion picture based on *Titanic* would be released. Even though he would be disappointed in the film, Cussler had every reason to be optimistic. He was on his way to becoming one of the most famous American authors of his time, a career that allowed him to follow his passion wherever it lay. And usually, his passion lay offshore.

Cussler had built a fictional world around an underwater adventurer named Dirk Pitt. The name was carefully chosen—two syllables, the kind a villain could easily spit out in disgust. Cussler had taken his son's name and added the surname of a former British prime minister for his hero. But Pitt, the special projects director of the National Underwater and Marine Agency, bore more similarities to Cussler himself. Both men were 6′3″ with green eyes, both loved exploration and history, both were addicted to adventure. Only Cussler's beard set him apart. Dirk Pitt saved the world as he raised ocean liners and found lost airplanes, and Cussler discovered that Pitt's adventures afforded him the time and money to do likewise.

Cussler was born in Aurora, Illinois, but his parents—Eric and Amy—had moved to Alhambra, California, when he was young. On the outskirts of Los Angeles, young Clive fell in love with the outdoors and honed skills that would last him a lifetime. He became an Eagle Scout by the time he was 14, devoured Horatio Hornblower books, watched *Flash Gordon* and the other serials of the day—things that would later inform his fiction. But he also had a more studious side. When his parents would go out at night, sometimes Cussler would park himself at the local library, and there he found a world just as amazing as anything Flash Gordon ever encountered. He was particularly drawn to one Civil War series featuring two brothers, one a Confederate soldier, the other fighting for the Union. The sweep of history overwhelmed Cussler, and he would never lose interest.

Cussler was most intrigued by the tales of John Paul Jones, the father of the U.S. Navy. Jones, a native of Scotland, spent his early career on British merchant ships. Controversy forced him to abandon his fortune and immigrate to the United States, where he soon volunteered to join the colonists in the fight against his homeland. He served aboard a number of American ships before taking command of a former French merchant ship, refitted for combat and rechristened the *Bonhomme Richard*. The *Richard* terrorized the British coast in the late summer of 1779, but finally met up with the Royal Navy on September 23. It was during this famous battle that Jones answered a taunt from the British with his famous quote "I have not yet begun to fight." But in fact he had, and the *Bonhomme Richard* would pay the price.

During the Battle of Flamborough Head, the *Richard* caught on fire and began to sink. Jones and his crew would transfer to other ships, but the *Bonhomme Richard* was lost somewhere in the North Sea. Two centuries later, those exploits would fascinate a growing young author. The ocean was an endless source of adventure and imagination.

The love of those sea stories led Cussler to writing fiction, and his exploits in the Korean War, where he served in the U.S. Air Force as a flight engineer, gave him more inspiration. In the air force, Cussler improbably became interested in sport diving, which offered him an entirely new world to explore. Years later, those experiences convinced him to walk away from a job in advertising to try his hand at writing. Success did not come overnight, but it did not take long, relatively speaking.

After publishing two novels in paperback, *The Mediterranean Caper* and *Iceberg*, Cussler found huge success with the novel *Raise the Titanic!* Pitt, his hero, was an American James Bond with more than a little in common with John D. MacDonald's immortal Travis McGee. He had found a new stage for the detective/adventurer hero— the ocean—and it proved popular with readers. Cussler's cinematic novels allowed him the success to begin collecting antique cars, which soon found their way into Dirk Pitt's converted airport hangar home.

But Cussler was not content to simply collect cars and write adventures. He wanted action himself—action he could not find behind a typewriter. Years later, he would say it was a lark that led him to become a shipwreck hunter—a lark, plenty of time and a healthy imagination.

It was just a passing comment that set him on his path. One day he was reading *Diving for Treasure* by Peter Throckmorton, a journalist and a pioneer of underwater archaeology; some would even call him the father of the field. Throckmorton theorized that the *Bonhomme Richard* was still out there and could be found by the right search team. In fact, he suggested a man from Wales had discovered a promising target. Cussler used his English literary contacts to get in touch with Throckmorton, and he had one question: How much would such an expedition cost? Throckmorton estimated $60,000.

It was a number that no longer gave Cussler any pause.

In 1978, Cussler assembled a team of divers and archaeologists—including Throckmorton—to scour the North Sea off Flamborough Head. Sidney Wignall, the man whom Throckmorton believed had possibly found the *Richard*, had a side-scan sonar image of three shipwrecks off Flamborough Head. One of them, he insisted, had to be the *Bonhomme Richard*. Wignall had previously discovered a Spanish Armada galleon, so he had a track record. Cussler was intrigued by his findings. The author started making plans, and writing checks.

Eventually Cussler rented a boat—a barely seaworthy old minesweeper called the *Keltic Lord*—and bought dive equipment. He even secured an old decompression chamber, just one of the many things he really wouldn't need. There was more equipment than assembled knowledge on the expedition, and it was an expensive learning curve.

The search was a disaster.

The team gathered in Bridlington, England, in August 1978.

Cussler's daughter Teri had gone ahead early with her husband to meet Wignall and prepare for the search. Cussler's wife, Barbara, and their two other children—Dana and Dirk—came along. Walt Schob and some divers from the University of Wales also joined the group. Cussler had yet to learn one truth in underwater archaeology: the larger the search party, the worse the results.

Nothing went as planned. Bad weather stymied the crew many days, forcing late starts and flaring tempers. Some of the hired hands seemed less than motivated. At one point, Cussler was left behind on the boarding boat, where he struggled to move gear onto the *Keltic Lord*. When he finally got aboard the minesweeper, muttering a long string of curses, Cussler got the group's attention and showed them his right hand.

"Whatever happens," he said, "a fire aboard ship, we strike an iceberg, or we're torpedoed by the crew of a U-boat who forgot to surrender, you save this hand."

When they asked why, Cussler pointed out the first rule of the expedition: "Because this is the hand that writes the checks."

Very quickly, the team and the crew of the *Keltic Lord* figured out that Cussler, not Wignall, was in charge.

For weeks, the group scanned the seas with their sonar. They found one wreck that looked promising, but divers determined it was a freighter torpedoed during World War I. The other two targets Wignall had located were both victims of U-boats. They had found nothing older than the twentieth century. They were about 200 years off the mark.

One of the divers recovered a faucet from one of the old wrecks, and it would become the only souvenir Cussler ever kept from any expedition. Every time he looked at that faucet, which he kept in his writing office, he remembered that it had cost him $80,000. Throckmorton had seriously underestimated the cost of maritime expeditions.

But Cussler was a determined man, and he did not give up easily.

In June of 1979, he returned to England—the dream of finding the ship from those boyhood stories was too great to ignore. For this expedition, he brought on Eric Berryman, a former navy commander; Bill Shea; and Throckmorton himself to join the search. Wayne Gronquist, a Texas attorney and Cussler friend, suggested the group incorporate as a nonprofit. The primary reason, at least initially, was to help with Cussler's tax burden—but there were other benefits to becoming a bona fide search organization.

Incorporating gave the group clout, turned them into something more official than a bunch of friends out looking for lost boats. Eventually, many of the people involved in the *Bonhomme Richard* search would become board members on this new nonprofit. Against the author's wishes, they named the outfit after the fictional agency that employed Dirk Pitt: the National Underwater and Marine Agency. Cussler was not crazy about the idea, but liked it better than the only other suggestion—the Clive Cussler Foundation. Slowly, Cussler's fiction was seeping into his real life.

A Scottish skipper named Jimmy Flett provided the team with a new search boat, the *Arvor II*. The *Keltic Lord* had since been lost at sea, along with some of the crew from the first expedition. Cussler was distraught by the prospects, but had to concede the *Arvor* was a definite upgrade for the search. It was a fine boat, one that Cussler would not forget.

For this expedition, Cussler focused on a tantalizing story that was nearly three decades old. In the 1950s, a fisherman had snagged the remains of a French musket thought to have come off the *Richard*. This catch was made six miles offshore, and it seemed as good a place as any to start the search. Because historical records indicated the *Bonhomme Richard* had drifted for perhaps a day-and-a-half before sinking, the NUMA team let the *Arvor* drift from the battle site for 36 hours. Luckily the tide and weather matched the conditions during the battle almost perfectly—a fact discovered through admiralty records.

The crew decided the ship would have ended up about 13 miles northeast of Flamborough Head. For weeks they searched the area, eventually covering 116 miles. The expedition turned up more than a dozen shipwrecks, but none of them the one Cussler wanted. Eventually, the author decided the ship had gone down much farther out to sea. It would take a crew running day and night for six weeks straight in fair weather to find it, he figured. Cussler decided the best he could do was offer a reward to anyone who provided NUMA with a target that turned out to be the *Bonhomme Richard*.

For the time being that was the end of the search, but in other ways it was only the beginning. Cussler had two deep-sea expeditions under his weight belt and little to show for it. But he was hooked, and his band of NUMA adventurers would continue to search the world's oceans for decades. And he would come back for the *Bonhomme Richard*.

The *H. L. Hunley* first caught Clive Cussler's attention in 1979. He read about it in the wake of the *Bonhomme Richard* expedition, while poring through Civil War history. In the darkest days of the war, a group of men had built an iron submarine and used it to sink a navy warship, the USS *Housatonic*. This happened 50 years before submarines became regular additions to navies around the world, before the science of underwater travel had been perfected. Somehow, a group of men with limited resources and scant knowledge had made maritime history, and left behind a lingering mystery. It was simply a great story—and Cussler could not resist a great story.

Cussler thought the *Hunley*, which had disappeared in coastal waters near Charleston, South Carolina, would be easier quarry than the *Richard*. The search area would be smaller and offshore conditions would be less of a factor. But Cussler also knew that he had been wrong before. He was sailing into uncharted waters, in more ways than he realized.

The *Hunley* was not as famous as the *Richard*, but it was legend in South Carolina. The most prominent mention of the sub had come in Shelby Foote's three-volume series on the Civil War, in which the great historian mistakenly said the *Hunley* had been found alongside its victim. A little research by Cussler and his NUMA staff had proven that wasn't the case. In truth, the *Hunley* had disappeared on February 17, 1864, and there had not been one confirmed sighting of it since.

The mystery of that appealed to Cussler's sense of imagination and, once again, he began to plan.

Because the search for the *Hunley* would be conducted inside state territorial waters, Cussler needed a license for the search. This brought him to Alan Albright at the Institute of Archeology and Anthropology, a relatively new organization headquartered at the University of South Carolina. Albright was initially suspicious of Cussler, figuring him for an amateur treasure hunter. The institute ran across no small number of men who looked for shipwrecks with visions of treasure in their eyes. There were a few well-known scalawags in the Charleston area alone that plundered shipwrecks and sold what they found, which was technically illegal.

Cussler did not seem like one of these types—they usually didn't ask for licenses—but Albright decided to quiz the author. They talked about the sub, the *Bonhomme Richard*. When they finally discussed the particulars of the license, Albright had a simple question: "If you find the *Hunley*, what then?"

"That's your problem," Cussler said.

In 1980, Charleston was a quiet town. Once among the largest cities in the United States, it had quickly been outpaced in the nineteenth century as the nation's economy grew beyond plantations and the slave trade. There was no place for Charleston, or much of the South, in the Industrial Age. The war that began in Charleston Harbor in 1861 had nearly destroyed the city, and it was still on a long road back to prominence. Reconstruction, an earthquake and a terrible economy conspired to keep the once defiantly proud town on its knees for more than a century. These days it was just another midsized coastal town with an aging navy base. But much of the historic downtown remained intact, even if its residents were "too poor to paint, too proud to whitewash"—a favorite saying among locals. That would be the key to its salvation.

Clive Cussler and his NUMA team would map out the day's search over breakfast in the dining room of their Isle of Palms motel. "The Great Trauma of 1980"—as Cussler would later call the expedition—had its share of distractions, but NUMA took its work seriously. Courtesy of Ralph Wilbanks.

The first historic preservation laws in the country left a considerable portion of Charleston frozen in time; it looked much as it had during the war. And now it was beginning to show signs of life. A new hotel and shopping complex was attracting tourists, and within decades the city would become one of the top vacation spots in the country. For now, Cussler found the sleepy town charming. In the dead of summer a famous man could wander among tourists unnoticed, or at least without being harassed.

Walt Schob, serving as NUMA's advance man, managed to find the team an old concrete-block beach motel on the Isle of Palms to rent—they needed a lot of rooms because most of the men brought their wives or girlfriends. When Cussler saw NUMA's Charleston base of operations, he figured it had probably seen a lot of action during Prohibition. It was certainly not part of the historic district—at least not any chapter of history that Charleston cared to tell.

The team took up residence in their shabby beach quarters just after the July 4th holiday. By now, this had become routine for Cussler's crew and, despite its casual atmosphere, the expedition boasted an amazing amount of talent. Aside from Schob, Koski-Karell, Shea and Cussler's son, Dirk, the team included Gronquist, Adm. Bill Thompson, Doc Harold Edgerton and even a psychic. Cussler had used psychics on the North Sea expeditions, for all the good it had done. But he would try anything and, although he held faith, Cussler later said the psychic was much better at predicting the weather than finding the remains of Civil War submarines.

Cussler had been working on his plan for months, and he'd done his homework. There were two prevailing theories on the *Hunley*: either it sank on the way back in, after it torpedoed the *Housatonic*, or it was lost shortly after the attack. Cussler believed the most likely scenario was that it had gone down on its return voyage. One account, which Cussler could not forget, spoke of a blue light on the water that was spotted 45 minutes after the attack. The light, almost certainly coming from the *Hunley*, had been seen directly in the path of a blockade ship coming to the aid of *Housatonic* survivors. Had the sub been hit? And, where had it gone after that?

The team would conduct two searches—one close to shore and another several miles out. Cussler's son, Dirk, would man the Zodiac with Shea and Koski-Karell running a magnetometer and sonar through the shallows just beyond the breakers. For the offshore search, Schob had rented a boat called the *Coastal Explorer*, a rickety craft with a small cabin and bright red gunwales. The water off Charleston was littered with wrecks, predominately from the Civil War, and there would be no shortage of targets. The trick was finding the ones that might be a 40-foot iron submarine.

The Institute of Archeology and Anthropology sent Ralph Wilbanks to monitor the expedition. Although he was ostensibly there to provide support, in truth the state wanted one of its own to keep an eye on Cussler, to "make sure everything went according to Hoyle," as Wilbanks later said. South Carolina famously didn't trust outsiders, and Wilbanks was the perfect man to watch them. He had been with the institute five years, was a seasoned professional and had grown up on the Isle of Palms—he knew the waters around Charleston well. Wilbanks also didn't suffer fools, and at first he wasn't sure about most of the NUMA crew. But he was assured by the presence of Throckmorton, a famous man in archaeological circles.

Wilbanks, like many South Carolina natives, knew the *Hunley* story by heart. Men had searched for the sub before and come away empty. One diver had claimed to have found it a decade earlier, but he offered no proof and Wilbanks knew the man as a bit of a loon. Wilbanks joked that, at one point or another, just about everyone in Charleston had claimed to have found the *Hunley*.

Wilbanks was not a man easily impressed, but he found that he liked Cussler and his team, even if they were wasting their time. Finding the *Hunley*, in his view, was a "pipe dream." Cussler got along with this young curmudgeon from the start. Although the author was not a trained archaeologist, he was smart, had common sense and good instincts. Wilbanks did not take long to come to the conclusion that the NUMA people were not dangerous amateurs— just well-intentioned optimists. And he could play along. A bad day on the water beat a good day in the office.

Except the first day.

Wilbanks had joined the search already in progress, and he got his initial introduction to the team on the cramped deck of the *Coastal Explorer*. The expedition turned up little that day, but the NUMA crew was still optimistic. They bragged to Wilbanks that they had found a good boat for the search. He wasn't so sure, especially when the captain decided to take a shortcut. Although the coastline was visible from the entire survey area, the trip into the harbor took nearly an hour—a long and boring trudge. The reason for this was the harbor jetties.

In the late nineteenth century, the Army Corps of Engineers had built two rock jetties leading into Charleston Harbor to keep the channel from silting in. These jetties kept the channel clear for nearly a century, but they interrupted the flow of sand along the coast, changing the offshore stratigraphy. The jetties had saved the government millions of dollars in dredging costs, but they also stood out as massive hazards to navigation.

The only real course into the harbor is to steer around the jetties, as they stick out of the water a couple of feet most of the time. But on this day, the *Coastal Explorer* captain decided to save three miles and cut across the north jetty. There was a particularly high tide, and he figured the 32-foot boat could clear the rocks. He was wrong. Just when he thought he'd cleared the obstruction, the *Coastal Explorer* stopped bouncing and came to an abrupt and violent halt.

The boat was lodged on top of the jetties, a small hole in its hull, water streaming into its engine compartment.

Cussler went into action as quickly as Dirk Pitt. He jumped overboard to assess the damage and found the boat lodged between two of the craggy rocks. The *Explorer* hadn't been going fast, so it could have been worse. Still, it was stuck—and no motor had the horsepower to push it off, not without tearing an even larger hole in the hull. Cussler thought for a minute. As he did, he leaned against the *Coastal Explorer* and found that, with a little effort, he could move the boat slightly when the swells rose around him.

He began to push.

Edgerton quickly joined him in the water and the two men were soon timing their pushes to inch the *Coastal Explorer* off the rocks. At one point they looked up and realized that all the youngsters— the crew and a newspaper reporter—were standing on deck, just watching the oldest men in the group do all the heavy lifting.

Within several minutes of well-timed shoves, the *Coastal Explorer* eventually broke free of the jetties. Cussler and Edgerton climbed back onboard and the trip inside became a literal race against time. Even with everyone bailing, the boat had taken on nearly two feet of water by the time it reached the dock on the Isle of Palms. They were lucky to make it back.

Soon the search fell into an easy rhythm. The hole in the *Coastal Explorer* was fixed within a day and the expedition continued. The NUMA crew was professional, thoughtful and conducted their survey the same as any university archaeological crew would. They sat in a meeting room at the hotel, going over charts, formulating a search plan with maps and computer readouts hanging from the wall. Cussler was always at the head of the table, usually with a cigar in his mouth.

The team used the most modern science available and employed well-established search practices. On the water they trolled back and forth, cutting one sea lane after another as they scanned the bottom. It got to be boring, a tedium that Wilbanks sometimes broke up by dancing on deck whenever they got a hit. Wilbanks could work hard, and play even harder. He fit in perfectly with the NUMA crew.

A week into the expedition, the team hit their first significant target. The *Coastal Explorer* crew surveyed the wreck of the *Housatonic*, which they found scattered and buried in the silt more than four miles off the Isle of Palms. In the decades after it sank, engineers had dynamited the old hulk at least twice to clear the channel, and that left very little of the *Housatonic* intact. Divers probed the wreck, but there was little left to see. And there was no piece as large as a submarine. They quickly came to one conclusion— the *Hunley* was not lying alongside its victim.

Walt Schob was appointed NUMA spokesman, and he announced the find to the local newspaper, the *Evening Post*. Schob said NUMA had found three fields of debris, any one of which could be the *Hunley*—not bothering to point out that he had his doubts. Proving any of these targets was the *Hunley* would require underwater excavation, and the team was not planning to attempt that. Cussler, Schob said, wasn't looking to gain anything from the search; he would simply turn over this information to the state.

Other shipwreck hunters weren't so noble. As soon as news of Cussler's search was reported in local papers, a man filed a claim in federal court that maintained he had salvage rights to both the *Housatonic* and *Hunley*. "Salvage rights" was a loaded term that suggested he intended to profit from artifacts recovered from the wrecks. The man claimed the rights to everything within a circle that extended miles in each direction from the *Housatonic*. It looked like an educated guess, and an insurance policy, and the court was not inclined to go along with such a scheme. For the time being, Cussler would ignore the delusional claim. But he would not forget the lesson.

Shipwrecks were in danger from the moment their location was put on a map.

For weeks, the *Coastal Explorer* searched the Atlantic. The team turned up a half-dozen hits on sonar, but did no further diving. For the moment, they were just looking for targets. It was a slow, tedious process, made all the worse by the stifling South Carolina heat. The bugs were terrible, the humidity suffocating, and it helped little that the *Coastal Explorer* constantly broke down. While the 32-footer languished offshore, the TIMEOUT BOATS Zodiac kept mowing lanes farther away from the beach, turning up very little.

Later, Cussler would call the expedition "The Great Trauma of 1980." In more charitable times, he referred to it as a working vacation. Between the long days on the water, the team spent long nights drinking and cutting up at the Isle of Palms hotel. Once they sabotaged Throckmorton's community supper of sautéed shrimp by throwing an old sock into the pot. They would do anything for a

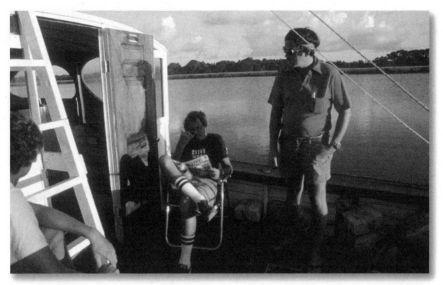

It took nearly an hour to get offshore from the Isle of Palms dock. The Coastal Explorer *would not cut through Breach Inlet, instead taking the team through the creek behind Sullivan's Island—near the spot where the* Hunley *moored—and into the harbor before heading out to sea. Ralph Wilbanks (standing) spent enough time with Cussler to figure out the author was serious about his shipwreck hunting. Courtesy of Ralph Wilbanks.*

laugh, anything to relieve the tension that came from another expedition that was turning up nothing. On the water, Cussler's team was sometimes distracted by Gronquist's girlfriend, who sunned herself on the *Explorer*'s bow, and by the occasional fighting between Cussler and Throckmorton.

At least there was comic relief. The *Coastal Explorer* carried two mates on break from The Citadel to help run the boat. Heckle and Jeckle, as Cussler dubbed them, were not exactly old salts. They once tore a porthole cover off the boat to keep it from clanging, and when the door to the *Explorer*'s cabin kept banging, Heckle and Jeckle thought the solution was to drive a spike through it, nailing it to the deck. Those two clowns and the patchwork boat, which once ran out of gas within sight of the docks, amused Cussler. But none of this entertainment, he realized, was helping him find the *Hunley*.

The expedition lasted nearly three weeks. Occasionally, a local reporter would wander out for an update, but there wasn't much to tell. Mostly, these journalists wanted time with Cussler, who made for a rare celebrity sighting in town. The former advertising copywriter was a marvel with the quotes and displayed a good humor toward his lack of success. It wasn't as if NUMA had come up empty. The team found several interesting targets offshore—but nothing that approached a smoking gun. After the expedition, Gronquist would say NUMA had identified between six and ten possible targets that could have been the *Hunley*. But they would have to check them out later. The expedition's time was running out.

Cussler could not spend the entire summer in Charleston. He had plans to travel from Charleston to Norfolk, Virginia, to search the waters off Hampton Roads for Civil War wrecks before flying to Boston for the premiere of *Raise the Titanic!* It was a busy summer, and the *Hunley* was proving no easier to find than the *Bonhomme Richard*. Cussler was only mildly frustrated. But he wanted something to show for his work.

On Sunday, July 20, Cussler came up with the idea to have Johnson swing by Morris Island. The island, which lay south of the channel, had been a strategic staging area for both Confederate and Union soldiers during the war. In fact, Charleston's deadliest battle was fought there in July 1863 when federal troops tried to take Battery Wagner, an earthen fort at the island's northern tip. Several Union ironclads had sunk in the area during battles throughout the siege.

The *Coastal Explorer* cruised back and forth just off the island for hours, rocking violently in the treacherous water. The island had eroded heavily in the past century, as the harbor jetties blocked its natural flow of replenishing sand, and the undulating ocean floor gave the ocean fits. Around Morris Island, the bottom could come up fast—and it was littered with junk. And soon, they found some of it. The magnetometer hit two big targets that were too promising not to check out. Cussler ordered divers into the water.

Using air hoses to blast through bottom sand, the divers dug down nearly eight feet and eventually found two famous Civil War iron-clads: the *Keokuk* and the *Weehawken*. These were not insignificant finds. The *Keokuk*, a 160-foot ship, had a short history of service. A month after it was commissioned in March 1863, it was one of dozens of ships that attacked Fort Sumter in an aggressive, and ultimately futile, attempt to take the city. The old fort not only held, but the Confederates trained their extensive firepower on the *Keokuk* when it wandered too close. In a half-hour, the ironclad took 90 direct hits, tearing its armor sheeting to shreds. The next day the crippled ship began to take on water, and finally sank.

The *Weehawken* vanished off Morris Island months later, in December 1863. The 200-foot ship was severely overloaded with ammunition and began to take on water in the same heavy winter seas that had kept the *Hunley* docked for a month. The crew tried to call for help, but no one saw their signal save for the troops at Fort Sumter. There was no way to save the ship, it was going down. Between the *Weehawken* and the *Keokuk*, the Union lost 64 sailors.

The location of the two ships had never been in much dispute—Confederates actually salvaged guns from both the ironclads during the war—but their exact locations had become lost to time. NUMA had found two significant Civil War vessels, their first major discoveries. As a result, the expedition made *U.S. News and World Report*—a picture of Cussler and Wilbanks gracing the magazine's pages.

Bill Shea was livid.

Shea had been manning the search equipment all day as the *Coastal Explorer* rocked through the swells off Morris Island. Finally, his infamous seasickness overwhelmed him and he had to take a break. Shea plodded off to lie down and asked Wilbanks to take over for him. Not long after that, during the last hour of the search, the *Keokuk* was found with Wilbanks at the controls. And he got the credit.

Shea groused for the rest of the day, which gave Wilbanks no small amount of pleasure. But in truth everyone on the expedition was ecstatic. Even without a Confederate submarine to show for it, NUMA was finally getting some attention. The team had found a lost shipwreck.

Although the day salvaged Cussler's spirits, he could not help but be frustrated. The search for the *Hunley* was over. He had spent three weeks fighting the humidity, the weather and an uncooperative boat. They had turned up a few good targets, but nothing that was clearly a Confederate submarine. Despite two great finds—the *Keokuk* and *Weehawken*—Cussler joked that it was an inauspicious start for NUMA: three expeditions hunting the two most elusive shipwrecks in the world had turned up little.

Cussler had spent months researching the *Hunley*, and nothing he found—or didn't find—on this expedition convinced him he was wrong. The *Hunley* was out there somewhere and he would get it. It simply wasn't ready to be found. But it would be one day.

Clive Cussler left Charleston with the knowledge that this was only the beginning. Everyone had to start somewhere.

CHAPTER 2

1861
New Orleans

It looked very much like a "huge whale in the water," Capt. Henry French would later recall. The menacing dark craft made almost no noise as it slipped across the surface and would have been practically invisible had it not belched black smoke so thick that it could be seen through the mist blanketing the river, even in the dead of night.

When French first spotted the curious vessel, it was 3:40 A.M. on Saturday, October 12, 1861, and his ship was anchored at the Head of Passes—traditionally considered the mouth of the Mississippi River. A midshipman had woken him with news of a "steamer right alongside of us," and the captain of the USS *Preble* looked out of a port to see the dark mass just 20 yards away. It was moving with "great velocity" toward the USS *Richmond*, another blockade ship just a few hundred yards downstream. The moon had set for the night or the clouds obscured it—he wasn't sure—but French was certain that this low vessel with the rounded hull was the Confederate ram he had heard so much about.

The Union blockade was under attack.

French did not realize the plume of black smoke from the mysterious boat was the result of its engine revving up power to ram the *Richmond*; he simply knew that he must stop it. French arrived on deck within seconds and found one of his mates already trying to alert the *Richmond* crew of the danger. The captain ordered the *Preble*'s gun trained on the craft, which seemed to be picking up speed. In short order, his three broadside guns hit the whale boat three times, glancing blows that echoed through the still night but appeared to do little damage. It was almost as if the cannon balls bounced off the dark ship, which was a disturbing prospect. The whale kept moving despite the attack and, to his surprise, fired a rocket into the air. As the *Preble*'s commanding officer wondered what this could mean, he looked upstream and caught sight of the fire-rafts.

There were three of the burning rafts, flaming hazards of navigation, and they appeared to be headed straight for the *Preble*. The fire-rafts—trademarks of Confederate guerrilla warfare—had been launched in response to the rocket fired from the mystery ship and were intended to create further havoc among the Union fleet. The rocket had been released prematurely. It was a calculated, but not flawless, attack.

French quickly ordered evasive maneuvers. If the fire-rafts collided with his ship, it might catch on fire, and he could not allow that. But the rafts did their job anyway: they distracted the *Preble* crew long enough for the Confederate mystery ship to complete its mission. Downstream, the whale rammed the *Richmond*'s flank, tearing away three planks of the ship's siding just below the waterline. On its own, this would not be enough to sink the boat—if the crew reacted quickly enough. But it was still a serious blow.

The four Union ships blockading the mouth of the Mississippi did not respond well to the attack. The old steamer *Water Witch* fired blindly into the darkness, hitting nothing. Filling with water, the *Richmond* attempted to chase the whale boat and ran aground. The *Vincennes* mistakenly steered out of the channel and quickly joined the *Richmond* on the river's muddy bottom. In a few minutes' time, the Yankees did as much damage to themselves as the Confederates had. And while the Union sailors worked to free their ships from the muck, the strange ship lurched off upstream, disappearing in the darkness.

The Confederate ram, christened the CSS *Manassas*, had suffered too much damage—both from Union gunfire and the impact of ramming the *Richmond*—to attack the other ships, as its crew originally had planned. It was not the outcome the men onboard had wanted; they had scarcely broken the blockade of New Orleans, but they had drawn blood. And they would escape. The whale boat would survive to attack again.

The era of the Confederate ironclad had begun.

The CSS *Manassas* had been launched six years earlier as the *Enoch Train*, a steam icebreaker out of Massachusetts. The boat was brought to New Orleans to serve as a privateer—a ship that would sink Union ships for the promise of Confederate bounties. The 143-foot *Enoch Train* had been stripped to the waterline and covered with 1.25-inch thick iron plating. Its topsides were rebuilt in a smooth sloping shape that resembled a turtle's shell, or a cigar. Less than five feet of the hull stood above the water, save for its huge smokestack. It was a fearsome vessel—and the Confederate's first ironclad. It was named in honor of the South's great victory in Virginia just months prior to its relaunch.

New Orleans was an ideal incubator for the latest in naval technology. The largest city in the South also had perhaps its biggest port, with eight dry docks and several modern shipyards. And soon after the war began, business picked up. Most of those shipyards began building new ships to aid the Confederacy's cause, either out of patriotism or—more likely—profit. The war, at least at its outset, was good for the economy. The politicians had inadvertently made sure of that.

The threat of disunion and the inevitable war that would follow had been building for years. Southern politicians had watched with dismay as the U.S. government placed increasing restrictions on the slave industry, which cut into the livelihood of the South's upper class. This was done not out of a concern for human rights, but as a means for Northern states to level the economic playing field. But that fact mattered little. These new laws were choking the South, or at least its most influential men.

The fire-eaters and the politicians sold secession to the Southern people by explaining it away as a matter of states' rights, without ever specifying which rights exactly were being denied them. The men who pushed for disunion knew that the vast majority of the nation's 4 million slaves were owned by 3 percent of the population, and that was not an issue that would likely inspire an army of young Southern men. So the politicians turned their squabble into a crusade for the Southern states' freedom, the irony apparently escaping them.

The men who longed for a separate Southern nation were fortunate that some people still harbored ill feelings toward the United States. The reason, of course, was taxes. Decades earlier, the federal government had levied what some considered increasingly unfair tariffs on goods produced primarily by the South. It amounted to an economic war of sectionalism. The Northern lawmakers who controlled the Congress had stacked the deck against their neighbors.

South Carolina seceded first, in December 1860, and six other states followed in the early months of 1861. The original Confederacy consisted of only seven states, but others would soon join. By the time Southern forces fired on Fort Sumter in April of 1861, thousands of men were signing up every week to fight for their new Confederate States of America. Soon, four more states joined the Southern cause; two others sent representatives to its Congress. The nation was divided.

The men who led the Confederacy believed their soldiers would be much more motivated to fight than Union troops, and that would help them overcome the disadvantage of having a new, and smaller, army. The Confederate leaders tried to make the most of that edge by painting the conflict as a war of Northern aggression, as an invasion of their homeland. They knew all too well that there was no short supply of patriotism in the South.

But the Confederacy's march to war had commenced with little thought of the Union's vast superiority at sea. While some Southerners hoped that disunion could occur without major, protracted conflict, most politicians gave it little thought. They were eager to secede while public sentiment was on their side. War was inevitable, and the Confederacy would suffer from slipshod planning. After winning several land battles, the Confederates' first losses came at the hands of the U.S. Navy.

The lack of a Southern Navy was a costly oversight. Much of the country's manufacturing base was in the north and since the Confederate States of America had no business relations with the very people it was fighting, the South had to depend on trade with other nations. Everything the southern states needed had to be shipped in, and the U.S. Navy was quickly moving to blockade all the South's ports—or invade those with inadequate defenses. It was perhaps the Confederacy's greatest problem. They could not keep their own ports open, or defend them on the water.

The South did not have the resources, or the time, to simply build its own fleet of ships. The only possible way to compete on the water was to lure private businesses into the war. The Confederate government found the easiest way to entice entrepreneurs was to offer obscene rewards—$50,000 in most cases—to any private ship that could sink or even disable Union vessels. That amount of cash—the twenty-first century equivalent of $1.3 million—had a way of stirring patriotism in even the most bottom-line oriented businessmen. But building massive sloops of war was time-consuming and not particularly cost effective. The solution, many shipwrights found, was to build small stealth crafts that could sneak up on massive U.S. Navy vessels and sink them before they knew what hit them.

War, and the necessities of it, was truly the mother of invention.

The timing could not have been more fortuitous. Engineers in both the North and South had begun to experiment with ironclad ships and odd-shaped rams, and the war only escalated this arms race. The same month that the *Manassas* attacked the *Richmond*, the New Orleans *Daily Delta* reported that some of the city's wealthiest men were planning to build a fleet of such ironclads, both to reopen the port—and to collect Confederate bounties. The attack on the *Richmond*, and the panic it stirred in the U.S. Navy, could only have been reassuring to these investors.

The *Manassas* was only the first of these ships. It would not be the last.

There is little chance the *Manassas*'s attack on the Union blockade escaped the notice of Horace Lawson Hunley. By the fall of 1861, Hunley had developed a keen interest in naval technology and, to a greater degree, the profits to be made from war. The *Manassas* appealed to both those interests, and Hunley was not a man who let opportunity pass. He was ambitious, even though he had already succeeded far more than most men of his time.

Hunley, 37, was the deputy collector of customs in New Orleans—a job he took to supplement the income from his modestly successful law practice. He had served in the state legislature even before he graduated law school and traveled in a circle of the city's richest and most influential people. He had recently bought himself a small plantation in La Fourche Parish, with plans to further add to his portfolio. Hunley had western land on his mind as the country divided into civil war.

He had been born to modest means in Sumner County, Tennessee, in December 1823, the first son of John and Louisa Lawson Hunley. His sister, Volumnia, joined the family two years later, and Louisa lost two other children while they were still babies. John Hunley found it tough to make a living in the rugged Tennessee countryside, and in 1830 he moved his family to New Orleans. Hunley knew the city well—he'd fought there under Andrew Jackson in 1812 and had family living in Orleans Parish when he took work there as a cotton broker. It was a generational migration that had begun in Virginia before the Revolutionary War. Several members of the Hunley family saw opportunity in the South's largest city.

The move changed young Horace Hunley's life, but not in the way he might have expected. Four years after settling in Louisiana, John Hunley succumbed to an unnamed illness, leaving Louisa widowed with two young children. She struggled to get by for a few years until she eventually married James R. Connor, another New Orleans cotton broker and plantation owner from New Jersey. Her new husband offered Louisa and her children a much more comfortable life and entry into an entirely different social circle.

Horace Lawson Hunley was a lawyer, deputy collector of customs in New Orleans and an ambitious man. Although he had a low opinion of the war, he saw it as an avenue to distinguish himself as a Great Man. This photograph, the only known image of Hunley, was taken in 1860—a year before he had the idea to build a submarine. Courtesy of the Collections of the Louisiana State Museum. Gift of Mrs. Kathleen Grosclose.

Growing up, Horace and Volumnia were coached in the ways of society like all scions of Southern aristocracy—even those who had only married into it. Their mother taught them an appreciation of music and English literature. Both children warmed to their stepfather good-naturedly and would remain close to him well into adulthood. Horace, a teenager by the time his mother remarried, took full advantage of his new standing by pursuing a law degree and politics—luxuries he likely would not have had as the son of a mere cotton broker. His work at the custom house not only insinuated him into one of the city's largest industries, it also paid the bills. Hunley's salary as deputy chief collector of customs was $1,500 annually—the twenty-first–century equivalent of nearly $38,000. Along with the profits of his law practice, this made Hunley a wealthy man. But it never seemed to be enough. He still remembered a life plagued by poverty and had no desire to return to it.

Horace Hunley did not simply want to live comfortably. Behind his dark eyes and thick beard lurked the mind of a dreamer—he was a man with grand plans. He kept a notebook in which he wrote down motivational sayings ("Procrastination is the thief of time") and his own dreams: "Build in New Orleans an octagonal brick tower, three hundred to six hundred feet high." He scheduled his days down to the hour, ate his dinner promptly at 4 P.M., and spent the rest of the night studying, corresponding with friends, or reading books borrowed from Volumnia.

Politics was something of a hobby for Hunley. When talk of war began, he made a list of the states he thought might secede, missing only Delaware and the western territories. As the 1860 election approached, he made bets on which candidate would win in each state. Hunley was fascinated by power. He also kept copious notes about the qualities of Great Men. *What makes a Great Man? What diseases do they get?* It was little secret to any of his friends that Hunley longed to become a Great Man himself.

It probably only fueled Hunley's ambition that his closest associates were far more successful than he. His friend Henry Leovy was both a lawyer and part-owner of a local newspaper. Perhaps his greatest confidante was Robert Ruffin Barrow, a wealthy plantation owner who had married Hunley's sister, Volumnia. Although Barrow was 27 years older than Volumnia, the couple seemed to share much in common—or else Hunley's sister shared her brother's disdain for poverty.

Hunley handled all of his brother-in-law's business and largely shared his political opinions, at least on the Confederacy. Both owned slaves—Barrow far more than the handful Horace Hunley had amassed—but they nevertheless thought secession was a bad idea. Their spirited conversations against the Confederacy, which focused on the hubris of politicians and the adverse economic effects of war, worried Volumnia. She often urged them to quiet their talk, because surely few in New Orleans felt as they did.

"When I hear Horace or yourself speak against our President and Government and (others too) it hurts me worse than for us to lose a battle," Volumnia wrote to her husband, who often stayed in the city overnight to conduct his business.

Even if Hunley did not initially share the goals of the Confederacy, he saw a way to profit from the cause. Just months after the first battle at Fort Sumter, Hunley became involved with a blockade-running scheme to secure guns for the Confederate Army. The idea likely originated with his custom house boss, Francis Hatch, who had taken a leave of absence to act as an agent for the Confederacy. Hunley took a similar leave—business at the custom house was no doubt slow as a result of the blockade.

In early June of 1861, Hatch took $1,000 from the Confederate government to outfit the schooner *W. R. King*—which was renamed the *Adela*—with the idea of meeting a British ship off the coast of Cuba to buy a load of guns. There were never enough guns. Hunley led the expedition, either for profit or to curry favor with Hatch, even though he had little experience with open water sailing. It was little surprise that the voyage did not go as planned.

Winds blew the *Adela* off course for several days, sending the ship down to the Yucatan peninsula before it finally reached the southwest tip of Cuba. By the time the sailing was good enough to head east for the rendezvous, Hunley determined that the chance of actually intercepting the British was not worth making the voyage. He limped back to New Orleans, unsuccessful.

"On arriving off the coast of Cuba, it was deemed too late to dispatch the *Bamberg* to Havana and St. Thomas as had been contemplated," Hunley wrote to Hatch. "We could not have reached Havana before the 23rd. This would have incurred an expense for a very improbable chance of success."

Failure was not acceptable to a potentially Great Man, and the experience onboard the *Adela* left Hunley frustrated. Although he did not fully approve of the war, he longed for action. He needed to be involved in the historic events transpiring around him. The only way to do that, he realized, was to become even more intimately involved with the Confederacy. Soon, the flurry of activity around the New Orleans port caught his attention. He had an idea.

Hunley never said where he first got the notion to experiment with submarine boats, but it could have come to him after reading a letter published in several Southern newspapers over the summer. The Rev. Franklin Smith, a chemist and inventor, urged the businessmen building privateers to invest in the idea of "Submarine Warfare" to aid the Confederate cause.

"The new vessel must be cigar shaped for speed—made of plate iron, joined without external rivet heads; about thirty feet long, with a central section about 4 × 3 feet—driven by a spiral propeller. The new Aneroid barometer made for increased pressure, will enable the adventurer easily to decide his exact distance below the surface."

Smith had provided both a generic and quite specific description of the properties a sub-marine boat should include. Such a craft was hardly a new idea. Europeans as far back as Leonardo da Vinci had toyed with the idea, and during the Revolutionary War a Yale graduate named David Bushnell had built a wooden submarine he called the *Turtle*. Bushnell employed a hand crank to turn his sub's propeller, as motors did not exist and sails would have hardly provided stealth— or allow his boat to operate beneath the surface.

Napoleon commissioned Robert Fulton to build a submarine a few years later, and he did use a sail for surface propulsion. But like Bushnell, he relied on hand cranks to propel the sub while it was underwater. Fulton was able to launch his submarine in 1800, years before his first commercial steamboat. The sub, which carried a crew of three men, performed admirably but it leaked and never managed to sink a ship. Napoleon thought Fulton had swindled him and the French Navy soon gave up on the experiment.

Although several submarines had proven it was possible to travel underwater, they remained little more than a curiosity. None of them had ever accomplished their primary purpose. No submarine had ever sunk an enemy warship in battle.

Horace Hunley knew any ship that achieved such a feat would surely designate its originator a Great Man. And even though he never spoke of it, it would have been quite a coincidence if Hunley did not see Smith's letter. Because by August 1861, he and James McClintock were planning to build a boat that could have been the very craft the preacher had described.

James McClintock proved the perfect foil to Horace Hunley. Although neither man had much investment in Southern politics, at least at the war's beginning, Hunley was simply an idea man. He could dream, promote and sell his plans, but the mechanics eluded him. McClintock, conversely, knew how to turn ideas into reality. He could build anything.

A native of Cincinnati, McClintock, 32, had been one of the youngest steamboat captains on the Mississippi before he settled down to open a machine shop with Baxter Watson on Front Levee Street in New Orleans. The two men built steam gauges and fabricated other parts for steamboats in their storefront near the French Quarter. It was a modest living, but their prospects had recently improved. McClintock and Watson had secured a lucrative contract to make bullets for the Confederate Army. The work was theirs without a bid, since they had built the machine that made the bullets—at a pace of "10,000 Minie-balls of perfect uniform and shape per hour."

McClintock was considered an engineering prodigy—he was not

only exceedingly proficient, he was self-taught. He was just the sort of innovator that a Great Man needed to see his dreams realized. It's not clear how Hunley met McClintock, but Henry Leovy may have pointed his friend in the right direction. That summer, Leovy's newspaper had published a story praising the genius of McClintock and Watson for their work in designing the system that produced ammunition for the Confederates. It was a marvel of manufacturing, one that displayed the sort of skill a man would need to build Hunley's submarine. But at its core, McClintock and Hunley shared one thing in common: they both wanted to make a profit.

James McClintock gave up a career as a steamboat captain to open a machine shop with Baxter Watson in New Orleans. He was a self-taught engineering genius. It took him only a few months to design and build his and Horace Hunley's first submarine, the Pioneer. *Courtesy of the U.S. Naval History and Heritage Command.*

Later, McClintock would claim he knew nothing of earlier attempts to build submarines—not even by Fulton, a man who should have been extremely familiar to a riverboat captain. Regardless, Smith's letter and Hunley's vision apparently provided McClintock enough inspiration to become the father of the modern submarine (even if Watson would claim he was the primary inventor of the group).

McClintock and Watson fussed over the boat's design through the fall; construction began before the year ended. They initially worked at their own shop with financial backing from Hunley, Leovy and, most likely, Barrow. Soon the project outgrew their modest storefront and they moved operations to the Leeds Foundry, which sat just upriver from the city near the Government Yards on the New Basin Canal.

McClintock started with a frame that was 35 feet long and cigar-shaped. Some would call it a cigar boat, presumably people who had never read Smith's letter. McClintock fastened quarter-inch boiler plate to the skeletal frame, firing the pieces until they formed the sleek, rounded contours he wanted. The boat would be pointed at both ends and almost completely round—four feet wide and four feet tall. It had a single hatch topside, and two external rods that controlled the rudder, which protruded from behind its shrouded propeller. On its side, the boat had two short, squat fins the pilot could move to dive or surface. They painted the hull black, the color of stealth.

There was little room inside the boat. The tapered ends, each ten feet long, served as ballast tanks to take in and expel the water needed to submerge and surface. The crew compartment was crowded with pumps for the ballast tanks, a tiller to control the rudder and a barometer that served as a depth gauge. The rest of the cramped cockpit was filled with the boat's rudimentary propulsion system: a crank that one or two men turned to power the propeller. The captain stood, perhaps with his head in the hatch, and steered by compass, although it never functioned properly inside the iron hull. But a faulty compass was all the ship had to steer by. McClintock would later say that he put no ports in the *Pioneer*, as they came to call it. It looked like an eyeless, prehistoric fish.

There was also no snorkel system on the fish-boat, nor any way to store air. Although Fulton had used compressed air in his submarine, McClintock presumed his crew could get by with whatever oxygen they sealed inside with them. The crew could surface to replenish their air supply, a practice that would continue on McClintock submarines even after he had devised a way to avoid such primitive means of getting air to the crew.

The first tests of this fish-boat did not go well. Some would later claim that two slaves suffocated inside the submerged craft, although McClintock disputed that. He said the boat could stay underwater for two hours, once the crew calmed down and learned to regulate their breathing. The crew's prospect for calm likely improved once McClintock and Watson figured out how to stop the *Pioneer* from leaking.

They first tested the boat in the New Basin Canal, near the foundry. Hunley's friend John K. Scott—a former riverboat captain whom Hunley knew from the custom house—volunteered to serve as the sub's pilot. The initial trials were stressful—the men were nervous and the boat leaked. Within weeks, both problems were overcome and the *Pioneer* was towed to Lake Pontchartrain for further tests. In the lake's brackish water, the crew discovered additional problems with the submarine that weren't so easily overcome. Without any way to see outside, the boat would sometimes get stuck in the mud. The crew—oblivious to this—would continue to crank the propeller furiously, going nowhere, quickly wearing themselves out.

At the same time, whenever one of the men shifted their weight or tried to move inside the crew compartment, the *Pioneer* rolled— such was the curse of a completely round hull. McClintock himself would concede the design flaw eventually, noting that his first submarine was "faulty in shape" and needed more weight in its keel— even though it was so heavily ballasted that when it floated the conning tower was barely above the surface. But McClintock took great satisfaction from one thing: he had proven that such a boat could be built.

Later, McClintock claimed the *Pioneer* sank a schooner and two barges in practice on the lake. The method of attack they had chosen was as simplistic as the boat itself. The sub towed a contact mine at the end of a long rope. It would approach its target, dive beneath it and then drag the explosive into the ship's hull. By the time the mine detonated, the sub would be on the other side of the ship, where it was shielded from the blast. The floating mine was critical to the sub's success—the *Pioneer* was far too small to be used as a ram. Hunley must have been ecstatic—this little boat showed even more promise than the *Manassas*.

As McClintock tested his new boat on Lake Pontchartrain, the era of the ironclad officially arrived nearly 1,000 miles away. On March 8, the CSS *Virginia* attacked the U.S. Navy fleet off Hampton Roads, Virginia. In a single afternoon, the *Virginia* sank two ships and forced another to run aground. The 263-foot boat, formerly the *Merrimack*, had been stripped to the waterline and covered with an iron skin that made it almost impervious to cannon fire. Its sloping hull resembled a floating butter dish, albeit a heavily armed one. It was 120 feet longer, and immeasurably more formidable, than the *Manassas*.

The next day, the *Virginia* reappeared to finish off the assembled Union vessels. And there the crew of the Confederate ironclad first caught sight of the USS *Monitor*. At 179 feet, the U.S. Navy's first

The battle of the USS Monitor *(right) and CSS* Virginia *(the former* Merrimack*) on March 9, 1862, at Hampton Roads, Virginia, changed naval history. It was the first battle of ironclad ships and changed the way navies around the world approached warfare. The two ships fought to a standstill, neither able to deliver a killing blow. The Union blockade of the Chesapeake Bay remained intact. Courtesy of the Virginia Historical Society, Robert Knox Sneden Diary.*

ironclad was much smaller than the *Virginia*, but its design was unnerving. The *Monitor* was almost completely flat, with a single gun turret rising from its mid-section. And the *Virginia* soon felt the blast power housed in that turret.

The two oddly shaped ships fired at each other for four hours, neither doing significant damage to the other. At one point, the Confederates tried to ram the *Monitor*, but landed only a glancing blow. Later, the *Virginia* scored a solid hit on the Union ironclad's pilot house, forcing it to break off the attack. By that time, the outgoing tide made it impossible for the Confederates to finish off the *Minnesota*. The *Virginia*'s crew sailed away from a battle that would become immediately famous.

Three weeks after the battle of the *Monitor* and the *Virginia*, John Scott applied for the *Pioneer*'s letter of marque—basically a license that allowed the submarine to attack Union ships on the Confederate government's behalf (and claim reward money). Hunley and Leovy put up a $5,000 surety bond to obtain the letter, and the *Pioneer* became the only submarine officially recognized by the Confederate States of America for the duration of the war.

But she would never see action.

On April 18, 1862, the Union fleet opened fire on Fort Jackson and Fort St. Philips 70 miles south of New Orleans. For five days, the Union fleet commanded by Adm. David Farragut traded shots with the two forts, which sat on opposite banks of the Mississippi. The forts had been designed to form a gauntlet through which no enemy ship could pass. It worked, at least temporarily. For nearly a week, the forts took heavy fire and returned it well enough to disable a few U.S. ships—even sinking one. But on April 23, the fleet got past the forts and steamed for the Crescent City.

The CSS *Manassas* would see action one final time. The first Confederate ironclad attempted to intercept Farragut's fleet as it made its way up the Mississippi. The *Manassas* tried to ram the USS

Pensacola, the *Mississippi* and the *Brooklyn*, but could not damage the boats or even slow them down. The fleet kept on course, hell bent for New Orleans. The *Manassas* gave chase until suddenly the USS *Mississippi* turned on it, ramming the ironclad with enough force to run it aground. While it was stranded, the Union took advantage. The *Mississippi* unloaded its guns on the *Manassas* until the ship caught fire and eventually sank. The South's first ironclad had barely lasted eight months.

The *Pioneer* would not earn the dignity of being lost in battle. Once Farragut's boats arrived in New Orleans, armed Union soldiers took the city with little resistance. The U.S. troops would occupy the city for the rest of the war, and would largely spare it. But McClintock and Hunley had no such luxury with their submarine. It was no longer safe to keep the *Pioneer* afloat.

David Farragut took command of the Union Navy's Gulf Coast Blockading Squadron in early 1862 and captured New Orleans in April of that year. Within months, he became the U.S. Navy's first rear admiral (and eventually its first admiral). His famous, although not entirely accurate, quote "Damn the torpedoes, full speed ahead" came during the Battle of Mobile Bay in 1864. Courtesy National Archives.

When it became apparent that New Orleans was lost, McClintock and Hunley decided to scuttle their boat to keep it out of Union hands. The prospect of having their secret weapon exposed was bad enough; they did not want the *Pioneer* confiscated and used against Confederate forces. McClintock took the cigar-shaped boat to the New Basin Canal and opened its hatch, allowing the dark water to pour inside. Within a few minutes, the boat disappeared into the mud below.

The *Pioneer* would lay hidden in the canal for more than a year

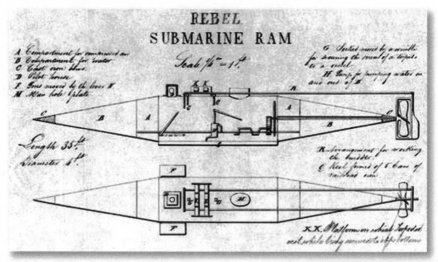

The only image of the Pioneer *that survives is this schematic made in December 1863, after occupying Union forces found the sub in a New Orleans canal. The detailed drawing was sent to Washington to alert navy officials that the Confederates were experimenting with underwater craft. By that time, James McClintock's third submarine was already prowling the waters off Charleston. Courtesy Friends of the* Hunley.

and a half. In December 1863, Union troops discovered the submarine in the muck, retrieved it and made a detailed schematic of it mechanics—the most complete record of the submarine that survives. The Union troops at New Orleans would send that drawing to Washington to warn U.S. Navy officials what the Confederates were testing, what they were capable of doing.

That intelligence filtered down the U.S. Navy's chain of command and, in January 1864, reached the South Atlantic Blockading fleet off Charleston. This disturbing news would help them prepare for an attack they hoped would never come, but was only a month away.

Because even though the *Pioneer* did not survive the fall of New Orleans, Hunley and McClintock did. They would escape with their research, their plans and the knowledge that they could build a boat that actually traveled underwater.

And next time, they would do better.

CHAPTER 3

1981 Charleston

This time would be better.

Clive Cussler felt confident of that when he arrived in Charleston just after Memorial Day. It had been barely 10 months since his first search for the *H. L. Hunley* ended, but so much had changed. This time they would spend nearly four weeks on the water—a serious, multifaceted expedition. This time the Institute of Archeology and Anthropology welcomed his presence, even supplied a boat and two divers. And in the past year, even the technology of underwater exploration had improved.

Motorola had developed a method of more effectively tracking offshore search grids, and even offered to send technicians down to help deploy the machinery. Cussler gladly accepted. He felt great about his prospects; everything was falling into place. This time there would be no problems. His crew had become a group of seasoned old salts, the result of three summers of steady shipwreck hunting. NUMA was still a casual organization—ultimately, they were a group of friends on a grand adventure—but it was becoming an increasingly businesslike endeavor.

Business was good for Cussler these days. He had a new publisher and his fifth Dirk Pitt adventure, *Night Probe!*, would be released in just two months. The new book helped fund the shipwreck hunting, which was turning into much more than a hobby for the author. Pitt's increasing popularity kept NUMA in business, and Cussler poked fun at himself and his growing celebrity by wearing T-shirts that read "Clive who?" Everyone thought it was hilarious, especially Cussler.

This year his team would spend more time in the water. They would not only search for targets, they would dive on them—allowing them to identify every target they found. There were still dozens— perhaps hundreds—of unexplored wrecks in the waters off Charleston, and, if he could, Cussler would put a name on them all. This was not a lark, it was a mission. The sweep of history inspired Cussler, and he had grand plans to seek out as much of it as he could find.

Just the sight of all that new diving equipment brought on a flood of memories. In some ways, SCUBA diving had led Cussler to this point. He had started diving for sport in the Pacific three decades earlier, back when most people had never heard of such a thing. In 1951 Cussler had been with the Military Air Transport Service, stationed at Hickman Field on Oahu. The air force had brought him to Hawaii, but it wasn't the world above the clouds that interested him. He was much more intrigued by the unexplored universe beneath the azure water surrounding the island.

Cussler and his friends had pooled their money and ordered SCUBA equipment from the only place it was available at the time— Jacques Cousteau. The gear was rudimentary and faulty, but it worked. The mask covered his entire face, the two snorkels had ping pong balls in them to stop incoming water, and the tank was bulky. But to Cussler, these toys were like tickets to another world.

Adventure had always been at the top of Cussler's agenda. As a teenager in California, he and his friends spent their days producing slick black-and-white films—cops and robber shorts, satiric takes on monster movies—just for the fun of making them, and the excuse to have a car chase or two. In the air force, Cussler's new posse would spend days exploring caves or swimming off the volcanic beaches of

Oahu. There was always something new waiting for his attention. Looking back, it seemed like everything he did was training for his future life, either writing books or hunting shipwrecks. Even the people he met left lasting impressions. One of his friends from Hawaii, an Italian named Al Giordano, would see his name changed by one letter and become forever immortalized as the faithful sidekick of Dirk Pitt.

When the SCUBA equipment arrived at Hickman, Cussler and his cohorts filled the tank with stale air from a hanger compressor and set off for new horizons. They took turns diving on reefs, enchanted by the quiet, blue world they found. Diving became such an obsession that Cussler carried his SCUBA equipment on refueling stops across the Pacific, taking any chance to dive around Midway or Wake Island. In those days, he was alone underwater. Cussler was doing nothing less than pioneering a new sport.

After he returned to the States, after his gas station and the jobs in advertising, Cussler returned to diving. He took a job at the Aquatic Center Dive Shop in Newport Beach when his wife pointed out an ad in the paper. She said that if he wanted to pen sea adventures, what better place to pick up material—and have time to write. It seemed like another lark, but there was a purpose. He had already written one novel, tapped out at night while his wife worked and his children slept. It had not turned out like he wanted, but he would try again.

The dive shop would allow him more time to be creative, but it also gave him on-the-job training. Cussler became a dive master, led charters off Catalina Island. He got his first taste of celebrity when he started broadcasting dive reports under the name Horace P. Quagmire. In some parts of California, he was still better-known for his hilarious weather reports than his literary success.

During the slow afternoons at the dive shop, he wrote in the back room. Cussler was composing the book that his publisher would eventually title *The Mediterranean Caper*, a title he would never particularly like. The words flowed, and this one was better. Dirk Pitt was becoming a living, breathing character and Cussler just had to sit back and enjoy the ride. When the book sold, and his writing prospects seemed brighter, Cussler quit the dive shop. The owners gave him a Doxa dive watch as a parting gift, a grand timepiece with a large orange face. He would give Pitt the same watch, and he would make it famous. The books came more easily after that, and soon Cussler had little time for sport diving.

The rest was history.

Looking at the dive equipment on the SCIAA boat, Cussler had to marvel at how the technology—the science—of diving and underwater archaeology had advanced since those days. Sometimes it was a trick just to keep Dirk Pitt's gear ahead of the times. This year, the *Hunley* expedition would use Motorola's new positioning equipment to run

Most of the people involved in the 1980 Hunley *expedition returned to Charleston for the 1981 search, including state archaeologist Ralph Wilbanks (seated, with bandana). That year, NUMA employed new fixed-point positioning equipment from Motorola that allowed crews onshore to direct the boats searching off Sullivan's Island. The equipment would make the team's search much more accurate, but lead to headaches years later. Courtesy of Ralph Wilbanks.*

search lanes. Using fixed points, his son Dirk could sit in a rental van onshore and triangulate the boat's position, tell the men on the water when to turn, where to look next. It was simply amazing.

They would run a lot of lanes this year. On their last trip, the NUMA explorers had searched two areas—a 1-mile by 3-mile grid inshore, and another 2 miles by 2.5 miles offshore. This time the state had issued Cussler a permit allowing him to explore nearly twice as much ocean. Their stage was a grid three miles wide—with Breach Inlet as its center point—and more than five miles out to sea. Cussler had chosen the location; based on his calculations, it was where the *Hunley* most likely ended up. He would joke that it wasn't rocket science, but it was decidedly scientific. Cussler relied on cold logic, as well as an intuition that even a trained archaeologist such as Wilbanks had to conclude was extraordinary.

Most of the 1980 team returned to Charleston with Cussler—Shea and Schob, Dirk and Wilbanks. Eventually the crew would include more than 17 people, including Coast Guardsman Tim Firmey, a couple of students from East Carolina University, two Motorola technicians, and Cussler's son-in-law, Bob Toft. For this longer expedition, they would get a change of scenery. Schob opted not to book the team into the old beach motel this year. Instead, he rented the team a rambling beach house on the Isle of Palms and hired a cook—memories of Throckmorton's sabotaged cooking still on his mind. Besides, who wanted to cook after a day on the water? Their host was gracious and her Southernisms a constant source of amusement. But the grits were fantastic.

There would be no return charter for the *Coastal Explorer* either. Shortly after he arrived, Cussler spied the boat chopped up and abandoned in the marsh behind Sullivan's Island. It had been on its last legs during the 1980 expedition, Cussler realized, but he was still sad to see her meet such a fate. The *Coastal Explorer* brought back fond memories and others that he did not want to relive. If he never saw another jetty, Cussler thought, it would be too soon.

This year Cussler chartered the *Sweet Sue* from a local captain. It was a newer boat than the *Explorer* and would handle the offshore searches while Schob used the university's outboard for running lanes closer inshore. For some reason never quite clear, the crew took to calling this the *Steak Boat*. The team sailed out of Toler's Cove in Mount Pleasant, behind Sullivan's Island. It shortened the trip outside considerably.

They would avoid Breach Inlet this year.

Cussler had his state-of-the-art equipment, a new boat and a team of veterans—but he wasn't ready to dive into the *Hunley* search just yet. He decided to start by relocating the *Keokuk* and *Weehawken* as kind of a warm-up. On the first day, the *Sweet Sue* steered for the waters off what remained of Morris Island, where the old lighthouse stood completely in the water at high tide. It made for a good reference point. There, the 1981 expedition began.

Before they dropped the magnetometer, Cussler bet Wilbanks a half-gallon of Bombay gin that he could find the *Keokuk* on their first pass—that's how confident he was. If they didn't get it on the first look, he would pay extra for each lane searched until they did. Wilbanks happily took the bet—he liked gin.

They didn't find the *Keokuk* on the first pass. Or the second. It took a little while, although not long. The old ironclad was still there, of course, and divers surveyed the wreck that afternoon. Wilbanks won the bet and proceeded to get sick on the Bombay, which he shared with Cussler. He may have liked gin, but apparently Wilbanks' stomach couldn't abide the good stuff. Cussler thought this was hilarious. Yes, this time would be better.

Diving would be a chore for the entire expedition. Off Charleston, the water is murky and visibility is often less than two feet. It was a world away from the clear waters of Hawaii, and it made the job tricky. Divers had to use their hands to see much more than their eyes. It complicated the search, but wasn't insurmountable—especially for a veteran diver such as Wilbanks, who had grown up in Charleston water. Soon, NUMA was finding and identifying wrecks almost every day.

The *Sweet Sue* crew located the *Weehawken* after the *Keokuk* and then moved into the harbor, where they found the Union Monitor-class ironclad *Patapsco*. The *Patapsco* sank in January of 1865 after sneaking into the harbor mouth between Sumter and Moultrie. There, drifting through the fog, the ironclad hit a floating mine that blew a hole in its side. More than 60 sailors died in the explosion and sinking, likely the Union's last casualties in Charleston.

The *Patapsco* had been missing for more than a century, but it took NUMA less than a day to find it—the result of good advance research. The ironclad was buried in the muck beneath the harbor channel, which made diving on the wreck difficult. There was always another ship sailing into the port, and the *Sweet Sue* constantly had to dodge traffic. It made little difference; they couldn't excavate the site anyway. The navy considered the *Patapsco* a burial site, putting it strictly off-limits. They could look, but they couldn't touch. That was fine with Cussler. The *Patapsco* wasn't their main target, just another notch in NUMA's belt.

Cussler did not limit his interest to military vessels—he had decided NUMA would search for anything that sailed. During the war, Charleston had been the home port of several blockade runners, and dozens of others called on the city regularly. It was one of the South's largest ports, and there was money to be made by any enterprising ship captain who could get past the South Atlantic Blockading Squadron. Every week these ships sailed in, often from Nassau, carrying nails, cloth or even booze. Many of the ships never made port, however—the Union fleet sank countless blockade runners and ran at least a half-dozen onto the beaches surrounding the city. That had been the *Housatonic*'s job, in fact.

One day when it was too rough to take the *Sweet Sue* out to sea,

Cussler decided to look around the Isle of Palms beach for some of those blockade runners, particularly the *Stonewall Jackson*. In the spring of 1863, the ship had been run aground on the island and blasted to bits while trying to deliver 40,000 shoes to the people of Charleston. The Union sailors took great joy in firing on blockade runners when they foundered, complicating Confederate efforts to salvage their cargo. Beached ships were good target practice.

Cussler had studied an 1864 chart of the coastline and realized that the beach now stretched at least a quarter-mile farther out to sea than it did in the nineteenth century, back when the Isle of Palms was known as Long Island. By that reckoning, Cussler figured, the *Stonewall Jackson* and some of those other wrecks might lie under the current beach.

The team laid out a grid around Fifth Avenue and started walking lanes up and down the beach with a metal detector. It was a much more difficult process than pulling a magnetometer behind a boat, but Cussler would not let a day pass without doing some work. Standing alone on the beach, Cussler tried to calibrate the metal detector's settings but found that it didn't want to cooperate. Its gauges were reading off the scales and he couldn't tune it down. He fiddled with the knobs for a minute and finally realized why he was having trouble.

He was standing on top of a metal wreck.

Cussler's son, Dirk, and the two East Carolina students began pushing into the sand with metal probes and soon hit something. After they consulted with some locals, the Isle of Palms sent out a mainte-nance crew with a backhoe. A crowd gathered, giving NUMA its first audience. For most of the day, dozens of bikini-clad spectators watched the backhoe cut into the beach. The sun bunnies got a history lesson that day, as Cussler and his crew dug deep into the nineteenth century.

They soon had an eight-foot trench, which quickly filled with water. After a few frustrating attempts, they decided to work exactly as they did underwater: they used a water pump and a plastic pipe to shoot water into the bottom of the trench, churning up the sand and digging an even deeper hole. Within minutes they had blasted down 15 feet. Suddenly, coal and pieces of mahogany surfaced. The only thing missing were the shoes.

Eventually the team would find two other blockade runners—the *Ruby* and the *Raccoon*—using a magnetometer and historic records that suggested where they sank. NUMA was adding more ships to its list every day, but these were simple tune-ups for the long days searching for the *Hunley*.

Soon, the crew fell into a daily routine: the *Sweet Sue* would run 30-meter lanes, the magnetometer recording every anomaly they passed over. Onshore, Dirk sat in the back of a hot, rented Budget van with the Motorola Mini-Ranger team and radioed directions to the team. Every target was recorded and listed, and Cussler kept track. In 17 days, the team had 19 potential targets. Finally, the *Sweet Sue* went back to investigate the most interesting, or likely, sites. A team of two divers would go in the water and survey the bottom using air lifts, like a vacuum hose to blast through the sand.

It is romantic to think that most ships sit on the ocean floor, waiting to be discovered and explored. But, truth is, most are buried beneath years of sand and silt and can only be reached through time-consuming digging. The divers did this much the same way they had on the beach, using compressed air to bore through the muck. It churned up the water terribly, but then the visibility underwater couldn't get much worse.

Once this process started, Cussler limited the team to one goal: finding the *Hunley*. Divers would investigate a site only long enough to figure out if they'd hit something that could be a 40-foot iron submarine. Any clue to the contrary and they packed up and moved on. Otherwise they could be on a single site for days. And Cussler did not have days to spare.

It became a grind, the search interminable, but the crew was working hard and Cussler felt they were making real progress. To break up the monotony, the author sometimes scheduled field trips for the late afternoon. They visited Fort Sumter and Fort Moultrie to get into the spirit of the expedition, and to connect with the city's past. One day, the team drove to an old bank in downtown Charleston and marveled at a little-known tourist attraction in its basement. There, in a dungeon-like room, sat a life-size replica of the *H. L. Hunley.*

Students at a local technical college had built the model in the 1960s, using sketches from one of the sub's builders as reference. The iron hull was bulky, dominated by huge rivet heads and a wooden spar. A couple of the hull plates had been left off to give visitors a look inside the strange contraption. Mannequins had been placed inside, their hands frozen on the sub's propeller crank. Cussler's crew examined the model for nearly half an hour. This, one of them said, is what we're looking for—and the real thing was probably not even 10 miles away.

And they would find it.

One day, a local television crew showed up unannounced at Toler's Cove. The reporter and cameraman, a couple of interns, wanted to do a story on the expedition. But they were not interested in interviewing the divers—"only Clive Cussler." With this attitude, it took about five seconds to piss off an entire boatload of people. When they were told Clive wasn't available at the moment, the TV crew decided to wait. Even interns knew better than to leave without the story.

Wilbanks got an idea.

The crew was invited to go along on the search, and this was not a calm day. Wilbanks, who had some experience with taking land-lubbers offshore, sat back and quietly predicted what would happen next. Within minutes of clearing the jetties, the boat was rocking steadily and the interns were lying on the deck, violently seasick.

Although it was only 8:30 in the morning, Wilbanks suggested the team break for lunch. The NUMA guys and Wilbanks sat in a circle around the two amateurs, passing sandwiches back and forth and laughing maniacally.

The sight of the food was nearly as bad as the motion to the visitors, and they writhed around, becoming what Wilbanks called "deck meat." Eventually the team took pity on the aspiring journalists and presented Cussler for an interview. The author was his usual jovial self, but it was all the reporters could do to hold a camera. They got through it just in time for the *Sweet Sue*'s captain to declare it too rough to search that day.

The plan was to take the TV crew back to shore and then resume the hunt. But Wilbanks had seen this too many times and estimated how it would go. As the *Sweet Sue* reached the relatively smooth waters between the jetties, he said, the reporter and cameraman would start to perk up. By the time they sailed into the harbor, both of them would be up and around, even joking. When they got to Toler's Cove, Wilbanks promised, the pair would be ready to go again.

As the NUMA guys tied up at the dock, the interns thanked them for a great day. Before they walked away, the young reporter asked if it would be possible for them to go out with the team again another day—just as Wilbanks had predicted.

The water remained rough for most of June, sometimes proving too much for even veteran divers. But Cussler would not let conditions dictate the expedition's schedule; he was in full search mode. If offshore conditions were too rough, he would spend the day looking elsewhere. On one particularly choppy afternoon, he steered the team into Charleston Harbor to hunt for local ironclads.

When the Confederates evacuated Charleston in February 1865, they had burned the city's trio of ironclads—the *Chicora*, the *Charleston* and the *Palmetto State*—at the docks near the foot of Calhoun Street. A local legend claimed that as the *Palmetto State* burned to the waterline, the image of a palmetto tree had shown through the smoke. In some ways, these were the city's most famous ships—and they had been lost to history for more than a century.

The *Sweet Sue* ran lanes along the peninsula's edge all afternoon, from Union Pier up to the Pearman and Grace bridges that connected Charleston and Mount Pleasant. It was frustrating work. There were several targets, but years of Army Corps of Engineering dredging and demolition had scattered and destroyed any remnants of the old ironclads. They were down there, but they were in pieces, and the NUMA team could not get a solid lock on anything identifiable. When the weather improved, Cussler abandoned the harbor search and turned his attention back to the *Hunley*.

They found an average of one good target each day. There was a lot of trash littering the ocean floor off Charleston: old coast guard buoys, equipment from shrimp boats and the remains of the Stone Fleet—a bunch of whaling ships intentionally sank by the Union to make the passage into the harbor more treacherous. Four of the targets were identified quickly, and most of the others were discounted immediately. Only one gave Cussler any real hope.

One afternoon the *Sweet Sue* was motoring back to the dock after a long day of running lanes. Everyone was tired, and they hadn't particularly found anything of interest that day. The crew was just ready to get back to shore and drink. The magnetometer had been left on by accident, and someone noticed the graph stylus jump as the device registered a huge metal object beneath the boat. Cussler ordered the captain to turn around, and the *Sweet Sue* circled until it hit the target again.

Firmey and the two East Carolina students—Bob Browning and Wilson West—dove in and began probing the site. They were only down there a few minutes before West surfaced and said they had something that appeared to be at least 30 feet long and probably four feet wide. It was the final detail that gave Cussler chills.

"Don't quote me," West said, "but the ends appear to be tapered."

The dreams of beers onshore died immediately. Wilbanks put a buoy on the site, and the *Sweet Sue* headed for the docks to retrieve the suction dredge. It was already 6 P.M., but in June they knew there would be at least two more hours of daylight. Suddenly, no one was tired anymore. Heading back out, they passed Schob and Shea in the *Steak Boat*. The two men wondered why the *Sweet Sue* was going the wrong way, but all they could do was wave. Cussler wasn't stopping for anything.

Back on the site, Wilbanks and Rodney Warren went over the gunwale with the suction dredge and got to work. A dredge churns up all matter of sea life, violently disrupting the tranquil underwater landscape. The commotion on this evening soon attracted at least one shark, trolling for an easy meal. Cussler and the others on the boat threw Pepsi cans at the great fish and eventually it went away, Wilbanks and Warren none the wiser. They were too busy.

It was almost dark before the two divers came back up. They had dug a two-foot hole and hit something, but didn't know what it was. The visibility that deep had been non-existent, and the fading evening light hadn't helped. Wilbanks sketched a fin that he'd found on the object. It was quarter-inch iron, some kind of a plate. And it was triangular. Whatever the fin was attached to was farther down in the silt and they were running out of time; there had been no time to dig deeper.

The plate was interesting, Wilbanks said, but something didn't feel right. He saw no rivets on it anywhere, which led him to assume it had been welded to whatever was underneath it. That did not bode well. There was no welding in 1863—the *Hunley* had been put together with rivets. As dusk fell on the *Sweet Sue*, Wilbanks stood on deck and talked it out with Cussler. It had to be a coast guard buoy, he decided—it was about the right size, and based on the magnetometer readings, it was the right shape, too. The ocean floor off Charleston was littered with these things, abandoned markers alerting ships to hazards of navigation.

That must be it, Wilbanks said. Cussler agreed.

Reluctantly, the crew gave up and the *Sweet Sue* motored back to the dock. Cussler and Wilbanks continued to talk about their find, but there was nothing else they could do. They had decided early on that, to keep the search moving, they stopped investigating sites once they found something that suggested their target was not the *Hunley*. And a welded metal plate didn't fit. So they moved on.

Long after he left Charleston, Cussler would think back to that night and wonder, as he did in all his books, *What if?* Wilbanks would remain haunted by that dive for more than a decade. Neither man could decide if it was curiosity or intuition. But for years both would repeatedly ask themselves the same question: What was that thing?

There was little else of note, and time was running out. Cussler had book appearances starting in little more than a month and he had

On June 26, 1981, Clive Cussler held a news conference at his rented beach house to talk about NUMA's just-concluded expedition. They had found nearly a dozen shipwrecks in just a few weeks. Although they didn't find the Hunley, *they had some promising leads—one of which would haunt Cussler and Wilbanks for more than a decade. Courtesy of Ralph Wilbanks.*

already spent $75,000 looking for the *Hunley*. Finally, on June 26, NUMA called a rare press conference on the screened porch of their rented house to talk about the findings of their expedition. Cussler, wearing his "Clive Who?" shirt and the Doxa watch he had made famous, was his usual good-natured self.

"Let's face it—what can you do?" Cussler told reporters. "We didn't find the *Hunley* but not all went down the tube."

They had surveyed 16 square miles of ocean, much of it beyond the wreck of the *Housatonic*. Cussler recounted the day his divers touched the *Weehawken*, the *Keokuk* and the *Patapsco*. He said NUMA had ultimately found the remains of five blockade runners— the *Rattle Snake* and *Norseman*, in addition to the *Ruby*, *Raccoon* and *Stonewall Jackson*. It had been a successful month.

But the *Hunley*'s location remained a mystery. Cussler admitted that he had begun to fear the sub, like the *Bonhomme Richard*, may have floated a long time before it eventually sank.

"We don't know where the *Hunley* is, but we know where it ain't," Cussler said. "If it floated out to sea, we may never find it."

It was a bittersweet admission, and one that Cussler didn't really believe. The expedition had been great, far better than the previous year's, and the author hated to leave. He had spent a lot of time in Charleston, and the town was starting to grow on him. Cussler joked to reporters that he and his wife had considered moving to Sullivan's Island—after two summers in Charleston, he felt quite at home. But duty called.

For the time being, Cussler's tenure in Charleston was over. The *Hunley* had proven as elusive as the *Bonhomme Richard*, and not even he could continue to pour money into the ocean. Although he talked about returning next summer, he knew in his heart that, until new information turned up, he was pumping a dry hole.

"I'm a writer, not an oil company," Cussler said.

Cussler's adventures with NUMA, and Dirk Pitt, were just beginning. He would go on to other shipwrecks, greater adventures, but the *Hunley* would never be far from his mind. Cussler did not tell reporters what he really thought. He believed the *Hunley* was out there and, when it was ready to be found, he would be the one who got it.

When Cussler left Charleston he was confident that, when the time was right, he would return—and find the *Hunley*.

CHAPTER 4

1862
Mobile

Horace Hunley arrived in Alabama the last week of April, feeling surprisingly confident considering the baggage he was carrying. He was a refugee, his property had been confiscated by the Union Army and he had been forced to abandon the submarine that he believed would make him a Great Man. But for the moment, Hunley would allow none of this to distract him. He felt that success was firmly within his grasp.

He found Mobile very much like the city that he had just escaped, only smaller and refreshingly calm. The Alabama port resembled New Orleans in several ways, from its architecture to its diverse culture. Cotton exports kept the city alive, although the blockade just offshore had tempered business considerably. Hunley felt right at home. He had James McClintock and Baxter Watson to help him continue his work and soon discovered that his old friend and boss, Francis Hatch, had taken up residence in the city. All the ingredients he needed to build a new submarine were in place.

In the spring of 1862, Mobile was as secure as any city in the Confederacy. The town of 30,000 souls sat inland on Mobile Bay, far from both the Union blockade ships in the Gulf and the fighting in the countryside. The Confederate troops stationed there had it easier than most of their counterparts across the South. There were still dangers, of course—there were rumors that spies lurked around every corner and the city's forces were often sent to fight in other places, most recently Shiloh.

The Mobile port was still busy, even though the U.S. fleet had cut off much of its traffic. Blockade runners managed to come in and out of the harbor almost daily, but the Union clearly had the upper hand. Local shipwrights were frantically building privateer ships in hopes of breaking the Gulf Coast Blockading Squadron and restoring commerce. The city had just gotten something of a reprieve when Confederate officials received word that Union Adm. David Farragut had set out for Vicksburg. For the moment, it seemed, no invasion of Mobile was imminent. It was a great relief for Mobile residents. The city would not suffer New Orleans' fate.

That bit of good news did little to slow construction at the port. For the most part, the Alabama shipbuilders were more conservative than their New Orleans counterparts. Their idea of cutting edge technology was to attach iron plating to the hulls of traditional

The CSS Tennessee *was one of the first full-fledged ironclads built by Confederates in Alabama during the war. When it was launched in February 1863, around the time of the* American Diver *trials, it became the flagship of Confederate Adm. Franklin Buchanan. The admiral much preferred this type of ironclad to McClintock's experimental submarines and offered the engineer little assistance in his efforts. Courtesy National Archives.*

gunboats like the *Gaines* and the *Morgan*. But it would not be long before locals graduated to the unorthodox design of full-fledged ironclads. Already, two such ships—the *Tennessee* and the *Nashville* —were under construction upstream in Selma. The Confederates held hope that those two ironclads would prove every bit as effective as the CSS *Virginia* had at Hampton Roads. They even dreamed of decimating the blockade in Farragut's absence.

Hunley and his engineers believed Mobile was the ideal city in which they could continue their work. The town had clearly embraced the innovative concepts of maritime technology and there was no shortage of machine shops where they might find willing partners. All they needed was proper introductions. Shortly after arriving, Hunley and McClintock sought an audience with the Confederate command. They wanted the military's blessing and support—but mostly they wanted its money. Cut off from most of the *Pioneer* investors, Hunley and McClintock worried about financing their new boat alone. McClintock had almost no cash and Hunley's resources were limited, thanks to the Yankees.

The trio could not have gotten a more receptive welcome from Gen. Dabney H. Maury. The Confederate commander at Mobile was just 40, a contemporary of Hunley, and already a seasoned military veteran. Maury was impressed with their work, due in part to familial connections. His uncle, the oceanographer and former U.S. Navy commander Matthew Maury, was an underwater explosives expert— himself a pioneer of sorts. The general felt he understood this technology and fancied himself as something of an innovator, too.

Hunley, McClintock and Watson showed Maury their schematics of *Pioneer* and recounted the boat's successful trial runs on Lake Pontchartrain. They lamented the necessity of sinking the submarine to keep it out of Yankee hands. Maury understood, but agreed they had done the right thing. Maury saw great opportunity in Hunley and his companions. These men, if they were to be believed, had built a boat "for running under the water, at any required depth from the surface," as McClintock had said. And that, Maury knew, could change naval warfare forever.

The general understood that technology was advancing at a remarkable rate, perhaps even faster than his uncle could have imagined. If it were possible for boats to travel under the water, Maury knew this could level the playing field—perhaps even give the Confederacy a chance for naval superiority. He immediately gave the project his blessing. Maury had no money for the inventors, but promised manpower and the cooperation of local machinists. It was the best he could do.

Maury put Hunley and Mc-Clintock back in business, but he also inadvertently would make their work more difficult. As the overall Confederate commander at Mobile, he could do

Dabney H. Maury was one of several U.S. military officers who resigned their commissions when the Civil War began. As the Confederate commander at Mobile in 1862, Maury helped James McClintock and Horace Hunley resume their submarine project, but inadvertently put them at odds with the Confederate Navy. The army's support of the fish-boat project ensured Adm. Franklin Buchanan would never embrace the project. Courtesy National Archives.

whatever he wanted. But his support put them in the middle of a brewing turf war between the army and navy. While the blue-water fleet was strictly the domain of the Confederate Navy, the army controlled all ships that sailed the South's rivers. With Maury's blessing, the army was promoting a project that would operate on the navy's battlefield. And some navy officials would not appreciate the intrusion. Hunley did not realize this at first. He only knew that he was about to build his second submarine.

Maury soon introduced Hunley and McClintock to two engineers who had a good reputation and a profitable working relationship with the Confederate government. Together, Thomas Park and Thomas Lyons owned one of the city's best machine shops—a large brick building at the corner of State and Water streets with two cranes out back and ample space inside. When the New Orleans refugees arrived at Park and Lyons' shop near the riverfront, McClintock and Watson finally felt the same as Hunley: as if they were home.

Park and Lyons were busy churning out bullets for the Confederate Army, just as McClintock and Watson had done back in New Orleans. Most machine shops were living off government work these days, so this was not much of a coincidence. But Park and Lyons had even closer ties to the cause. At that moment, they had a lucrative contract reboring rifles for larger-caliber ammunition. The work was progressing steadily, because the Mobile engineers had no shortage of help.

Maury had assigned members of the Twenty-first Alabama to Park and Lyons for light duty in the days following Shiloh. The regiment had taken heavy casualties in the Tennessee countryside, and the general felt the men needed time away from the front lines after that battle—the war's worst yet. The Twenty-first Alabama had landed this assignment in part because there were a few gifted engineers in the regiment. When Maury spoke to Park and Lyons about the submarine, he mentioned William Alexander specifically.

Alexander was an engineering prodigy—a man who could not only rebore guns but who also designed and built them. He had shown such talent that he would never have to fight on the front lines again; the Confederates would not risk losing a gifted engineer. That was fine with Alexander. A native of England, he had emigrated to America for just such opportunities. Maury thought McClintock could use Alexander, and the two seemed to get along immediately. Alexander was intrigued by McClintock's boat, even though he quickly recognized that Hunley was the more passionate man, the driving force behind the project.

It would take months to draw up plans for the new boat, and that much longer for Alexander to find the materials to build it. McClintock overcomplicated the process, determined to learn from his mistakes with the *Pioneer*. His design would reflect the lessons learned from his first submarine. This one should have more defined edges, like a traditional ship—the rounded hull had been too difficult to keep on an even keel. McClintock also believed the *Pioneer* had been too wide, that its beam had cut down on its speed. The new boat would be much sleeker than his original, and much narrower, to the chagrin of its eventual crew.

When McClintock finished his drawings, he put Alexander in charge of building it. The young engineer would draw the patterns for the individual pieces that others would cut, and he set out to salvage iron from old boilers he found around the city. McClintock had little role in this aspect of the construction. For the moment, he was most concerned with the submarine's source of power.

McClintock thought the hand-cranked propeller on the *Pioneer* was too laborious, even barbaric. He wanted something far more advanced and elegant. He wanted his boat to have an engine. Some would later claim McClintock experimented with steam for his second submarine. But he likely knew that such a scheme would never work. At the very least, a steam engine would foul the crew's air, or potentially turn the entire boat into a boiler—or a bomb. McClintock later said that, from the start, he envisioned his futuristic ship powered by an electromagnetic engine.

McClintock passed the entire summer and part of the fall experimenting with electromagnetics. Although Watson assured him that such engines existed, McClintock could not build one small enough to both fit into the submarine and provide the power needed to turn the propeller. McClintock grew frustrated, but he would not give up. The technology was almost there. While Alexander constructed the submarine's hull, McClintock stubbornly continued to tinker.

Horace Hunley spent weeks trying to find investors for this new boat. In New Orleans he had a stable of rich friends to draw on, but he had few connections with wealthy Mobile residents. Hatch could not help him, and Hunley chose not to bother his brother-in-law for the money. Robert Barrow had never been entirely committed to the idea of the first boat, and perhaps Hunley knew better than to ask a second time.

But Hunley had complete faith in McClintock, enough so that he eventually gave up his search for partners and financed the entire project himself. He had been paying for materials as Alexander collected them anyway, and Hunley felt certain his investment would pay off tenfold. It was not an insignificant risk. By the time McClintock finished his work, the boat would cost Hunley $15,000. The submarine took all but his last cent.

Progress on the boat was slow through the summer, and Hunley soon became restless. McClintock's incessant talk of electromagnetics bored him immeasurably. Hunley needed adventure, as well as a new source of income. General Maury's kind reception had given him second thoughts about his disdain for the Confederacy, so he eventually offered to put his talents to work for the South. The aspiring architect offered the military a simplistic and wildly impractical idea to make Mobile more defensible. He outlined a plan to build iron walls at obtuse angles—to better repel enemy fire—throughout the city. But there was barely enough iron available for a small submarine, much less a wall several miles long. The Confederates politely declined his proposal.

As it became increasingly apparent that Vicksburg would become a key battleground in the defense of the South, Hunley set out for Mississippi. Perhaps he had gotten the idea from his old boss, Hatch, who was still working as a Confederate agent. Or maybe Hunley was just looking for new ways to become a Great Man. There was little for him to do in Mobile, so he stayed away most of the summer. Not even his sister could keep up with his whereabouts.

"My poor Brother! Where is he?" Volumnia wrote to her husband at one point.

～

The hull of the new submarine, initially—and unimaginatively—called *Pioneer II*, began to take shape in the early fall. Alexander built the sub's frame and had most of the forged boiler plates in place, but he could not finish his work because he didn't have the dimensions for whatever motor McClintock intended to install. The engineer's obsession with an electromagnetic engine delayed construction by months. Alexander was confident he could have the submarine completed shortly after McClintock delivered its propulsion system. But there seemed no end in sight to McClintock's experiments.

The submarine had caught the attention of the workers at Park and Lyons' shop, and Alexander had no shortage of extra hands willing to help. It seemed everyone wanted to be involved with the secret project. One of the men most drawn to the sub was Alexander's friend from the Twenty-first Alabama Infantry, George E. Dixon. And Dixon soon became as obsessed with the boat as McClintock was with his engine.

Dixon may have been attracted to McClintock's submarine for any number of reasons. He was an engineer, so he admired the concept behind the boat. He also had spent his share of time on the water. Dixon had worked on steamboats on the Mississippi and Ohio rivers before the war—including a gambling boat called the *Flirt*—but was stranded in Mobile once the fighting began. He had adjusted well to his adopted hometown, as different as it was from Cincinnati, where he had lived just a few years earlier. He joined a local Masonic lodge and the Mobile Grays, a volunteer police force. Dixon even began to court a local girl.

Dixon said little about himself, or his past, but he made friends easily. He was an impressive man, lean and a few inches shy of six feet tall, with fair hair and the mannerisms of the Southern gentry. Friends would later say that Dixon had an "attractive presence." He also knew his business well, and he and Alexander had become almost inseparable.

The Mobile Grays joined the Confederacy as a single unit in the fall of 1861. They soon became the Twenty-first Alabama Infantry Regiment, and Dixon and Alexander were assigned to Company A. When the regiment shipped out for Tennessee in March of the following year, the ladies of Mobile turned out to see them off in style. Just before they boarded the train, one of these ladies—apparently Dixon's sweetheart—gave him a $20 gold piece to keep for her sake.

That romantic gesture would save his life.

The Twenty-first Alabama was sent to Corinth, Mississippi, where Southern forces were amassing for a surprise attack. The Union Army led by Maj. Gen. Ulysses S. Grant had advanced to Pittsburg Landing in Tennessee and the Confederates wanted to stop these Yankees before they drove deeper into the South. The Battle of Shiloh, as it would be called, turned out to be the bloodiest engagement of the young war. The Twenty-first Alabama was nearly decimated.

Early in the battle, on April 6, the Alabama soldiers fell into a brutal firefight. The Union Army was relentless and viciously efficient on that day. The Twenty-first lost six color-bearers in quick succession; eventually, 200 of the regiment's 650 men were killed or wounded. Dixon was one of the first shot. An errant bullet hit Dixon in his left thigh, dropping him immediately. The ball should have severed his artery, leaving him to bleed to death on the battlefield.

Instead, the bullet hit the gold coin in his pocket.

The impact of the shot was so strong that it warped the coin and drove it into the meat of Dixon's leg. The coin-wrapped bullet burrowed so deep into his thigh that it left a trench in his femur, but somehow the gold absorbed most of the impact. Dixon would walk with a limp for the rest of his life, but he had survived. This miracle was the talk of the Twenty-first Alabama for weeks after the battle.

"George Dixon, shot in the hip, the ball striking a gold piece ranged upwards and came out of his side; will probably recover if he can be well cared for," one member of the Twenty-first Alabama wrote to his wife, assessing the regiment's casualties the day after the battle.

Everyone agreed that the coin had saved his life, even Dixon. When he returned to Mobile, he took the coin to a jeweler who added an inscription to the mangled gold:

Shiloh

April 6th 1862

My life Preserver

G.E.D.

He would never part with the coin, or go anywhere without it. It was a battle-tested good luck charm. Every day it reminded Dixon not only of his extraordinary good fortune but of one other inarguable fact: He was a survivor.

William Alexander no doubt stoked Dixon's interest in the submarine. He was excited to be involved in the project, and the feeling was infectious. After spending months working on its construction, Dixon began to get ideas about serving on its crew—just as Alexander had. Dixon was attracted to this new method of warfare. He was convinced it would work, and he wanted to be a part of this grand experiment. At the very least, sailing aboard a submarine boat would require minimal walking.

McClintock gave up on the electromagnetic engine in the fall. It was folly, he realized, and he had spent more time on an unworkable motor than it had taken him to build the entire *Pioneer*. He was dejected, but still determined to make this boat more powerful and more efficient than its predecessor. Even though the *American Diver*—as the boat was eventually christened—had less room in its interior than the *Pioneer*, McClintock doubled the crew size. He built four cranking stations in the *Diver*'s main compartment and attached them to the sub's propeller shaft.

McClintock believed that by increasing the manpower, he could double the boat's speed. It was a terrible miscalculation for an engineer, and he would not be pleased with the outcome. Later, McClintock would say the *American Diver*—despite its improved hydrodynamics and the amount of time put into its development—was every bit as flawed as his first effort.

"To obtain room for the machinery and persons," McClintock later wrote, "she was built 36 feet long, 3 feet wide and 4 feet high, 12 feet at each end was built tapering or modeled to make her easy to pass through the water. There was much time and money lost in efforts to build an electromagnetic engine for propelling the boat ... I afterwards fitted cranks to turn the propeller by hand, working four men at a time, but the air being so closed, and the work so hard, that we were unable to get a speed sufficient to make the boat of service against vessels, blockading the port."

The *American Diver* was launched in the winter of 1863, nearly nine months after the New Orleans refugees arrived in Mobile. It was first tested in the safe waters of Mobile Bay, and its five-man crew may have included local captain George Cook as its pilot, and Dixon as a crewmember. The men found the interior cramped and uncomfortable—far too narrow for any grown man. The sub itself was dreadfully slow. By some accounts, it would not go any faster than two knots. The extra manpower did nothing to improve speed.

Neither Hunley nor McClintock would ever say much about the *American Diver*, probably because it was such an abysmal failure. Its design flaws were apparent soon after it was launched, and its short time in service was a disaster. The sub could barely operate in Mobile Bay, and the light chop of the Gulf of Mexico taxed the *American Diver* beyond its meager abilities. Contrary to local rumors, however, no one ever died aboard the submarine. That was about the only good thing that could be said about McClintock's second sub.

A Confederate deserter offered the most detailed account of the *American Diver*'s time in service. He told U.S. Navy officials that the secret weapon had set out to attack the Gulf Coast Blockading Squadron in early February, but could not reach the fleet. The *American Diver* had sailed from Fort Morgan near the mouth of Mobile Bay around 8 P.M. one evening. The crew planned to travel underwater to Sand Island, about three miles offshore, and then take bearings on the nearest Union ship.

Originally, McClintock wanted the sub to dive beneath its prey and attach a mine to its keel. But that plan was too complicated and eventually the *Diver* was set up to attack in the same manner that *Pioneer* had employed: by dragging a contact mine at the end of a 100-foot rope and drawing it into the flank of the enemy ship. But the *Diver* would never get the chance.

Once the crew surfaced off Sand Island, they realized the current was quickly dragging the submarine out to sea. They had no choice but to turn back. The first officer cut the mine loose, pulled the rope inside and the *American Diver* set a course for Fort Morgan. It took the men several hours to reach the fort's dock, and they arrived exhausted and defeated. Farragut's fleet was never in danger.

The *Diver* allegedly tried again several days later, but it still could not get close to the fleet. The crew simply didn't have enough power, or stamina, to travel four miles out to sea. McClintock suggested that a small ship might tow the sub within a mile of the fleet. The crew could board the submarine at sea, blow up a ship, and then return to their tender. It was not an ideal solution, but given the limits of the boat, it was the only choice.

Confederate officials later suggested the *Diver* made several attempts just as McClintock planned, but it never worked. And soon, they ran out of chances. One night the *American Diver* was swamped while under tow, perhaps as the men tried to climb aboard. For years, people in Mobile would whisper that the crew let the sub sink intentionally, just so they wouldn't have to spend another hour behind those damned cranks.

Confederate Adm. Franklin Buchanan informed the navy secretary in Richmond of the *Diver*'s loss on February 14. He did not bother to suppress his skepticism. The entire project was a failure, Buchanan said. Even with a full crew cranking the propeller, he said, "On that occasion its speed was not more than two miles per hour."

"Since then other trials have been made all proving failures. The last trial was made about a week since when the boat was lost off this harbor and was sunk, the men came very near being lost," Buchanan wrote. "I never entertained but one opinion as to the result of this boat, that it should prove to be a failure, and such has been the case ... I considered the whole affair impracticable from the commencement."

Buchanan could not have done more to sabotage the *Diver* if he'd left the hatches open himself. From the start, he made no secret of his disdain for the submarine, perhaps a lingering resentment of the army meddling in naval affairs. But Buchanan's sharp criticism was somewhat surprising, as he was one of the least likely candidates to eschew new technology. Prior to his arrival in Mobile, Buchanan had been the first captain of the CSS *Virginia*.

Buchanan had commanded the *Virginia* on the day it sank the *Congress* and the *Cumberland* at Hampton Roads. He sustained an injury in the battle and was not onboard the following day when the former *Merrimack* had its famous battle with the USS *Monitor*. But he harbored no ill feelings toward these innovative ships—he was one of the Confederacy's biggest proponents of the *Tennessee*, the new ironclad under construction at Selma.

Whatever his reasons, Buchanan made it clear he had no use for Hunley, McClintock or their submarine. And he would not help them attempt to recover the sub, which sank somewhere near the mouth of Mobile Bay. Later, some Confederates would hint that there was a cursory search for the *American Diver*, but it was never found. Buchanan would not devote much manpower—much less a ship—to any search. Eventually Baxter Watson wrote to Secretary of the Navy Stephen Mallory, asking him to intervene. The attempt to go over Buchanan's head failed miserably. Mallory only passed the request back to Buchanan, giving him another excuse to insult the *Diver*.

"The boat cannot possibly be of any practical use in Mobile Bay in consequence of its shallowness, nor do I think it could be made effective against the enemy off the harbor as the blockading vessels are anchored in water too shallow to permit the boat to pass under them," Buchanan wrote.

And that was it for the *American Diver*. The second Hunley and McClintock submarine was gone.

Horace Hunley had returned to Mobile to watch the *American Diver*'s launch, only to find that he had lost another submarine—and $15,000. He quickly sank into one of his dark moods, a depression that would linger for months. James McClintock felt like a failure. He was sure his two boats had been great advancements in naval technology. Very few ships in history had been able to submerge, travel underwater and then surface again. McClintock was close, he knew it. If only he had another opportunity, the engineer felt that he could take the knowledge and experience he had amassed and build an even better submarine.

But no one wanted to give them another chance.

By March of 1863, McClintock was a man out of options. The failure of the *American Diver* had cooled the Confederate brass to his plans, and Hunley did not have the money or the will to finance another project. By some estimates, Horace Hunley had literally sunk more than $20,000 into his venture. It was the end of the submarine project—until luck intervened.

In March, as spring and despair descended on Hunley and McClintock, a chance at redemption arrived in Mobile. Edgar C. Singer, fresh from the Texas coast, came to town and took a strong interest in their submarine boats. He had been experimenting with his own new underwater technology and Singer had talent, ideas—and money.

Singer was the nephew of Isaac Merrit Singer, creator of the first widely produced sewing machine, and an inventor in his own right. In fact, he had made improvements to his uncle's sewing machine. Singer had been serving in the Texas military since 1862, when the Union took his adopted home town with such ease that it made his blood boil. He decided to turn his talents to warfare and began to experiment with underwater mines. One thing led to another.

Singer had come to Mobile to mine the bay with his underwater explosives. There was little chance any blockade ships could get past Fort Morgan, but Singer was a good salesman and the Confederates accepted his offer. While he was in town, Singer met Hunley and McClintock and saw promise in their sad story. He agreed to put $5,000 into the submarine project. Some of his associates, including B. A. "Gus" Whitney, bought another $5,000 worth of shares in the project. As depressed as Hunley was, he somehow managed to find another $5,000—a sign that he had not yet completely given up on McClintock or submarines.

Singer soon left town, but Whitney and some others stayed behind to help McClintock build another boat. The engineer was either too polite or too indebted to his new partners to protest. The men had to be there anyway to build more mines for the Confederacy. Hunley left town with Singer. The pair headed for Mississippi, one of the South's most active war zones.

McClintock began work on the plans for his new submarine immediately, with the help of Whitney and Alexander. The men returned to the Park and Lyons Machine Shop, although they would quickly outgrow the cramped brick building. McClintock was determined to make this new boat bigger, faster and more advanced than the first two submarines. He desperately wanted to show all his detractors that he could do it—he could build a working submarine capable of sinking Yankee ships.

There were a lot of ships out there, McClintock thought, and he would get them yet.

CHAPTER 5

1984
At Sea

Somewhere down there, more than 100 feet below the *Arvor III*'s keel, the *Leopoldville* called out to them.

The NUMA team had picked up a 500-foot mass on the boat's onboard echo sounder and knew it had to be the Belgian ship. The SS *Leopoldville* had been sunk by a German U-boat in the English Channel on Christmas Eve 1944. At the time, it was serving as a transport ship for the Allies, carrying more than 2,200 American troops from the U.S. Army's Sixty-sixth Infantry. They were on their way to the Battle of the Bulge, but nearly 800 of those soldiers would never make it. They died in the water that night, just months before the war in Europe ended.

Clive Cussler's crew had been searching for the ship less than 90 minutes. To get a hit so quickly was an amazing stroke of luck, but these days NUMA seemingly could do no wrong. In the three years since the 1981 *Hunley* expedition, the National Underwater and Marine Agency had found nearly a dozen lost ships. On this trip alone they already had located the *U-21*, the second submarine to sink an enemy ship; the HMS *Pathfinder*, the *U-21*'s victim; and the *U-20*. After a tour of World War I history, the team was on to the mysteries of World War II. Now it appeared they had the *Leopoldville*, and they wanted a better look.

The trouble was NUMA had found their target just off the coast of France—where the French Navy had denied their permit to search for the Confederate raider *Alabama*. In fact, the French had been most inhospitable and no one could understand why. After two weeks of bureaucratic red tape, a frustrated Cussler had decided it was time to go. He asked Jimmy Flett, captain of the *Arvor*—the boat they'd previously used to hunt for the *Bonhomme Richard*—to take the crew to England. But on the way across, they decided to take a quick peek to see if they could locate the *Leopoldville*. And now, although Cussler was satisfied, the rest of the NUMA crew—Bill Shea, Wayne Gronquist and Dirk Cussler—wanted another look.

"Throw out the side-scan sonar," Dirk said.

"Be nice to see more of her," Flett agreed.

When Shea finally allowed that he wasn't ready to give up either, Cussler reluctantly agreed. They had come this far, and Cussler knew they were close to a significant find. The *Leopoldville* was an often forgotten story of the Second World War, and he hoped the ship's discovery would resurrect the memories of those soldiers who had died so needlessly. Within a minute, the side-scan sonar went over the side and they powered up the recorder. But just seconds after the sonar hummed to life, the *Arvor*'s radio began to crackle—a message coming over the speaker in perfect English.

"Will the boat five miles north of Cherbourg please return to port immediately," the voice said.

Cussler was beyond surprised. *Did the French have technology to detect side-scan sonar? How did they catch on so quickly? And, more importantly, why was the French government watching them so closely?* For the past two weeks, Cussler had thought he was becoming paranoid—people searching the ship while they were out, frogmen in the water around the dock. He looked to Flett for answers and quickly realized the captain knew all too well. They were smack in the middle of restricted French water, Flett said. Apparently the French government thought NUMA was snooping around.

"Will the boat five miles north of Cherbourg please return to port immediately," the radio voice said again.

Cussler looked to Shea, for once not battling seasickness, and asked if they'd at least gotten a good reading. Shea told him the bad news: "Not the best."

The ship looked to be fairly well-preserved, Shea said, and was probably lying on its starboard side. The *Leopoldville* was just an immense shadow on the sonar's recorder. There was little detail in the image, but this was probably all they would get without another pass. As they studied the image, the radio came to life once more: "Will the boat five miles north of Cherbourg please return to port immediately."

NUMA was on the cusp of a potential international incident. For all they knew, the French Navy was already en route. Cussler looked to Flett once more, as if to say *now what do we do?*

The radio crackled to life once again.

Since the second *Hunley* expedition ended, Clive Cussler had been a busy man.

At the urging of Bantam, he'd taken his first Dirk Pitt novel out of a drawer and spent three months rewriting it. The book, originally entitled *The Sea Dwellers*, was published in paperback as *Pacific Vortex!* in late 1982. After two weeks, it was No. 2 on the *New York Times* best-seller list. Cussler was getting more popular with each book, and the publishing community was forced to take notice. As so many villains had learned over the years, Dirk Pitt was unstoppable.

Cussler earned his first $1 million advance for the next Pitt adventure, *Deep Six*, which was published just prior to his trip to Europe for the *U-21/Leopoldville* mission. Already he'd begun a new Pitt book, *Cyclops*, which would come out in early 1986. His writing career was in its heyday, and the demand for his books was growing exponentially every year—both from the public and his publishers.

When he wasn't behind a keyboard sending Dirk Pitt to the far corners of the world's oceans, Cussler was going there himself. The

European trip was his fifth NUMA expedition since the last *Hunley* search. A few months after he left Charleston in the summer of 1981, he'd taken a small crew to New Orleans for an extensive survey of Mississippi River wrecks. Nursing a broken ankle, Cussler scoured the river from a lawn chair propped up in a skiff he'd chartered from a Cajun fisherman. The team found the *Louisiana*, the gunboats *Governor Moore* and *Varuna*, as well as the first Confederate iron-clad, the *Manassas*—the ship that may have inspired Horace Hunley to get into the stealth boat business.

Finally, NUMA was having some luck. Cussler was particularly pleased to find the *Manassas*. Although he would do no diving on the trip, he turned over the coordinates to Louisiana officials and offered to fund an expedition to survey the first Southern ironclad. No one would take him up on the offer, perhaps because the wreck was almost completely under a levee. But at least the ship had been located. Cussler hadn't found the *Hunley* yet, but he'd gotten one of her ancestors.

From New Orleans, Cussler and his entourage had moved on to Baton Rouge, where they embarked on a search for the ironclad CSS *Arkansas*. In July 1862, the *Arkansas* had blown through a group of U.S. Navy ships assembled near Vicksburg, inflicting heavy damage on Farragut's fleet. But a few weeks later the *Arkansas* was lost after the Battle of Baton Rouge. As the *Arkansas* moved into position to attack the USS *Essex*, her engines failed. Helpless and adrift, the crew had abandoned the ironclad and set it on fire to keep the ship from falling into enemy hands. After the captain dived overboard, the burning *Arkansas* floated close to federal warships, where it exploded.

In Baton Rouge, Cussler got in touch with the sheriff's office, both to alert local authorities to NUMA's presence and to ask for the use of a boat. The sheriff was more than happy to lend him an old outboard, especially after the answer Cussler gave when the lawman asked why he wanted to waste his time looking for an old Confederate ship.

"It was the only Confederate boat that kicked hell out of them damned Yankees," Cussler told the sheriff.

As usual, Cussler knew his audience.

The sheriff's boat carried Cussler and the NUMA team up and down the Mississippi, covering seven miles of the waterway in just a couple of days. The *Arkansas* gave Cussler the same problem he'd encountered with the *Bonhomme Richard*—the ship had drifted, and no one was sure exactly where it had finally gone down. Historical accounts suggested the ship had been set afire while aground on the river's western bank just north of the city. But no one knew how far it traveled before it exploded and sank.

Cussler had found an account of the *Arkansas*'s demise in the diary of a young Confederate girl who witnessed the battle. Sarah Morgan Dawson's journal even documented her vantage point for this spectacle, which provided a good starting point. Dawson claimed the *Arkansas* went down at a place that locals called the old Thompson Gravel Pit. But that was allegedly the final resting place of another boat, the Union Navy frigate *Mississippi*. Cussler was skeptical. The *Mississippi* allegedly had been sunk at Port Hudson, nearly 15 miles upriver. He did not believe the ship could have drifted all the way to Baton Rouge. It was a mystery, but one he didn't dwell on. He wanted the *Arkansas*.

For days, NUMA ran lanes in the river, turning up nothing. It was amazing how little ship-sized debris there was in the Midwest's primary waterway. Later, Cussler would kick himself for waiting until the last day of the search to actually survey the Mississippi's west bank. There, the magnetometer detected a mass 165 feet long by 35 feet wide. It was the exact size of the *Arkansas*. And it was buried beneath a rock levee.

Later, after Cussler had turned the coordinates over to the state, one Louisiana archaeologist would ask a longtime local exactly where the Thompson Gravel Pit had been. The man pointed out the exact spot in the river where Cussler's target was, the only shipwreck he'd found in a seven-mile stretch of river. It was exactly where Sarah Morgan Dawson had said it was.

~~~~~

Five months later, Cussler flew to Cincinnati to search for the remains of another ironclad, the USS *Carondelet*. The ship survived the war only to be decommissioned and left to rot—the sad fate of many Civil War vessels. According to legend, a spring flood in 1873 had washed the *Carondelet* down the Ohio River until it came to rest at Manchester Island. There, it quickly disappeared into the muck.

Cussler thought he knew where to look for the *Carondelet*, but the search was delayed when the local sheriff asked if NUMA could use their fancy gear to help them hunt for a woman who had disappeared three years earlier. The team spent hours assisting local authorities with their search and eventually came up with a few targets for divers to explore. That work took most of the day.

When Cussler and his band finally reached Manchester Island, they found a huge dredge boat anchored nearby. The dredge captain told them he'd gone through the river around Manchester Island just hours earlier. They'd hit something—and eventually brought up wood, a bracket plate and a piece of steam pipe. Steering the boat around the island, the NUMA magnetometer picked up the remains of the lower hull and keel of the *Carondelet*, still buried in the muck. If only they'd been earlier, Cussler thought. It was an important lesson—shipwrecks are never safe.

In 1982, Cussler spent nearly as much time on NUMA business as his books. In July he returned to Hampton Roads to continue his search for the USS *Cumberland* and the *Florida*, a Confederate raider. He had first looked for the ships after the 1980 *Hunley* expedition, but that search did not go well and Cussler wanted to try again. He felt reasonably sure he knew where the *Florida* was and had the location of the *Cumberland* narrowed down to a small search area. This should be easy, he figured, especially given NUMA's recent track record.

In some ways, the expedition was more trouble than it was worth.

The *Cumberland* would be a great find for NUMA. The sailing frigate had been the first victim of the CSS *Virginia*, a day before its famous battle with the *Monitor*. The *Florida* had sunk under mysterious circumstances. It was off the coast of Brazil in October 1864 when it was captured by a U.S. warship. Ignoring Brazilian sovereignty, the *Florida* was hauled back to Virginia. And there the *Florida* sank in a collision with a troop transport ship—probably an intentional accident to avoid returning it to Brazil, which had a legal claim to the ship.

Virginia officials were wary of NUMA's motives. The state had seen too many ships plundered by scavengers, and they were suspicious of the novelist. But Cussler was working with four former state archaeologists who had formed their own company—Underwater Archaeological Joint Ventures—and they vouched for Cussler. He was no treasure hunter. NUMA eventually got permits to search for the ships. But it wasn't easy.

The NUMA team interviewed local crabbers, fishermen and sport divers, hoping for any lead that might make the search go easier. One clam digger led them to a wreck site he'd found while trying to retrieve some tongs he'd lost overboard. Cussler never failed to be amazed by how innocent accidents often made for the best discoveries. The man had led them directly to the *Cumberland*.

Cussler's team dived on the wreckage for several days, and before long there was no doubt they had the *Virginia*'s first victim. They recovered the ship's bell—perhaps the best, most identifiable thing they could have found. Within days, the crew moved on to a site off the Horne Brothers Shipyard Dock that they had surveyed two years earlier. There they found evidence just as significant—a bowl inscribed from a pharmacy in Brest, France. The *Florida* had been in that French port just months before she was lost. Cussler made a compelling case that NUMA had found both its targets.

For the first time Cussler got involved in the preservation of artifacts his divers had recovered—and it taught him a lesson he wouldn't forget. One organization that promised to fund the preservation backed out. Finally, a conservationist at the College of William and Mary offered to split the cost of restoring the artifacts with the idea that they would eventually go into the Mariners' Museum in Newport News—one of the finest maritime museums in the nation. But then the U.S. Navy got involved and claimed the artifacts as spoils of war.

Cussler had records that proved salvage rights to both ships had been sold by none other than the Secretary of the Navy, but it made little difference. The artifacts were confiscated and taken to the Norfolk Naval Museum. Later, some locals would whisper that NUMA had looted the *Cumberland* and *Florida*. That rumor lingered for nearly a decade, until the FBI raided another museum and found that a group of local treasure hunters had been selling the museum's curators artifacts stolen off the two ships.

Cussler was frustrated, but NUMA was doing too much good work to let a little federal bureaucracy stop him. He would return to Virginia two months later, looking for the CSS *Virginia*—the former *Merrimack*—itself. He hired the same archaeology team and together they dragged a magnetometer through the Elizabeth River. They hit a few targets, but nothing they could prove was the famous *Monitor*'s adversary. While in Portsmouth, he was invited to a Civil War reenactment that inspired the ending for *Deep Six*.

It was the only thing Cussler was able to salvage from the trip.

Cussler took some time off the water in 1983 to finish the manuscript for *Deep Six*. His publishers were hounding him for one book a year, and more if possible. They were riding their new show horse hard. Even though Cussler wasn't particularly interested in matching their pace, he did his best to oblige. He limited NUMA to one expedition in 1983—a search for Cornelius Vanderbilt's luxurious passenger steamboat, the *Lexington*. The boat had caught fire and gone down somewhere in Long Island Sound in 1840. After a quick search, Cussler and Bill Shea had not only found the once elegant steamer, but pulled up a handful of artifacts that Cussler donated to the Vanderbilt Museum on Long Island.

The 1984 European expedition was supposed to make up for lost time. Cussler and his NUMA team would spend six weeks on the water—part of that time in the North Sea, the rest in the English Channel. The first leg of the trip began in Denmark, where Cussler wanted to find a handful of German U-boats. He'd hired Flett and the *Arvor III* from the second *Bonhomme Richard* search—a nod to practicality more than nostalgia, and they met in Aberdeen.

It took four days for their equipment to catch up to them in Denmark, and Cussler spent that time ingratiating himself to the locals. The short respite would be the only rest he'd get for a while. When the equipment arrived and the team was finally ready to set out in search of the *Pathfinder*, Cussler asked for a short detour to look for the *U-12*, a German sub sank by the British ship *Ariel* in 1915. It took only about four hours to find the sub, which was two miles from where Admiralty charts listed her. By the next morning, the *Pathfinder*'s location had been captured as well.

The frigid waters of the North Sea proved to be excellent hunting grounds for NUMA. While en route to search for the *U-20*, the sub that sank the *Lusitania*, Cussler's crew ran across the HMS *Hawke*, which had been a victim of the *U-9*. Their main target was not much more difficult to find. Within days, Cussler had Danish divers inspecting the wreck of *U-20* 400 yards off Vielby Beach. The infamous German submarine had run aground there nearly seven decades earlier.

The weather soon deteriorated, and the North Sea violently protested the changing meteorology. By the time the *Arvor III* reached the location Cussler had chosen to search for the *U-21*, Bill Shea wasn't the only one onboard suffering from seasickness. The crew determined to muscle on and threw the side-scan sonar in the water. For six hours, the boat rocked through six-foot swells running search lanes. Eventually, Cussler had to take the controls of the sonar himself as Shea went down, greener than seawater. Soon, Cussler saw a tiny blip and thought *that's it*.

Flett made a few more passes and then they had the target nailed down. It had the exact dimensions of the *U-21*, and it was just where Cussler had predicted it would be. This trip was a little befuddling. NUMA was finding lost ships at every turn—even in the fickle North Sea—so why had the *Hunley* eluded them? Cussler had to look at the upside. He had not found the first submarine to sink an enemy ship in battle, but now he'd found the second.

It was on to France, and near disaster.

The problems began as soon as the *Arvor III* docked in Cherbourg. Talking to the marina's dock master, Cussler mentioned that he'd come to France in search of the *Alabama*. It was a casual remark that came up in conversation, but suddenly the dock master seemed very interested. He asked questions. He wanted to know when they intended to start searching. The next day, Cussler said.

Not likely.

The following morning, six French custom agents showed up at the marina and detained the *Arvor III*. The agents caught them early, just as they were preparing to cast off, and proceeded to search the boat from stem to stern. They rifled through every cabinet on the boat, dug through every suitcase and even inspected the engine. They looked suspiciously at the side-scan sonar equipment and asked a lot of insinuating questions. Cussler did his best to remain polite, all the while wondering exactly what the hell was going on.

After more than an hour of this harassment, the agents finally asked Cussler why he was in France. When he explained that they were looking for the CSS *Alabama*, the customs men informed him that no one could conduct such a search without approval of the French Navy. It was the worst thing the author could hear. NUMA was now ensnared in bureaucracy. Cussler knew they would be lucky to get a reply from the navy—much less permission to search French waters. At least they weren't arrested.

Cussler dispatched Wayne Gronquist, who had joined the expedition in England, to talk with the navy brass. When that went nowhere, Gronquist boarded a train for Paris to enlist the aid of the U.S. Embassy. Meanwhile NUMA approached the French Embassy in Washington. It all had the air of international intrigue—Dirk Pitt's world intruding on Cussler's. Usually, it was the other way around. This was supposed to be shipwreck hunting, not espionage.

But that is exactly what it felt like to Cussler. As he sat grounded in Cherbourg with Shea and Flett, the group began to get the feeling that someone was watching them. One day, helicopters flew over the *Arvor III* with a cameraman hanging out the door. A few days later, an American couple in port told Cussler that they thought the *Arvor III* had been bugged while the crew was out to dinner. A number of men were seen snooping around the boat, the couple reported.

Cussler and Flett searched the boat, but could not find any portable listening devices. As a precaution, or perhaps out of boredom, they began conversing in odd accents in the hope that someone actually was listening. They talked about the economy in Antarctica and played some of Cussler's jazz tapes. Everything was going fine until the Scottish crew that Flett had brought along started making derisive comments about the "Frogs," and how they'd never won a war. If the boat was bugged, Cussler thought, this would not help them get a permit.

For two weeks Cussler and company were forced to waste their days sightseeing while Gronquist worked on the diplomats. The French Embassy in Washington apologized for the confusion but said there wasn't anything they could do. The navy refused to budge. Finally Cussler took to the airwaves, using the press to make his case. Nothing did any good. When Cussler's son, Dirk, showed up to join the expedition, he found that he'd flown a long ways to sit on the deck of a docked boat.

Cussler and Flett were smoking cigars on the *Arvor III*'s deck one evening when they saw bubbles in the water next to the boat. Cussler recognized what was happening immediately, so he stepped into the cabin and called Shea. "Turn on the underwater video equipment," he said. As Shea fired up the electronics, Cussler lowered a camera into the water. When the camera was activated, Shea hit the underwater lights. And there on the screen suddenly appeared the faces of two very surprised French Navy frogmen.

When the divers saw the cameras, they swam off in another burst of bubbles.

Cussler could not imagine what had caused the French Navy to be so wary of him. *Did they think he was a treasure hunter? Were they afraid he was going to steal artifacts that they considered property of the French government? Could they actually think he was a spy?* It stumped him. He considered all this while he and Dirk and Bill Shea toured the beaches of Normandy. One day, Cussler visited a monument to American soldiers, some of whom had been lost on the *Leopoldville*.

Finally, Cussler gave up. The French would not give in, and after two weeks the author decided he'd waited long enough. Some admiral had it in for him—that was all Cussler could figure. He would not continue to waste money on an expedition that included no actual shipwreck hunting, so Cussler asked Flett to take them back to England. They set off before dawn for the short trip across the English Channel.

On the way out of port, Cussler briefly thought about making a quick pass through the area where he thought the *Alabama* rested. But that was a fairly wide area and he was certain the French Navy would watch the *Arvor III*'s departure. He figured they would pay particular attention if the boat drifted into any area connected with the *Alabama*'s last known whereabouts. They couldn't take the chance. But as the boat cleared the harbor, Cussler realized he'd never mentioned that he was also searching for the *Leopoldville*. He thought about the monument and realized he could not forget the men who'd gone down with it.

Cussler suspected that if they ran the side-scan sonar long enough, French intelligence could pick up some sort of faint signal. But surely that wouldn't happen immediately. If a navy vessel came along and caught them in the act of violating orders to not search French waters, however, there could be trouble. Cussler didn't want to spark an international incident. He also did not want to seem paranoid, but the previous two weeks had convinced him nothing was impossible. For all he knew there were more frogmen clinging to the keel.

He decided to risk it anyway.

As the *Arvor III* motored away from the French coast, Cussler asked Flett to fire up the onboard echo sounder. It was not nearly as good as side-scan sonar—they would have to pass directly over the *Leopoldville* to pick up any kind of reading—but it was their only option. They would start at the admiralty chart's mismarked location of the ship and make a few expansive passes. Maybe it would look like they were just killing time.

The *Arvor III* cruised around for nearly an hour and a half, turning lazy circles and trying to "sail casual." Finally, the echo sounder hit something. It was 500 feet long, resting on the bottom about 160 feet below. There was no question—it was the *Leopoldville*. Cussler stared down into the water, thinking *this is a grave*. Beneath the *Arvor*'s keel, hundreds of American servicemen had perished. Cussler wished that he had a wreath to throw, some sort of ceremony planned. But there was no time. Cussler decided they were pushing their luck already. They had to move on.

Shea and Dirk wanted to turn on the side-scan sonar and get a better image of the wreck. They insisted, and finally Cussler acquiesced. But seconds after they had thrown the switch on the sonar, the radio sparked to life with the ominous command: "Will the boat five miles north of Cherbourg please return to port immediately."

Sometimes you aren't paranoid, Cussler thought. Sometimes they really are out to get you.

The monotone voice continued at regular intervals, ordering the *Arvor III* into port. It sounded as if it could have been a recording, but they knew it was just a bureaucrat. Cussler and Flett talked over the drone of the radio, weighing their options. If they went back France, the boat might be impounded and they could be arrested. If they resisted, or tried to escape to England, the French Navy could probably overtake them. But would the French risk the adverse publicity of attacking a British ship carrying four Americans?

Finally, Cussler asked the most important question: *How far is it to British waters?*

"Just about 18 miles," Flett answered.

"What do you think, skipper?" the author asked.

Flett looked out on the horizon and as the voice came back over the speaker, he reached up, turned the radio off and gunned the motor.

They were headed for England.

Cussler announced the discovery of the *U-20* and *Leopoldville* on the deck of the aircraft carrier USS *Intrepid* in New York City later that summer. Wearing a seersucker suit, Cussler told the American press that the U.S. government had suppressed information on the sinking of the transport ship because it was a "screw-up." The attack had been left out of encyclopedias and military histories for years. It was an oversight that he challenged politicians to rectify. The author said the U.S. government should designate the *Leopoldville* wreck site a war memorial.

"It is still a tomb for hundreds of American GIs just like Arlington Cemetery or any other resting place," Cussler said.

Safely back in the United States, Cussler took the opportunity to lambaste the French Navy for its treatment of a nonprofit shipwreck hunting organization. He recounted the spying frogmen, the orders to return to port, the suspected search of his boat. The press devoured the entertaining yarn and included all the salacious details in their dispatches. The *Washington Post* even called the French Embassy for comment. The consul confirmed the story while defending his navy's actions.

"I am not surprised. Would you like us to search in your territorial waters?"

There was, unsurprisingly, no apology.

It would be months before Cussler learned what actually had happened in France.

Shortly after he returned home to Colorado, Cussler read that the French government had launched its own search for the *Alabama*—and found it. Did they do it for spite, or did the French fear that NUMA was about to jump its claim? It must have been internal politics, he decided. The news stung Cussler—they found the *Alabama* just where he had planned to look. It could have been his discovery, perhaps one of NUMA's most significant finds to date.

But the French hadn't sabotaged Cussler's search simply to jump his claim. Months later, Cussler got a call from a deputy director at the CIA in Virginia. The man said he wanted to talk about the author's actions in Cherbourg over the summer. Cussler apologized for the potato incident, but the director had no idea what he was talking about. The *Arvor III* had only seen one French ship on its way back into port—a missile cruiser that passed them in Weymouth Harbor. Cussler had directed Flett to pull alongside, where he and the rest of the NUMA team pelted the ship with potatoes.

"I haven't heard about that one," the deputy director said.

Cussler let it pass.

It seemed, according to the CIA, that NUMA had stumbled into French waters just as the navy was preparing to test its newest nuclear submarine. Fearing the NUMA boat was cover for foreign spies, the French postponed the test run for six months—much to the chagrin of the CIA, the KGB and a dozen other foreign intelligence agencies that were, in fact, hidden in the waters off Cherbourg to observe the tests.

The French did not realize it, but Cussler had inadvertently done them a favor. Although the incident had screwed up months of planning by the CIA, the deputy director told the author that NUMA had made the right call that day in the English Channel. The French Navy was so certain they were spies that, had they returned to Cherbourg, they would have been imprisoned and the boat seized.

Cussler apologized for fouling up American intelligence gathering, but the CIA wrote it off to bad luck. The French sub would eventually be tested, and they would be there. The deputy director did ask Cussler for one favor: please let them know the next time he was snooping around in international waters—particularly waters where sensitive military equipment was tested. Cussler promised them a postcard.

Cussler remained mildly frustrated that his attempt to find the *Alabama* had been thwarted, but he could not complain too much. In six years, NUMA had established itself as one of the most competent and successful nonprofit shipwreck hunting outfits in the world. Cussler and his merry adventurers had discovered more than 30 shipwrecks to date. And now they were certainly on everyone's radar. He would continue to search, and even venture back into international waters. NUMA's fortunes were catching up to his success on the best-sellers' list. And it was a good thing. In less than six years, Cussler had spent $500,000 on his hobby.

"Some men play golf," Cussler explained to reporters. "I've got this crazy thing about maintaining our nation's maritime heritage."

Even as he amassed new discoveries, or took a moment of pride for all that he had accomplished, Cussler could not forget about the ones that got away. He had looked briefly for the *Richard* during the 1984 expedition, but turned up nothing. He would look again. And he would search for the *Hunley* again. He had considered a 1982 expedition for the lost submarine, but was distracted by other ships.

The *Hunley* would wait. Cussler knew it was out there, and he would get back to Charleston someday—when the technology improved, when his team had a few more notches on his belt. The Confederate submarine called to him, just as the *Leopoldville* had, and he would not forget it.

At the time, Cussler had no idea it would be another decade before he was back on the *Hunley*'s trail.

CHAPTER 6

1863
Mobile

In early March, the commander of every ship in the East Gulf Blockading Squadron received a distressing telegram from the U.S. Secretary of the Navy. The new intelligence coming out of the South, according to Gideon Welles, was most unsettling.

"Spy just returned from Selma and Meridian reports two large ironclads building at Montgomery, two launched at Selma February 1 and two others building there for the Tombigbee and Alabama rivers. At Mobile five ironclads and two wooden gunboats."

Shipwrights were busy in the Cotton State, and Welles feared this could have serious repercussions for Farragut and his fleet. Alabama had been quiet for much of the war—almost too quiet. The U.S. Navy had engaged the occasional blockade runner out of Mobile, but there had been little in the way of actual Confederate attacks on navy ships. Welles believed that might change soon. He sent the short dispatch along to his captains without comment, assuming they would understand its importance. He was warning them to monitor the mouth of Mobile Bay very carefully in the coming months.

The Union's tally of Confederate warships under construction in Alabama that spring did not include James McClintock's new submarine. As the Deep South's spring thaw began, few people even knew the engineer was beginning work on a third sub. McClintock felt confident as he sat down to design his new boat, but he also struggled under the enormous pressure to succeed. He knew this might be his last chance.

It was nothing less than luck that Singer had stumbled into Mobile at precisely the right time. McClintock and Hunley were broke, and the loss of the *American Diver* had nearly forced them to abandon their dream of a new technology. Singer and his men—fellow engineers—recognized that McClintock was on the verge of a significant new invention and were willing to invest in it. But failure was not an option now. McClintock and Hunley likely would not find another group of benefactors so farsighted—or generous. This boat had to work or no one would ever give them another dollar.

There was little money to be had in Mobile. The city's moribund economy was struggling through the war as much, if not worse, than most Southern towns. Shipping was Mobile's lifeblood, and the blockade had cut the city's import/export business considerably. Not far from McClintock's rented room, ships filled with cotton awaited orders to set sail for Cuba, where they could sell the state's crops to British merchants and perhaps even bring back much-needed guns. But Alabama's governor would not even allow that.

A group of citizens had complained that a quick payday for blockade runners was not worth the risk of losing these ships to the Yankee cruisers anchored offshore. They feared Mobile would be invaded, just as New Orleans had been, and they needed every ship available to defend their homes. The governor was inclined to agree with them, at least until all those ironclads under construction were ready to provide some cover. What little commerce Mobile had managed to maintain dried up almost instantly.

McClintock believed his new submarine would solve all Mobile's problems. It could pick off Union blockaders before they realized they were under attack, a prospect that may have made him smile. McClintock worked with the confidence born from nearly two years of trial and error—what men in the twenty-first century would call research and development. In that time, he felt he had come to understand underwater travel. McClintock believed he could build a perfect stealth weapon.

Some of that confidence was justifiable. The *Pioneer* had demonstrated that McClintock could design a boat that would dive, surface and travel underwater at will. The *American Diver* had, if nothing else, improved upon the hull shape. But the *Diver* suffered from over-correction—its design was too extreme. The *Pioneer* had been too round; the *Diver* perhaps not enough. And McClintock had wasted far too much time trying to develop a new method of propulsion for his second boat. That damn electromagnetic engine had caused him to neglect far too many other details. McClintock believed this had doomed the *American Diver*.

The third boat would be more advanced, more sophisticated than anything McClintock had ever built.

Matthew Fontaine Maury, the uncle of Confederate Gen. Dabney H. Maury, was a man of many talents—including a study of the world's oceans. A former U.S. Navy official, he resigned when his home state of Virginia seceded and became the South's chief of sea coast, rivers and harbor defences. Maury is credited with building the torpedo (akin to a modern-day mine) that sank many U.S. Navy vessels during the war. In the years following the war, James McClintock—who considered Maury a kindred spirit—would recount his submarine experiments in letters to the famous author and cartographer. Courtesy National Archives.

He had kept track of every flaw in his previous efforts. Years later, McClintock would write to Matthew Maury—the underwater explosives expert and uncle of Dabney Maury—that for this third submarine, he took "more pains with her model, and the machinery."

McClintock obsessed over the submarine's design for weeks. He started with the idea that it would have an "elliptic shape" much closer to the *Diver* than the *Pioneer*. But this boat would be larger than the *American Diver* in every respect. His last submarine had been too narrow, only 36 inches wide, and the crew had complained about the cramped quarters. McClintock would allow this boat to be six inches wider, but feared more girth might slow it down too much.

He would also add to the submarine's length. At 40 feet, it would be 4 feet longer than the *Diver*. The reason for this, as McClintock explained to Maury, was because "(t)his boat was built expressly for hand power." If it had to be powered by hand, he reasoned, he would simply add more hands. The main compartment of the submarine would be nearly 25 feet long. With that additional space, he could expand the crew to eight men.

McClintock was forced to concede that more hands did not necessarily produce better results—additional manpower had not made the *Diver* faster than the *Pioneer*. The *Diver*'s crew had reported suffering from back-breaking fatigue and the boat was still just as slow as the *Pioneer*. McClintock decided that constant toil inside cramped quarters, where oxygen was at a premium, was too intense to make a submarine effective. This led to perhaps his most innovative concept for the third boat.

Instead of attaching the hand cranks directly to the propeller shaft, he would install a series of reduction gears and a flywheel. The crew would be able to wind up the propeller like a child's toy, which would give the men periods of rest and perhaps even allow them to work in shifts. It would cut down on exhaustion, which would potentially increase the submarine's range.

Other improvements came to McClintock each week. He designed the boat to have two hatches, both to accommodate the larger crew and provide greater air circulation. The submarine would include a snorkel system as well, but it was at best a back-up system to be used only when the crew could not surface. The sub's two hatches—each two feet long and 15 inches wide—could be opened periodically to admit far greater amounts of air when the boat was riding atop the water.

The boat's design was a decided improvement over McClintock's previous efforts. The "elliptic shape" would allow the boat to cut through the water more effortlessly than its predecessors. The bow would be only an inch wide, the submarine expanding to its broadest point at the crew compartment. Beyond that, the sub tapered toward the stern. This was not a cigar boat; it looked more like a shark.

McClintock even added thin, three-foot dorsal fins in front of the hatches to slice through the water, which would help cut down on drag when the boat traveled on the surface. He also designed small fins to be mounted in front of the boat's diving wings. These fins would deflect rope or seaweed—anything that might jam the dive planes' operation. The shroud around the propeller served the same purpose. With these added safety features, McClintock believed he was significantly increasing the sub's odds of success.

The most notable improvements to this boat, however, would be internal. Like his previous submarines, this one would include forward and aft ballast tanks, which held enough water weight to allow the boat to submerge. Each tank had its own pump, but McClintock added fail-safe redundancies with a network of pipes running beneath the crew bench. With the switch of a lever, water could be pumped from one tank to the other, equalizing distribution. If one of the pumps broke, the other could be used to expel water from both tanks. It was an ingenious backup plan and made the most of the crew compartment's sparse space.

The ballast pumps also included a setting that would allow the crew to suck water out of the cabin and into the ballast tanks, where it could then be vented into the ocean. This was perhaps the boat's greatest safety feature. The sub's buoyancy was fragile—the difference between gliding beneath the waves and sinking to the ocean floor was a matter of mere pounds. McClintock had seen it happen with the

American Diver. A few gallons of water could send a submarine to the bottom like a stone.

McClintock amended his plans throughout the submarine's construction, likely taking suggestions from Gus Whitney or his machine shop partner, Baxter Watson. In the first draft of history, men would call McClintock's submarine a converted boiler, suggesting it was a primitive contraption barely able to stay afloat. But that was far too simplistic a description. With this boat, McClintock had designed a sleek, hydrodynamic, complex sailing vessel. For years, engineers would copy his basic design elements. Future subs would be much larger, faster and more complicated. But well into the twentieth century, they all followed McClintock's basic vision. He would never get the recognition he deserved as the father of the modern submarine, but as the war dragged on into the Alabama spring, the engineer gave that notion little thought. He knew only that this submarine would work.

Now all he needed was for William Alexander to build it.

The war's second anniversary passed quietly while McClintock toiled. Had he not been so preoccupied, perhaps the engineer might have noticed the changing climate in the South. The strains of "Dixie" were heard less often in the street, and the economy—and not states' rights—was the foremost concern of most people. The mounting casualty rate was beginning to take its toll, and even the most enthusiastic patriots were growing weary of the conflict.

In January, U.S. President Abraham Lincoln had signed the Emancipation Proclamation, freeing slaves in the Confederate States. Southerners called it a cheap political stunt to bolster his popularity among Northern abolitionists. The Confederates said the proclamation carried no weight since Lincoln was not their president. The act marked a historic turning point that would be remembered for more than a century; but at the moment it actually accomplished little. It would take the war's end for any meaningful change to come.

No doubt Lincoln had to do something to stir his people—the declining enthusiasm for war was not limited to the South. Already the fighting had gone on far longer than Union officials predicted, forcing the United States to pass a conscription act—a draft basically—that called on all able men between the ages of 20 and 45 to enter military service. Northern residents claimed the conscription discriminated against the poor and working class. It was the same argument Southern critics had used when the Confederacy enacted its own conscription a year earlier. Both sides were losing men much more quickly than new recruits were enlisting, and neither side could afford to concede the battle of attrition. There was no end in sight to the War Between the States—even though everyone was tired of fighting.

Despite that growing reluctance, the frequency of battles across the South would actually increase in the coming months. The Civil War was escalating into its most violent period, both sides determined to deliver a killing blow. In the first week of May, Union and Confederate forces fought for seven days at Chancellorsville, Virginia. Southern forces took the victory, although 1,600 Confederate soldiers were killed, nearly 10,000 were wounded and another 6,000 were missing or captured. The North lost fewer men but had been forced to retreat. Before the month's end, Union Gen. Ulysses S. Grant would lay siege on Vicksburg, Mississippi. By the time it ended, Confederate Gen. Robert E. Lee and his Army of Northern Virginia would be preparing to engage the Union at Gettysburg, Pennsylvania.

Around the time McClintock delivered his plans to William Alexander, he learned from Southern newspapers that Union engineers were also experimenting with submarines—and had suffered similar setbacks. The USS *Alligator* had been built in Philadelphia about the same time McClintock was testing the *Pioneer*. Although it was similar in shape to the *Pioneer*, the 30-foot *Alligator* was perhaps even more rudimentary. In its first incarnation, the iron sub was propelled with oars. It was a horrible design flaw, and one that Union engineers rectified by fitting the sub with hand cranks, the same as McClintock's boats.

A year of trials had brought the Yankees no more luck than McClintock. Test runs in the Potomac River—one of which was observed by Lincoln himself—were utter failures. The boat designed to take out the CSS *Virginia* could go no faster than the doomed *American Diver*. Union officials dubbed the project a failure, but they had invested so much time in it they were not willing to give up.

That spring, U.S. Navy officials decided the *Alligator* might best serve them in Charleston, one of the few places Southerners had actually tried to engage the blockade. Plans were made for the USS *Sumpter* to tow the submarine down the coast to Port Royal—a large, natural South Carolina harbor that the Union had taken early in the war. But on April 2, somewhere off the Outer Banks of North Carolina, the *Sumpter* ran into violent weather. To keep the ship afloat, the crew was forced to cut the *Alligator* loose. The sub drifted for a while, but soon sank beneath the waves.

The United States had lost its first submarine; the Confederacy would soon have its third under construction.

William Alexander began work on McClintock's new boat late that spring. The submarine's frame was assembled at the Park and Lyons machine shop in April, the iron scavenged from whatever scrap the men had available to them. Some of those pieces were indeed cut from old boilers—iron, like everything else, was at a premium in the South. That likely led to the later speculation about the sub's origins. But this boat would be far more than a boiler with fins. McClintock's third boat was built from the ground up as a submarine.

The pieces of the sub were fashioned to fit together seamlessly. Each of the 16 hull plates, all 33 inches wide, abutted one another instead of overlapping. They were fastened to flat ribs and then reinforced with thicker support beams that sat halfway between the rivet strips. Tar was used to waterproof the seams. Although it might

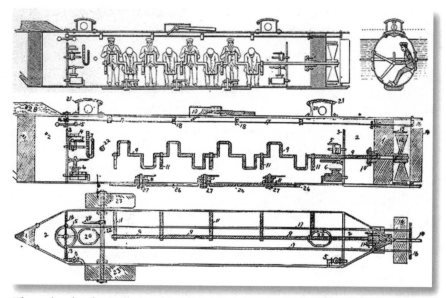

These sketches by William Alexander, made nearly 40 years after he helped James McClintock build the fish-boat, offer highly detailed yet rudimentary descriptions of the Hunley. *Although some elements in the drawings are accurate, many others—such as the steering wheel—are so far off the mark that some believe Alexander must have mingled design elements from the* American Diver *in this drawing. Alexander offered these descriptions for the numbers on his sketch: (1) bow and stern castings. (2) water ballast tanks. (3) tank bulkheads. (4) compass. (5) sea cocks. (6) pumps. (7) mercury gauge. (8) keel ballast scuffing boxes. (9) propeller shaft and cranks. (10) stern bearing and gland. (11) shaft braces. (12) propeller. (13) wrought iron around propellers. (14) rudder. (15) steering wheel. (16) steering lever. (17) steering rods. (18) rod braces. (19) air box. (20) hatchways. (21) hatch covers. (22) shaft of side fins. (26) cast-iron keel ballast. (27) bolts. (28) butt end of torpedo boom. (23) side fins. (24) shaft levers. (25) one of the crew turning propeller shaft. (31) keel ballast. Courtesy of the U.S. Naval History and Heritage Command.*

still leak some, McClintock believed the hydrodynamic benefits were worth avoiding overlapping plates.

The upper and lower hull plates were fastened to a flat strip of iron that ran down both flanks of the sub. Alexander called them expansion strakes. This "expansion" gave the submarine its oval shape and added interior height. Although this allowed for more headway in the main compartment, the interior was still so cramped that the crew would have to sit hunched over. The sub would stand four feet and three inches tall, most of it beneath the waterline even when the boat was traveling on the surface.

The bow, stern and conning towers were made of cast iron, molded into shape by local craftsmen. This took time, but was worth the effort. The fitted pieces of the bow and stern gave the sub a sleek, menacing look unlike any other sailing craft. From above, it looked as sharp as a knife. The boat was engineered to glide through the water with little effort, and McClintock no doubt took its shape from marine life.

By the time the cast iron caps were ready to be installed, Alexander had moved the operation out of Park and Lyons' shop. The boat was just too big and took up too much room in the machine shop. But the move may have had as much to do with secrecy. The men wanted more privacy to finish building their secret weapon, and there were rumors of deserters and Union spies wandering the streets of Mobile. McClintock and Alexander desperately wanted to avoid any chance that the Yankees might learn of their new project.

Alexander found a more secluded work space at the Seaman's Bethel Church, an unused building eight blocks south of Park and Lyons' shop. The port's declining business meant that there were few sailors coming into port seeking spiritual guidance. The hall provided ample room for the submarine, but it wasn't entirely secure. Some days, local kids would come into the church and play beneath the submarine, their heads precariously close to the iron blocks McClintock had attached to the boat's keel. This heavy ballast would keep the sub upright and also serve as another fail-safe. T-bolts inside the main hull could be turned to drop the blocks, allowing the sub to rise to the surface. McClintock would leave nothing to chance this time. He would not surrender another boat to the sea.

As the work progressed, McClintock made several last-minute adjustments to the design. He had the men install ten small deadlights—topside ports—between the two hatches. These ports would provide some natural light when the sub was on the surface or in a shallow dive. The engineers added hinged covers so the crew could hide any interior light when they approached enemy ships—McClintock and Alexander did not want these ports to become targets in an attack. The ports in the conning towers had no covers; there simply wasn't enough room.

Whitney lingered among the workers during much of the construction, and his $3,000 contribution gave him the authority to offer suggestions. McClintock did not mind—Whitney was a capable man—but it seemed the investors required constant attention. McClintock felt he was struggling to maintain control of the project, and there were too many distractions. It did not help that he had to take additional time to answer the occasional query from Hunley himself, who wanted constant updates.

In early May, Hunley was en route to Vicksburg, the front line of fighting in the west. He claimed that he was doing some sort of work for General Maury. When he stopped in Canton—barely 60 miles out of Mobile—Hunley sent a letter to his New Orleans friend Henry Leovy, lamenting that he had heard no news of the "seegar boat." In truth he had other things on his mind at the moment. Hunley was riding into a war zone and knew he might not make it back. He mailed Leovy a new version of his will, although it's unclear whether it was done for dramatic effect or just precaution. Either way, it was a practical concern—all hell was about to break loose in the Mississippi river town.

"I have some idea of joining our forces in defense of Vicksburg, and should any accident befall me, I wish you to take charge of my affairs," Hunley wrote.

He sent Leovy specific instructions for selling his sugar and tobacco holdings and suggested he invest the money in blockade running to turn a better profit. Hunley also mentioned a couple of people who owed him money. One of these men, identified only as "Dixon," was indebted to him for $82 on an old score. Hunley may have been talking about George Dixon, whom he had met in Mobile at the Park and Lyons' machine shop.

Horace Hunley was in a foul mood and appeared to be floundering without a purpose. He displayed the classic symptoms of depression, a malady he likely suffered from most of his life. He needed action, yearned to be important. Hunley could not sit idle in Mobile, while the new submarine was built, and was so desperate for adventure that he was willing to take up arms for a cause he didn't particularly support. But he would not linger for long in Vicksburg. There was little he could do there, so he quickly left Mississippi.

For much of the summer, Hunley traveled the South aimlessly. Perhaps he fancied himself a secret agent of sort and may have done some work at the behest of his old boss, Francis Hatch. Like Hunley, Hatch was deeply involved in the war effort without actually serving in the Confederate military. Hatch was constantly entangled in some plot—usually one that he hoped would fill his pockets. Hunley often went along with these plans. For the moment, he had nothing else to do.

Hunley's Louisiana plantation and slaves had been seized by the Union military and, despite his sister's constant entreaties, he saw little reason to return home. There was nothing there for him anymore. By late July Hunley was in Rome, Georgia, trying to secure some sugar owned jointly by him and his brother-in-law. The sugar had been seized earlier in the war, and he wanted it back. It was just about all he had left.

While Hunley was roaming the countryside, trying to turn a profit and find his purpose, he missed the launch of the boat that would bring him immortality.

By the middle of June, the submarine was nearly finished. Inside the Seaman's Bethel Church, the boat's hull was completely assembled save for the topside hull plates. These were left off while workers installed the axle for the diving fins and the intricate network of pipes that would move ballast water from one tank to the next. The interior had to be finished before the top hull plates could be attached because the hatches were too small for most of the sub's machinery to fit through.

One of the last things installed was the crew's bench. The bench was made of hardwood and cut into pieces, each mounted on brackets attached to the portside bulkhead. The crew would sit with their feet against the starboard bulkhead, their torsos positioned over the massive cranks. In this attitude, the men would more evenly distribute the weight inside the submarine—and avoid hitting their heads. Alexander later complained that the cranks took up so much room it was nearly impossible to pass through the crew compartment. But at the time he said nothing; Alexander did not feel he had the authority to question McClintock.

The long crank shaft certainly dominated the interior of the submarine, and most of the crew would have little to do but operate it. The commander's station, however, was a complex work space. It included a tiller that operated the rudder and a large lever that controlled the attitude of the dive fins. The captain was also responsible for opening and closing the valve to the forward ballast tank's seacock. Next to that valve, McClintock installed a depth gauge—a glass tube filled with mercury that measured pressure inside the sub to estimate its depth beneath the surface. On the forward ballast tank wall, Alexander added a small wooden shelf with enough room for a candle and the ship's compass. It was just about the only flat surface inside the sub.

The cramped space would leave the captain standing with his head in the forward conning tower much of the time, but Alexander built a small wooden seat with a lip that fit snugly over some of the internal piping. At the same time, he added a long handle to the forward ballast tank pump that would allow the first man on the bench to operate it. The captain had enough to do, and little room to do it in— although he enjoyed significantly more space, and comfort, than most of the men sitting on the crew bench.

McClintock had thought of nearly everything, but Alexander—and the sub's first crew—would find ways to improve upon the sub. There was just enough room between the bench and the ballast piping to store canteens and other equipment. Alexander had the walls painted white to help with illumination. And the first officer would eventually saw off the corner of the bench, most likely because he tired of rapping his knuckles while working the aft ballast pump.

After the ballast system was tested and the bellows for the snorkels had been installed, the topside hull plates were attached by rivets. The rivet heads would be sanded down, the seams packed with more tar. Then the hull may have been painted black, which would not only improve its stealth but add another layer of sealant. And then it was finished. In less than three months, William Alexander had built the boat just as McClintock had drawn it.

Alexander had his differences with McClintock and his design. For one thing, he thought it was foolish to leave the ballast tank walls open at the top. McClintock may have thought this would give the crew another option to bail water from the main compartment, but Alexander knew the pumping system would do that far more efficiently. Alexander believed the open ballast tanks were a fatal flaw in the submarine. But again, he said nothing—he was just a soldier following orders.

Despite these quibbles, Alexander took as much pride in the boat as McClintock. This submarine was as close to perfection as they could build, at least with the materials available to them. It looked like an ocean predator, a whale or a shark. That's why, even after they decided to name the sub in honor of Horace Hunley, most of the men continued to simply call it the fish-boat.

The *H. L. Hunley* was launched in mid-July.

Alexander had workers hoist the submarine onto a wagon for the short trip to the water, but they quickly found the boat was too wide to fit through the Bethel's doors. With the two dive planes, both of which were eight inches wide, the submarine measured nearly five feet across. Workers tried to maneuver the sub out but finally had to cut two columns to get to the street. After the slight delay, the crew found a growing crowd of spectators gathering to watch this curious contraption parade down Water Street toward the Theatre Street dock.

The crowd let out a cheer when the workers finally wrestled the *Hunley* off the cart and it slipped into the dark river.

The South was desperate for something to cheer about at that moment. Earlier that month, the Confederacy had suffered a humiliating defeat in the Pennsylvania countryside. Robert E. Lee's army had lost nearly 5,000 men, with another 12,000 wounded and 5,000 missing at Gettysburg. The debacle ended Lee's plan for a northern campaign that he hoped would break the spirit of Union politicians. Along with the fall of Vicksburg, July had been the Confederacy's most devastating month—a turning point in the war. A new secret weapon was, if nothing else, a reason for some measure of optimism.

From the beginning, the *Hunley* performed much better than either of its predecessors. In its initial test runs, the crew found this boat was easier to operate than the *American Diver*, even though it was not significantly faster. McClintock knew it was too slow, but there was little he could do. Other than its plodding speed—about four miles per hour—the engineer later told Matthew Maury that the sub "worked to perfection." The *Hunley* cut through the water easily and dived swiftly. The sub responded to its controls much more quickly than either of the previous subs. But it was still, to be sure, a delicate piece of machinery.

McClintock would fret over its operation in those weeks of trials, constantly barking orders to the men who operated it. He was nervous, but it was clear he had done it—McClintock had built a real submarine. Whitney was so proud he would barely leave the boat's side, and he even offered to serve on the crew. There was no shortage of prospective sailors for the fish-boat. George Dixon volunteered, as did Alexander. Years later, William Alexander would describe the fantastic capabilities of the *Hunley* to veterans' groups, or just about anyone else who would listen.

"The first officer steered and handled the boat forward, and the second attended to the after-tank and pumps and the air supply, all hands turning on the cranks except the first officer," Alexander recalled. "There was just sufficient room for these two to stand in their places with their heads in the hatchways and take observations through the lights in the combings.

"All hands aboard and ready, they would fasten the hatch covers down tight, light a candle, then let the water in from the sea into the ballast tanks until the top of the shell was about three inches under water. This could be seen by the water level showing through the glasses in the hatch combings. The seacocks were then closed and the boat put under way. The captain would then lower the lever and depress the forward ends of the fins slightly, noting on the mercury gauge the depth of the boat beneath the surface; then bring the fins to a level; the boat would remain and travel at that depth. To rise to a higher level in the water he would raise the lever and elevate the forward end of the fins, and the boat would rise to its original position in the water.

"If the boat was not underway, in order to rise to the surface, it was necessary to start the pumps and lighten the boat by ejecting the water from the tanks into the sea. In making a landing, the second officer would open his hatch cover, climb out and pass a line to shore."

The *Hunley* appeared much easier to operate than it actually was, and that worried McClintock. For most of July, he tried to train a crew largely comprised of men from Park and Lyons'. He was too technical in his instructions and sometimes talked over the heads of his prospective submariners. But McClintock worried that carelessness, or a lack of attention to detail, could cost him what was certainly his last chance to prove that submarine technology worked.

"The boat and machinery was so very simple that many persons at the first inspection believed that they could work the boat without practice, or experience," McClintock recalled years later. "Although I endeavored to prevent inexperienced persons from going under the water in the boat, I was not always successful in preventing them. I was at all times willing to instruct any person who wished it, to tell them, the difficulties, which in my own mind was want of speed and power."

After two weeks of successful trials in Mobile Bay—perhaps with George Dixon at the helm—McClintock felt confident enough to invite Confederate military officials to the waterfront for a demonstration of his machine's capabilities. On Friday, July 31, Mobile commander Dabney Maury, Adm. Franklin Buchanan and Gen. James Slaughter gathered on the riverbank while a flat barge loaded with lumber was anchored in the middle of the Mobile River.

On cue, the *Hunley* appeared upriver. The sub sailed toward the barge with little more than its hatches breaking the surface. Trailing behind, at the end of a 150-foot rope, a floating contact mine bobbed in the *Hunley*'s wake. The mine seemed to travel separately, as if it operated under its own power. The military men realized that, at night, the submarine would be nearly invisible even without submerging.

As the *Hunley* approached the barge, it slipped gracefully beneath the surface. The mine stayed on the surface, advancing toward the barge slowly. When it made contact there was a tremendous explosion, a wall of water thrown high into the air, timbers—and its cargo of lumber—raining down on the surface. The barge lurched and dipped, and soon began to sink. Within minutes it was gone.

Moments later, the *Hunley* surfaced 400 yards downstream, the captain popping out of the forward hatch. McClintock could not have been more proud.

The *Hunley* made quite an impression on its small audience. Later that day, Slaughter sent a note to his friend Gen. P. G. T. Beauregard, the commander at Charleston, to boast of the submarine's feat. The letter would serve as an introduction for Baxter Watson and Gus Whitney, who were already making their way east toward South Carolina. The two men, Slaughter wrote, wanted an audience. They would like to test their submarine boat in Charleston Harbor.

"So far as I am able to judge I can see no reason why it should not answer all our sanguine expectations," Slaughter wrote to Beauregard.

The suggestion of Charleston as a home port for the *Hunley* seemed to come out of nowhere. Slaughter may have had the idea, or perhaps it came from Whitney. He believed the submarine should tour ports across the South, breaking blockades—and collect-

Gen. Pierre Gustave Toutant Beauregard, the Confederate commander at Charleston, was initially impressed with the fish-boat and ordered it sent to Charleston shortly after its trials in Mobile. He believed the Hunley *could help break the city's blockade, but would come to loathe and fear the submarine. Courtesy National Archives.*

ing bounties—as it went. But it's most likely that the idea of sending the *Hunley* to Charleston initially came from Buchanan, the man who had said such venomous things about its predecessor.

While Buchanan could not have failed to be impressed by the *Hunley*'s demonstration, he was both old-fashioned and territorial. He had his own ironclad under construction in Selma, and he did not want this machine—which he did not trust—to steal any of its glory. Military politics also played a role. The *Hunley*, while a civilian vessel, had been promoted tirelessly by the Confederate Army, and Buchanan had no control over it. And he would not have any vessel sailing his waters that he didn't ultimately command. So the day after he watched the *Hunley* blow up the barge, he sent a note to his counterpart in Charleston. Buchanan enthusiastically recommended the *Hunley* for duty in South Carolina.

"If it can operate in smooth water where the current is not strong as was the case yesterday, I can recommend it to your favorable consideration," Buchanan wrote. "I am fully satisfied it can be used successfully in blowing up one or more of the enemy's Iron Clads in your harbor."

Buchanan closed by asking that Beauregard be informed immediately. He would take no chance that his very pointed suggestion might be ignored.

Charleston was in particular need of assistance at that moment. In the past month, Union forces had invaded Morris Island outside the harbor and now held two-thirds of the barrier island. A gallant attempt to take Battery Wagner on the island's north end—led by a regiment of black troops from Massachusetts, the Fifty-fourth—had failed. But the Confederates knew it was only a matter of time before they would have to cede the earthen fort. And then what? As the *Charleston Mercury* had made abundantly clear, if Wagner falls, Sumter falls. And if Sumter falls, Charleston falls.

General Beauregard was consumed by that scenario in early August, the very moment the letters from Slaughter and Buchanan hit his desk. Beauregard was under siege—his men worn down, his forts taking heavy shelling and his own ironclads nearly worthless. He needed some sort of advantage or Charleston would likely be lost. For that reason, he was intrigued by what he read about this submarine. A secret weapon might give him that edge. It could not have hurt that its builder and its namesake were both from New Orleans, Beauregard's hometown.

Sometime shortly after those letters arrived, Watson and Whitney showed up on Beauregard's doorstep. They carried a letter of introduction from Slaughter and a detailed description of how their submarine operated. The idea showed promise, although at that point it did not take much to convince the general. That same day, August 5, Beauregard hurriedly sent out a series of telegrams. The first, to Dabney Maury, said: "Have seen Whitney and Watson. Have accepted their submarine boat. Please assist them to get it here as soon as possible."

And then, to all railroad agents between Mobile and Charleston, Beauregard sent this note: "Please expedite transportation of Whitney's submarine boat from Mobile here. It is much needed."

It would take dozens of men, a crane and nearly two days to lift the *Hunley* out of the Mobile River and load it onto two train cars. Some locals believed they were witness to the coming of a new development in naval warfare and regretted they wouldn't be able to see it in action. Lt. George Washington Gift, who operated the crane that moved the *Hunley*, predicted the submarine boat will "in a very short time become one of the great celebrities in the art of defence and attack by floating objects."

In a letter to his wife, Gift described the machine in great detail and said he had watched the experiment in the Mobile River, when the sub dived beneath the barge and "smashed her side to atoms." He declared the boat "perfectly safe and perfectly sure." He was

The South Atlantic Blockading Squadron off Charleston, seen here in a photograph taken from Morris Island, had effectively cut off the port city's supply line by the summer of 1863. Desperate to break the blockade, Confederates in the city embraced Horace Hunley and James McClintock's fish-boat as their best hope to defeat the viciously efficient U.S. Navy. Courtesy National Archives.

confident the sub would soon sink every ironclad off Morris Island. McClintock would have been pleased to know how much he had impressed the locals.

By August 7, the *Hunley* was secured and ready for a trip across the South. It took up two train cars, and workers fashioned a tarp over the sub to hide its shape. When the train finally pulled out of the station, the *Hunley* left Mobile as quietly as it had slipped into the river three weeks earlier.

The *Hunley*'s departure was devastating to the men at the Park and Lyons shop. They had invested months in construction of the boat and did not want to lose it now. Alexander and Dixon took the news hardest. They wanted to sail on it, but they were stationed in Mobile and probably didn't think to ask if they could go along. Only McClintock would travel with the boat.

As Alexander and Dixon watched the train steam out of sight, they feared they would never see the *Hunley* again. Dixon could only hope that soon McClintock would send word that they were needed in Charleston.

Part Two

Into Charleston

CHAPTER 7

1994
Off Sullivan's

The *Divercity* cut through rolling swells, dragging a magnetometer and fighting the Atlantic Ocean to stay on course. The sea was particularly rough that morning, the Isle of Palms bouncing erratically on the horizon. It was not a good day for precision—the boat was running search lanes that were, at best, educated guesses. Bill Shea would soon be seasick, and he might have company.

Ralph Wilbanks was having the time of his life.

He was back on the hunt and could not have been happier. Wilbanks preferred spending his days on the water, chasing adventure like the guys on *Sea Hunt*. He had loved that show as a kid growing up on the Isle of Palms. Now he was living it. Part Jacques Cousteau, part Quint—the captain from *Jaws*—Wilbanks somehow conveyed the dual and sometimes conflicting presence of a scholar and a good ol' boy. As he steered through confused seas, Wilbanks danced a jig and kept the *Divercity*'s crew and passengers entertained with his antics.

"Boy, we're magging now!" he yelled out.

Clive Cussler had to laugh. In the thirteen years since he'd last worked with Wilbanks, the South Carolina native had only gotten more colorful, more opinionated and more stubborn. And, if possible,

Ralph Wilbanks was an even better underwater archaeologist than he had been as a young man. This guy was the real deal, Cussler realized, a true professional. He would have to use him more often—definitely. NUMA could use a guy like Ralph.

In the past five days, Wilbanks and his partner—the North Carolina archaeologist/diver Wes Hall—had already relocated four targets that NUMA found more than a decade earlier. Any one of the sites might be the final resting place of the *H. L. Hunley*, and they were there to remove all doubt. Wilbanks worked quickly, efficiently and seemingly without effort, and Hall appeared to read his mind. They worked together like a symphony orchestra, Cussler thought, perfectly in concert. Locate a target, mark it with a buoy and then radio the coordinates to a boat full of divers who would then go down for a closer look.

The only trouble was, the pilot of the other boat could never find the buoys.

Idiots, Wilbanks thought—and wasn't afraid to say so. He had come to the conclusion that most of the people on the dive boat were incompetent, and it was wearing on his paper-thin patience. Even the amiable Cussler was growing weary of the miscues, but he had to wonder if he didn't share some of the blame. Already, the author wished he had not agreed to work with the amateur divers hired by the man from the South Carolina Institute of Archaeology and Anthropology. The 1994 expedition was not going well.

～

After 11 years away from Charleston, Cussler's thoughts had returned to South Carolina and the Confederate submarine in 1992. He wasn't sure why. It's possible that *Sahara* was to blame. Cussler had spent nearly a year writing the eleventh Dirk Pitt adventure, an ambitious novel that sent the fictional underwater archaeologist into the North African desert to find a lost Confederate ironclad. In the book, the CSS *Texas* had disappeared near the end of the Civil War and conflicting stories of its demise still circulated more than a century later.

Cussler's alter ego traipsed through the largest desert on the planet looking for a lost river and a ship that was in the last place it should have been. It was a complex story, one of Cussler's best and most popular books to date. The author couldn't help but see the subconscious similarities between his story and that of the *Hunley*.

Or perhaps Cussler's renewed interest in the sub had more to do with something that the diver and side-scan sonar expert Garry Kozak had once said: shipwrecks aren't found until they are ready to be found. That had stuck with Cussler over the years. Maybe the *Hunley* was ready now. At the very least, Cussler was ready. NUMA was ready.

In the decade since the author and his entourage had sailed out of Charleston, the technology for underwater searches had improved markedly. But Cussler had uncovered no new information that might lead him to the sub, and the author had said he wouldn't return without a new clue—an edge of some kind. But here he was again, back at the scene of NUMA's first stateside expedition. Cussler just couldn't let go of the *Hunley*. This one should be easy, he knew, and Cussler desperately wanted to find it. He decided his edge was NUMA's experience. The team was a lot more seasoned these days.

Since 1981, Cussler and NUMA had become remarkably efficient, locating dozens of lost shipwrecks around the world. The sea hunters had even solved the mystery of a train that vanished in the nineteenth century. In 1878, a flood had washed away a bridge over the Kiowa Creek in Colorado, and Engine 51 went tumbling into the rushing water. Or so the railroad said. Cussler's team showed up to look for the train, but their research suggested that the Lost Locomotive of Kiowa Creek was likely nothing more than an insurance scam.

These days, NUMA found what it was looking for more often than not. But for all his success, Cussler was haunted by the ones that got away: the *Bonhomme Richard* and the *Hunley*. He had not searched for the elusive *Richard* since that cursory glance in 1984, but was considering a fourth expedition. But first, he thought, it was time to give Charleston another look.

Cussler had phoned the South Carolina Institute of Archaeology and Anthropology (SCIAA) in 1992 to get a new search permit. The call was answered by Mark Newell, the man who had taken Wilbanks's old job when he'd quit years earlier. Newell wasn't the state agency's underwater archaeologist but he had been interested in the *Hunley* for years—had even written an article about one of the early Cussler expeditions for a diving magazine. To Newell, Cussler's voice on the other end of the line was opportunity calling.

Newell suggested that NUMA avoid the red tape of a permit and team up with SCIAA for a joint expedition. The agency formerly known simply as the Institute would supply equipment and manpower; Cussler would provide the money. It would be the biggest, most extensive search to date for the lost Confederate submarine. The author mulled it over and finally decided he couldn't see any reason to decline the invitation—the more people looking, the better.

In retrospect, Cussler decided, he should have known better.

It had taken nearly two years to arrange everything and clear the NUMA crew's schedule. Cussler and Newell planned a nine-day expedition, and their primary goal would be to relocate and identify seven unidentified magnetic anomalies from the 1981 search. Cussler's team had found several interesting possibilities but had dived on few of them. While SCIAA put a label on the old targets, some of the NUMA team would expand the search grid.

NUMA advance man Walt Schob arrived in Charleston in early August 1994. He booked the team rooms at a Mount Pleasant Holiday Inn and then tracked down Wilbanks. Schob found him on a survey expedition in Delaware, where he was doing contract work. Wilbanks had left the institute in 1984 and was freelancing for several companies when he wasn't leading dive charters in Charleston. In the past decade, Wilbanks had amassed a lot of experience with the tools of underwater archaeology—sub bottom profilers, positioning systems and magnetometers. Schob offered him a new gig, closer to home.

These days Wilbanks was doing a lot of work with Wes Hall. Hall had his own business in North Carolina, one similar to Diversified Wilbanks, but the men often teamed up for surveys. After a quick phone call, the two archaeologists agreed to return to Charleston, supply their time and Wilbanks's boat. Cussler had a great eye for talent, and he had recognized it in Wilbanks years earlier. He took an immediate liking to Hall as well. The former marine was more than competent in the water and as an archaeologist. But then, Cussler would expect no less from a friend of Ralph's. Wilbanks famously didn't suffer fools.

And that was a problem from the beginning of the expedition, because the men onboard the *Divercity* felt they were surrounded by them.

Wilbanks started out with a low opinion of his SCIAA replacement, and Cussler soon had his own misgivings. The author learned that the divers Newell had provided for the search were not professionals, but enthusiastic members of a local Sons of Confederate Veterans camp. The men had actually paid Newell for the privilege of joining the expedition. That was the first red flag. The second was an actual red flag—a Confederate banner the divers carried to rub on the *Hunley*'s hull once they found it. This did not bode well for serious science.

Even before the search began, Cussler could sense tension in the SCIAA ranks. Carl Naylor, a thoughtful scientist and SCIAA official, seemed to be at odds with Newell. Naylor would not take responsibility for the amateur divers, many of whom did not have trustworthy equipment—one man even wore sweat pants for a wetsuit. Naylor's consternation was a telling sign. Cussler realized he had embarked on an expedition with a man who was not even respected by his own colleagues.

Newell had been right about one thing, however. This would be the largest search for the *Hunley* yet, and also the most complex. Three boats were on the water most of the time. Cussler's son, Dirk, and a small crew ran search lanes in a small outboard close to shore while the author sailed on *Divercity* with Wilbanks and Hall, relocating NUMA's old targets. Newell took the SCIAA boat and the divers, following behind. The divers would investigate every site the *Divercity* team located.

In theory, it was an efficient system for a search. But the SCIAA boat was the weak link. More often than not, Newell could not find the peanut buoys Hall dropped to mark the targets. Wilbanks would wait for the inevitable call, and then have to circle back and lead the other boat to the site. Once the SCIAA divers arrived, there were often other problems. A few times they forgot important equipment— probes, dredges—and had to rendezvous with *Divercity* to borrow tools. It was all very unscientific. Amateur hour, Wilbanks called it.

It took NUMA only three days to find six of the seven old targets. But several of the sites were never explored. Newell dismissed some of them out of hand because they did not give off the gamma signals he thought the iron hull of the *Hunley* should emit. Metal objects affect the Earth's magnetic core, and these slight deviations can be detected at close range with a magnetometer. It was never clear how Newell had calculated the strength of signal the *Hunley* would give off since so little was known about the sub's actual construction. He was just pulling a number out of his ass, Wilbanks suspected.

Cussler did not protest, at least not initially.

At first, Cussler was simply happy to be back in Charleston. He loved the city—its history, its culinary sophistication and its people. But he soon found this was not the same Charleston he had visited a decade earlier. It had changed dramatically, irrevocably, and the author could sense that the cause of all this change had damaged the city's entire psyche.

In 1989, a category 4 hurricane called Hugo had ravaged the coast of South Carolina. It was a direct hit—the eye had actually passed through Charleston Harbor. In a few hours, the storm literally changed the city's landscape. Hugo chewed away Folly Beach, dumped seven feet of water into the mansions on The Battery and destroyed hundreds of homes on the barrier islands. The old concrete-block motel on the Isle of Palms where the NUMA team stayed in 1980 was gone.

In the summer of 1994, the city was still rebuilding—even the steeple of St. Philip's Church remained encased in scaffolding. It would take years for the city to fully recover and, as it did, a new Charleston was born. This was not a sleepy beach town any longer. It was quickly becoming a destination, a tourist attraction, a cruise ship port of call. Charleston was still beautiful, still the place he had once considered calling home. But Cussler found that he missed some of the old charms, which were now literally gone with the wind.

Above all, Cussler realized that such a major storm might have churned up more wrecks on the ocean floor—that was the power of a category 4 hurricane. In the months following Hugo, archaeologists with the Charleston Museum had found the remains of a Union camp on the north end of Folly Beach. The artifacts dated to the summer of 1863, when U.S. soldiers had been planning their assault on Morris Island. After more than a century buried in the sand, the remnants of the Union camp were now simply lying on the beach, exposed. The entire place had been upended.

Cussler had changed, too. At 63, he was much more famous than he had been a decade before. In the early 1980s, he was a best-selling author; now he was a phenomenon. He had sold nearly 100 million books and was in the middle of negotiating a new publishing deal that would earn him $14 million for the next two Dirk Pitt adventures. Although he was still the same unpretentious, good-natured guy from decades past, he was now also one of the most famous authors in the world.

That sort of success did not lend itself to anonymity, even in an off-the-beaten-path town like Charleston. So Cussler was not surprised when one evening, after returning from a day at sea, he was recognized on the docks. But he was quickly amused to find that it wasn't his famous face that sparked the encounter: the man had spotted the orange dial of his Doxa dive watch. It was the same one the famous Dirk Pitt wore, the man said—he had read about it in a book. He simply assumed it was the famous author attached to the Doxa.

Cussler seldom returned to the scene of the crime. If he didn't find a shipwreck on a single expedition, he rarely went back. But he had made an exception for Charleston, for the *Hunley*. The story of the first combat submarine still fascinated him, and a decade had not squelched that enthusiasm. His friends considered him a man possessed, and they had serious circumstantial evidence. Had Cussler not been obsessed with finding the *Hunley*, he would not have put up with all that he endured in 1994.

At first, nothing seemed out of the ordinary.

Cussler, Wilbanks and Hall worked well together and quickly fell into an easy pattern. They launched *Divercity* at the Isle of Palms marina each morning at 8 A.M. and almost never returned before 8 P.M. This was not the working vacation of year's past—this was an intense, almost frenetic schedule. The *Divercity* covered 10 square miles in a little over a week. Dirk Cussler searched several more miles before finally abandoning the team's unreliable outboard and joining the *Divercity* crew.

The plan was simple: they would investigate each of the sites NUMA had found in the earlier expeditions and if anything else showed up on sonar, look at that, too. The trouble was the old sites were not easy to find—at least initially. Cussler had given Wilbanks all the notes and coordinates from the 1981 expedition, but the numbers made no sense. They didn't represent latitude/longitude lines, State Plane or universal transverse Mercators (UTMs). Finally, they remembered that the team had used the Motorola Mini-ranger that year, and more than a decade later that system was woefully out of date.

The Mini-ranger system set its coordinates based on distances to fixed points of reference—and those points of reference were long forgotten. Without them, all of Cussler's notes were useless. The team was in a panic until Wilbanks' wife, Frances, stepped in. She had a degree in mathematics and a knack for solving puzzles. She started crunching the numbers, fed them into a computer and worked for 24 hours straight.

The men from Motorola, long since retired, had created a grid system that started at a zero point in the ocean. Finally, Frances Wilbanks found the zero point scribbled in the margin of one of the dog-eared pages and set to work replotting the entire search area. As Wilbanks and Hall headed out the door on the first morning, Frances was printing off modern coordinates for the men to follow.

After that, the team found the old targets with relative ease. Only one of their previous sites had disappeared, and they later learned that the object had been snagged by shrimpers and moved. Whatever it was, it certainly wasn't a 40-foot submarine. The sites they did find revealed nothing of great interest. But then, Cussler and Wilbanks did not realize that the SCIAA team was dismissing some of their targets without a single dive.

It soon became apparent to Cussler and Wilbanks that Newell wanted to focus on the place he thought the *Hunley* rested—Maffitt's Channel, an old blockade runner shortcut into the harbor that ran along the Sullivan's Island beach. Newell had a theory. He believed that, from their low vantage point on the water, the *Hunley* crew could not have found Breach Inlet after the attack. Instead they would have steered for Fort Sumter, a much more visible landmark. Newell thought the sub was trying to reach the harbor when it sank.

The basis for that hypothesis most likely came from early accounts of the sub's disappearance. In 1864, the troops at Battery Marshall did not report the *Hunley* missing for a couple of days. At first, they simply didn't notice that the fish-boat was not at the dock; when they finally did, the Confederates assumed it had returned to the harbor.

The *Hunley* had sailed out of the harbor mouth several times. But that was before it was moved to the northern tip of Sullivan's Island.

The troops on Battery Marshall did not fully understand the submarine—or its range. But then, few people did. Some people in Charleston suggested that after its attack on the blockade the *Hunley* had sailed for Georgetown, nearly 50 miles up the coast. None of these rumors took into account the simple fact that the *Hunley* could not travel that far. Even reaching the harbor from the *Housatonic*'s location would have been ambitious for the crew. But Newell believed that is exactly what had happened.

Wilbanks thought the theory was not only illogical, it was loony. Cussler was also skeptical. In fiction, you stretch the bounds of credibility without breaking it. And this hypothesis didn't pass any reality smell test. The author knew there was no way the *Hunley* crew, already tired from hours of labor, would have willingly added several miles to their journey. They had a compass to steer by, and had even requested Battery Marshall troops light a signal fire that they could steer by. Newell's theory didn't make sense to Cussler.

For several days, Cussler and Wilbanks resisted Newell's pleas to drag the magnetometer through Maffitt's Channel. They thought it was a waste of time. They wanted to relocate and identify all the targets they'd already found. One of those targets, No. 1, was of particular interest to both Cussler and Wilbanks. That was where Wilbanks had found the odd triangular fin in 1981. They had decided then that the precise craftsmanship suggested welding, which precluded any chance it was a Civil War–era vessel. But they hadn't actually seen any weld seams. Now they wanted to be sure, to satisfy their curiosity if nothing else.

Newell wasn't interested in target 1. He dismissed it out of hand because its gamma reading fell below the levels he expected to find on the *Hunley*. Couldn't be it, he declared. At NUMA's insistence, however, Newell finally took a quick look. Harry Pecorelli, an underwater archaeology graduate student—one of the few professional divers on the SCIAA boat—went into the water one day to check out target 1.

The ocean was relatively shallow at the site—less than 30 feet. Pecorelli reached the coordinates with ease, but found a thick layer of oyster shells covering the sand over the target. He tried using a probe for a few minutes, but couldn't get through the shell. Whatever it was, Pecorelli thought, it's covered up pretty good. He surfaced and explained the situation to Newell. And that was all the excuse he needed—the SCIAA man was out of patience. He told Pecorelli to climb aboard. They were leaving. That's not it.

The tension between the two teams escalated quickly and threatened to wreck the entire expedition. Barely a day passed without some miscue, miscommunication or drama. Equipment was left at the dock, a boat got lost or Newell renewed his push for a search of Maffitt's Channel. At one point, Newell transferred to *Divercity* and when Naylor called to unleash a tirade on his colleague, Cussler was actually on the receiving end of the radio. Cussler didn't hold it against Naylor, but he feared Wilbanks was right to be skeptical about this bunch.

The greatest drama came on the final day of the expedition, more than a week after it began. One of the volunteer divers got disoriented when saltwater leaked into his dive mask. Swimming blind he was lost at sea within minutes, and the boat crew quickly lost sight of him. Pecorelli went into the water to find the man. And soon, he was gone, too. The SCIAA boat had two men overboard.

Pecorelli searched the water for several tense minutes before he finally found the lost man drifting helplessly. The young diver calmed the man down and helped him to the surface. There, the two quickly realized they were far beyond the range of the boat. And from that distance, the SCIAA team couldn't see them bobbing on the surface, the man clinging to Pecorelli. The two men treaded water until Wilbanks and Cussler spotted them and hauled them aboard the *Divercity*.

Later that day, August 13, Wilbanks finally trolled Maffitt's Channel for Newell. Within a few minutes, they actually hit a target. The SCIAA boat had already returned to the dock by the time Wilbanks got on the radio and announced that they had something. He said it registered about 1,000 gammas on the magnetometer, which put it squarely in Newell's estimated range for the *Hunley*. The SCIAA crew scrambled to cast off and race back to the site.

Fighting the changing tide, Newell rushed his divers into the water to probe the site. The water was shallow, the current was tricky, but they soon determined they had found a metal object between 30 and 40 feet long, six feet wide—with a curved upper surface. It was too good to be true, and it fit Newell's theory perfectly.

He was confident they had found the *H. L. Hunley*.

Newell was excited, but he did not want to excavate the site—not yet. He wanted to bring in more sophisticated equipment to analyze the target before uncovering it. Newell said that, by next summer, he could bring in tools that would examine the object using sound waves, offering them a much clearer picture of what they had. Wilbanks and Cussler thought Newell was stalling. They didn't believe this target— No. 8—was the *Hunley*. But by then, their relationship with SCIAA had deteriorated to the point that they didn't say anything.

Newell was frustrated by the way things had turned out. He believed that if the expedition had started in Maffitt's Channel, as he suggested, they already could have verified target 8 was the *Hunley*. He asked Cussler to extend the expedition by two days—in other words, pay for two more days of work—but the author wasn't interested. He was finished with the joint expedition.

Cussler thought the entire search had been a terrible mistake, but it had not driven him to the point of giving up. In fact, he was now more determined than ever to find the *Hunley*. He just wouldn't spend any more time working with SCIAA. Before he left Charleston, Cussler put Diversified Wilbanks on retainer. He asked Wilbanks to keep searching for the *Hunley* in his spare time between other jobs.

Suddenly, the man once sent to watch NUMA was now part of the team.

In September, Wilbanks and Hall resumed their search. They would set out for two or three days at a time, dragging a magnetometer through the waters off Sullivan's Island. Cussler kept in touch with Wilbanks throughout the fall. The author would study maps of the ocean floor off Charleston and fax Wilbanks charts of the areas he wanted to search. Their playground was expanding every month. Wilbanks went out when he could, sometimes with Hall and other times with his wife. He never found anything of interest. In some ways, Wilbanks felt like he was plowing old ground. But Cussler was a kindred spirit, and Wilbanks understood his drive. He knew it had to be there, somewhere.

About a month after the 1994 expedition ended, Wilbanks and Hall went back to Maffitt's Channel. Mostly it was curiosity, but Wilbanks believed in marking potential targets off the list. The two men probed target 8 one morning and decided it was 35 feet long and six feet wide. Despite its promising size, Wilbanks decided it was nothing more than an old boiler—just as he'd predicted. But Wilbanks didn't bother to share this information with Newell. He figured the SCIAA folks didn't care what he thought, so why waste his breath?

Wilbanks continued his search without fanfare, and without saying anything about it to anyone.

On January 28, 1995, the Charleston *Post and Courier* carried a front-page headline that proclaimed, "Divers may have located *Hunley*."

In the story, Mark Newell said that he had a "very provocative target"—"the only target of its kind in a huge body of ocean." Newell was publicly announcing that target 8 was the *H. L. Hunley*, even though he would not disclose the location. The SCIAA team had also gone back to the site after the expedition, and Newell thought the size and shape verified it was the submarine. Newell was so certain he had found the lost sub that he could not help but leak the news to the local paper.

Newell said that he would lead an expedition to the site in the spring with acoustic remote sensing devices, gear that would help confirm the identity. He claimed Cussler was still involved in the project, but it may have been an attempt to make amends publicly. In truth, Newell blamed Cussler and Wilbanks for the failures of the 1994 expedition. He thought the men were condescending and had treated him disrespectfully. And he believed they had intentionally waited until the last moment to search Maffitt's Channel. If they had only cooperated, they might already have the submarine.

Around friends, Newell had taken to calling Cussler a "glory-hunting millionaire."

The glory-hunter wasn't the one talking to newspapers, however. Cussler was at his home in Colorado when he heard about Newell's announcement. The author was furious and called Newell immediately. Cussler told him it was unprofessional to identify a target that had not been surveyed. That would serve no purpose, would do nothing except to get people's hopes up. Cussler also knew that if Newell was wrong, it would make the entire expedition look unprofessional. And he did not want NUMA associated with such nonsense.

The outburst was out of character for the easygoing author, and his friends later said they had never seen him so angry. They assumed Cussler was as annoyed at himself as anyone. Cussler had worked too hard, and NUMA was too respectable, to be dragged into some amateur "Eureka!" moment.

Ralph Wilbanks took a completely different view of the article. He thought it was hilarious. Wilbanks knew that Newell was wrong and was more than content to sit back and let him keep talking. That winter, as the town whispered about the possible discovery of the *Hunley,* he and Hall continued their search. But foul weather and other jobs delayed their work through much of the winter of 1995. They would pick up where they'd left off in April 1995.

Shortly after Newell's announcement, Wilbanks explained the situation to Cussler. The author immediately relaxed and even had a good laugh. Cussler realized that he'd found something nearly as good as the *Hunley*—he now had Wilbanks on the NUMA team.

And if the *Hunley* was out there, Cussler was confident that he and Ralph Wilbanks would eventually find it.

CHAPTER 8

1863
James Island

The train carrying the camouflaged *H. L. Hunley* traveled northeast out of Alabama, steamed through the plains of Georgia and, at Augusta, finally crossed into South Carolina. The trip across the barren landscape of the South would take five days. And that was not nearly fast enough for Gen. Pierre Gustave Toutant Beauregard.

On August 11, Beauregard sent a frantic telegram to his counterpart in Mobile, Gen. Dabney H. Maury, asking if the submarine boat was on its way and, if so, when it had left Alabama. Two weeks before, the Charleston commander had not even heard of this new secret weapon, and now he allowed himself to imagine that it might be the solution to all his many troubles. For that reason, he could not wait—he wanted it immediately. The general was desperate. Charleston was desperate.

Since the battle on Morris Island nearly three weeks earlier, the fighting around the city had barely abated. Just two days after the unsuccessful attack on Battery Wagner, Union gunboats sailed into range and opened fire on both Wagner and Sumter. Four men died and 11 others were wounded before the ships were chased off by heavy Confederate cannon fire. The naval assault resumed two days later and lasted the rest of the week. At one point, 19 Union gunboats were firing on the city's forts simultaneously.

On August 4, Confederate troops had discovered a barge attempting to land Union soldiers on the high ground between Morris and James Island. It was all Beauregard's men could do to stop the boat, and they knew it would return eventually. There were just too many Yankees and, at this rate, the general didn't know how long he could fend them off. It seemed that more U.S. troops arrived every day, but the Confederate government wouldn't send reinforcements. Charleston was running out of men.

Beauregard had become so short-handed that he asked local plantation owners to supply more slaves to help shore up the city's defenses. Although the *Charleston Mercury* editorially supported Beauregard's position, most plantation owners refused to give up a single man. They told the paper that the military had taken "as much negro labor as is requisite for the proper and energetic prosecution of the work upon our defences, and that, therefore, no more slaves are needed."

They did not seem to understand that, if Charleston fell, it would not matter if their crops were harvested on time.

The reaction of plantation owners should not have been a surprise to Beauregard. The patriotism of local residents was undeniably flagging. Between the humiliating defeats at Vicksburg and Gettysburg, there was very little in the way of good news coming out of the war. But locals did not have to read the papers to see their cause slipping away. They only had to look out across the harbor, where Fort Sumter—the icon of Charleston's defense—had been reduced to rubble by the near-constant shelling. Already, people who could afford to leave the city were packing their belongings and moving inland. Charleston had become its own corner of hell.

To stem this outgoing tide, Beauregard needed an edge. He prayed that the *Hunley* was it.

The train carrying the *Hunley* arrived at the Charleston depot on August 12, the day after Beauregard sent his telegram to Maury. The journey had been tense, the men onboard wary the entire time, careful not to stop anywhere that Union spies might get a good look at the two camouflaged cars. By the late summer of 1863, Southerners no longer trusted anyone they didn't know.

James McClintock had made the trip with the submarine, and Gus Whitney and Baxter Watson were among the crowd waiting at the depot to greet the train. Soon, most of the other investors would join them in the city. Singer was en route, and Horace Hunley would not be able to stay away for long—especially after hearing the news that McClintock received upon his arrival.

The Charleston import-export firm of John Fraser and Co. had offered $100,000 to anyone who could sink the USS *Wabash* or the *New Ironsides*—the ship that led most of the attacks on Sumter and Wagner. The blockade had been bad for Fraser's business, and the company was willing to pay generously for revenge. Fraser and Co., which operated many of the city's most successful blockade runners, also promised a $50,000 award for every Union ironclad sunk by the sub. The $15,000 investment Singer and his associates had made in the *Hunley* suddenly held great promise.

When Beauregard got his first look at the fish-boat, however, his optimism waned considerably. His secret weapon appeared to be little more than a long iron tube with fins on the side. "From its shape it came to be known as the 'fish torpedo boat,'" Beauregard would later write. This was the secret weapon that was supposed to break the blockade? It barely looked as if it could float, let alone sink the United States' most formidable warships. Beauregard was wary, but offered the men whatever assistance he could to speed the project along. He sent his quartermaster a note instructing the man to give Gus Whitney whatever he needed.

At that point, Beauregard had no other choice.

The *Hunley* had to be unloaded from the train by crane, and then it was hauled to the Cooper River docks. Once the sub was in the water, it was most likely towed to the back side of Sullivan's Island, where it was moored at a small dock just behind Fort Moultrie. From that quiet spot, away from curious onlookers in Charleston, James McClintock finally launched his submarine project.

From the moment the *Hunley* arrived, Charleston residents talked of little else. There was a decided difference of opinion among the chattering class. Some thought the strange contraption might be their salvation; others doubted it was even seaworthy. But most everyone was willing to give it a chance. Soon, letters from the war zone began to include mentions of the "man from New Orleans" who had arrived to rid the city of those damn Yankees. From these detailed—and accurate—accounts of the submarine's brief history, it was clear that Charleston's new secret weapon was not much of a secret.

"It was tested in Mobile on an old vessel with most satisfactory results," one local woman wrote. "The boat is 40 feet long, pointed at both ends with a kind of fish tail + can remain under water 1 hour + ½. We are full of hope + hear it is soon to make an attack. May it be successful."

McClintock's first priority was to raise a crew that could actually sail the *Hunley*. He needed six men at the very least, as McClintock would serve as the sub's captain while Gus Whitney took on the duties of first officer. No one knew the craft as well as they did, and there was simply no one else who could train a crew. The Confederates had volunteered one man, but McClintock declined their offer. He suspected the military simply wanted an officer onboard to keep tabs on the project, and the engineer did not want anyone watching him. His secrecy immediately raised the suspicions of Charleston military officials. The pace of his work did little to ease those concerns. They would soon begin to fear they were being conned.

McClintock moved slowly by almost any measure. He was cautious, even hesitant, with the machine. He knew how easily his previous subs had sunk, and he had no desire to lose another—especially with himself onboard. So he trained his new crew at the dock by day and took the sub out in the evenings, often staying in the harbor for hours.

Many Charleston residents watched the fish-boat sail across the harbor on those late summer evenings. In fact, too many people saw it. One Confederate officer later noted that several people began to call the *Hunley* the "cigar boat" in a nod to its shape. The secret weapon became such a common sight that finally two blockade runners spied the sub. Their detailed eyewitness accounts—which included some inaccuracies—would soon make it into the hands of U.S. Navy intelligence.

The tests continued for a week, but the crew never attempted to venture beyond the mouth of the harbor. Beauregard was not amused by this apparent lack of progress and had officers try to prod McClintock along. McClintock said he needed more time. But that was yet another commodity the Confederacy did not have. The two sides became almost adversarial, and even the troops at the harbor forts could tell that something was wrong.

"You doubtless remember and perhaps you saw while in the City the iron torpedo boat which certain parties brought from Mobile to blow up the Ironsides," one private in the Washington Light Infantry wrote to his wife. "They have been out three times without accomplishing anything and the government suspecting something wrong, proposed to allow a Naval officer to go with them on their next trial, which they refused."

McClintock resented the military interference and believed their impatience stemmed from a basic misunderstanding of his machine. He explained to the Confederates several times that the *Hunley* was a delicate machine, and not nearly as easy to operate as it appeared. But that did not stop anyone from telling him what he should be doing. Even Horace Hunley was applying pressure. Shortly after McClintock reached Charleston, he received a letter from Hunley, who was in Enterprise, Alabama. He apologized that he was not in Charleston—and asked leading questions. It was clear that Hunley desperately wanted good news, preferably confirmation that the sub had collected its first bounty on a Yankee ship.

"I have been extremely anxious about your experiment at Charleston," Hunley wrote. "It is not at all on the question whether you will succeed in blowing up a vessel of the enemy for I think that is more than probable and of itself only a small matter. It is whether your success will be made available in effecting a real solid benefit for the Confederacy and conferring glory on its originators."

Hunley believed a successful attack by the sub might start a panic among the Yankees, break the blockade and perhaps even drive Union troops from Morris Island—a very optimistic outlook. He even had the audacity to suggest that McClintock lay out this battle plan to Beauregard, as if the general needed instructions from a civilian. But Hunley was not lacking in hubris. He even took the time to jot down a few motivational notes for McClintock to relay to his team.

"Remind your crew of Manassas and Shiloh and the consequences of faltering in the hour of success," Hunley wrote, "and make one grand effort & you may have cause to rejoice as long as you live over the fruits of your labor, and that like men in more exalted positions you did stop to rejoice over your small gain let slip a vast success and an immortal honor."

Hunley was so pleased with his words that he asked McClintock to read them to Whitney. But the more Hunley considered all that was happening in Charleston, and the opportunity for glory that awaited him, he decided that he could not stand to miss it. By the time James McClintock received the letter, Hunley was already headed east.

On August 21, as McClintock continued his crew's training, a demoralized Charleston fasted. Confederate President Jefferson Davis had requested that the entire South participate in this day of "fasting, humiliation and prayer" as a gesture of solidarity and renewed commitment to the cause. There was barely enough food to go around, so this was not an onerous request. The *Charleston Mercury* called on residents to pray for deliverance from all the city's troubles. But the trouble was actually just beginning.

When the Hunley *reached Charleston in August 1863, Battery Wagner on Morris Island was still recovering from two unsuccessful attacks by Union troops the prior month. At that moment the earthen fort was on its last legs, unable to prevent the Union from setting up a battery in the middle of the island that would bombard Charleston from late August 1863 until two months before the war ended. Courtesy of the Virginia Historical Society, Robert Knox Sneden Diary.*

Soon, Charleston would know real humiliation.

Just before 11 P.M. that evening, a Union messenger arrived outside Battery Wagner on Morris Island carrying a note addressed to General Beauregard. The letter from Brig. Gen. Quincy Gillmore demanded the immediate evacuation of Fort Sumter and Wagner. On the surface, it seemed a bizarre request. Why would the Confederates simply hand over two forts they had been defending successfully for more than two years? It would have been a laughable request had it not come with an ultimatum that threatened the entire city.

"Should you refuse compliance with this demand, or should I receive no reply thereto, within four hours ... I shall open fire on the city of Charleston from batteries already established, within easy and effective (range) of the heart of the city."

Beauregard was not on Morris Island that evening, or even in Charleston. His staff claimed the general was out inspecting field batteries in the countryside, perhaps a strange activity for a Friday night. The Confederates felt they had been set up to fail. Even if Beauregard had been in his office, there was little way to carry the note to the city, formulate a response and reply within four hours. Officers at Battery Wagner tried to stall. They sent the note back, claiming it could not be accepted because it was unsigned.

The Yankees saw through the ruse immediately.

At 1:30 A.M. on August 22, Union soldiers fired a 150-pound projectile from the Marsh Battery in the middle of Morris Island. The eight-inch Parrott gun known as the Swamp Angel would hurl 16 shells at the city that night, each one exploding among the fine homes of Charleston's lower peninsula. The damage was minimal, but the noise alone brought panic to the city. Guests dashed from their rooms at the Charleston Hotel, a few not even bothering to dress. One man ran along The Battery, trying to wake up his neighbors to warn them, as if his yelling could be heard above the sound of the mighty cannon fire.

If the *Hunley* was in the harbor the night that the Siege of Charleston began, no one ever said. McClintock often waited until dusk to set out on training missions, and it was not unusual for the crew to spend hours in the protected waters between the peninsula and the barrier islands. Whether McClintock went out or not, that evening marked the end of his tenure as captain of the *Hunley*.

The next night, Union gunboats sailed into the mouth of Charleston Harbor and opened fire on Fort Sumter. As Sumter and Moultrie fought back into the early morning hours, a wall of fog descended on the harbor—the leading edge of a tropical depression. When the mist broke momentarily, the Confederates saw that one of the Yankee ships had run aground at the edge of Sullivan's Island. The fog rolled back in before Moultrie's guns could open fire, masking the ship's location long enough for the stranded crew to muscle it back into deeper water and escape.

Gen. Thomas Clingman, the commander on Sullivan's, was forced to report his troops' missed opportunity the next day. At the same time, he also documented the *Hunley*'s failure to take advantage of a helpless ship that had run aground less than a mile from its own dock. Clingman was frustrated, not only at the failings of his own men, but at what he considered a decided lack of effort on McClintock's part.

"The torpedo boat started at sunset but returned as they state because of an accident," Clingman wrote. "Whitney says that though McClintock is timid yet it shall go tonight unless the weather is bad."

The weather was bad the next night—the tropical depression had arrived. The wind blew in strong gusts and the rain fell incessantly throughout the evening. The *Hunley*

Gen. Thomas Lanier Clingman, Confederate commander at Sullivan's Island, was the first Charleston military official to become disillusioned with the Hunley. *The former U.S. senator complained to General Beauregard's office that McClintock and his fish-boat were ineffectual and "would not render any service under present management." A few days later, the Confederates seized the privateer submarine. Courtesy National Archives.*

did not venture away from the dock that night, and it would never sail again under McClintock's command. The Confederates were livid, and Clingman would not accept the weather as an excuse. He reported to Beauregard that "The torpedo boat has not gone out. I do not think it will render any service under present management."

Whitney, already suffering from the beginnings of serious illness, made half-hearted excuses for McClintock. He was willing to go out, but the weather would not cooperate. The crew was still learning the boat. Whitney asked that they give McClintock another chance, but the Confederates were in no mood for leniency. They had just suffered through the city's most horrible weekend yet, and they had had enough. Within 24 hours, the government seized the *H. L. Hunley*.

The privateer was suddenly a Confederate States Ship.

⁓

The Confederates believed McClintock had wasted a full week paddling around the harbor. Perhaps if the torpedo boat had put some pressure on the Yankees, they would not have been bold enough to launch this new offensive. Now Charleston was under siege and the military felt they had no more time. They would launch the fish-boat immediately. A day after it was seized, Lt. John Payne volunteered to take command of the submarine. Beauregard gave him four days to raise a crew and attack the *New Ironsides*.

Payne was as good a candidate as the Confederates had to command the fish-boat. He had been serving aboard the ironclad *Chicora*, which was so sluggish and untrustworthy that the military barely used it. Payne was mostly watching the war from the deck of the decrepit gunboat and, even if he had reservations about the *Hunley*, he was eager to give it a try. Payne had taken an interest in the strange boat when Whitney came to get supplies for the *Hunley* from the *Chicora*'s stores.

The Virginia native was not intimidated by new technology; he'd seen it before. Aside from his time aboard the *Chicora*, where he learned the fickle ways of iron ships, he had been in Hampton Roads to witness the CSS *Virginia*'s two-day run of attacks on the U.S. Navy. These next generation warships were strange, but effective. Payne realized the world was changing, war was changing, and he was willing to go along with it.

It did not take long for Payne to find several men just as intrigued—or bored—as he was. Most of the crew he selected came from the ranks of the *Chicora*, men he knew and trusted. William Robinson, Michael Cane, Nicholas Davis, John Kelly, Frank Doyle and Absolum Williams would be the first, and only, crew of the

Hunley to come entirely from within the ranks of the Confederate States Navy. These men volunteered to work aboard the sub without knowing exactly what that entailed. And no one would offer them much in the way of details.

McClintock was so upset the *Hunley* had been seized that he refused to train Payne or his crew. Whitney, who was coming down with pneumonia, was little help but Singer may have offered some advice. The torpedo expert had just arrived in Charleston, probably to check on his investment. Either he or Whitney recommended that Payne hire Charles Sprague, a man who knew much about torpedoes, to round out the crew.

Singer's generosity may have had something to do with the military's appraisal of the sub. The Confederates had offered to buy the *Hunley* from its investors, and they settled on a price of $27,500— nearly twice the amount it had cost to build the boat. Although that sum was far less than the bounty Fraser and Co. offered, Singer and his partners would nearly double their money in less than six months. But the government never paid Singer or any of the other investors. There simply wasn't time.

Payne and his crew took the *Hunley* out on trial runs every day during the last week of August. They practiced in Charleston Harbor, which was an ideal and safe place to test the sub's capabilities. Soon they were able to make the *Hunley* dive and surface, and possibly even cruised beneath anchored ships. Payne proved a capable captain, an impressive feat since he was largely self-taught. With Singer's departure, he was on his own. Whitney's pneumonia, no doubt contracted during the nights he spent inside the wet fish-boat, had left him bedridden. He would soon die, and for years his friends would consider him the *Hunley*'s first victim.

On Saturday afternoon, August 29, Payne and his crew took the sub out one final time. They planned to attack the blockade that night, and Payne wanted to make sure his men were prepared. They worked about an hour in the harbor before stopping to wait for sundown at the Fort Johnson docks—Payne did not want his crew exhausted. From James Island the *Hunley* crew would launch its first assault on the U.S. Navy, something Beauregard had anticipated for nearly a month.

Payne felt confident the crew was ready, but he was a man short. Either Charles Sprague had not yet joined the crew, or was absent that day for some reason. It was not easy to find a replacement. Payne had gone aboard the *Chicora* earlier that day and offered Lt. C. L. Stanton a seat on the sub. Stanton wanted to sail on the *Hunley*, but could not get relieved from his shift on deck watch. Finally, Payne ended up giving the seat to Lt. Charles Hasker, another *Chicora* sailor.

Hasker, a native of London, had been around ships most of his life. He'd served in the Royal Navy before immigrating to the United States and had even served aboard the *Virginia* earlier in the war. He was fascinated by the *Hunley*, probably for the same reason as Payne, and had volunteered to serve on the crew earlier that week. His brief tenure as a member of the *Hunley* crew gave him a story that he would recount for the rest of his life—although not the one he had hoped to tell.

Around dusk, Payne gave his crew the order to load up. The men climbed through the tight hatches and took their seats along the bench, ready for hours of laborious cranking on the propeller. Robinson served as the first mate and took his seat directly under the aft hatch. Perhaps because he was unfamiliar with the sub, Payne assigned Hasker to the first seat on the bench, directly behind the captain's station.

The first position on the crew bench came with one of the most difficult jobs on the submarine. The person who sat there not only had to help crank the propeller but also operated the forward ballast tank pump as well as the sub's snorkel system. It was a lot of work, but Payne must have thought Hasker needed instruction, and it was important to keep him close. That decision would save Hasker's life.

Later, no one could agree on exactly what happened at the Fort Johnson dock that evening. Some claimed a passing steamer, the *Etiwan*, threw a wake that swamped the *Hunley*, filling it with enough water to send it plunging to the bottom of the harbor. The official report said that lines from another boat departing the dock got tangled up with the sub, pulling it onto its side until its open hatches dipped beneath the surface.

Either way, the result was the same. With Hasker halfway through the forward hatch and Payne standing atop the hull, the *Hunley* began to sink.

Payne jumped free and found himself treading water in the harbor until the crew of the *Etiwan* eventually fished him out. The burly Robinson fought the water rushing into the aft hatch and finally got away as well. But Hasker and the rest of the crew were trapped and rode the sub to the bottom of the harbor. The Englishman fought against the water pouring into the forward hatch, but found himself snagged in the handle that controlled the dive fins.

As the *Hunley* descended into the black water, Hasker tried not to panic. Everything was working against him: He was not familiar with the sub's interior and could not figure out how to get free of the dive plane controls. The rushing water left him disoriented and blind as the sub tumbled into the depths, and soon Hasker wasn't even sure which way was up. But he survived to give the most vivid account of the *Hunley* sinking ever told.

"I had to get over the bar which connected the fins and through the manhole," Hasker later wrote. "This I did by forcing myself through a column of water which was rapidly filling the boat. The manhole plate came down on my back; but I worked my way out until my left leg was caught in the plate, pressing the calf of my leg in two. Held in this manner, I was carried to the bottom in forty-two feet of water. When the boat touched bottom, I felt the pressure relax. Stooping down, I took hold of the manhole plate, drew out my wounded limb, and swam to the surface."

Hasker later said he was more dead than alive when he broke the surface. A member of the *Chicora's* crew saw him emerge from the bubbling water and jumped in after him. The sailor pulled Hasker toward the ironclad, where the crew hoisted him aboard. He would never get his ride on the *Hunley*, but Hasker reveled in telling the story for the rest of his life. He was fond of saying, "I was the only man who went to the bottom with the 'Fish-Boat' and came up to tell the tale."

The sinking of the *Hunley* was an unmitigated disaster.

Military officials had recklessly rushed the submarine into service, and they would pay for their impatience. Although the crew's lack of training had little to do with the accident, perception was all that mattered. The sight of a boat full of men helplessly drowning just out of reach of the shore haunted the troops at Fort Johnson. The accident eroded their shaky morale nearly as much as the siege. One Confederate private wrote to his wife that those "poor fellows, they are five in one coffin." Over the following days, several men stationed at the fort would mention the accident in their letters.

"They were all volunteers for the expedition and fine men too, the best we had," Augustine Smythe, a Charleston native who served on the *Palmetto State*, wrote the next day. "It has cast quite a gloom over us. Strange, isn't it, that while we hear with indifference of men being killed all around us, the drowning of one should affect us so."

News of the accident spread through the city quickly, and the residents of Charleston were less than kind in their assessment. They were shocked by the senseless loss of Southern sailors and focused their ire on the military. The most popular shorthand version of the story was that the Confederate Navy had seized the submarine and, within a week, managed to sink it.

"It seems a pity that the Fish-boat should have been turned over to the Government," one local wrote, "we might have had a better chance at the '*Ironsides*' if she had been bought by Trenholm and taken out by Jefferson Bennett, as was proposed—it is too bad to have her lying at the bottom of the bay, when so many long-headed men who understood machinery saw no reason why she should not succeed in sending the enemy down there."

In retrospect, McClintock looked prescient. His warnings about the fragile nature of the submarine had gone unheeded and men had died. Even if some locals had their doubts about the *Hunley*, most were anxious to see it in action. Now that hope, along with the fish-boat, was at the bottom of Charleston Harbor.

The *Charleston Mercury* and *Daily Courier* were careful to avoid reporting specific details of the incident. Both newspapers were heavily invested in the Southern cause: the *Mercury* had been a leading voice in the secession movement, and the *Courier*'s editor was a Confederate officer. Neither wanted sensitive information to end up in the hands of Union officials—a very real concern. The Monday, August 31, edition of the *Charleston Daily Courier* carried only a brief mention of the deaths on the harbor.

"On Saturday last, while Lts. Payne and Hasker, of the C.S. Navy, were experimenting with a boat in the harbor, she parted from her moorings and became suddenly submerged, carrying down with her five seamen, who were drowned. The boat and bodies had not been recovered up to a late hour on Sunday. Four of the men belonged to the gunboat *Chicora* and were named Frank Doyle, John Kelly, Michael Cane, and Nicholas Davis. The fifth man, whose name we did not learn, was attached to the *Palmetto State*."

The fifth man to die on the *Hunley*, Absolum Williams, would perish in relative anonymity, his name lost for more than a century. Some would speculate that the newspapers had not bothered to report his name because he was black.

Over the years, the *Hunley* mythology would grow to near epic proportions. Survivors of the war told tales of the fish-boat well into the twentieth century, and their stories became more outlandish as the years passed. Some claimed the sub sank five—even six—times, killing upwards of 50 men. Most of these stories confused details, mingled fact with fiction, or were based on the faulty memories of aging Confederates.

Several people insisted the boat once sank in the Stono River. Others said that following the accident at the Fort Johnson dock the *Hunley* sank again two days later off Fort Sumter, claiming yet another crew. But that simply did not happen. Two days after the accident at Fort Johnson, the *Hunley* was still at the bottom of the harbor.

The same day Charleston newspapers subtly reported the tragedy at Fort Johnson, Beauregard was contemplating a move that might cost him the city. The general feared he would soon have to abandon Battery Wagner. The men on Morris Island were close to their breaking point. Their earthen fort was under siege daily and the troops were running low on provisions, particularly drinking water. What little fresh water there was to be found on the island had been contaminated by the decaying bodies of hundreds of soldiers who had died there in the July battle. The island was rotting out from under them.

Beauregard knew that he needed to evacuate his men, but was hesitant to give the order—the general realized the ramifications of retreat. The Union Army would take over the fort, giving them a direct line of fire on Fort Sumter, which was already being shelled into so much rubble. As the *Mercury* and several top Confederate military officials had speculated, the fall of Battery Wagner would lead to the fall of Sumter. And the fall of Sumter would quickly lead to the fall of Charleston. But Beauregard felt he had no choice.

Perhaps that's why the general sent an order that day to have the *Hunley* raised. He would not allow the sub to become a coffin for his men; at the very least he wanted the sailors to have a proper burial in the Seaman's Burial Ground. But he also had not given up hope on the fish-boat—Charleston could not afford to do that. Not now.

The accident at Fort Johnson had been just that, and there was still a chance the boat could be used to attack the blockade. And at that moment Beauregard did not have many other options. If he lost Wagner, he needed something that would give him a chance to level the playing field at sea—even if it was a slim chance. He needed something to give Charleston hope.

Beauregard sent orders to have the *Hunley* raised and to inform Lieutenant Payne of his decision. He obviously meant for his submarine captain to try again. At this point, Payne knew the boat better than just about anyone in Charleston. Perhaps he and Sprague could raise another crew. But Payne would never get the chance. Before the *Hunley* could be recovered, Beauregard would find another option— one that required far less risk on his part. And that was perfectly fine with him. These days, he was taking enough risks.

The Confederates hired two local divers, Angus Smith and David Broadfoot, to retrieve the sub from the harbor floor, a task that would take them nearly a week. They found the *Hunley* easily—it had not drifted far from the Fort Johnson dock—but it took days of work in hard helmets and canvas dive suits to attach the rope and chain needed to hoist it out of the muck. It was not an ideal work environment. Most days they had to work within earshot of cannon fire. And that Sunday, the water around Fort Johnson was cluttered with barges delivering the soldiers evacuating Battery Wagner.

Eventually, a Confederate ship pulled the *Hunley* out of the mud and towed it to shore. Since its hatches had not been locked, workers had no trouble opening the submarine. Getting the bodies out was not so easy, however. Edmund Ruffin, the famous fire-eater who spent time in Charleston, later said the crew had become so bloated that the divers had to chop the dead sailors into pieces just to get them through the impossibly small hatches. The grisly work further demoralized the men at Fort Johnson.

After the bodies of the *Hunley*'s crew were buried at the Seaman's Burial Ground in Charleston, Payne sent a note to Beauregard's office apologizing for the price of the services. He had been forced to commission oversized coffins to hold the bloated remains of his crew, and the cost had been extraordinary for the Confederates—in more ways than one.

On September 14 the *Hunley* was moved to downtown Charleston, where it would be re-fitted and prepared for launch. Payne was in charge of the operations. The sub would have to air out for more than a week, and the lieutenant likely used slave labor to scrub its interior. Most of the sap and tar used to make the iron boat watertight would have to be replaced, its gears oiled. Otherwise, the machine was in good shape. Before that work was finished, however, Horace Hunley decided to take control of the situation. On September 19 he asked Beauregard to return the submarine to him.

"Sir—I am part owner of the torpedo boat the *Hunley*. I have been interested in building this description of boat since the beginning of the war, and furnished the means entirely of building the predecessor of this boat which was lost in an attempt to blow up a Federal vessel off Fort Morgan, Mobile Harbor," Hunley wrote. "I feel therefore a deep interest in its success. I propose if you will place the boat in my hands to furnish a crew (in whole or in part) from Mobile who are well acquainted with its management and make the attempt to destroy a vessel of the enemy as early as practicable."

A veteran politician, Hunley proved infinitely more diplomatic than McClintock. The engineer had put himself at odds with the Confederates from the start; Hunley was smart enough to offer a compromise. He suggested that military officers could be a part of the crew, illustrating he had nothing to hide, but Hunley also suggested he supply other men who knew how to operate the boat. The promise of a crew "well acquainted" with the boat had to be appealing to Beauregard—it only increased the odds of success. But there were other benefits as well. He would not have to risk more men.

By the time Hunley made his request, Beauregard had already changed his mind and decided to scrap the submarine project. The general had relieved Payne of his command days earlier. Payne had learned to operate the sub well enough to sail it in the harbor, but he had also allowed it to sink. Beauregard was loath to lose more soldiers—soldiers he could not spare—on an unproven ship. He did not tell Hunley any of this; Beauregard simply accepted the offer.

Three days after Beauregard received Hunley's note, his chief of staff sent out orders instructing officers to fulfill any request made by Hunley "with the utmost celerity and to supply material as he will requisition as the mechanics under his control can apply." The Confederates wanted the submarine ready to sail within two weeks, and Hunley happily agreed to those terms. He was through traveling and felt he had finally found his calling. He would command the secret weapon that bore his name.

Hunley immediately sent a telegram to Mobile asking for volunteers. Within a day, he got more men than he needed—all of them from the Park and Lyons machine shop. William Alexander, who had directed the submarine's construction, was among those initially chosen to go, but at the last minute Thomas W. Park—son of the machine shop's co-owner—asked to go in his place. There was no shortage of men in Mobile eager to sail on the fish-boat, at least among those who had helped build it. Alexander reluctantly gave up his seat, perhaps because he knew Confederate officials were less than enthusiastic about losing his talents. And Park was connected. It was politics.

George Dixon, who had become so interested in the submarine during its construction, was not among the group selected to serve on the *Hunley*'s new crew. He would not give up easily, however, and fought with military officials. Finally, on October 1, General Maury agreed to give him 30 days' leave. Dixon boarded a train for South Carolina that afternoon, anxious for another chance to serve aboard the *Hunley*. He was several days behind the rest of the Mobile crew and worried he would not reach Charleston before the sub sailed. He knew that, if he arrived in time, he could help Horace Hunley succeed.

But he would not be able to save him.

CHAPTER 9

1995
Isle of Palms

Clive Cussler's phone rang at 6 A.M., unceremoniously rousting him from a deep sleep.

It was early—damn early. Thursday morning, May 4. The first strains of daylight were just filtering into the sky above Denver, 12 miles east of his home on top of Lookout Mountain. Cussler looked at the clock, noted the muted gray light coming through his window, and was mildly annoyed.

Although he normally wrote in the morning, to Cussler "morning" meant a much more civilized hour. Anyone who knew him realized that he no longer got up with the sunrise—and no one who did not know him had his phone number. Still half asleep, he had no idea who would be calling. The kids wouldn't phone unless it was an emergency. His friends would not be so rude. And it was too early, even on the East Coast, for his publisher to be bugging him.

The phone rang again.

Although this was not one of those critical periods in publishing— the weeks when editors, graphic designers and publicists called nearly every day—Cussler was busier than he'd ever been. The paperback of *Inca Gold* had been released two months earlier, he'd just turned in the manuscript for *Shock Wave*, the thirteenth Dirk Pitt book, and was now at work on his first book of nonfiction, The *Sea Hunters*, with NUMA special projects director Craig Dirgo. It was a lot of writing. Some days he felt that he did little else but feed the Cussler publishing machine.

After nearly 20 years of shipwreck hunting, Cussler had decided it was time to chronicle his own adventures with NUMA. Maybe he could recoup some of that cash he'd spent—call it research—and appease his accountants. They all thought he was crazy to spend so much money on something that he did simply for a love of history. Well, that and the fun of it. Maybe this would shut them up, since these days any book with the Cussler name on it was a guaranteed best seller. No, Cussler concluded, they will still think I belong in a padded room.

The phone rang again.

Cussler picked up the receiver and heard the Southern drawl of Ralph Wilbanks on the other end of the line. He had last talked to Wilbanks weeks before, when he'd faxed him the latest batch of coordinates to search for the *Hunley*. Wilbanks was a morning person, and his cheery voice on this day only irritated Cussler more. He thought: *What now?* This could not be good, he knew. Wilbanks was not the kind of guy who called just to chat.

"Well, I guess we're sending the final invoice on the *Hunley*," Cussler heard Wilbanks say.

This was not what Cussler wanted to hear. They were close, so close. He knew it. Ralph and Wes Hall had only resumed their search for the *Hunley* in April. Quitting now didn't make any sense. But Wilbanks didn't joke around—not about archaeology. Cussler figured he had a new job, and NUMA had just been pushed to the back burner. He told Wilbanks to take it easy, that they'd find it—if he kept looking.

"Are you giving up?" Cussler asked, trying to mask his disappointment.

"No," Wilbanks said. Then he paused.

The previous 24 hours had been a blur for Ralph Wilbanks. He was up well before the sun on May 3, leaving his oceanfront home on the Isle of Palms for the short drive to the marina where he would launch *Divercity*. As he'd pulled out of his driveway, he cast a glance across the gray Atlantic, where hints of the light shown on the horizon. It was out there, he thought, and today they would find it.

He and Wes Hall had a new target, one they liked a lot. It was the right size, the right shape—it could be the *Hunley*. The target was directly between the *Housatonic* wreck site and Breach Inlet, exactly where archaeologists, treasure hunters and divers had always expected to find the submarine. He couldn't believe they had missed it. Wilbanks was so confident he'd decided they would need an extra hand and invited Harry Pecorelli—the young marine archaeology student from the 1994 search. Pecorelli was the only man on the SCIAA team who had actually impressed him, so Wilbanks had called him the day before with a single question that made it impossible for Pecorelli to say no.

"Do you want to help us go find the *Hunley* tomorrow?"

Wilbanks had laughed at that—it was shameless. He knew the kid couldn't resist. What archaeology student would refuse that offer? But at first Pecorelli was silent. Wilbanks thought Pecorelli was hesitant, maybe had something else to do. So he repeated the question: "Do you want to go?" As it turned out, Pecorelli just couldn't believe his luck—he was momentarily speechless.

"Hell, yeah," Pecorelli said.

That morning Pecorelli was early. He knew better than to be late and risk the ire of Wilbanks. But in truth, Pecorelli was just excited, even if he was only the grunt man on the trip. He would go into the water first, he would man the probe. It wouldn't be easy, Wilbanks had explained, but Cussler paid well. Pecorelli didn't care how much work it was. This was what he was trained to do. And this was what they called an opportunity of a lifetime.

The young archaeologist was in awe of Hall and Wilbanks. The two men worked together easily, seemed to intuit each other's moves, and Pecorelli fell into an easy rhythm with them. They prepared the boat, secured their gear—including a cooler of Corona—and pushed away from the dock. Wilbanks steered out of the marina, into the Intracoastal and soon *Divercity* was passing the remnants of the old Battery Marshall dock on Sullivan's Island. The sun was just beginning to rise.

The trip offshore took nearly an hour. Once *Divercity* reached the harbor, Wilbanks turned east, passed Fort Sumter and cut between the jetties. As he steered, Wilbanks explained the job at hand to Pecorelli. They had a target that was in relatively shallow water and within cannon shot of the *Housatonic* wreckage. They were going to dig down and expose it, no matter how long it took. He told Pecorelli to be ready for a long day on the water.

Wilbanks was beginning to feel a little guilty. He'd made more than 10 daytrips to search for the *Hunley* since the 1994 expedition ended—often with Hall, other times with his wife, Frances—and he had come up with nothing. He had dutifully followed Cussler's instructions, running grids up and down the coast of Charleston's barrier islands. And all that came of it was more checks from Cussler. Wilbanks hated to take the man's money and not have any more to show for it. He had a disdain for failure that matched Cussler's own.

There would be no giving up, however, Wilbanks was certain of that. Cussler was a man possessed—he had to find the *Hunley*. They had searched 1,100 miles off the coast already, and the author just kept pushing them. The more Wilbanks and Hall looked without finding the sub, the more Cussler expanded the search area. Eventually, both men feared Cussler would want to run 250-mile search lanes from Savannah to Wilmington.

Pecorelli may have briefly thought they were going to look at target 8, the one Newell had crowed about in the *Post and Courier* a few months earlier. But Wilbanks put that notion to rest. With a laugh, he told Pecorelli that he and Hall had dug up the site a month after the expedition and figured out that target 8 was little more than sea junk. Pecorelli immediately got the joke—nobody had told Newell.

The *Hunley* is out there somewhere, Wilbanks said, but it's not in Maffitt's Channel.

Hall found their target with his Geometrics marine magnetometer just after 9 A.M. He alerted Wilbanks. They soon had the site marked with a buoy and *Divercity* anchored. At this rate, they might have the *Hunley* before 10 A.M., Pecorelli thought. This was much better than last year's expedition. Wilbanks and Hall worked fast, but were perfectionists—real underwater archaeologists. Pecorelli suited up, put on his air tank, took a few last-minute instructions from Wilbanks and went over the side. He had felt like he would never get in the water.

Pecorelli spotted it as soon as he reached the bottom—something metal sticking out of the sand. He briefly wondered how something exposed could have avoided detection for so long, and then it hit him: Hugo. Perhaps the hurricane that decimated Charleston more than five years earlier had uncovered it. Pecorelli could see his target clearly—it was rusty and had a length of chain attached to it. Odd, he'd never heard anything about chains on the *Hunley*. But maybe it had gotten fouled in something; that could even be the reason it sank. Pecorelli examined the object closely—he didn't want to be wrong.

He quickly realized that this was no submarine.

Whatever it was, it certainly looked too modern to be a nineteenth-century vessel. Pecorelli swam around for a few more minutes, careful to make sure he didn't misidentify what he had. Another look did not change his assessment. Finally he decided it was a winch, the kind they used on modern shrimp boats, or an early-twentieth-century windlass. Whatever—it was sea trash, not a piece of history. Pecorelli hadn't figured it would be that easy, so he was not particularly crestfallen. But he worried that his shipmates would be. He looked a third time and, finally, surfaced to deliver the bad news.

Not the *Hunley*.

Wilbanks and Hall were disappointed. They had allowed themselves to get excited by the target, something they both knew better than to do. Wilbanks sat in the captain's chair, munching pickled okra and trying to figure out what to do next. He was so frustrated that he considered heading back to the marina. *I thought we had it.* But he looked at his watch, looked at Hall, and decided to keep going. Cussler wouldn't give up, Wilbanks knew; he'd keep going. Besides, His Authorship—as Hall called Cussler—paid by the day, and it wasn't even 10 A.M. No way would they cheat the man.

Wilbanks took out his records and started looking at the coordinates of their old targets. He asked Pecorelli how carefully Newell's team had probed each of them. Not very well, Pecorelli conceded. Newell had been afraid to introduce oxygen to the sites and discounted some targets based on their gamma readings. That was all well and good, Wilbanks said, but it didn't do much for figuring out what these things were. They counted four of the old targets that had not been labeled. Since they had no other leads, Wilbanks said, they would go look at each one of them and not leave until they were identified.

"Let's put them on the map for what they are," he said.

And he would start with target 1, the mysterious object that had haunted him for more than a decade.

The site was close by.

Hall and Wilbanks had decided to recheck their targets based on the strength of their magnetic signatures. And it just so happened that the target Wilbanks was most interested in also had the most promising magnetometer reading. Because target 1 was about 1,000 feet farther out to sea than the *Housatonic*, no one had ever seriously considered it. For more than a century all searches for the *H. L. Hunley* had been confined to the area between its victim and the shore. Everyone assumed the submarine was headed back to Sullivan's Island when it was lost. Why would the submarine be seaward of the ship it attacked?

But Wilbanks was curious. He had dived on the site in 1981—it was where he'd found that odd triangular fin. And he and Cussler had wondered about it ever since. Something about the target was unsettling, but they never figured out what it was. Wilbanks was determined to change that. He pored over his notes, found the coordinates and steered toward target 1.

It took only a few minutes to find the site and, when they did, Wilbanks noticed something odd. The magnetometer recorded only a short spike on the graph when they floated over it in one direction. But when they passed over again, from a different angle, they got a long, continuous reading for a couple of boat lengths. The mag signature suggested something long and narrow—and metal—was down there.

"This is exactly what that thing would look like," Wilbanks told Hall and Pecorelli.

As *Divercity* anchored over the site, Pecorelli mentioned that he had dived there the previous summer as part of the 1994 expedition. He remembered the site in particular because it was encased in a thick scattering of oyster shells that went down at least two feet. He hadn't been able to get through the shell with a metal probe, and Newell quickly called him off.

This time Pecorelli would get a better look. In addition to a four-foot metal rod to push through the sand, Wilbanks and Hall sent him down with a water jet. The probe used water pressure, shot from its nozzle with tremendous pressure, to blast the shell and sand out of the way. It was an underwater archaeologist's best friend, and Wilbanks would take no chances with anything less. He was not leaving the site—not this time—until he knew what was down there.

In the water for the second time that morning, Pecorelli quickly made his way to the ocean floor nearly 30 feet below. Off Charleston, the Atlantic is notoriously dark and foreboding, a result of ebb tides pulling pluff mud and vegetation out of the Lowcountry marshes. Visibility underwater was rarely more than two feet, and this morning was no different. But once Pecorelli reached the bottom, he could see one thing clearly: the oyster shells were still there.

Pecorelli turned on the water jet and all hell exploded. The probe blasted the shells out of his way with little effort, and Pecorelli began to move it in an expanding circle. This was much better. Within a few minutes, he hit something solid less than four feet down. Pecorelli moved the probe and pushed it down in another spot, and then another, the sand melting away under the pressure. He quickly realized he had found something big—at least 10 feet long. And it was most likely cylindrical. He could tell from the way the probe hit it.

Pecorelli turned off the water jet and reached into the hole he'd made. He could faintly see something that he assumed was metal and reached out to touch it. It was covered in hardened sand, but had once been smooth. This object, whatever it was, appeared to be in good shape—too good for something that was more than 100 years old. Maybe, he thought, it's a dredge pipe. No, it's too big for that, he decided. Pecorelli explored the site a little longer, but didn't find any more clues. Finally, he kicked to the surface.

"I don't know what it is, but it's not the *Hunley*," Pecorelli said.

That answer did not suit Wilbanks. He wanted to know exactly what they had, once and for all. It had been bugging him for nearly 15 years, and he wanted to mark it off his list of unfinished business. Wilbanks told Pecorelli to go back down there, figure it out. Meanwhile, Hall suited up to follow him. The kid, Hall thought, is going to need help.

Hall had grown accustomed to working in black water over 25 years of diving in rivers and swamps. Visibility meant little to him. The former marine had studied under Gordon Watts, the underwater archaeology pioneer who had surveyed the wreck of the CSS *Alabama* and served as co-investigator on the search for the USS *Monitor*. Wilbanks often said that Hall could "see" with his hands—a most useful talent in the murky world of underwater archaeology.

There is a method to identifying objects that lie beneath the ocean floor. Once an archaeologist finds a target, they probe in all different directions to determine its size. And then they find its shallowest point—the part of it that sticks up farther than the rest. That allows divers to do as little digging as possible to actually touch what they've discovered. Pecorelli had probed the site well; he had found its highest point, and that's where he had dug down.

Hall immediately swam into the hole Pecorelli had made and began to feel his way around the exposed metal. The thing had a huge, gnarled knob on it—its highest point—and Hall hugged it to his body, estimating its size. He first assumed that Pecorelli had dug up a nineteenth-century ship's boiler. But the protruding knob—it looked somewhat like a tree stump—intrigued him. Maybe it was the boiler's steam dome. Hall moved his hands around the knob, feeling every square inch of it. And then his hand landed on something that Hall was almost certain was a hinge. His heart raced.

Hall turned to Pecorelli and put his hands in the young man's face, just in front of his dive mask, opening and closing them. Pecorelli didn't understand, but the normally sedate Hall was becoming more and more animated. He opened and closed his hands again and again, like a clam. *What is he trying to tell me?* Pecorelli wondered. He didn't get it. Finally, Hall pointed to the surface and shot up, toward the *Divercity*.

Wilbanks was standing on the deck when Hall surfaced. They hadn't been gone that long, so he expected bad news. Wilbanks was sure that his friend had figured out what the mysterious object was. And if he'd determined it this quickly, the news was either really good—or really bad. Hall gave nothing away, not even in his eyes, as he treaded water. He pulled his mask off, took the regulator out of his mouth and looked up at his partner.

"It's the *Hunley*. That's it. That's all it can be. We've come down on one of the hatch covers."

Wilbanks, rarely a man at a loss of words, was speechless.

Slipping into his wetsuit had been a blur.

Wilbanks was in the water minutes after Hall dropped the bombshell—he had to see it. And once he reached the bottom, he was not disappointed. The three men worked together for nearly two hours, digging, looking, feeling their way around the site. The hole that Pecorelli had dug, the shallowest point, was fortuitous. In that small spot, they not only found the hatch but a square box with two pipes protruding from it. Wilbanks knew from his research that this was the sub's snorkel system. He could not believe their luck. They had uncovered the two most easily identifiable features of the long-lost Confederate submarine.

It was the *Hunley*, without a doubt.

The *Hunley* was lying at about a 45-degree angle, listing to starboard, and covered in shell and hardened sand—what archaeologists call concretion. Wilbanks, Hall and Pecorelli explored the small patch of hull methodically, looking for more identifiable features, but that was just the scientist in them. They knew they had it. Finally, the men felt their way down the port side of the sub and found the long, thin dive plane. It was pointed upward, as if the sub had been trying to surface.

The three men lingered on the site for a little longer. They probed around trying to get an accurate measurement of the submarine's length, deciding it was at least 34 feet long and perhaps even longer. None of them wanted to leave, but they realized there was nothing more to be done. They filled in the hole Pecorelli had dug, covered their tracks as best they could, and kicked for the surface.

Back onboard *Divercity*, Wilbanks felt the weight of history on his shoulders. The *Hunley* was a monumental find and, frankly, he was a little surprised they'd actually made it. Now he was carrying a big secret, and everything he did was aimed at keeping it to himself. Wilbanks left the site quickly, lest anyone see the boat lingering over the spot, and headed for the harbor. This is big, he thought.

Pecorelli was a little surprised by the ride back to the marina. There was no celebration, no conversation, and no sound save for the occasional clinking of Corona bottles. Wilbanks and Hall were solemn, because they had been around a lot longer. And both of them realized that a shit storm was coming. Everyone was going to want a piece of this.

Wes Hall, Ralph Wilbanks and Harry Pecorelli found the Hunley *on May 3, 1995— a day on which they had set out to explore another site in the ongoing search for McClintock's long-lost submarine. Their discovery would remain secret for more than a week, but Wilbanks marked the occasion by having the three pose for this photograph in front of the* Divercity *while holding a copy of Conrad Wise Chapman's famous image of the sub. Courtesy of Ralph Wilbanks.*

Back at the marina, they trailered the boat quickly and drove to Wilbanks' house a few blocks away. Wilbanks told Hall and Pecorelli to get cleaned up—he was taking them out for dinner. This occasion called for steak. Wilbanks tried to call Cussler, but didn't get an answer. The news would have to wait. Before they piled into the car for the drive into town, Wilbanks had his stepson take a photo of the three of them standing in front of *Divercity* holding a framed copy of Conrad Wise Chapman's famous painting of the *H. L. Hunley*.

They ate at Breck's Place in North Charleston, the three divers and Wilbanks's wife, Frances. Throughout dinner they talked about everything in the world except Confederate submarines. Later, Wilbanks admitted they all shared the same fear: if they even thought about the *Hunley*, someone would figure it all out. Afterward, they drove downtown to the Charleston Museum, where a life-sized replica of the *Hunley* was parked on the sidewalk.

It was the same model that had once sat in a bank's basement downtown, the one that the NUMA team had visited on their second expedition in 1981. The model was based on sketches that William Alexander had drawn from memory more than 30 years after the sub disappeared. And it was suddenly clear to Wilbanks that Alexander had a faulty memory. He told Hall and Pecorelli they were the first people to be able to compare the model to the real thing.

"That's wrong, that's wrong and that's wrong," Wilbanks said. "And we're the only people who know it."

Wilbanks called Cussler the next morning, still so excited that he forgot about the time difference between Charleston and Denver.

After apologizing for waking him up, Wilbanks teased Cussler for a minute, rattling on about how he was sending the final bill. Hilarious, Wilbanks thought. The author sounded sleepy, perhaps a little grouchy, and he set up the punch line perfectly when he asked if they'd given up the search. "No," Wilbanks had said before pausing and delivering the biggest headline of NUMA's long history.

"We found it."

After that, he had Cussler's attention.

Wilbanks recounted the previous day, the disappointment with the first target, the decision to label all the old sites. The *Hunley* had been the first one, he said. Wilbanks described the snorkel box, the dive plane and the forward hatch—"It looks like a Derby hat." There was no doubt, no question, Wilbanks said. They had the *Hunley*.

"It's a done deal."

Cussler hung up the phone before Wilbanks even finished talking. The author was so excited he'd disconnected before he meant to. He was already thinking ahead. This was NUMA's greatest find, he knew, but an announcement would have to wait. They could not risk making a mistake—the entire organization's credibility was on the line. The nonprofit shipwreck business may have been strictly for fun, but he did not want anything to mar the good work his team had done. He picked up the phone and called Wilbanks back.

"We must have absolute proof," Cussler said. "People have been claiming they found the *Hunley* since 1867, but none of them ever produced a shred of proof. We've got to have photos."

"We can do better than that," Wilbanks said. "We'll go back and shoot video."

Finally, Cussler's curiosity took over and he asked, "Where is it?" When Wilbanks explained the *Hunley* was 1,000 yards east and just south of the *Housatonic*, Cussler realized it was target 1, the mysterious object found in the final days of the second *Hunley* expedition 14 years earlier.

"Isn't that where we dove in '81?"

Wilbanks confirmed that it was, and both men took turns saying it was their fault that they'd given up on the site so quickly. In some ways, however, they knew it was fortunate the submarine hadn't been discovered then. In the early 1980s, the technology to raise and preserve such a fragile—and big—historic artifact did not exist. Had anyone bothered to recover the *Hunley* back then, it would have probably rusted away by now.

Cussler told Wilbanks to make a dozen copies of the video. Wilbanks wasn't sure he knew how to dub tapes, but Cussler insisted he find a way. There was no way a lost videotape was going to ruin this moment. It had finally started to sink in. NUMA had found a lot of ships, but probably none of them had been lost under such mysterious circumstances—none of them had been as elusive—as the *Hunley*.

This was going to be big.

On Sunday, May 7, the divers returned to the *Hunley*'s grave site. They went out early to avoid the pleasure boaters who would soon crowd the offshore water. With paranoia setting in, they even snuck the underwater video camera over the side of the boat. Wilbanks was desperate to not attract any attention. He and Hall knew all too well what vandals and treasure hunters could do to an untended ship-wreck.

They uncovered the same section of the sub easily and spent hours filming the most identifiable features of the *Hunley*: the forward con-ning tower, the snorkel box, the dive fin. Even in the murky water, the dark shapes showed up fairly well on film. In fact, because the camera filtered artificial light better than the human eye, the film would produce their best view of the *Hunley* yet.

Later, Wilbanks would find a video technician from a local tele-vision station to dub copies of the video. He told the guy he wanted the tapes to be high-quality enough for TV newscasts. The guy asked if he wanted any narration on the tape. No. He asked if Wilbanks wanted a soundtrack. No.

"Why are you so sure the TV stations will air this?" the technician asked.

"They will, trust me," Wilbanks said.

This went on for more than an hour, Wilbanks refusing to elabo-rate. Finally, the technician said, "You're acting like you found the *Hunley* or something."

"Of course not," Wilbanks said.

This time they measured several features of the sub for documen-tary purposes. The hatch was 16 inches long and 14 inches wide. On the forward hatch, they discovered that the viewing port was broken out, as well as a U-shaped, grapefruit-sized hole in the conning tower.

Wilbanks believed this hole was either a result of the *Hunley*'s impact with the *Housatonic*, or an anchor snag after it sank. Otherwise, the submarine appeared to be in surprisingly good condition.

Before they departed, Wilbanks and Hall left something behind to prove they had been there. They had decided to leave a calling card of sorts in the conning tower hole, and they had prepared it in advance. It was Hall's idea to use Wilbanks' own words, the ones he said as punctuation to a good day on the water. They scribbled the message hastily on a piece of NUMA stationery, taking Cussler's signature off another letter and pasting it on. The sheet was laminated and put into a watertight box. The note read:

Today, May 3, 1995
One hundred thirty-one years and seventy-five days
after your sinking.
Veni, Vidi, Vici!
Dude
Yours respectively,
Clive Cussler
Chairman, National Underwater & Marine Agency

Hall crammed the NUMA package deep into the conning tower, and then he and Wilbanks and Pecorelli took more than an hour covering the *Hunley* with the sand they had dug away. The sand had effectively protected the submarine and hidden it from treasure hunters for more than a century. Now it was all that stood between a piece of history and looters. It didn't seem like enough, but it would have to do.

Soon, the whole world would know the *Hunley* was still out there.

The trouble started almost immediately.

NUMA scheduled its press conference for Thursday, May 11, in Charleston. If the location of the announcement—in front of Charleston Museum—didn't give away the news, then the *New York*

Times did. On May 10th the *Times* announced that Cussler had found the long-lost Confederate submarine. It was, without a doubt, the most prominent story about NUMA in the organization's 17-year history. In the opinion of the nation's largest newspaper, Cussler had arrived as a serious underwater explorer.

"There's absolutely no doubt," Cussler had confirmed. "It's the *Hunley.*"

The Charleston *Post and Courier* rushed its own story into print and the city went wild. It was 1863 all over again—everyone was talking about the fish-boat. People who had never heard of the *Hunley* were immediately transfixed by the story: a small submarine built during the darkest days of the war attacked a huge Union blockader ... and then vanished. It was a story straight out of Cussler's Dirk Pitt books, and everyone was hooked.

The NUMA crew was staying at the Mount Pleasant Holiday Inn just across the Cooper River bridges from downtown Charleston— the same hotel they'd used as a base during the 1994 expedition. Cussler was there with Wilbanks. Hall and Pecorelli had been on a survey job in New Jersey, and Cussler flew them in for the press conference. They were having a grand time when Mark Newell showed up.

Newell has gotten a call from the *Times* and was confused. At first he believed Cussler had gone back to Maffitt's Channel without him, and he feared his claim had been jumped. He wanted answers. Cussler was patient with the SCIAA man. He told him that the *Hunley* was not in Maffitt's Channel. Cussler led Newell to the hotel conference room, set up a monitor and showed him the tape that would soon be broadcast all over the world—without a soundtrack.

The images on the film were stark, the shape of the submarine unmistakable. There, captured on video, were the first photographic images of a lost legend. Anyone who saw the tape and knew anything about the *Hunley* realized NUMA had it. When the video ended, no one said a word. The room was silent for several moments before Newell finally spoke up.

"Well, that's a very provocative target," he said.

It was the understatement of the century, Wilbanks thought, and he hit the roof. He wanted to tell Newell that he could have been part of the discovery had he not been so quick to dismiss target 1. But Cussler didn't want anyone to know where the submarine was, so Wilbanks only mocked Newell.

"Provocative?" Wilbanks said. "That's the *Hunley*, and we found it."

The next day, Cussler told the media the same thing as he stood in front of the *Hunley* model: we found it. And he provided photos and that compelling video. More than a century earlier, P. T. Barnum had offered $100,000 to anyone who could deliver the sub to him and on this day it seemed the old showman knew what he was doing. There was a carnival atmosphere in front of the normally quiet Charleston Museum. Several citizens showed up just to get a glance of the famous author.

The reporters were in a good mood as well. A Cussler press conference was not like most stuffy media briefings. Cussler told funny stories, offered interesting insights and gave good quote—he was far more entertaining than any politician, even the crazy ones that infested South Carolina. But he wasn't there to promote himself, only the sub. Cussler knew what fellow writers needed to do their job and he provided it. On this day, he had a lot of material.

"This is without a doubt the greatest underwater find since the *Monitor* was located," Cussler said.

Cussler said the *Hunley* was much more modern than he had anticipated, far more advanced than the model he stood before. "It looks like an early Nautilus submarine." He speculated on the cause of the sinking—he said because the snorkel was up, they were probably trying to get air into the sub. "I think they paddled like hell and just didn't make it."

Cussler had only the video to go by; he had yet to see the submarine in person. Wilbanks had taken him to the site the previous morning, but heavy seas prevented them from diving. Cussler was disappointed but there was nothing he could do. Sitting on the gunwale of *Divercity*, the coast in plain sight, the author realized how vulnerable and unprotected the *Hunley* actually was. If for no other reason, the trip was not a complete bust. It alerted Cussler to the very real security concerns the sub faced.

He was reminded of those concerns when the questions began. The first ones, of course, were about the sub's location. Cussler decided he would hedge to throw off looters. He said only that the *Hunley* was "far" from shore and claimed it was in about 18 or 19 feet of water. Earlier some scientists from SCIAA had suggested they put a buoy on the site. It was one of the few times that Cussler lost his cool.

"Why not just put up a sign that says 'Vandals, come one, come all'"?

He thought the buoy idea was the most asinine thing he'd ever heard, and began to fear that this state was decidedly amateur. But the question of where the sub was dominated the press conference; he would not easily evade that most important detail. One reporter approached Pecorelli and asked if the sub was in Maffitt's Channel, as Newell had claimed. The young man did not want to lie, but he was not about to break Cussler's trust. Pecorelli allowed himself to say only one thing: he promised the *Hunley* was not in Maffitt's Channel.

Chris Amer, the state underwater archaeologist from SCIAA, was more cool-headed than some of the other scientists. Like Cussler, he knew what was at stake and would never allow a buoy on the *Hunley* site even if NUMA had given him the coordinates. Amer was cautious in his comments and focused on the state's commitment to keep the sub safe.

"It's an icon for the South," Amer said. "The South is not going to let anyone rush to defile its heritage."

Despite that assurance, Cussler continued his subterfuge—there were too many people listening. He claimed it was far from the *Housatonic*, a relative term he hoped would throw off any people who would desecrate the site. Already he was hearing rumors that collectors were offering thousands of dollars for one of the *Hunley*'s hatch covers. It made him shudder to think that he might lead treasure hunters—or inept bureaucrats—to the sub.

"I didn't spend fifteen years looking for it only to have it broke up by amateurs," Cussler said. "Until I see a comprehensive plan put together by qualified people, they won't get any cooperation from me."

Ralph Wilbanks had seen it coming.

From the moment Wes Hall popped out of the water and told him they'd found the *Hunley*, Wilbanks knew there would be trouble. He'd spent his entire life in South Carolina, had witnessed the hoopla stirred up when the remains of a single Confederate soldier were unearthed. Now they had found an entire crew of Southern sailors, and perhaps the world's only intact Civil War vessel. He was certain it would set off a feeding frenzy. But even Wilbanks could not have imagined how big it would become.

Within two weeks of the NUMA announcement, South Carolina congressman Mark Sanford filed legislation claiming the submarine for his state. Already the U.S. Navy, the Smithsonian and the state of Alabama were maintaining the sub belonged to them. Sanford said since the sub had been in South Carolina for 131 years, it should remain there for the next 131. An Alabama congressman filed competing legislation, arguing the sub should be returned to the city where it was built.

The navy claimed the *Hunley* was "spoils of war" as the U.S. government had taken possession of all Confederate assets at the end of the Civil War. But the *Hunley* never really belonged to the Confederate States of America. The South's military had seized the submarine in August 1863 and offered to buy it. But after it sank,

General Beauregard returned the *Hunley* to its owners—no cash ever changed hands. Until the night it disappeared, the submarine had remained a private vessel—even if some persisted in mistakenly calling it the "CSS *Hunley.*"

That fact did not stop federal officials from claiming the U.S. General Services Administration held title to the fish-boat. South Carolina officials, as usual, saw things differently. The records showed the federal government had a weak case, and lawyers for the state worked on creative legal arguments as to why the *Hunley* actually belonged to South Carolina.

At the same time, the South Carolina Institute of Archaeology and Anthropology continued to try and pry the coordinates out of Cussler. First, they considered an expedition to find the sub independently. Then, they relieved Newell from his duties as leader of the institute's *Hunley* project. Newell said he was reassigned to appease Cussler, but SCIAA officials said he was never supposed to have been in charge of such a sensitive project. Cussler approved of the move, but he still wanted to see a competent plan for recovering the submarine in writing before he would reveal the *Hunley*'s location.

The seeds of that competent recovery plan were actually sprouting a few blocks away from SCIAA's offices in downtown Columbia—at the state Capitol.

On the same day Cussler announced his find to the world, state senator Glenn McConnell sat in the South Carolina Senate chambers reading an advance report of the submarine's discovery in Charleston's *Post and Courier*. The story fascinated McConnell. He could remember visiting the model of the *Hunley* in the basement of a downtown Charleston bank in the 1960s, its interior filled with mannequins clad in Confederate soldier uniforms. The tale of the fish-boat captivated him then, and now it filled him with a new sense of purpose.

McConnell had been a student of history since his undergraduate days at the College of Charleston, but had recently taken his studies to an entirely new level. Several years earlier, the senator had fought for the return of a South Carolina Civil War soldier whose remains were unearthed by developers in Virginia. His efforts won him the praise of the Sons of Confederate Veterans, and suddenly a new world opened up to him. McConnell became so consumed by his state's wartime history that he eventually gave up his law practice and opened a store that sold Civil War memorabilia—paintings, flags and even some historic collectibles. The past became his future.

This circuitous career path now all made sense to McConnell. As he read the newspaper article, he felt the familiar pull of history. He felt the *Hunley* calling to him. McConnell leaned over and showed the story to a friend, Sen. Ernie Passailaigue. We've got to save the *Hunley*, he told Passailaigue. His colleague agreed. They quickly devised a plan to pass a law creating a commission that would oversee the submarine, deal with the federal government and claim the *Hunley* for South Carolina.

McConnell was uniquely qualified to lead this crusade. He had the passion, he had the history, and he was quickly on his way to becoming the most powerful politician in South Carolina. If the *Hunley* remained in this state, McConnell knew, it would be safe. He would make sure of it.

When the press conference ended, Wilbanks offered to drive Hall and Pecorelli back to the airport. They were celebrities now, at least locally, but fun time was over—they had to get back to their survey job in New Jersey. But first Wilbanks decided that a detour was in order. Off Meeting Street, Wilbanks drove through the gates of Magnolia Cemetery, an antebellum graveyard that was the final resting place of many of Charleston's most historic—and colorful—characters, not to mention hundreds of Confederate soldiers.

Wilbanks steered through the cemetery's sandy roads until he reached its terminus near the Cooper River. There, across the way from the tombstone of Robert Barnwell Rhett Jr.—wartime editor of the *Charleston Mercury*—they found the grave of Horace Lawson Hunley.

Wilbanks got out of the car carrying a bottle of Gosling's Black Seal Bermuda Black Rum. Standing over Captain Hunley's grave, he mixed the rum with a local ginger ale and a wedge of lime. Wilbanks called it a Dark 'n' Stormy, and it was his favorite drink. He gave Hall and Pecorelli a glass, and then poured himself a stout mugful.

The three men toasted the *Hunley*, laughed at all that was happening around them, and splashed a little into the ground for old Horace. They had done it—they had found the long-lost Confederate submarine. There was no doubt they had become part of the history they wanted so desperately to preserve. They enjoyed the calm under the shade of a giant live oak and tried to forget about all the headaches that accompanied their achievement.

It would be the last peace they would know for a while. At the same time these men were toasting the *Hunley*, 100 miles away state officials already were trying to figure out how to get their hands on the submarine. But first they had to find it. And those three men drinking Dark 'n' Stormys with Horace Hunley were the only people in the state who knew exactly where it was.

Perhaps, one state official suggested, they should just arrest the divers. Or better yet, maybe they would put out a warrant to arrest Clive Cussler.

CHAPTER 10

1863
Adger's Wharf

The Union sailors spotted the curious little boat around nine o'clock that night, just as it was closing in on the starboard beam of their ship.

It was coming at them from seaward, which confused the men. Either this strange craft was a long way from home or it had come out of Charleston and somehow managed to slip through the South Atlantic Blockading Squadron. That seemed improbable to the sailors, who considered their fleet the finest in the world. The puzzled crew tried to hail the little boat four times, but it kept coming—on a collision course for the flank of the USS *New Ironsides*.

The most amazing thing about the vessel was that they had seen it at all. It rode low in the water, made almost no noise and had a sleek cigar-shaped hull that they estimated was about 40 to 50 feet long. In the water, it looked like nothing more than a whale's back. If this was a Confederate weapon, which the men on the *Ironsides'* deck watch assumed, it was built for stealth.

When the boat did not reply to the crew's hails, the sailors opened fire with their muskets. They would take no chances or allow themselves to be caught off guard. The craft retaliated almost immediately—small arms fire—and one of the gunshots hit the officer of the deck, Ensign C. W. Howard. A few sailors tended to his wounds while the others kept firing at the boat. And still it kept coming.

When the odd little boat got within 20 feet of the *New Ironsides*, a great explosion rocked the mighty warship off its keel. They were under attack.

The *David* had slipped out of Charleston Harbor just after dark that evening, October 5. It sailed past Fort Sumter and crept between the U.S. Navy blockade ships, as it had been built to do, before finding the *New Ironsides* at anchor off Morris Island. The *David* was a smaller version of the CSS *Manassas*, the Confederates' first ironclad, with a few differences. It carried a crew of just four men in an open cockpit. The boat ran on steam and its jet black smokestack was the only thing on it that stood more than two feet above the waterline. The engine even burned anthracite coal, so that it belched clear smoke. The Union men were correct; the *David* had been decidedly built for stealth.

The CSS David *was considered a cousin to the* Hunley. *The semi-submersible coal-fired torpedo boat had an open cockpit, a crew of four and rode low in the water—but did not dive below the surface. There were an undetermined number of these boats built in Charleston during the war, and one would eventually beat the* Hunley *into battle, attacking the USS* New *Ironsides in October 1863. This* David *was photographed lying in the mud on the Charleston Battery. Its fate remains unknown. Courtesy of the U.S. Naval History and Heritage Command.*

Several of these ships, of varying sizes, were under construction in Charleston by late 1863. The name of these boats may have been taken from one of the builders, David C. Ebaugh, but most people ascribed it to the Biblical tale of the man who took down the giant Goliath. Whether it was true, the sentiment certainly applied. The boats carried a 20-foot iron spar on their bow with a contact mine at the end. They were designed to ram their prey, blowing a hole in an enemy ship's flank big enough to sink it in minutes.

This *David* was the first of the fleet to see combat, and its target was not coincidental. The 230-foot *New Ironsides* had led the attacks on Fort Sumter for most of the year and the Confederates were desperate to take out the ship that they simply called "Ironsides" with a mix of disdain and grudging respect. John Fraser & Co. had good reason to reserve its largest bounty for sinking it. The *New Ironsides* carried more than a dozen big guns, was powered by sail and steam, and had metal sheeting over its hull to protect it from enemy fire. For most of the war, it had seemed invincible. But the "Ironsides" could not easily fend off a point-blank attack.

The explosion from the *David*'s contact mine—which held 70 pounds of powder—rocked the *New Ironsides* to port and rattled its iron skin, but did not sink it. The blast also unexpectedly threw a huge wall of water into the air. That water drenched the sailors on deck, and enough of it splashed into the *David*'s smokestack to extinguish the engine's fire. With its one torpedo already fired and the men onboard out of ammunition, the little boat was suddenly defenseless and adrift. The crew of the *New Ironsides* would have blasted it out of the water had they not been preoccupied with the damage to their own ship.

As the *David* floated farther away from the *Ironsides* and out to sea, its captain—Lt. William T. Glassell—decided the only alternative they had was to abandon ship. If the *New Ironsides* recovered from the blast and pursued the torpedo boat, or another blockader came upon them, they would certainly be sunk. Glassell ordered his crew out of the cockpit. They quickly dove into cold, inky water and began to paddle toward the shore.

The *David*'s engineer, J. H. Tomb, did not swim far before deciding that he would rather take his chances on a crippled boat than alone at sea. He kicked back to the *David*'s silhouette on the water. There he found another crewman, J. W. Cannon, clinging to the smokestack. Cannon could not swim, but had been afraid to tell Glassell. Cannon helped Tomb back aboard and the two worked for several minutes until they finally re-lit the *David*'s fire. The boat slowly picked up speed as they steered for Fort Sumter. It was time to get the hell out of there.

On their way back into the harbor, Tomb and Cannon scanned the water for their crewmates, but by then it was too late. They had been picked up by Union boats and were now prisoners of war; Charleston would not learn of their fate for weeks. Tomb and Cannon struggled against the current for a while and did not make it back to the docks until after midnight. When Tomb reported in, he could only speculate on the damage to the great warship. They may not have delivered a killing blow, but they had hurt it.

News of the battle was heralded in the *Mercury* within days, but the paper was careful not to reveal too many details. Regardless, by the time the story was printed most Charleston residents knew it had been the *David* that had attacked the "Ironsides." The little ship—and Tomb—became very popular in the city, especially after the *New Ironsides* limped over the horizon, headed to a friendly port for repairs.

It was the most encouraging news the city had received in a long time.

⌒

Horace Hunley could not help but be a little jealous.

The *David* was suddenly the stealth weapon of choice in Charleston, and Hunley felt that he'd been cheated of his opportunity to strike first. He blamed the Confederates. If they had not sunk his ship, if they had allowed McClintock more time, perhaps the *Hunley* could have beaten the *David* into combat. And the submarine would have sunk its target, not merely damaged it. He was frustrated. His moment was passing him by, and Hunley feared he was losing the chance to prove himself a Great Man.

It was up to him now. Whitney was dead and all the other investors were gone. Now all that remained was his dream, his submarine. The trouble was that, frankly, Hunley knew very little about actually operating the boat. He'd always been the ideas man, and the trifling details mattered little. He had lost patience with the project during construction of the *American Diver*, had spent more than a year wandering the South—Mississippi, Georgia—looking for some way to distinguish himself.

In that time, Hunley had lost touch with the project. But now he realized this boat was his best chance for immortality. Just one successful attack would replenish his bank account and make his name known and respected throughout the South. His inability to actually pilot the thing was just another small detail to overcome, Hunley decided—another trifling matter.

The men from Mobile arrived that first week in October, around the time the *David* attacked the *New Ironsides*. By then, several workers—most likely slaves appropriated from local plantations—had finished cleaning the sub. The boat still carried the stench of death, a feeling more than an actual smell. But there was nothing that Hunley could do about that. Again, he blamed the Confederates.

In those early weeks of October 1863, Hunley behaved like a man possessed. He had lost all patience and seemed almost desperate to launch his attack. This reckless impatience was a condition his family had long recognized in Horace Hunley. His younger sister, Volumnia, had spent much of the war awaiting news of her brother's whereabouts and fretting for his safety. She begged her husband to talk some sense into him. When they learned that Hunley was in Charleston making plans to pilot his submarine, Robert Barrow tried to persuade him to return to Louisiana. Either out of genuine concern or simply to placate his young bride, Barrow appealed to Horace's sense of family. In that September 1863 letter, Barrow asked Hunley to give up this quest before he got himself killed on some anonymous battlefield.

"*This is the* place for you and you ought to be here and you should be here," Barrow wrote in his letter, underlining his point for emphasis. "So come home."

Whether Hunley responded to the letter, he certainly ignored the sentiment. He had a job to do, and nothing—not his sister, his brother-in-law, or his friends—could stop him.

The submarine was nearly ready to sail by the time General Maury allowed George Dixon to leave Mobile. Dixon was given only one month—starting October 1—to travel to Charleston, pilot the *Hunley* on an attack, and return to Alabama. It was not as much time as he had hoped for, but it was a start. Dixon was several days behind the rest of the crew, and feared he might miss his chance to be aboard the sub when it claimed its first victim. The men from Park and Lyons—Robert Brockbank, Joseph Patterson, Henry Beard, John Marshall and Charles McHugh, in addition to Thomas W. Park—were already in South Carolina.

Dixon left Mobile by train the same day his orders came through. He was excited to sail aboard the fish-boat again, but regretted that Alexander was not joining him. Dixon believed that Alexander, who had essentially built the submarine, should be allowed to serve on the crew. But politics had intervened—Park had connections—and there was nothing he could do for now. Perhaps he could arrange a leave for Alexander from Charleston.

By the time Dixon reached the city, the Mobile crew had patched the sub's leaks, oiled its gears and replaced all the onboard equipment ruined in the sinking. Hunley was in a hurry not only to prove his machine superior to the *David*, but to restore its tarnished reputation. Around town, folks had begun to call the *Hunley* a "peripatetic coffin," the "murder machine" and other even less-flattering names. The crew from Mobile ignored this idle talk. Like Hunley, they blamed the military. They knew the boat would work.

Later, Beauregard would claim Horace Hunley immediately appointed Dixon captain of the submarine's crew. It made perfect sense. Certainly none of the others understood the delicate mechanics of the boat as well as he did—especially not Hunley. While the other men from Park and Lyons had helped build the submarine—and probably sailed on it—Dixon, who had worked alongside Alexander every day the previous spring, knew it best.

The second crew of the *Hunley* would not have much time to get reacquainted with the sub. Although Charleston was quiet for most of the first two weeks of October, locals knew it was only a temporary respite. The Confederates had captured two Union soldiers who claimed that Robert Parker Parrott, inventor of the infamous gun that bore his name, was on Morris Island and allegedly building an even larger weapon than the Swamp Angel. This new gun would be able to fire shells up to six miles, putting most of the city well within its range. The news did little to soothe Charleston's fragile psyche.

The entire city seemed despondent. Deep into the war's third year, even the most patriotic Southerners could find little to celebrate. The local papers brought nothing but bad news from the front lines. Charleston itself was in disarray, a shell of its former self. Hundreds of buildings had been lost to fire, others had been abandoned, and a few carried fresh wounds from Yankee shelling. By the fall of 1863, Charleston was more a military base than a real city. There was no relief from the damned war to be had on any day. When some young boys were killed near Confederate headquarters while playing with undetonated Yankee shells, the city was shocked by the senseless deaths.

But anymore, it seemed that all the deaths associated with this war were senseless.

Beauregard encouraged the new crew to take their time training aboard the boat. Although he was anxious for progress, he had seen what happened when men tried to sail the *Hunley* without adequate practice. And even though these sailors were not his own troops, Beauregard did not want to lose them. Charleston could not take the deaths of more men. He fervently hoped the submarine would succeed, for his sake—and the city's.

Horace Hunley was not nearly as concerned with Charleston's morale as Beauregard. His motivation was glory and, in no small part, money. He had sunk nearly all of his cash into the submarine project and with a war on there was no new revenue streaming into his bank accounts. There was no job at the Custom House in New Orleans awaiting him, no new clients for his tiny law firm. Even his sugar had been confiscated. He desperately needed the bounty that came with sinking enemy ships. But more than all that, Horace Hunley simply needed to have his name posted in the ledger of Southern heroes. And so he pushed his men.

Years later Beauregard would recall that, during the first half of October, Dixon trained with his crew regularly in Charleston Harbor. The *Hunley* was moored downtown at that point, partly out of convenience but also because the military had abandoned any pretense of secrecy. The Mobile men stayed in a hotel on King Street and practiced during the day. Dixon would load up his crew and take them up and down the Cooper River for hours at a time.

A receiving ship anchored in the middle of the harbor became the *Hunley* crew's favorite mock target. Most of Dixon's "repeated descents," as Beauregard called them, were beneath the CSS *Indian Chief*. It was close to the same size as some of the blockade ships, but was easier to dive beneath—the *Indian Chief* anchored in the channel during the day, which meant there was more water under its keel than most of the ships parked just offshore. Regardless, the receiving ship offered a respectable substitute for the Yankees.

This went on for more than a week, and by mid-October Horace Hunley believed his new crew was ready to attack. He had enlisted the aid of Charles Sprague, the explosives expert recommended by Singer, as the final crew member—probably at the request of local military officials. Sprague had been slated to be aboard the submarine when it sank the first time, but good fortune had intervened. Finally, he would get his chance.

Hunley was so eager to prove the value of his submarine that he scheduled a demonstration of its capabilities for October 15. Nothing would stop him—not the foul weather that descended on the harbor, or even the mysterious absence of George Dixon. It's unclear why the lieutenant was not at the docks that morning, or what he might have had to do in Charleston that superseded his commitment to the *Hunley*. Some would say he had not arrived in the city yet, but Confederate records suggest otherwise. Beauregard cryptically said later only that Dixon was "absent from the city."

As a result, Dixon would not pilot the *Hunley* during the October 15 public demonstration. Instead, Horace Hunley had decided that he should assume command of the ship that bore his name. Perhaps he even thought it was his destiny.

A crowd gathered near Adger's Wharf that morning, ignoring the light drizzle that had lingered for hours. News of the test had spread throughout the city, either by word of mouth or because Hunley himself advertised it. By Thursday morning, it seemed everyone knew. And this suited Hunley fine—he wanted Charleston to see how well his boat worked. If the people watched the sub dive beneath the water, and then surface again, they would realize just how unique it was. Much better than the *David*.

Hunley was something of a showman, and he played to the crowd well. He told his audience to take note of the *Indian Chief* at anchor in the harbor. His submarine would sail toward it and then dive beneath it, surfacing far on the other side. It was a very simple exercise for his amazing boat, Hunley noted. There was not another ship in the South that could accomplish such a feat. Hunley had no reason to believe he would have any trouble with this; Dixon had done the same thing on several occasions.

The *Hunley* pulled away from the dock at 9:25 A.M. It moved slowly, churning through the water silently. The crowd followed the sub by watching its conning towers, which stuck out of the water—16 feet apart—like twin tree trunks. The fish-boat's oversized propeller threw a barely perceptible wake; it hardly seemed to move. For 10 minutes the *Hunley* followed an invisible straight line. And then, about a hundred yards from the *Indian Chief*, it slipped beneath the surface.

Aboard the *Indian Chief*, Confederate sailors watched the demonstration as closely as the people onshore. The sailors had monitored the movements of the little boat for weeks, had cheered when it dove beneath them and surfaced on the other side of the ship. It was without question an impressive display. This morning, one of the sailors onboard the receiving ship—Charles Stanton—watched with particular interest. Stanton had been promised a seat on the *Hunley* only to lose it when his other duties interfered. But he had seen the boat operating several times, and knew what it should do—and what it shouldn't.

And on this morning, Stanton was worried. Within moments, he could tell that something was wrong.

"I happened to be aboard the receiving ship *Indian Chief* on some temporary duty off Adger's Wharf when the Fishboat was observed approaching the vessel on the starboard side," Stanton wrote years later, "and when within a biscuit throw disappeared and successfully dived under the ship, reappearing on the port side a short distance from the docks. Presently she dived again, and when, after half an hour elapsed, she failed to come to the surface we knew the men in her were dead."

Stanton claimed the sub made one successful dive with Horace Hunley at the helm, but other witnesses say that the *Hunley* never reappeared once it submerged that morning. J. H. Tomb, hero of the

David attack on the *New Ironsides*, later claimed that he watched the *Hunley*'s demonstration onshore with George Dixon. And as soon as they saw bubbles appear on the surface they knew something aboard the submarine had gone horribly amiss.

Inside the *Hunley*, the trouble most likely was not detected immediately. When Horace Hunley gave the order to submerge, he pulled the dive fins lever toward him and opened the seacock for the forward ballast tank. Park, the first officer, opened the aft seacock. The tanks began to fill with harbor water and the men inside—furiously cranking the propeller shaft—felt the pressure begin to build.

At some point, the submarine was supposed to stabilize. Normally, the *Hunley* dived nose first until leveling off when the captain reached the depth he wanted. But on this morning the descent continued longer than normal, its bow dipping far lower than its stern. Soon, the men felt the tug of gravity pulling them toward the bow. This was not right, they realized. Hunley likely tried to adjust the dive fins, to bring them to a neutral attitude, or even point them up to surface. But the dive planes could not change the sub's course while the ballast tanks were still filling with water.

The submarine kept going down, and nothing could stop it.

The crew probably never figured out what had gone wrong. First they felt the cold water hit their ankles, rising at a furious rate. They tried to pump out the compartment, using the sub's plumbing system just as McClintock had designed. But it was no use—the water was cascading over the forward ballast tank wall. Hunley had forgotten to close the forward seacock—a trifling detail that would doom him. There was no way to pump the sub dry. There was just too much water.

Within minutes, the *Hunley* filled enough to send it plunging into the harbor floor. The men were in a panic—the water was now up to their chests, save for Thomas Park. The sub hit bottom, its bow in the mud, but its stern still floated free. Park had pumped the aft ballast tank dry, and that gave the sub some buoyancy. He did not think to adjust his pump setting and try to empty the forward ballast tank. But it would not have mattered.

As the water climbed within inches of the sub's ceiling, the men fought to hold their heads above it. Some of them had the presence of mind to plunge into the cold blackness and try to release the sub's keel weights. Finally they attempted to open the hatches, but the water pressure would not allow it until the *Hunley* was completely filled with water. By that time, most of the men had drowned.

Park and Horace Hunley were the last to succumb. There were pockets of air in the sub's conning towers, and that is where they would be found—their heads just above the interior waterline. They would suffocate as the last remaining oxygen ebbed out of the *Hunley*. Horace Hunley clutched a candle in his hand, which suggests it survived the rushing water that poured into the crew compartment. Or perhaps Hunley had held it absently as he considered whether this was the way Great Men died.

In his final moments, Horace Lawson Hunley could not avoid the obvious irony: the ship that carried his name—and his grandest dream—would be the death of him.

It would be weeks before anyone figured out what happened.

The submarine was there on the surface one minute and then it simply disappeared. The crowd at Adger's Wharf stood in silence for long minutes, awaiting a cheer from the *Indian Chief* that never came. Since most people had no idea of the *Hunley*'s capabilities, they weren't sure how long it could remain underwater. But it became apparent soon enough that the showman Hunley would not be returning to the dock.

The loss of the *Hunley* for a second time was just another setback in a city that had become all too accustomed to them. That day, Beauregard's officers noted the sad event in their journal of operations, writing that "an unfortunate accident occurred this morning with the submarine boat, by which Capt. H. L. Hunley and 7 men lost their lives in an attempt to run under the navy receiving ship." Whoever wrote that entry speculated that the accident was due to some error on the part of the crew.

"As soon as she sunk air bubbles were seen to rise to the surface of the water, and from this fact it is supposed the hole in the top of the boat by which the men entered was not properly closed. It was impossible at the time to make any effort to rescue the unfortunate men, as the water was some 9 fathoms deep."

The next day—Friday, October 16—the *Charleston Daily Courier* published a cryptic notice of the accident under the headline "Melancholy Occurrence." The article included the names of the eight sailors who had gone down on an anonymous ship. There were no details that might allow Yankees to discern exactly what the Confederates were planning. It mattered little; most of the paper's readership already knew far more than the scant information in the *Mercury*'s one-sentence account.

"On Thursday morning an accident occurred in a small boat in Cooper River, containing eight persons, all of whom were drowned."

And that was it. Beauregard ordered his staff to make arrangements for the *Hunley* to be recovered, and they would again contract Angus Smith and David Broadfoot to raise it. This would not be nearly as easy as it had been the first time. It would take the divers two days just to find the *Hunley* in the city's great harbor, and even longer to bring it up. The nasty weather of October 15 lingered and would cast a pall over the city for weeks.

The day after the accident, Confederate headquarters issued orders allowing George Dixon to travel to Mobile "on business connected with the Submarine Torpedo Boat." The note made no mention of the lieutenant's recent absence, or what business he had in Mobile. But it seemed the Confederates were confused about the fish-boat's status. As far as Beauregard was concerned, there was no business to be had with the *Hunley*, other than recovering it. The experiment was over.

Nearly three weeks passed before Smith and Broadfoot delivered the *Hunley* to shore. The weather was miserable throughout October, churning the harbor into a violent froth most days, making it nearly impossible to stage salvage efforts. The Confederates filled the divers' orders for more rope and chain, but in those conditions there was no boat that could actually handle the delicate work of hoisting the submarine out of the depths—much less tow it to the dock.

Smith and Broadfoot had found the submarine sitting on the harbor bottom at a 35-degree angle. Its bow was in the mud, but its stern floated. This at least made it easier for Smith and Broadfoot to wrap the *Hunley* in the ropes and chains they would use to pull it out of the muck. It was the only break they would get for weeks.

Finally, on November 7, the *Hunley* was brought ashore at the Cooper River docks. The morbid ceremony near the foot of Calhoun Street drew dozens of curious spectators—perhaps more than had watched it depart weeks earlier. The workers found it easy to open the hatches; they were not latched. But still they were heavy, and it took several men to get a handle on the lids and pry them up. As they worked, there were murmurs in the crowd that another crew had already volunteered to take the place of the men inside. If he heard such talk, General Beauregard likely did not bother to correct it. He was too shaken by his first glimpse of the men who had perished aboard the *Hunley*.

"When the boat was discovered, raised and opened the spectacle was indescribably ghastly; the unfortunate men were contorted into all kinds of horrible attitudes, some clutching candles, evidently endeavoring to force open the manholes; others lying in the bottom, tightly grappled together, and the blackened faces of all presented the expression of their despair and agony," the general wrote years later.

The stench was overwhelming—three weeks of accumulated gas from the decomposing bodies wafted out of the submarine. Some people recoiled, but most Charleston residents had become all too familiar with the smells of war. Sometimes it seemed the city wallowed in the scent. Once the bodies were removed, workers explored the submarine's interior for clues that would tell them what had happened, why the *Hunley* had failed to surface.

Slowly, the story became clear. Workers found the aft ballast tank nearly empty, but the front tank was full of water. The wrench used to open the forward seacock was on the floor. It could have fallen while the sub was under tow, but perhaps Horace Hunley had dropped the small tool and lost it in the darkness. That would explain why he had not closed the ballast tank valve. Others assumed he had merely forgotten to close it, as he was not overly familiar with the boat's operations. The bolts that held the sub's keel weights had been partially turned, but not enough to drop them.

The attitude of the bolts suggested that the men only thought of dropping the keel weights at the last moment, after the sub had hit bottom. Had they remembered the keel weights earlier, before the sub completely filled with water, they might have been able to surface. But the water had come in faster than the men could react. By then, they were doomed.

Even before Beauregard saw the horrible expression on Hunley's face that day, he had ordered his staff to arrange a military funeral for him. Although Horace Lawson Hunley had never officially joined the Confederacy—captain was a term of endearment, not a title— the general nonetheless believed he deserved the respect of a proper military burial. He had given his life for the cause.

They buried him next to the river where he had died.

The honor guard marched through the gates of Magnolia Cemetery at 4 P.M. on November 8, the Rev. W. B. Gates following behind. Although the deceased was not a Charleston resident, a surprising number of locals trailed behind the procession as it made its way to the back of the cemetery that Sunday afternoon. The carriage carrying his coffin stopped at a quiet spot beneath a grand live oak.

Here, Gates would deliver the final remarks on Capt. Horace Lawson Hunley. His burial was the most significant event that would occur in Charleston that day.

Even the *Mercury* sent a reporter to cover the funeral. The next day, the paper carried a front-page obituary of Hunley under the headline "Last Honors to a Devoted Patriot."

"Possessed of an ample fortune, in the prime of his manhood—for he was only thirty-six (sic) at the time of his death—with everything before him to make life attractive, he came to Charleston, and voluntarily joined in a patriotic enterprise which promised success, but which was attended with great peril. Though feeling, as it appears from the last letter which he wrote to his friends, a presentiment that he would perish in the adventure, he gave his whole heart, undeterred by the foreboding, to the undertaking, declaring that he would gladly sacrifice his life in the cause. That presentiment has been mournfully fulfilled."

Hunley's family did not attend the services. Volumnia Hunley Barrow would get her only account of the burial from Gardner Smith, a friend of the family. Hunley had summoned Smith to Charleston in the days before the accident—for what reason Smith never said. But he arrived after the accident, just in time to pick out a coffin and simple tombstone for his friend. He suggested Volumnia visit her brother's grave, and perhaps pick out a more appropriate headstone. Smith could do no more; he was heartbroken.

"At the grave I could not refrain from tears as the casket of the spirit of a noble and generous man was being lowered, 'earth to earth'—to its final resting place," Smith wrote to Volumnia. "I lost in him my best friend. My wife had also become much attached to him. He was so gentlemanly and kind. When I came home and related the death and burial, she wept as though it had been a dear relative."

Henry Leovy had arrived in town earlier that month on business. Leovy would carry his friend's waterlogged pocket watch, a pair of sleeve buttons and two gold studs back to Volumnia as keepsakes. But Smith sent the most heartbreaking artifact in his letter informing her of her brother's death. There, in the folds of blue paper, he had tucked in a single lock of Horace Lawson Hunley's hair.

It would be all that Volumnia had left of him.

With Hunley's death, General Beauregard declared the submarine project a complete failure. McClintock was gone, the Singer Submarine Corps had moved on, and the general would not risk any more of his men on this futile experiment. The fish-boat had sunk twice in three months, killing 13 men—none of them Yankees. Beauregard had decided that the submarine should die with its namesake.

This was a moral decision for the general. Beauregard knew he could raise another crew—he had heard the rumors that more men were willing to volunteer. These were certainly desperate times, but still he was amazed that some continued to hold faith in the gallant, but dangerous, little death trap. Beauregard was unsurprised, however, when he received a telegram from Mobile. Lieutenant Dixon had inquired about the condition of the submarine days before Hunley's funeral. He wanted permission to raise another crew.

Dixon was ambitious, headstrong and determined. The two accidents had done nothing to erode his faith in the *Hunley*. He had secured another leave of absence from Maury and the Twenty-first Alabama and was ready to return to Charleston. Beauregard admired Dixon's courage, but he could not allow the submarine to sail again. He did not want any more blood on his hands. Beauregard had sent men to be killed—this was war, after all—but he did not have soldiers to spare on such a foolhardy endeavor. It would be suicide. So on November 5, Beauregard personally replied to Dixon's telegram with what he believed would be the final word on the fish-boat project.

"Lieutenant Dixon: I can have nothing more to do with that submarine boat. Tis more dangerous to those who use it than to the enemy."

By that time, Dixon was already on his way back to Charleston— and he would not accept the general's answer. Dixon was determined that the *Hunley* would sail again.

CHAPTER 11

1995–1997 Columbia

Glenn McConnell was not sure where this path might lead, or what kind of fight lay ahead. He only knew that he was ready for battle, and that "No" was not an answer he was prepared to accept.

The South Carolina senator rushed through the halls of the L. Marion Gressette Building on August 2, 1995—his first steps toward bringing the *H. L. Hunley* home. In a few minutes, McConnell would launch the opening salvo in the state's battle to claim the submarine, and he had to wonder what he'd gotten himself into. He feared this competition for the sub might start another Civil War, and that concerned him. After all, his adversary was the federal government—and South Carolina did not have a great record against Washington.

The idea of fighting the feds—and other states—did not appeal to him. But if it came down to that, McConnell thought, so be it. At least the location of the battle was fitting.

The Gressette Building, home to the South Carolina Senate, had been named after one of the state's longest-serving legislators, a man whose biography reflected the changing history of the South. Marion Gressette had fought the federal government's effort to desegregate schools in the 1950s and '60s, but in later years not only accepted change—he tried to facilitate it. Gressette had even sponsored legislation to make Martin Luther King Jr. Day a state holiday. Ultimately he failed, but his efforts spoke volumes about winds of change blowing through Dixie.

McConnell now held Gressette's post as chairman of the Senate Judiciary Committee, and in a few years would take over his role as President Pro Tem. McConnell, however, had never been such a controversial politician. He was a conservative Republican, but labels meant little to him. He could work across the aisle, and even Democrats in the General Assembly respected his mind, his allegiance to the legislative process and his sense of fairness. McConnell was a rare South Carolina politician never accused of playing political games or stoking the fires of controversy.

His campaign to keep the *H. L. Hunley* in South Carolina would change all of that. McConnell soon would be linked to the politics of the Civil War, and that was still an open wound in his home state. Some people believed that support for anything related to the war was tacit approval of the politics of the Confederacy, or even segregation. To be sure, McConnell—a history major in his days at the College of Charleston—revered his state's colorful past. And years earlier he had worked to bring home the remains of a South Carolina Confederate soldier found in Virginia. But this quest to do the same for the *Hunley* was not political. For McConnell, this was personal. He simply had to bring those men home.

And their home, to his thinking, was South Carolina.

As he walked into the committee meeting room, McConnell relaxed. This was his home field and these were his people. He had managed to set up the state *Hunley* Commission in the waning days of the legislative session—a testament to his political prowess. Permanent legislation would not come until next year, but McConnell could not wait. They had to start now. By next year, it would be too late to save the *Hunley*.

A week earlier, a congressional subcommittee in Washington had debated the fate of the *H. L. Hunley*, and it did not look good for South Carolina. An Alabama congressman argued that his state had a greater right to the submarine. Federal bureaucrats insisted it belonged to the navy, that it was the "spoils of war." If McConnell didn't move fast, he feared the first successful attack sub would end up on display in the Smithsonian Institution.

The *Hunley* Commission gave the state a little leverage in the fight. McConnell had stacked the panel with influential lawmakers and friends, including Sen. Ernie Passailaigue and Rep. Rick Quinn— the House Majority Leader and son of South Carolina's most influential political consultant. He had appointed his friend Randy Burbage, commander of McConnell's Sons of Confederate Veterans (SCV) camp, as well as the SCV's state commander. Finally, he brought in Charleston resident William Schachte, a retired navy rear admiral who had served as a judge advocate general. Schachte would act as the state's unofficial diplomat when dealing with the Naval Historical Center, which had taken a strong interest in the *Hunley*.

McConnell also had the state's attorney general on his side, and he was happy to let the controversial and flamboyant Charlie Condon make the headlines and take the heat. Condon, sounding every bit as stubborn and determined as his nineteenth-century forefathers, had told the congressional subcommittee several days earlier that he—that South Carolina—would not just roll over for Washington.

"I am fully prepared to back up South Carolina's claim in court if I have to," Condon had said.

The first shot had been fired. And as was custom, it had come from South Carolina.

The *Hunley* Commission spent three hours mapping out a battle plan. A delegation would travel to Washington to negotiate a deal with the navy, but if that failed they would take the fight to court. Both McConnell and Condon had prepared complex legal arguments to back up the state's claim to the sub. Although the federal General

Services Administration declared that it owned the sub, Condon said nineteenth-century records proved otherwise. After the war, the government had awarded a man named Benjamin Maillefert a contract to salvage both the *Housatonic* and *Hunley*. Condon argued that amounted to the government releasing its claim. Maillefert had found the *Housatonic* but never mentioned the *Hunley*, a fact Condon conveniently ignored. The attorney general said when the government signed a contract with Maillefert, ownership had transferred to him. And if Maillefert abandoned the *Hunley*—which he apparently had— then title reverted to South Carolina.

McConnell's argument was completely different, but it bolstered Condon's. The estate of Henry Leovy, a close friend of Horace Hunley, claimed one-third ownership of the submarine. Military records showed that the Confederates had returned the submarine to Hunley in September 1863 which, McConnell said, proved the submarine was not "spoils of war" confiscated from the Confederacy. At the time of its loss, the *Hunley* was a private vessel.

Both arguments cast doubt on the federal government's ownership, but did not prove the state's claim. For that, McConnell and Condon relied on a trick of mapping. Federal jurisdiction extends three miles off the U.S. coast. The *Hunley* was resting on the ocean floor four miles offshore, beyond federal reach. However, the sub was reportedly within two miles of the Charleston Harbor jetties. That, McConnell insisted, put the submarine squarely in South Carolina territory.

The biggest problem with these arguments was that no one knew exactly where the *Hunley* was. They weren't even sure the submarine had been found. During the *Hunley* Commission meeting, one member of the panel asked state archaeologist Jonathan Leader if he was certain Clive Cussler's team had indeed found the *Hunley*.

"No, sir, I am not," Leader said. "It may very well be the *Hunley*. There is a difference between a person asserting and scientific proof. And that's very true in shipwrecks."

For the time being, the state had to take Clive Cussler at his word.

Clive Cussler was not talking.

The author had vowed to not reveal the *Hunley*'s location until he saw a workable plan to protect the sub and possibly recover it. Three months later that still had not happened. The politicians could talk all they wanted, but nothing they said made Cussler feel any better—especially when he heard rumors that the state of South Carolina might try to arrest him and his divers in an attempt to make them turn over the *Hunley* coordinates.

In fact, the rumor was just that. No state official was willing to consider such a stunt. State officials knew the public backlash would be horrible and realized that any decent attorney, which Cussler could certainly afford, would have the charges dismissed within a few hours. The rumor began when one disgruntled state employee had suggested South Carolina lock them all up until they talked, and Ralph Wilbanks heard about it. But no one ever came for Wilbanks, and Cussler was on the other side of the country with no plans to return to South Carolina anytime soon.

Cussler was a thousand miles away in Colorado, making final edits to the new Dirk Pitt adventure *Shock Wave*, which would be released in January 1996. This new title—he had originally called the book *Diamonds*—had an unintended resonance for the author. He could feel the shock waves from South Carolina all the way from his perch in the Rocky Mountains.

It was annoying. Cussler had done nothing but try to protect the *Hunley*, to show some responsibility for the safety of a historic artifact. Now his name was being dragged through the mud, hardly the show of gratitude he should have expected. Southern Confederates claimed NUMA had desecrated a grave and now held a hallowed artifact hostage. They planned to burn Cussler's books in protest of his unwillingness to cooperate with the great state of South Carolina. Finally, the amiable Cussler had heard all he could take.

"I've been accused of ransoming the sovereign state of South Carolina, the Sons of Confederate Veterans wanted to burn my books and I was charged with desecrating the tomb of our glorified dead," Cussler wrote in a letter to the editor of the *Post and Courier* that September. "If that's the cost of saving the *Hunley* for future generations of Americans then, by gosh, it's worth it."

Cussler said that neither he nor NUMA made any claims to the submarine—"we were ready to turn our report over to the proper authorities and head home. But then the vultures came to rest like gargoyles brooding over a derelict cathedral. Everyone wanted a piece of the action, and they began fighting over the *Hunley* like a school of piranha attacking a ham tossed off the stern of a river boat."

The author said that none of those people had ever spent a dime or an hour of their time searching for the lost torpedo boat. They simply swooped in at the last minute and wanted the prize. Cussler wanted no prize. He said that he looked at the search for the *H. L. Hunley* as a challenge, and "our only profit was the satisfaction in achieving a revered goal." Cussler had finally had his say. But it would not be his last words.

Wilbanks spoke for Cussler at the next *Hunley* Commission meeting later that same month. NUMA would release the coordinates, Wilbanks said, when there was a realistic plan for the sub's future. But that did not appear likely to come anytime soon. The state was too caught up in its quest for the *Hunley*'s coordinates, and its fight to gain title of the sub, to actually consider a recovery plan. At the same meeting, the South Carolina Institute of Archaeology and Anthropology—Wilbanks' former employer and NUMA's previous partner—announced plans for a new *Hunley* search. The expedition would cost about $136,000, almost exactly what Cussler had spent to find the sub. The commission eventually offered $40,000.

Cussler was incredulous. A new expedition would be a huge waste of taxpayer money. The *Hunley* had been found, Cussler told reporters, and the state should devise a plan to salvage it—not spend money reinventing the wheel. Cussler said that Gordon Watts, the East Carolina University professor who found the USS *Monitor*, was working on a proposal to save the sub with the Naval Historical Center. The center had been designated by the General Services Administration as the agency to lead the recovery, and Cussler said Watts' plan was "within inches" of being finished. Cussler said he expected to release the coordinates before South Carolina could mount an expedition.

But no one in the state appeared to be listening.

Despite the *Hunley* Commission's efforts, the careful dance between the state and federal governments would drag into the fall. The sticking point was ownership and Washington officials were not prepared to budge. The *Hunley* was the property of the federal government, they claimed, and no nineteenth-century documents could convince them otherwise. The entire argument was reminiscent of South Carolina's attempt to negotiate a surrender of all federal property within its borders after the state seceded in December 1860. This negotiation was going almost as well. Bureaucrats, it seemed, had a long memory.

It was U.S. senator Strom Thurmond who finally broke the impasse. The South Carolina politician, nearly a century old, had been around Washington for 50 years since his failed presidential bid as a "Dixiecrat." As the longest-serving member of Congress at the time, he held considerable sway—and the chairmanship of the Senate Armed Services Committee. This gave South Carolina a considerable edge because Thurmond knew exactly how political games were won in the capital. When navy brass approached Thurmond for help on another project, the wily old senator played the worried grandfather. He couldn't even start to think about that, he said, until the *Hunley* was safe.

"The sooner differences between the navy and *Hunley* Commission are worked out, the sooner historians will be able to study what was a revolutionary development," Thurmond said.

Within weeks McConnell was in Washington, meeting with navy officials, who suddenly had become much more accommodating.

Still, the two sides would argue for months. Ownership of the sub remained the sticking point, but McConnell soon had nearly everything else he wanted: Once recovered, the *Hunley* would remain in South Carolina forever, and its crew would be buried in Magnolia Cemetery alongside Horace Hunley himself. McConnell and the *Hunley* Commission had a tentative deal that accomplished most of their goals.

Now all they needed was the submarine's current address.

On November 9, 1995, the phone rang in Bob Neyland's office at the Naval Historical Center in Washington. The archaeologist was new to the center and barely on the periphery of the *Hunley* negotiations. His boss, William Dudley, was handling most business related to the sub. But when Neyland answered his phone that day, he suddenly became part of the act. Clive Cussler was on the line.

Cussler and Neyland chatted about the submarine for a while. They discussed the plan to recover the *Hunley* and talked about the benefits of an expedition to examine it more closely. The NUMA team had not inspected the sub to discern its condition; they simply verified they had found it. Neyland was impressed by Cussler's knowledge of the *Hunley*'s history, and underwater archaeology, but he had to wonder exactly what this rambling conversation was all about. Finally, Cussler asked him a simple question:

"You got a pencil?"

Neyland froze. He realized Cussler intended to give him the *Hunley*'s coordinates. But Neyland did not want to be responsible for such information. He blathered on for a minute, at one point suggesting the author send the information over a secure fax line. This espionage amused Cussler, but he wouldn't play along. He calmly told Neyland, "Just get a pencil."

Cussler offered the location in traditional latitude/longitude coordinates: 32 degrees, 43 minutes, 15.01 seconds latitude; 79 degrees, 46 minutes, 28.81 seconds longitude. Neyland scribbled the numbers down in a shaky hand, unable to believe he now held the best-kept secret in the South on a scrap of paper. It was so simple. Basically, the *Hunley* was just north of the harbor jetties, about four miles from Sullivan's Island.

The navy now had the coordinates that would lead them directly to the wreck of the *H. L. Hunley*.

Divercity rounded the Charleston Harbor jetties early that morning, slicing through the Atlantic as easily as a Sunday drive. It was late April 1996, and Ralph Wilbanks was headed back to the *Hunley* site. It had been almost exactly a year since they had found the sub and so much had changed since then. The state and federal governments were playing nice for the moment, NUMA had released the coordinates, and South Carolina and the navy had reached a final deal. Now these partners all wanted a look at their prize, and they had asked Wilbanks to lead them to it.

An alphabet soup of state and federal agencies planned a six-week study of the submarine. For this expedition, the Naval Historical Center and the South Carolina Institute of Archaeology and Anthropology would follow the lead of the National Park Service's Submerged Cultural Resources Unit (SCRU, an acronym destined to be changed). But first, the group wanted Wilbanks to put a PVC pipe on the site where NUMA claimed to have found the submarine.

Wilbanks thought it was silly, a monumental waste of time to actually take them to the spot. Weren't the coordinates enough? But he played along.

The oversized expedition had set out days earlier and ran into its first trouble immediately. They had a magnetometer reading they believed was the *Hunley* but, trouble was, the location was more than 100 feet from Cussler's coordinates. Bureaucrats being bureaucrats, this discrepancy forced them to question NUMA's discovery.

Wilbanks was annoyed; he felt like he was auditioning. But Cussler wanted to cooperate, so Wilbanks grudgingly accommodated the government folks.

It took Wilbanks just minutes to find the *Hunley*—right where he'd left it—and he planted the PVC pipe as requested. He didn't understand the problem until he quizzed the search team. As it turned out, the government team was using a different global positioning system—and it differed from NUMA's by about 100 feet. Once the confusion was sorted out, Neyland realized that Cussler had put them right on top of the sub—or, as they called it, "the object."

Although Wilbanks led them to the *Hunley*, at first the scientists would not concede it was the lost submarine. They wanted proof. Prior to the expedition, the archaeologists decided they had to find five distinguishing features to safely verify that NUMA had found the *Hunley*. This would prove harder than they imagined. For one thing, the water off Charleston was so murky it was nearly impossible to see your hand in front of your face. Initially, the divers could not even find the PVC pipe Wilbanks left behind.

Finding "distinguishing characteristics" would prove difficult because the *Hunley* did not look anything like the old sketches suggested. The scientists compiled a list of seven features of the submarine based on the drawings William Alexander had made decades after the war. Wilbanks recognized the flaw in the plan immediately. He had compared the *Hunley* to its model outside the Charleston Museum, which was also based on the Alexander sketches. There were several striking differences, most likely due to Alexander's failing memory. That, Wilbanks thought, or Alexander just couldn't draw.

As soon as they had "the object" located, bad weather delayed the expedition for more than a week. It was May 9 before divers actually began to dig on the site. They were looking for some combination of the spar, dive planes, snorkel box, hatch, keel weights, propeller and rudder. But at first, they found nothing. It was nearly impossible to see what they were touching. Neyland had dived around the world, but he had never worked in such murky conditions.

Leonard Whitlock was more accustomed to the opaque water than anyone else on the dive. The ocean engineer had more than 25 years of experience exploring places much darker. He had supervised the first dives on the USS *Monitor* wreck site nearly two decades earlier. Whitlock also held the world record for the deepest simulated saturation dive as the result of his work on a Duke University project in the 1970s. Zero visibility meant nothing to him. Whitlock was just happy that Larry Murphy and the National Park Service had invited him to join the expedition. He had worked with the Submerged Cultural Resources Unit on several projects, including a survey of shipwrecks in the Dry Tortugas and study of the USS *Arizona* in Pearl Harbor.

Whitlock was amassing an impressive resume of dives on historic wrecks, but he knew the *Hunley* was special. This was very likely the only remaining intact Civil War shipwreck, and the first working submarine. The appeal of being part of such an expedition was overwhelming. Whitlock desperately wanted to touch the sub. He could not wait.

The work was slow and methodical. The divers had to dig through the muck while dodging the jellyfish that invade the South Carolina coast every spring. Five feet beneath the sand they hit "the object" and it looked promising. It took only a day to find four "distinguishing features." Divers identified the forward hatch, the snorkel box, a cutwater and the portside dive plane. At this point it was pretty clear they had the *Hunley*. But this was a bureaucratic process, and the bureaucrats had set five features as their goal. It would take another week to find that elusive final clue.

The rough weather returned after that day, and the dive team was stuck at the dock for nearly a week—victims of the fickle South Carolina spring. When they returned to the site, they found the sand had drifted back over the wreck. It took two more days to dig it back out and get their confirmation. Finally, on May 17, divers came across the rear hatch of the *H. L. Hunley*. That made it official, even for the most officious skeptic. NUMA had located the long-lost Confederate submarine. The next day, the *Post and Courier* announced the news under a front-page headline: "It's Official."

The Park Service's Larry Murphy joked that he was simply happy they finally could quit calling it "the object."

For two weeks scientists, archaeologists and divers inspected the submarine, going over its hull with measuring tapes and cameras. They found the note left by NUMA in the forward conning tower— yet more proof that Wilbanks and his team had been there first. Ultimately they uncovered about half the submarine, but would not risk exposing more of it. They worried the hull was unstable and did not want to remove sand that might be holding it together. But they dug out enough to put to rest all questions about the *Hunley*'s length.

Over the years, some had claimed the sub was only 20 feet long, while others insisted it was 40 feet. The official measurement was 39 feet, five inches. At its widest point, the hull was a mere 42 inches in diameter. The oval conning towers sat 16 feet, three inches apart and their hatches opened toward one another. The forward hatch was hinged on its back, the aft hatch to the front. The conning towers were each about two feet long, 14 inches tall and only 15 inches wide. It had been a tight squeeze just to get in the sub, and it was clear the accommodations inside could not have been much more luxurious.

The expedition was a success by any measure: they not only had the submarine but had determined it was largely intact and—as best the scientists could tell—structurally sound. Neyland realized, however, that this was the easy part. Recovering such a fragile artifact would not be so easy. They had not seen the bottom of the submarine, could not tell if its keel had rotted away. They also had no idea how much the *Hunley* might weigh, another important variable. The only thing Neyland knew for sure is that it would cost millions to bring her up.

Whitlock got the question he expected before the survey ended.

He knew why he had been invited: he was projects manager at Oceaneering International, a company that had recovered more than its share of lost vessels in recent years. Its engineers had become the gold standard in their field. If anyone could raise the *Hunley*, the archaeologists knew, it was Oceaneering. Eventually Neyland got around to asking the question.

"Do you think the *Hunley* can be raised?"

Whitlock didn't hesitate. "Certainly," he said.

"How?"

This time, Whitlock paused a moment. Finally he said, "Well, that's the question."

When the government verified the *Hunley*'s discovery, it raised old questions about who had actually found the sub first. Around South Carolina there were conflicting stories of the fish-boat's history. Local newspapers reported that the sub had been found as early as 1870, the "bleached bones" of her crew visible inside. The romanticized, and unsourced, story was probably a hoax—no one could have seen inside the sub at that depth. More recently, a local treasure hunter claimed he had found the *Hunley* decades earlier. But scientists were skeptical.

That summer, the *Hunley* Commission decided it would put the issue to rest and award credit for the submarine's discovery. Members of the commission spent months poring over the documentation and the data collected by scientists and finally held hearings in February 1997. One man who claimed to have found the sub submitted highly detailed—and contradictory—paperwork to the panel. His testimony was largely dismissed after Senator Passailaigue pointed out the obvious: this man's description of the submarine did not match the vessel that Park Service divers had studied in the least. In fact, the object described by the man—whose own "nonprofit" had awarded him his only academic degree—closely resembled a submerged buoy lying next to the wreck of the *Housatonic*.

Later, SCIAA and Coastal Carolina University scientists would report that all data collected at the site and from the sub's hull indicated that once it was buried in the late nineteenth century, the *Hunley* was never uncovered. It never sat exposed on the ocean floor during the twentieth century, as the man insisted. If for no other reason, the *Hunley* could not have sat exposed on the ocean floor because it lay in a path that Shem Creek shrimpers had dragged their nets over for decades—and they kept meticulous records of all "snags" in their hunting grounds. There was simply no way anyone ever stumbled over the sub sitting in plain sight. It just didn't happen.

In March 1997, the state *Hunley* Commission credited Clive Cussler and his NUMA dive team with the discovery of the long-lost Confederate submarine. Others could claim they had found it all they wanted, but NUMA had proven it. As Cussler himself had once said, what good is going to the moon if you can't prove it? The *Hunley* Commission's endorsement made national news and did much to smooth over the rift between NUMA and the state.

The *Hunley* Commission finding should have been the final word.

By the time Cussler received credit as the discoverer of the *Hunley*, the project was at a crossroads. The controversy of the previous two years had settled down; the state had made up with the feds and Cussler. Scientists had confirmed NUMA's find, and Glenn McConnell had its coordinates safely locked away. Now the collective feeling among all these parties was one big looming *now what?*

For McConnell and Cussler, there was no question: the *Hunley* should be raised and the men aboard her given a proper burial. But that was much easier said than done. No one knew exactly how to retrieve an intact Civil War submarine from the ocean floor. McConnell knew they needed a plan and a way to pay for it—even if no one was sure how much it might cost.

The "programmatic agreement" between the state and Washington would allow the *Hunley* to remain in South Carolina forever, although the federal government would retain title. McConnell assumed that as a result of that caveat he could secure some federal funding for the recovery—after all, it was the feds' ship. And given his position in the state legislature, he felt certain he could make a case that South Carolina should pay some as well. McConnell had sound basis for the investment: he envisioned a museum devoted to the *Hunley*—an attraction that would lure thousands of visitors to South Carolina.

But scientists had estimated the entire recovery and refurbishment of the sub could cost upwards of $20 million, and McConnell realized there was a limit to how much government money he could get his hands on. He knew some people would use any excuse to complain about excessive government spending. Private money would be a necessity. Donations and corporate sponsorships could finance a major part of the project and, perhaps, squelch the criticism he knew would come eventually.

McConnell decided the *Hunley* needed a fund-raising group, a nonprofit organization to raise the profile of the recovery project—and the cash it needed to raise the sub. That was something that he, as chairman of the state *Hunley* Commission, could not do. The senator was not too disappointed. He hated to ask people to open their wallets for campaign donations; fortunately, he was so popular he rarely had to ask. McConnell and his senate attorney, John Hazzard, set up a nonprofit that spring, initially calling it the "Save the *Hunley*" fund. When someone asked how to donate, McConnell could steer folks to that account, and within months the charity had $20,000. It was a start, but they would need much, much more.

Eventually the nonprofit would be renamed Friends of the *Hunley*, and McConnell became obsessed with finding the right person to lead it. This, he knew, was an important decision. The amount of money they had to raise would require someone who had connections, and just the right touch. It could not be a politician—No, too polarizing, McConnell realized. The senator soon decided that he should find a businessman.

That summer McConnell asked *Hunley* Commission member William Schachte for recommendations. The retired navy rear admiral dabbled in all facets of life—government, military, business—and he seemed to know everyone. Schachte understood how things worked in Charleston: who could make a go of such an endeavor, and who couldn't. He took his assignment seriously but didn't have to think long before he came back to the senator with a very short list of candidates.

There was one name on it.

Schachte had met Warren Lasch through Neil Robinson, a prominent Charleston attorney who did work for the State Ports Authority. To Schachte's thinking, Lasch was perfect: A native of Cleveland, Ohio, a self-made man, the son of a butcher. Lasch had worked his way up through the business world and now owned several companies across the country, including Bavarian Motor Transport—a trucking business that hauled luxury cars such as Mercedes, Porsches and BMWs. By any measure, Lasch was the American success story.

Lasch's company had been working on a logistics study for the Greenville, South Carolina–based arm of BMW when Schachte met him. The company was shipping cars into Charleston, putting them on a train for a 200-mile trip to Greenville and processing them there before distributing the cars throughout the southeast. Lasch, a friendly but direct man, told BMW officials they perhaps could save some money. Lasch said there was no need to move the cars twice. BMW asked him to prove it.

Lasch eventually determined BMW could save several million dollars each year by processing the cars in Charleston and distributing them from there. He had even found a new, unused building on the grounds of the recently shuttered Charleston Naval Base where BMW could set up shop. Ultimately, BMW decided against the idea for political reasons—they did not want to move jobs from the Upstate to Charleston. But the plan showed that Lasch was more than capable of strategic planning, and getting the most out of a dollar.

By 1997, Lasch was quickly learning his way around Charleston's insular business world. He and his wife, Donna, had recently moved from Michigan to Kiawah Island. The childhood sweethearts bought a three-story home overlooking the ocean and a golf course that would one day host the U.S. Open. Lasch joked that he had moved to the South to slow down, but his long work days suggested otherwise. Lasch was busier than he'd ever been, but still felt like he was looking for something more. He just hadn't found it yet.

In June 1997, Schachte invited the Lasches to dinner at his downtown home off Broad Street. After the meal, the admiral led Lasch to his upstairs office and said he would like to talk to him about the *Hunley*. Lasch said sure, but "What's a *Hunley*?"

Schachte took a long time relating the story of the world's first attack submarine, its discovery two years earlier and the efforts of the state *Hunley* Commission to raise it. It was a long story, and one without a conclusion. The commission recently had set up a fundraising organization to raise money for the recovery of the submarine, Schachte explained. Lasch listened politely, and figured he was about to be hit up for a donation. What came next was, to put it mildly, a surprise.

"You're the man we need for this project," Schachte said. "I'd like to introduce you to Glenn McConnell."

Lasch was stunned. He was gracious but noncommittal; he knew no one succeeded in business without knowing all the facts before jumping into a deal. But he was intrigued, and of course he had heard of McConnell. It was nearly impossible to run in certain Charleston circles without hearing stories of the city's famous senator. Lasch told Schachte he'd be more than happy to meet with McConnell.

The admiral quickly wrote McConnell a long note outlining Lasch's background and describing his businesses. He said that Lasch was direct and savvy—the kind of man who could get things done, the sort of person who did not take "No" for an answer. Lasch could see three moves down the chessboard and learned all the angles before he did anything. In some ways he was a business world version of McConnell himself. If anyone could make the Friends of the *Hunley* a success, Schachte said, it was Lasch.

"He's the person," Schachte said.

The senator did his own checking around, calling his extensive networks of contacts around Charleston. He liked what he heard. Lasch had no political affiliations in South Carolina, so it would not look like this was a good ol' boy appointment. He had no local enemies that would make his job harder. The man was running four businesses and called it "slowing down." That was just the sort of energy the Friends of the *Hunley* needed. But McConnell also may have seen another benefit to hiring Lasch, one that Schachte had not mentioned.

The senator had been around politics enough to know that any project associated with the Civil War—particularly the Confederacy— would suffer its share of bad publicity. Already the state was facing criticism for flying a Confederate Naval Jack from the dome of the statehouse. McConnell knew that if he appointed a Southern partisan to run the charity, it would start with a tremendous deficit. It would be marginalized, considered a regional project at best. And corporations rarely invested in regional projects. McConnell wanted this to be a world-class operation, one that was above the petty politics of the day. He wanted this to be a serious scientific and historical project about a vessel that just so happened to fight for the Confederacy. And there was no better way to show that this project was above politics than to hire a Yankee from Ohio to recover a Rebel sub.

Lasch met McConnell at his law offices in West Ashley, just a few miles outside of downtown Charleston. McConnell was slowly closing his practice down to go into business full-time with his brother, Sam. The two had opened a Civil War–themed gift shop that sold art, souvenirs, memorabilia and collectibles. The store was so popular that McConnell had to devote more and more time to it every month. He found it much more interesting than practicing law.

The meeting was cordial, but there was no job offer. Lasch recognized that it was simply a sit-down to get to know one another. Maybe they weren't interested in him, he realized, and this didn't disappoint him terribly. Although intrigued by the possibilities, Lasch had enough to do, and he worried about the time commitment. And in truth, what did he know about raising submarines?

Still, something about the project appealed to Lasch—so much so that he found himself thinking about it often. He had been surprised that there were submarines in the Civil War. The *Hunley* was not the only one, just the first to succeed. The idea that this piece of history was just a few miles offshore in 30 feet of water made recovery possible, he knew. Finally, Lasch thought volunteering for the project would be a perfect way to give back to his adopted hometown.

There were two other meetings, each one about two weeks after the last. Finally, at the third, McConnell offered Lasch the chairmanship of the Friends of the *Hunley*. Lasch was polite, but warned them he couldn't devote more than ten hours a week to the charity. He was willing to commit, but had plenty of other things to do. McConnell promised that wouldn't be a problem.

"Warren, that will be more than enough time," McConnell assured him.

McConnell had studied Lasch and realized he didn't do anything half-heartedly, did not take any commitment lightly. Perhaps he truly thought the Friends of the *Hunley* would not require more than ten hours a week. Or maybe the savvy politician realized that Lasch would not allow himself to do a poor job, no matter how much time it took. But McConnell could not foresee just how dedicated Lasch would become. Later, McConnell would joke that Lasch had been quickly "Hunleytized"—a word that became shorthand for anyone completely consumed by the submarine.

Within three months, Lasch was suffering through sleepless nights. Running a charity was an entirely new world to him. For the first time in his life Lasch did not have all the angles figured out. He did not even know how much cash he needed to raise, and that ate at him. Lasch knew he could not ask for money without a fund-raising goal, without a plan to show to potential contributors. There was a lot of work to be done and, in those first months, he wasn't sure exactly how to get started. It got to be so daunting that Lasch considered telling McConnell he was sorry but "I don't think I'm the guy."

But Schachte had been right: Lasch did not give up easily. He was stubborn, did not believe in quitting and would not accept failure. If he didn't have the answers, he would figure out how to get them. By the time the Friends of the *Hunley* first met on December 5, 1997, and formally installed him as chairman, Lasch was learning more about ocean recovery than he ever knew existed. It was an entirely new world to him, but one he would soon master.

McConnell had chosen well. He now had his own George Dixon—a captain to lead the team into unchartered waters. Within months, Lasch was putting together a plan to recover the *Hunley*. The journey would take years, money from his own pocket, and a whole lot more than ten hours a week. But Lasch was determined to make this work.

Warren Lasch did not realize it at the time, but—like the *Hunley* crew a century earlier—he was sailing into the darkness.

CHAPTER 12

1863
Mount Pleasant

The president's train arrived at the John Street depot around midday on Monday, November 2, and hundreds of curious onlookers met it at the station. The people cheered as Jefferson Davis stepped out of his car, there was a short military salute and then a sizeable delegation sent by the mayor formally welcomed him to town. It was as much pomp and circumstance as Charleston could muster on Day 73 of the Siege.

Davis was on his way back to the Confederate capital in Richmond after a trip to Mobile, but had decided to stop for a few days in Savannah and Charleston en route. Both cities were under extreme pressure from Union military forces, and perhaps he thought a state visit could raise morale. At the very least he could do a little politicking.

Davis had no idea what he was getting into.

The president had not been to Charleston—the site of the first secession, and the first shots of the war—since the Confederacy was formed. His support there was weak, due in no small part to constant criticism of his administration by Robert Barnwell Rhett and the *Charleston Mercury*. Rhett had coveted the Southern presidency for himself and, when it went to Davis, his newspaper retaliated by nitpicking every decision he made.

General Beauregard also met President Davis's train, and the two men exchanged an awkward greeting. Davis and Beauregard shared a mutual distrust and disdain, but for the moment they needed each other's support. Despite their differences, they would try to get along for a few days. So, as city officials arranged a parade of buggies to take the president to City Hall, Davis and Beauregard rode together in the lead carriage.

The parade made a long, circuitous route through the city, and the president could not help but notice that Charleston was in shambles. The Union troops on Morris Island were shelling Sumter and the city on nearly a daily basis, martial law had been declared and the streets just off the route appeared to be nearly deserted. The lower part of the peninsula had been partially abandoned since the Yankees acquired new guns capable of landing shells as far north as Calhoun Street. Even Beauregard had been forced to retreat from the Meeting Street house he had been using as an office.

When the carriage stopped in front of City Hall, Davis was greeted by a band playing "Hail to the Chief." The crowd was enthusiastic, but the ceremony was clumsy. Davis stumbled through remarks meant to stir local patriotism, but which had nearly the opposite effect. With Yankee guns blasting in the distance, the president said that if Charleston was ever taken, he hoped it would only be as "a mass of ruins." It was not the most uplifting thing he could have said. Between the bombing and the charred remains of an 1861 fire that still littered the peninsula, Charleston already closely resembled Davis's description.

Davis tried to recover, declaring that he did not think Charleston would ever find itself under Yankee rule. As he attempted to reassure residents, the president suggested that even if the city's forts fell, Charleston had "other means" to protect itself—things he "need not refer to" at this time. Beauregard was furious. It seemed that Davis was directly referring to either the *David*—or worse, the *Hunley*. But, true to his word, the president made no further mention of these "other means."

Davis kept busy during his four days in Charleston. He toured the forts that lined the harbor and surveyed the damage to Sumter. Every evening there was another party for the Confederate president, and Beauregard declined to attend one of them. The general had been upset by Davis's failure to mention him by name during a speech praising the defenders of Charleston. It was unclear whether the omission was an oversight or intentional, but that mattered little to Beauregard.

The president was harsh in his critique of Beauregard's operations throughout the visit. Davis said the troops were stretched too thin at Charleston's forts without mentioning the fact that soldiers had been taken from the city for duty elsewhere, or that Beauregard had not been given any reinforcements. Davis correctly noted that the bombardment was actually doing little damage to the city's buildings but had landed a tremendous blow to its morale. The recent loss of the city's secret weapon did not help matters, although that was never mentioned—at least not overtly.

Beauregard believed that Davis, through his careless remarks, had undermined his decision to abandon the *Hunley* experiment. Even if the president wasn't referring to the fish-boat in his City Hall speech, Beauregard feared that if he did not shore up the city's defenses and break the blockade Davis would not hesitate to replace him. This predicament would still be on the general's mind when he next saw George Dixon.

Dixon and William Alexander reached Charleston shortly after President Davis left town. Somehow Dixon had convinced Maury to grant Alexander leave when his own was extended. This was crucial to Dixon. Not only did he want his friend with him, he knew his chances of success increased exponentially with the aid of the man who had actually built the sub. No one, save for perhaps James McClintock, knew the machine better. Although Alexander had not considered it, he was fortunate to have lost his seat on the second crew. If he hadn't, he most likely would be dead. Fate, it seemed, had spared both Dixon and Alexander.

The two men arrived at the John Street depot, just as Davis had, and immediately set out to examine the *Hunley*. They found it a few blocks away, practically untended on a dock overlooking the Cooper River. The secret weapon apparently was not much of a secret anymore. The sub's iron hull showed no signs of serious problems, for which they were thankful, but the interior told a different story. Inside the crew compartment, the smell of death was overwhelming. The two men did their best to disregard the stench as they climbed in to assess the sub's condition.

Nothing they found contradicted the Confederates' own investigation of the sinking. Alexander noted that the aft ballast tank valve was closed properly but the seacock for the forward tank, the one Horace Hunley would have controlled, had been left open. The wrench that turned the valve was still lying on the floor. Perhaps Hunley had dropped it in the confusion, or maybe the sub had flooded because he had lost it during the descent and could not find it to close the valve.

Dixon and Alexander quickly realized that Horace Hunley's final moments had been chaotic and terrifying. The keel block release bolts had been partially turned and both hatches were unlatched—all signs the crew knew they were in trouble. But their efforts had been in vain. As Alexander later noted, the intense water pressure 60 feet below the surface would not have allowed them to open the hatches. The men had died fighting to escape what would become their iron coffin.

If the image of such a grisly death affected either of them, they said nothing of it. This analysis of the accident gave them some insight to the submarine's limits and capabilities. Both decided that pilot error was the cause of the sinking. They still had complete faith in their torpedo boat.

Dixon and Alexander concluded there was no serious damage to the *Hunley*. It would need some modest repairs, a thorough cleaning, and its machinery would have to be oiled, but it was still in remarkably good condition. Alexander believed they could have it ready to sail again within weeks. Armed with this information, Dixon sent another note to Beauregard on November 12, asking once again for permission to relaunch the *Hunley*.

Beauregard granted Dixon an audience almost immediately. The lieutenant met the general in his new headquarters on Ashley Avenue, where he had relocated after the Yankees began shelling the city. Thomas Jordan, the general's chief of staff, sat in on the meeting along with Francis D. Lee, an engineer and friend of Beauregard. Lee's presence was not coincidental and suggests Beauregard had already made up his mind about the fish-boat's status.

The *Hunley* had killed 13 men, Beauregard said, which meant it was too dangerous to allow it to sail again. Dixon diplomatically argued that the boat was perfectly safe so long as it was operated by people who understood it. He did not have to state the obvious: The Confederate Navy men who sank the sub had almost no training, and Hunley had been foolish to try and pilot the machine. Dixon noted he had helped build the boat and piloted it many times without incident, even before it was brought to Charleston. He was confident the sub was still in good order and could be refurbished in a few weeks' time. They only needed a new crew and the *Hunley* would work.

Beauregard respected Dixon. The lieutenant fought under him at Shiloh and had a reputation as a serious man. Although he did not share Dixon's optimism about the fish-boat's prospects, his chief of staff apparently did—and Jordan may have helped sway the general. The recent presidential visit also may have played a role. Beauregard knew he had to do something. The blockade became more efficient every week, and Charleston was struggling to survive without provisions from the outside world.

Finally, Beauregard told Dixon he would allow him to take

command of the *Hunley* on one condition: The sub must not dive. The general suggested the sub use a spar torpedo, like a *David*. It was a more practical, and proven, method of attack. Lee opposed the idea immediately. He had invented the spar torpedo two years earlier, in Port Royal, and did not want it associated with the boat. Lee believed the *Hunley* was too dangerous, barely seaworthy. He was certain the submarine would sink again, and he wanted no part of it. Lee argued the *Hunley* didn't have enough buoyancy to venture into the fickle Atlantic. But Dixon made a better argument and, in truth, Beauregard was desperate. Lee knew that he had lost.

Dixon saw where the discussion was going and agreed to Beauregard's terms. He knew the submarine worked best under-water—that element of surprise was its only edge—but he would ac-cept any terms it took to get the *Hunley* back on the water. Ultimately, Lee could not deny Beauregard's wishes either and agreed to forge a spar for the *Hunley*. It would be ready by the time the fish-boat was refurbished. The general seemed satisfied, happy to have an unappeal-ing decision behind him.

Two days later, Jordan sent a telegram to Mobile, requesting a leave of absence for Dixon through the end of the year. Beauregard no longer expected miracles from the *Hunley*.

Dixon and Alexander went to work immediately.

Jordan supplied them with lime and soap to scrub the sub's inte-rior as well as rope, a new compass and ten slaves to handle some of the labor. The *Hunley* was moved to the outskirts of Mount Pleasant. It would take longer to get supplies from across the harbor, but there were far more advantages to the location. Dixon wanted no interrup-tions and felt it best to take the sub as far away from the nosy residents of Charleston as possible. If there were spies in the city, as there had been in Mobile, it would be prudent to limit the number of people who saw the *Hunley* being repaired. The sub was set up on blocks on a dock overlooking the waterway between the mainland and Sullivan's Island. The spot was within seeing distance of the first place the *Hunley* had been moored, when McClintock had briefly commanded it. Neither Dixon nor Alexander probably realized the significance of the location.

The rehabilitation of the *Hunley* would take several weeks. Working inside the cramped submarine was slow and tedious. But they found no additional problems; it was structurally sound. The *Hunley*'s nose had set down gently in the muddy harbor bottom and its stern had not even touched the muck. Much of the machinery had begun to rust as a result of three weeks in brackish water, and the reduction gears between the hand cranks and propeller had to be reoiled. Dixon had workers scrub down the entire interior with the lime and soap. They put a fresh coat of white paint on the interior walls, both to mask the stench of death and improve illumination. Finally, the seams between the hull plates were waterproofed using tree sap or tar.

Dixon and Alexander toiled every day from early in the morning until it was too dark to see, at which point they crossed the harbor and returned to their rooms at a King Street hotel. They were too tired to participate in the city's weak attempts to maintain normalcy; they attended no parties or balls. They were there to work, and the intermittent sound of shells landing in the city was a constant reminder that they were under a deadline.

Even secluded in Mount Pleasant, the *Hunley* attracted its share of visitors. One day the rector from St. Philip's Church crossed the harbor to find Alexander working on the refit. The clergyman asked the engineer to reconsider his mission. He had seen two crews perish in the boat already and warned that sailing on the sub was a great risk. Alexander was touched by the man's concern and accepted his invitation to attend services at St. Philip's the following Sunday. But it would do nothing to change his mind. Alexander was as committed to the *Hunley* as Dixon.

By early December the *Hunley* was nearly ready. Lee had delivered an iron spar nearly 20 feet long and offered to help Alexander install it. The spar was a fairly complicated weapon: solid iron for its first few feet, the rest of the pole was hollow—which made it lighter and easier to maneuver. It was bolted to the bottom of the bow with a yoke, and its angle could be adjusted, most likely with ropes. This would allow the crew to pinpoint their target with a fair degree of accuracy and made it easier to attach a torpedo when the sub was moored. The new weapons system was just about the last thing the sub needed before it was re-launched. But before they could do that, the submarine had another visitor—one who would immortalize it.

Conrad Wise Chapman dropped by the dock one afternoon to ask if he could make a sketch of the strange little fish-boat. The 21-year-old artist was the son of John Gadsby Chapman, a famous Virginia painter whose work was in the U.S. Capitol. Chapman was not just another gawker; he was working. The artist believed that the *Hunley* would be a worthy inclusion to a series of new portraits he was painting.

Early in the war, Chapman defied his family's wishes, abandoned his studies abroad and joined the Confederacy. He was injured at Shiloh, his wound just bad enough to take him out of action for months. By the summer of 1863 he had made his way to Charleston, where Thomas Jordan commissioned him to paint scenes of the defense of Charleston. Jordan was trying to raise support for the war effort and hoped the paintings would restore patriotism. He also may have been trying to save the talented young man from the horrors of the battlefield.

Chapman would ultimately paint more than 30 scenes of Charleston during the course of the war, and all of them showed just as much promise—and talent—as his father's work. None of the paintings Chapman did, however, would become as famous as his rendering of the *H. L. Hunley*. It remains the classic image of the submarine.

Chapman made several sketches of the submarine that he would use as the basis for his painting. He depicted the sub prior to its spar fitting, sitting on blocks with the aft hatch open. The details in his work were amazing—he even included the deadlight in the top of the

The artist Conrad Wise Chapman painted the Hunley *based on sketches he made of the submarine on the docks at Mount Pleasant in December 1863. For years Chapman's painting would be considered a romanticized rendering of the submarine, depicting a machine much too sleek and advanced to have been built by Civil War–era engineers. In fact, the painting is the most accurate historical record of the* Hunley—*even the smallest details are accurate, down to the spar's yoke at the bottom of the bow. Scientists today consider Chapman's painting a map of the fish-boat.*

open hatch. Chapman painted himself into the scene, as well as another man leaning against the rudder. Some people claimed the man standing in the painting was supposed to be Horace Lawson Hunley, the doomed "lost patriot" himself.

For years Chapman's painting would be criticized as too romantic, too fanciful. It depicted a machine far too sleek and modern to actually be a Civil War vessel. More than a century later, these critics would learn that Chapman had produced the most accurate contemporary image of the submarine ever made, far better than the sketches Alexander later drew from memory. He even included the yoke that would attach the *Hunley*'s new weapon system to the bow. Chapman had painted a very accurate, careful portrait of a machine that was far ahead of its time.

As Alexander made the final adjustments to the *Hunley*'s mechanics, George Dixon searched for a new crew. At first, Beauregard refused to allow him to solicit army or navy men. Dixon and Alexander could risk their lives, but the general would not lose more of his own troops. Alexander and Dixon met several times with Jordan, and eventually the chief of staff convinced Beauregard to soften his stance. Dixon could take Charleston recruits so long as all were volunteers, and they understood the danger involved. They must have "full knowledge" of the accidents that had already occurred. Beauregard had to know there were few people left in the city who had not heard horror stories about the fish-boat. But he wanted these dangers spelled out very clearly to anyone who considered setting foot inside the peripatetic coffin.

In early December, Beauregard's office sent a short note to Charleston navy officials seeking their blessing for Dixon to use Confederate sailors on the boat. The note, most likely written by Jordan, expressed great faith in Dixon and said "(t)he destruction of the enemies ironclads would warrant in my opinion the approval of Lt. Dixon's application."

Dixon ultimately was allowed to address the crew of the *Indian Chief*, a receiving ship anchored in the harbor. The ship was sort of a way station for sailors on their way to one assignment or another, so it was a good place to find men unattached to other duties. But Beauregard may have steered him in that direction because of the *Indian Chief*'s history with the submarine: it was the ship the *Hunley* had been trying to dive beneath when it was lost with Horace Hunley at the helm. The general realized that no one onboard the *Indian Chief* was under any illusions about the boat; they had seen firsthand how quickly it could kill.

If military leaders thought Dixon would have any problem finding volunteers, they were mistaken. Aboard the *Indian Chief*, Dixon found at least five men who would serve on the *Hunley*'s final crew.

Alexander later suggested Dixon had his pick from any number of men, all of them eager to test this new technology. In truth, the sailors may have been attracted by the bounty wealthy Charleston residents had offered for sinking blockaders. At the very least, they may have believed the benefits of joining an elite team were infinitely preferable to suffering through the dreary life that regular military service had become.

Dixon may have been looking for some intangible quality in the men he recruited because none of them fit into a simple mold. Some were young, others well into middle age. Most of them had experience on boats, but a few had spent precious little time on the water— save for their service in the safe confines of Charleston Harbor. Some people assumed the crew had to be comprised of small men to fit in the unforgiving confines of the submarine, but Dixon selected some men shorter than average, and others who were over six feet tall.

Arnold Becker was the youngest of the men selected, and perhaps the smallest, but he had a background that certainly appealed to Dixon. Becker had emigrated from Europe just before the war and worked aboard a riverboat out of New Orleans. When the fighting began, Becker's paddleboat was converted to a gunboat and he enlisted along with the rest of the crew. For a while, he served as the ship's cook. The *General Polk* spent months defending the Mississippi River only to be lost in June 1862. Trapped in the Yazoo River, the *Polk*'s crew burned her rather than allowing the ship to fall into Union hands.

Becker moved on to Charleston that summer and had served aboard the ironclad *Chicora* before he was reassigned to the *Indian Chief*. There is little doubt Becker knew the history of the fish-boat. Four of the five men who had died aboard the sub in August were from the *Chicora*, and the ironclad had been nearby when it went down. In fact, Becker may have been one of the few men to witness both of the *Hunley*'s previous accidents. But still he volunteered, and that must have impressed Dixon.

Joseph Ridgaway, a quartermaster on the *Indian Chief*, was one of Dixon's most astute selections. Ridgaway hailed from a prominent maritime family on Maryland's Eastern Shore. The Ridgaways of Talbot County were affluent, due in no small part to their plantation and a fleet of merchant ships. Ridgaway worked on his father's ships from an early age, at first in the Chesapeake Bay and then on longer voyages. Joseph Ridgaway earned his Seaman's Protection Certificate, which identified him as an ocean-going sailor, when he was just 16—a distinction most men in that line of work did not receive until they were in their twenties. At 30, Ridgaway was one of the most experienced sailors Dixon would hire.

James Wicks was an old salt who had seen the war from both sides. A career navy man, the North Carolina native had been aboard the USS *Congress* on March 8, 1862, when the ironclad CSS *Virginia* attacked it at Hampton Roads. As the *Congress* sank into the muck, Wicks was taken prisoner and decided, at that moment, to join the Confederacy. It really wasn't a difficult choice.

Wicks was a born sailor. He'd joined the U.S. Navy in 1850 and was stationed in Brooklyn. There he met his wife, a young Irish woman, and the first of his four daughters was born shortly after. For more than a decade, the navy moved Wicks from one ship to another. It was a struggle to keep his growing family close by. Two more daughters arrived while his family lived in his native North Carolina, and the fourth arrived by the time Wicks had relocated his growing brood to Fernandina, a small town on Amelia Island in northern Florida.

When the war began, Wicks was conflicted. His home state had joined the Confederacy but like many Southern sailors, Wicks remained at his post. Navy men often had the most difficult time choosing sides in the War Between the States. They thought of home more as a country than any individual state. But when the *Congress* was sunk, Wicks knew his decision had been made for him: he belonged with the Confederacy. He enlisted in Richmond days after the

Battle of Hampton Roads and, already in his mid-forties, was assigned to the *Indian Chief*. He carried his heavy U.S. Navy peacoat with him to Charleston. Good jackets were hard to come by in the South in those days.

Those three men were natural picks for Dixon. They had significant experience on ships, which was the only sort of training even remotely similar to the work they would do on the *Hunley*. Wicks could decipher intelligence on navy ships, Becker showed no fear and Ridgaway was as accomplished as any sailor in the Confederate Navy. The other men he chose were less obvious, a sign that Dixon was running on gut instinct.

Frank Collins was in his early twenties, from Fredericksburg, and over six feet tall. He was hardly the model submariner, and not only because of his height. He'd grown up near the Rappahannock River, and if he had any experience on the water it likely came from working around the ships that operated out of the city. His mother had died at an early age and his father, Albert, left him and his brother with their grandfather, who worked as a cobbler. Albert Collins made a living as a portrait artist and, in 1860, had remarried. He did not bother to take in the two sons from his previous marriage.

Collins may have simply been patriotic, or perhaps his father's new family left him feeling rudderless and adrift. For whatever reason, Frank Collins joined the Confederate Navy at Richmond shortly after the fighting began. He had been assigned to the *Indian Chief* ever since. It was not the most exciting assignment, and Collins likely spent long days staring at the city of Charleston from the deck of the receiving ship. For a young man who did not smoke, it was a boring existence. Perhaps he was looking for adventure, and Dixon recognized that thirst.

The final sailor Dixon selected that day was a middle-aged man originally from Europe named Lumpkin. He was bulky, had lived a hard life, and it's unclear what—if any—sailing experience Lumpkin might have had. The *Indian Chief* had become, among other things, a support ship for Confederate mine operations, so it's possible Lumpkin had some knowledge of explosives. Whatever the reason, Dixon selected Lumpkin from among the dozens of other volunteers he interviewed that day.

These five men, along with Dixon and Alexander, would make up the new crew of the *H. L. Hunley*. Dixon had one more position open on the submarine, but chose not to fill it with another member of the *Indian Chief*'s crew. Alexander later said he and Dixon had traveled to Charleston with one or two other men, but at some point both decided against sailing on the fish-boat. Perhaps Dixon still hoped he could convince one of them to change their mind.

Dixon's crew would see the benefits of their new job immediately. The men moved off the ship and into a two-story house near the Mount Pleasant harbor front. The house, about halfway between Shem Creek and the dock where the *Hunley* had been refurbished, was infinitely more comfortable than their quarters on the *Indian Chief*. The food was not great, but it was better than the fare they received aboard a navy ship in 1863. Soon, these men realized the relative comfort they enjoyed was hardly a fair trade-off for the cramped conditions aboard the world's first attack submarine.

Dixon and Alexander kept their lodgings on King Street for a while. Later, Alexander would recall that for most of December, he and Dixon and two other men attached to the submarine stayed in a downtown hotel. Perhaps these were men Dixon had summoned from Mobile to fill out the crew—at various times Alexander mentioned two men, Dillingham and Lorrence. But in December, the only member of the crew who did not come from the *Indian Chief* was a man Alexander remembered only as Miller. He never specified which members of the crew stayed downtown, and Confederate records do not indicate who these men were. Whoever they were, they eventually joined the rest of the crew in the Mount Pleasant house.

Sometime in the second week of December, Dixon and Alexander took their new recruits out for their first trip aboard the *Hunley*. Those early cruises were confined to the creek behind Sullivan's Island and brief jaunts into the harbor. Dixon piloted the boat and Alexander served as first officer, operating the aft ballast tank from a spot beneath the rear hatch. It's most likely that Becker or Ridgaway was seated in the first station behind Dixon, where they would operate the pump for the forward ballast tank at Dixon's command, as well as the bellows that had been attached to the sub's snorkel to help draw in fresh air. The rest of the men simply learned to crank, their work finally falling into an easy rhythm.

Trained by the men who knew the *Hunley* best, it took this crew little time to grow comfortable enough with the boat to venture farther from the dock. Dixon kept Beauregard's chief of staff informed of their progress and, within a week, reported that they were ready. On December 14, the general issued orders giving Dixon permission to attack the blockade.

"First Lieut. Geo. E. Dixon, Twenty-first Regt. Ala. Vols., will take command and direction of the Submarine Torpedo-Boat 'H. L. Hunley' and proceed to-night to the mouth of the harbor, or as far as capacity of the vessel will allow, and will sink and destroy any vessel of the enemy with which he can come in conflict."

The general had instructed army and navy officers to provide any assistance needed but Dixon needed only one thing: a tow. J. H. Tomb, the hero of the *David*'s attack on the *New Ironsides*, provided that service often during December 1863. Tomb would later remember Dixon as a "brave and cool-headed" man with great confidence in his boat. Tomb even claimed he had watched the incident in which Horace Hunley died with Dixon. That suggested Dixon had not been out of town at the time the sub's namesake perished, one more mystery that would linger for more than a century.

At the time, the *David* was still trying to repeat its attack on the *New Ironsides*. Tomb had his sights on the USS *Wabash*, a ship Dixon desperately wanted to sink himself. It became a race to see which of the stealth boats might strike first, but the *David* was at a disadvantage: for the moment, it was designated as shore support for the fishboat. Tomb used the *David* to tow the *Hunley* away from the dock in Mount Pleasant. The two ships sailed into the harbor and just beyond Fort Sumter under the *David*'s power most nights. At that point, Dixon would cast off the tow line and the *Hunley* set out to sea. The sub ventured out an average of four nights a week, a limitation most likely imposed by the crew's stamina.

Traveling with the tide, which was not always possible, the *Hunley* could make about four knots. The strain of cranking the sub's propeller in the thick saltwater made for a long night of work. Most of the blockade ships swung at anchor several miles offshore, out of the range of Fort Sumter's guns, and it could take hours just to venture out that far. Dixon had to pace the crew to make sure they had enough strength to make it back. Even when the weather was calm and the tide running with them, Dixon found it was nearly impossible to reach the blockade.

Dixon kept up this routine until one night when tragedy nearly struck. The *Hunley* still carried its floating mine, either because the spar system had not been perfected or because they wanted the option to attack twice. Whatever the circumstances, Tomb said one night the contact mine fell off the submarine and its towline got caught in the *David*'s propeller. At the same time the *Hunley* drifted into the mud around Sullivan's Island. It was chaos, and Tomb and his crew had to scramble to stop the mine from blowing their ship out of the water. Years later, Alexander would concede the towline worked much better in rivers than it ever did in tidal waters.

When Tomb reported the floating mine incident, the *David* was no longer allowed to tow the *Hunley*. The Confederates would not risk both of their stealth weapons, particularly the one that had proven to work. The order was a serious setback for Dixon. He would have to abandon the floating mine completely, that was certain. But without a support ship, the *Hunley* could no longer sail from Mount Pleasant.

As the New Year arrived, Dixon worried he might never get a chance to attack the blockade. He had the right crew and the submarine worked fine, but it could not operate alone—not given the constraints of Charleston's geography. He was also getting contradictory signals from the Confederates. They wanted him to attack, but would not support him. It was frustrating, and Dixon felt his mood darkening.

But as 1864 began George Dixon had even more problems than he realized. In addition to all the other obstacles standing between him and the South Atlantic Blockading Squadron, he had also lost his one advantage, the *Hunley*'s single greatest weapon: surprise.

The Yankees knew he was coming.

CHAPTER 13

1998 The Tower of Babble

Warren Lasch felt his eyes starting to glaze over. And as the omnipresent bureaucracy sucked the last remaining air out of the room, he fought to stifle a yawn.

Lasch was sitting in the conference room of the Charleston Museum, where the representatives of a half-dozen groups and agencies were debating what to do with the *Hunley*. Some believed the sub should be raised immediately; others urged caution, a slow and deliberate planning process. A few thought the recovery would be a relatively simple task; others feared the challenges were insurmountable. Every few minutes, someone threw a new variable into the discussion: *What if we also do this?* The meeting was flying out of control, a headless beast without focus, without leadership, contradicting itself every minute. Lasch wondered *what have I gotten myself into?*

All the stakeholders—and there's a bureaucratic word, Lasch thought—in the *Hunley* project had gathered in the early winter of 1998 to discuss options for raising the submarine and delivering it safely to Charleston. The sub's new home would likely be the very museum where they sat; at least that seemed to be the direction in which things were moving. But nothing was settled—on any front. In fact, Lasch found this all most unsettling.

Between the *Hunley* Commission, the South Carolina Institute of Archaeology and Anthropology, the Naval Historical Center, the Friends of the *Hunley* and a few other interested parties, there was no shortage of expert opinion in the room. All of these people meant well and had good intentions, but it felt to Lasch as if some of these folks were most interested in jockeying for positions of authority on a project that was quickly gaining national prominence. Everyone wanted a piece of the *Hunley*, everyone had an agenda and on this day, everyone seemed to be talking at once.

Lasch would come to call this historic gathering the "Tower of Babble" conference.

To a businessman's view, it was the worst sort of management by committee. This was like the United Nations, and Lasch feared nothing good could come of it. In his companies Lasch hired good people, held them accountable for doing their jobs well and then got the hell out of the way. But he had learned very early on that success required, above everything else, a coach. Perhaps that is why the famous Green Bay Packers coach, Vince Lombardi (another son of a butcher), was one of his role models.

As Lasch fought catatonia, he realized this crew was in serious need of someone to teach them about the American zeal, as Lombardi called it—"that is to be first in what we do and to win, to win, to win." To Lasch, winning in this instance meant doing this project the right way. This philosophy had made Lasch, like Lombardi, a very successful man.

What are we trying to accomplish here? Lasch asked himself. The goal was simple: recover and preserve a historic artifact for future generations. But it seemed like everyone who spoke brought up another side issue, sending the meeting down another rabbit hole. Everyone had ideas, but no one seemed willing to take responsibility or take charge. This, Lasch knew, was no way to get to the finish line.

Soon, Lasch turned his attention to Bob Neyland. The archaeologist from the Naval Historical Center came across as meticulous, prepared and conservative. Perhaps too conservative, Lasch believed, but it was clear Neyland knew his subject matter. Neyland was a product of Texas A&M's vaunted maritime archaeology program and had not been with the navy for long. He was the man who'd taken the coordinates from Cussler in 1995 and later played a role in the 1996 expedition to the *Hunley* site. Neyland seemed focused on the task at hand.

He could work, Lasch thought.

When the meeting finally ended, Lasch invited Neyland to get lunch before he had to catch a plane back to Washington. With William Schachte in tow, Lasch guided the archaeologist to his new BMW parked outside. Neyland plopped into the front passenger seat, where Lasch wowed him with the car's GPS system—not exactly standard issue on cars in 1998. Neyland showed the appropriate interest, but it was clear he didn't understand exactly what was going on.

Lasch engaged Neyland with his usual amiable banter—a few jokes, some self-deprecating observations—trying to loosen him up. Then he hit him hard with full-on business talk.

"Bob, how much do you make?"

Neyland, taken aback, stuttered a bit. "Don't you think that's kind of a personal question?"

Lasch shrugged it off. He was in full sales pitch mode and quickly explained his line of thinking: someone had to direct the *Hunley* project. They needed a person who understood the archaeology and the government sides, someone who had more than a passing knowledge of the engineering required and the conservation that would follow. This can't be done by committee, Lasch explained— a very thinly veiled criticism of the meeting they'd just left.

Neyland seemed to agree with Lasch. No one could have walked out of that meeting and felt optimistic, at least no one Lasch would ever hire. Neyland was polite, but he did not commit to anything. The Friends of the *Hunley* chairman let the offer hang there for the rest of the day—but he wouldn't let the question linger for long. Within weeks, both Lasch and Schachte would talk to Neyland's boss, William Dudley, about borrowing the Naval Historical Center archaeologist for a while.

It took Lasch about a month.

By January 1998, just weeks after he formally became chairman of Friends of the *Hunley*, Lasch had rid himself of all doubts and regained his famous confidence. He might not know exactly how to raise a 130-year-old submarine, or how much money he needed to do it, but he knew what he knew—and that was organization and management. Those might not be the most fascinating pieces of the puzzle, but they got results. Lasch realized that if he could get the top people in their fields involved in this project, and put together the best recovery plan, the chances of success went up exponentially. And that's exactly what he intended to do.

Lasch worked for more than a month on a management structure for the *Hunley* project. His plan was to recover the sub as quickly as possible. He had heard the arguments for waiting, but he believed there was nothing to be gained by dragging out the process. The price of doing business would only go up, and it would be far easier to raise money while the *Hunley*'s profile was high. And it appeared that profile was about to get much higher. The media mogul Ted Turner had announced plans to film a *Hunley* television movie for his TNT network, and Lasch knew you couldn't buy that kind of advertising.

Lasch focused on the project's core mission—*What are we trying to do here?*—and filtered out the distractions that had crept into the conversation during the Tower of Babble meeting. There were only five prongs to this plan: raise the sub, conserve the sub, raise funds for both, use public relations to assist in the fund-raising, and administration. Anything that did not fit into one of those five categories had to be jettisoned.

Lasch did not realize it, but he was very quickly taking over the *Hunley* project.

Lasch delivered his management plan to the *Hunley* Commission in February 1998. He unveiled the concepts that would become the basic marketing strategy for the submarine, the roadmap they would use to raise the money for its recovery and restoration. The Friends would tell the story of the *Hunley* in historical context, he said, with a focus on education. They would cast this as an American story, not simply a Southern tale, to avoid the controversy everyone expected to follow. The *Hunley*, Lasch proclaimed, is a global story "steeped in history, not burdened by it."

Lasch was engaging, inspiring and even used the phrase that would become the project's motto: "We only have one chance to do this right." Lasch deftly steered the commission clear of trouble before it began—that is, a focus that was too dependent on Southern heritage, which was a phrase that raised red flags in the business community. He managed to say just the right things. That day, the commission voted to raise the *Hunley*.

Vince Lombardi would have been proud.

The decision to proceed with a recovery plan did not come without scientific endorsement. The South Carolina Institute of Archaeology and Anthropology had declared the *Hunley*'s hull stable, at least strong enough to withstand the trauma of being pulled from the muck and lifted out of the sea. It was a solid ship, this last surviving relic of the War Between the States. Apparently, James McClintock had built his submarine to last.

"It looks like it's in very good shape," state underwater archaeologist Chris Amer told the commission. "It looks like lifting it is going to be no particular problem."

That was a more optimistic assessment than Glenn McConnell could have hoped for, and it made him only more determined to bring the *Hunley*—and its crew—home quickly. Not all of his colleagues were sold on the idea. One commissioner refused to cast a vote. He suggested the state instead build a memorial on top of the *Hunley* similar to the one towering over the wreck of the USS *Arizona*, the battleship sank at Pearl Harbor. His colleagues politely ignored the idea. There was no question regarding the will of the commission.

The *Hunley* was coming home.

Using what information he had available to him, Lasch told the commissioners it would likely cost $15 million or more to fund the recovery, a figure that would rise to $20 million by year's end. The problem was that no one knew exactly how to retrieve the sub, and that remained the biggest variable. But it was not the only problem the commission faced. The state still needed somewhere to put the *Hunley* once they brought it home.

Several organizations had expressed interest in housing the sub, but so far McConnell had only one actual proposal. The Charleston Museum submitted a detailed plan to add a wing to its downtown facility, square footage that would serve as a conservation laboratory and, later, host a permanent *Hunley* exhibit. The reviews were mixed. Although the museum was a top-caliber institution with a collection far greater than its reputation, some commissioners were less than enthusiastic about the nondescript brick building.

The Charleston Museum was landlocked and abutted an emerging downtown neighborhood. Already, some residents had voiced concerns about living near the caustic chemicals that would be used to restore the sub's rusted hull. Some commissioners even worried that the museum did not have enough parking to handle the crowds that would flock in to see the *Hunley*. Every day someone found a new reason to turn down the museum's offer.

It was far from a perfect solution, but the museum staff was enthusiastic and no one else had offered. So for the moment, McConnell and Lasch would consider the museum a tentative plan while they focused on the first job—recovering the sub. That would turn out to be their first mistake.

In the spring, the first crews from TNT arrived in Charleston to begin principal photography on Ted Turner's *Hunley* movie. The producers had attached two famous actors to the movie—Donald Sutherland as General Beauregard and Armand Assante as George Dixon—and locals turned out by the hundreds to catch a glimpse of them. Eventually, the movie would hire dozens of those gawking locals as extras. McConnell even had a bit part with Sutherland as one of Beauregard's men. For months, the movie was the center of attention in Charleston—nothing excited the city like the Civil War.

The entire shoot was a circus. One day the crew covered Broad Street in dirt to recreate a wartime parade through the city. Newspaper photographers on the set got a picture of Sutherland between takes that gave the production some high-profile publicity. He was sitting on a horse in full Confederate general regalia, talking on a cell phone. The photograph was reproduced in newspapers and magazines, and even appeared on CNN. None of those news outlets used the photo in which Sutherland, as Beauregard, casually stared at the photographer and flipped him the bird.

Engineers built the movie *Hunley* based on William Alexander's late-nineteenth-century sketches of the submarine—but not entirely. The film's first controversy erupted when folks saw the mock-up, which included a spar mounted at the bottom of the *Hunley*'s bow. Most people believed the spar had sat atop the bow, and it was a source of great debate in Charleston. The movie engineers argued that a bottom-mounted spar was the only configuration that made any sense—no matter what the drawings showed. Scientists, and Civil War buffs, took a dim view of this logic. In Charleston, they took their history seriously.

The production used Lake Moultrie as a stand-in for the Atlantic Ocean, Charleston Harbor and the waterway behind Sullivan's Island. The crew also built a cutaway of the sub for interior scenes. They did most of this work on a soundstage Lasch had suggested: the empty navy base building that he had recommended to BMW years earlier. Ultimately, many of the film's interior shots would be filmed in the warehouse-like facility known as Building 255.

Throughout the summer, many local war buffs complained that the film took too many liberties with the story—the spar was only the tip of the submarine. The writers had created incredible back stories for most of the crew and even threw in a bar fight to keep the action moving. Some locals believed this took too much liberty with their history. McConnell did his best to ease concerns. He did not want the movie criticized before it even premiered. Like Lasch, the senator realized the Turner production was a potential gold mine in marketing and publicity.

~

Lasch intended to have Friends of the *Hunley* in full campaign mode by the time the film premiered in the summer of 1999. Strike while there's sizzle, he liked to say. Lasch spent much of the year consumed with the details of the project. He worked out a deal with William Dudley to use Neyland as project director and hired a public relations firm to develop the marketing plan. His friends saw a complete change in Lasch. The recovery project became his obsession. Everything else was of secondary importance.

Lasch was quickly taking control of every facet of the *Hunley*'s recovery and restoration plan, and his enthusiasm grew daily. It was a lot of work—much more than the ten hours a week McConnell had said would be "more than enough"—but Lasch seemed as excited as a kid. When he heard that the old Park and Lyons' machine shop—where the *Hunley* was built—had been disassembled, Lasch tried to buy it. He wanted to truck it to Charleston as part of the sub's museum. But someone else had already spoken for the building. When the TNT movie wrapped, McConnell convinced the producers to donate the sets—particularly the mock-up of the *Hunley* interior—for use in its eventual museum.

Movie sets and old buildings had little to do with their primary mission, but Lasch and McConnell could not resist. It suddenly seemed as if the *Hunley* was everywhere. Every day something else came along to keep the project in the news. The most significant development surfaced at the end of the summer, shortly after the Turner crew had left town. As it turned out, the submarine's third crew was not the only *Hunley* sailors missing in action.

State archaeologist Jonathan Leader called a press conference in August 1998 to outline his plans to find the *Hunley*'s first crew. Leader believed the men might be buried beneath The Citadel's football stadium. The idea had come from Randy Burbage, a member of the *Hunley* Commission and an ardent war historian. Burbage had spent more than a decade tracking the history of an old Confederate sailor's cemetery once located on the city's peninsula. It all started years earlier when he found a stone obelisk at Magnolia Cemetery that referenced four "Men of the Torpedo Boat." Burbage searched the entire cemetery, but could not find their graves.

With a little digging, Burbage learned that the men originally had been buried in an old seaman's cemetery located on the site of the current Johnson Hagood Stadium, where the military college's football team had played for decades. Charleston records showed that the city council had voted to move the cemetery to make way for the stadium in 1947, but the memo ordering the move said only "transfer of tombstones in the small cemetery adjacent to Johnson Hagood Stadium." Perhaps, Burbage thought, the workers had taken those orders literally.

There were other clues that he was on the right track. Five years earlier he and other members of the Confederate Heritage Trust had gotten the college's permission to dig up the stadium parking lot. There, they found the graves of a dozen Confederate sailors. Either by bureaucratic foul-up or sheer laziness, the city had left a number of coffins behind during the relocation. Burbage suspected there were more men on the property, but The Citadel would not allow him to tear up the stadium. But a few years later, when the college announced plans for a stadium renovation, Burbage had the excuse he needed to ask again. And this time the school told him he could rip up the concrete floor beneath the bleachers—after the 1998 football season ended. Burbage called in Leader.

In March 2000, the first crew to perish aboard the Hunley—*discovered months earlier beneath The Citadel's football stadium—was buried in Magnolia Cemetery alongside Horace Hunley and the second crew to die on the submarine. Today, all 21 men who died while serving aboard the* Hunley *are interred together in Magnolia. Courtesy Friends of the* Hunley.

The dig would commence in early 1999. Although Leader would not say anything definitive, Burbage was certain the first crew of the *Hunley* was in there somewhere—and he meant to find them. He wanted to rebury the men in Magnolia Cemetery beside Horace Hunley and the second crew. And one day, he hoped George Dixon and his crew would rest there as well. Burbage believed all three crews should be interred together. McConnell and Lasch could focus on the recovery; this was Burbage's priority.

Clive Cussler followed these developments from the other side of the country. He had not returned to South Carolina in the years since he announced the discovery of the *Hunley*. His job there was done, and he had moved on to other NUMA business and several new writing projects. Ralph Wilbanks kept Cussler up to date on *Hunley* happenings. Although the author was intrigued by the idea of finding the sub's first crew, he saw no role for NUMA in that hunt.

By 1998 the demand for Dirk Pitt adventures had forced Cussler to cut back on NUMA expeditions. The crew went out on fewer, but bigger, hunts. Cussler felt chained to a desk most days. His publisher and his significant fan base could not get enough, and Cussler did all he could to keep them happy. Finally, the author came up with an idea that would satisfy everyone. Working with coauthor Paul Kemprecos, Cussler developed a new series called the NUMA Files. These novels would feature Kurt Austin, a coworker of Pitt's, in his own adventures for the fictional government agency. Cussler's empire was growing even faster than the *Hunley* project.

The first NUMA Files book was titled *Serpent*, and it featured all the hallmarks of a Pitt novel: a madman bent on a dastardly scheme, a priceless ancient artifact and a famous shipwreck—in this story, the lost Italian luxury liner *Andrea Doria*. The book would come out in 1999, followed five months later by a new Pitt adventure, *Atlantis Found*.

Lasch wanted to get the famous author more involved with the *Hunley*. Cussler could bring considerable publicity to the project, and Lasch realized that the sea hunter also had amassed a good amount of knowledge of archaeology and maritime recovery. Frankly, the project could use his advice—it was all part of Lasch's plan to get the best people involved. In late August, Lasch invited Cussler to Charleston, where the Friends of the *Hunley* chairman was throwing a barbecue to honor the NUMA crew. Wilbanks, Wes Hall and Harry Pecorelli would attend, but not even a reunion with his old crew could tear Cussler away from his computer. He sent Lasch his regrets.

Slowly, the two men began to correspond and eventually Lasch asked Cussler to join the Friends of the *Hunley* board. Cussler had thought he was finished with the submarine—he'd found it, now let others save it. That was how he'd always done it in the past. But Lasch had other ideas, and he was persuasive. Finally Cussler accepted the invitation. He might have thought he was finished with the *Hunley*, but the *Hunley* was not finished with Cussler.

⁓

It seemed everyone wanted to raise the *Hunley*.

Every week, Lasch was bombarded with pitches and proposals from companies around the globe. They all bragged about their track records, hinted at the innovative plans they had for the submarine's recovery, and the low, low cost to the charity. One man hired a Charleston attorney to sell Lasch on a scheme to use a huge scoop to pick up the *Hunley* and all the sand around it. It did not seem like a safe idea, Lasch thought, and he let it lie. But the man would not go away easily.

Lasch was polite with all these suitors, but he remained wary. He realized most of these outfits saw dollar signs. They knew the government would fund at least part of the recovery, so they were sure to get paid. Plus there would be a great bonus in publicity for any company connected with the project. Lasch thought some of the plans plausible, others laughable. None of them passed his smell test, but he showed them to the scientists from SCIAA and Neyland, who had arrived in Charleston that August.

Neyland was not interested in unsolicited plans for the sub; he had his own ideas for the recovery. In September, he and Lasch flew north to meet with Leonard Whitlock at Oceaneering International's facilities in Maryland. Neyland was impressed with Oceaneering and Whitlock, whom the National Park Service had invited to join the 1996 *Hunley* dive. From the time he'd asked Whitlock if the *Hunley* could be raised, Neyland had believed Oceaneering was the company to do it. They had an amazing record of successful recoveries, and Lasch wanted a guarantee the sub would be recovered safely.

Oceaneering was about as close to a guarantee as there was. The subsea engineering and applied technology corporation had been in business more than 30 years. The company did a lot of work for offshore drilling operations, but was becoming nearly as well known for its deep sea recovery work. Teams from Oceaneering had recovered the solid rocket boosters from the *Challenger* disaster in 1986, a find that solved the mystery of the shuttle's explosion. Two years earlier, the company had found the cockpit voice recorder from a ValuJet crash in Florida, and then helped lead teams to the wreckage of TWA Flight 800 off Long Island.

Whitlock impressed Lasch from the start. He not only had the engineering chops and years of diving under his weight belt, he also had a healthy respect for history. Since supervising the first manned dives on the USS *Monitor*, Whitlock had become enchanted with historic shipwrecks. After the 1996 *Hunley* survey, Whitlock often thought about that question Neyland had posed to him. Raising the *Hunley* was an intriguing engineering puzzle. It also could be quite dangerous. One slip and a unique piece of history could be destroyed. Just like the *Cairo*.

The USS *Cairo* was perhaps the greatest nightmare in the history of maritime recovery, a story that sent chills through every marine archaeologist in the world. The Union gunboat became the first victim of a naval mine when it was lost in the Yazoo River in December of 1862. Ninety years later, Edwin Bearss of the Vicksburg National Military Park found the wreck and recovered several artifacts from it.

In 1964, an attempt to raise the entire ship ended in disaster. Crews wrapped steel cables around the hull in an attempt to lift the *Cairo* straight out of the water. But when the full weight of the ship rested on the cables, the steel wires sliced through the wooden hull— tearing the *Cairo* apart and spilling its contents into the river. Engineers were forced to cut the boat into three pieces. Whitlock did not want to see that happen to the *Hunley*. The thought made him ill.

Whitlock read the Park Service assessment of the *Hunley* following the 1996 survey and came away most worried about the rivets that held the sub's hull plates. They were the weak link. No matter how much weight load they had been designed to hold, it would not match the current tonnage of a submarine filled completely with sediment and sand. And no one was even sure how strong the rivets were after more than a century in saltwater. Under such stress, Whitlock knew there was a chance those rivets could pop and the *Hunley* would literally fall apart before it reached the surface. That would make the *Cairo* disaster look like a minor accident.

Whitlock knew there had to be a safer way to raise the submarine, one that would hold it together no matter how strong its weakest points were. He took an idea from history, a subject with which he was well-acquainted. He had been working as program manager for the U.S. Navy's submarine rescue system at Oceaneering. He had researched the history of submarine accidents from the early 1900s to the Deep Submergence Rescue Vehicles of the modern era. Years earlier, Whitlock had studied a top secret CIA operation to recover a sunken Russian submarine—a story that may have inspired Tom Clancy's *The Hunt for Red October*. In 1968, the *K-129* sank more than 1,500 miles north of Hawaii. The United States spent millions of dollars to recover the Cold War artifact and any secrets of Russian naval warfare it might hold.

Under the cover story of a mining operation, teams sailed to the wreck site in a ship that had bay doors in the hull. From those doors, they lowered a cradle that would lift the submarine into the ship. It was like something out of a Dirk Pitt novel. The cradle part of the operation intrigued Whitlock. If engineers could put a vessel into a sling that approximated its position and attitude on the ocean floor, it could be raised without putting additional stress on the hull. The *K-129* expedition—which was code named Project Azorian—was not perfect, but Whitlock saw promise. He believed that, 30 years later, Oceaneering could improve upon the design. It was fitting, Whitlock thought: one submarine recovery inspiring another.

The idea appealed to Lasch immediately, and he asked Oceaneering to bid on the project. For several months, he heard nothing from

Whitlock and Lasch feared he wasn't interested. But Whitlock was busy developing a plan that would impress even the most conservative critics. When Lasch finally saw Whitlock's scheme, he became convinced Oceaneering was as close as he could get to a guaranteed recovery.

After meeting Whitlock and touring Oceaneering, Lasch felt more confident turning down the avalanche of recovery proposals that crossed his desk. Some of these suitors did not take it well. The man with the scoop crane filed suit in an attempt to force the project to hire him. Scientists had dismissed the proposal as foolhardy, pointing out that the submarine would collapse under its own weight as sand seeped out of the crane. But the man didn't want to hear criticism, he simply wanted the job.

The Friends of the *Hunley*, set to embark on its first fund-raising drive, suddenly needed additional money just to defend a frivolous lawsuit. And it would not be the last. For months, the legal wrangling slowed the project to a crawl. None of this was getting us to the finish line, Lasch complained. The *Hunley* was still out there, so close yet millions of dollars and years away.

It's not about the money, McConnell and Lasch liked to say, it's the money.

But as 1999 dawned, the two men most responsible for the *Hunley* did not have anywhere near enough of it to recover the submarine. In the final week of January, McConnell—with Schachte in tow—boarded a plane for Washington to rectify that problem. McConnell knew that no matter how successful a private fund-raising campaign was, he would need government financing to reach that $20 million goal. The best place to get it was from the federal government, which was as flush as it had been in a long time. Besides, McConnell thought, the federal government argued that it owned the *Hunley*. By that measure, it should help pay for the recovery.

For several days, McConnell and Schachte navigated the halls of power, meeting with the most influential members of South Carolina's congressional delegation. He outlined the plans for recovery, explaining what they would need to ensure the submarine's safe recovery. Most of the politicians proved eager to help. Sen. Strom Thurmond agreed to secure funding, as did Sen. Fritz Hollings. Congressman Floyd Spence promised to find money on the House side of the Capitol. By the time McConnell and Schachte flew home, they had assurances that the project could expect at least $3 million from federal coffers.

That would not be enough, McConnell knew, but it was a significant bite. And he could use those commitments to leverage a similar amount out of the state. McConnell could safely make the argument that such an investment would probably come back to the state in tourism revenue generated by the submarine. In retrospect, McConnell would realize that even his optimistic appraisals seriously underestimated just how much of an economic benefit the *Hunley* held for South Carolina. The project was gaining more momentum than anyone could have imagined.

As McConnell and Schachte made their way back to South Carolina, the senator was already plotting a way to speed up the timeline for recovery. When the money came in, it would be important to move quickly. The longer the *Hunley* waited, the more costs would rise. And the truth was that Senator McConnell was worried about the sub. It sat out there unguarded, its location no longer much of a secret. The thought of the *Hunley* being looted on his watch scared McConnell more than anything ever had.

Still, he could not help but be somewhat optimistic. The trip to Washington had been an unqualified success. Most people seemed enthusiastic about the project and the navy had even offered McConnell an additional gift: the *Intelligent Whale*. The submarine had been built in 1863, but Union red tape kept it moored until well after the Civil War. McConnell knew little about the sub, other than the fact that John Holland had some connection to it.

The *Intelligent Whale* would be a nice addition to the eventual *Hunley* exhibit, perhaps even make it more of an American story, as Lasch had envisioned. A submarine from both sides of the Civil War could only make the *Hunley* project more significant. At the same time, McConnell also had commitments from Bosch for a life-size model of the *Pioneer*, James McClintock and Horace Hunley's first submarine. Trainees for the company had built the model from Union sketches, and it was impressive—and life-size. McConnell could see the *Hunley* becoming a world class exhibit about the beginnings of submarine warfare. Perhaps it deserved its own museum.

Months earlier the *Hunley* Commission had tentatively decided the *Hunley* could be raised in the spring of 2001. But that was not soon enough for McConnell. He would deliver the good news from his Washington trip to the commission in hopes of convincing its members to reconsider the schedule. Things were moving along nicely, and he did not want to lose momentum. He wanted to get the submarine before the project hit any snags. But mostly, he didn't want those men to have to spend any more time in the ocean than necessary. They had waited long enough to come home.

The *Hunley* Commission did exactly as McConnell had hoped. Before the end of the year, the commission voted to raise the submarine in the summer of 2000. In some ways it was a great leap of faith. The money had not come in yet, but they were confident it would. The important thing was to accelerate the project and get the *Hunley* to Charleston before anything went wrong. As soon as the commission voted, the clock was ticking on the *Hunley*.

The trouble started almost immediately.

The first setback came within a month of the commission's vote. Charleston officials had approved a *Hunley* wing at the Charleston Museum, but that blessing had not come with any money to finance the estimated $5 million upgrade. McConnell and Lasch realized that it would take months to secure that kind of funding from city and county governments, and that put the entire timeline in jeopardy. There was simply no way to get the museum ready for the submarine, not if it was going to be delivered in the summer of 2000.

Museum officials were not to blame, but McConnell and Lasch knew that staging the sub's conservation downtown was now a lost cause. As spring arrived in the Lowcountry, the two men were scrambling to find a new location to house the submarine. This was not just a problem, it was a potential deal breaker—and they were running out of time. It would do no good to raise the *Hunley* if they had nowhere to put it.

Things had been going so well, but this problem threatened the entire project. Soon Lasch was back to struggling through sleepless nights again. After McConnell's success with the federal politicians, the whole project now might be derailed by local ones. The *Hunley* was due to surface in little more than a year. They not only needed an approved recovery plan and a place to put the *Hunley*—they needed a miracle.

And the clock was ticking.

Part Three

Hunley Rising

CHAPTER 14

1864
Sullivan's Island

The men crept onto the deck of the *Indian Chief* just after midnight.

A heavy fog had fallen on Charleston Harbor that evening, the mist so thick they had to make their way across the ship's cluttered deck from memory. The fog would be a problem later, but for now it served as welcome cover: the sailors on watch could not see them. E. C. Belton considered this a stroke of luck, because he and the four men following him were about to commit treason.

Once amidships, they climbed over the ship's rail and into Capt. James Henry Rochelle's gig, which was tied up alongside. Belton had joined the crew of the Confederate receiving ship in October—the same week Rochelle took command—and was assigned to the captain's personal launch. Nearly three months later he knew the little boat well and was certain it would work. The gig was just big enough to get him and his friends the hell out of Charleston. It was January 5, and Belton was deserting.

By 1864 it was apparent the South's prospects had dimmed considerably. The Confederates were losing men, losing the war, and conditions for the troops grew worse every day. The military scarcely had enough food to feed its soldiers. For some, it came down to a choice between dying in combat, starving to death or risking court-martial for deserting. Escape, many decided, offered the best odds.

In the first week of January alone, nearly a dozen men would desert Charleston's military operations. Belton had more reasons to abandon than most; he wasn't even Southern. The Michigan native had worked his way South in the years before the war, picking up jobs as a mechanic along the way. He'd found himself in Mobile when the fighting started and took work on a railroad running back and forth to Montgomery. Confederates officers found him on the train and basically drafted him. They gave him only one choice: army or navy. Belton calculated that life onboard a ship would be far better than conditions in the field, so he chose to become a sailor. Plus, he figured it would be easier to escape from a ship. After less than three months, Belton saw his chance.

The men accompanying him had as little allegiance to the South as he did: two were Irish, one was from the North, the other from Baltimore. All were serving more or less against their will. They only shared a desire to get as far away from the war, and the Confederacy, as possible. They would rather face a firing squad—the usual outcome of a court martial—than spend another night aboard the *Indian Chief*.

Belton and his comrades slowly paddled out of Town Creek, where the receiving ship was anchored, and into the expansive harbor. They were sailing blind—the men had no compass and could not see any land to get their bearing. Belton tried to navigate from memory but he didn't know Charleston Harbor nearly as well as the deck of the *Indian Chief*. In the mist, he steered the small boat up Shem Creek and into Mount Pleasant. By the time the men realized their mistake, it was nearly dawn.

They spent the day hiding in the marsh, the rain so heavy that no one ever saw them. When darkness finally came they rowed out of the creek, hugging the shore all the way to Sullivan's Island. Late that night, they slipped between Forts Moultrie and Sumter, avoided a picket boat, and reached the open sea. In the early hours of January 7, a Union ship picked them up.

Fort Moultrie, on the southern end of Sullivan's Island, is an important landmark in Civil War history. Shortly after South Carolina seceded, U.S. troops stationed there abandoned the fort, moving across the mouth of the harbor to the more defensible Fort Sumter. The Confederates took over the fort immediately, declaring the movement by U.S. troops the first act of war between the states. When it arrived in Charleston, the Hunley was moored behind Fort Moultrie. Later, as Lt. George Dixon and his crew were testing the sub near the harbor's mouth, the fort stood witness to an accident that nearly ended in the sub's destruction. Courtesy National Archives.

George Shipp deserted from the *Indian Chief* the day after Belton and his compatriots made their escape, but he had a far easier journey. Shipp cast off at 4 P.M. that afternoon, pretending that he was going about his normal business. He sailed to Fort Johnson, where he loitered for hours talking with the fort's guards. At 8 P.M. he told the men he was returning to the *Indian Chief*, but instead rowed out of the harbor and into the Atlantic. Soon, Union sailors intercepted him and took him aboard a blockader.

Belton and Shipp turned out to be useful informants for the U.S. Navy. The men talked freely—and at length—about all they had learned in Charleston. They described the gun complements of the city's three ironclads, revealed the location of several land batteries and mapped harbor obstructions for naval commanders. They detailed the horrid conditions of life in the Southern military. But mostly, the two men wanted to talk about the torpedo boats in Charleston Harbor, especially the one that could dive completely under the water.

Belton claimed he had been in Mobile when the submarine was built; Shipp watched the sub sink in October and saw it dragged ashore in November. Both men said the boat was made of iron, spoke of the "manholes" on her topsides, and gave inaccurate, conflicting reports of its dimensions. Both men repeated erroneous rumors about the number of times the underwater torpedo boat had sunk. Oddly enough, Belton and Shipp both called it the "American Diver." Shipp said that although Beauregard had ordered the project abandoned, he believed it might sail again.

"They launched her again in about a week, but nothing was done with her until lately, when they fitted her up again and sent her down to Mount Pleasant, where she is now," Shipp's report claimed.

Belton, an engineer, was most intrigued by the torpedo boat. He said that although the sub had gone down several times, it was "owing to those in her not understanding her." The officer taking notes from Belton's testimony added that the deserter believed the boat "can be worked perfectly safe by people who understand her." Belton appeared to have nearly as much faith in the *Hunley* as George Dixon.

Even though Belton and Shipp were wrong about several details and offered sometimes contradictory testimony, they knew enough to provide the Union Navy with solid intelligence regarding the South's top secret naval project. Belton would even use his engineering skills to build a model of the torpedo boat for Union officers. Adm. John A. Dahlgren took this all very seriously. He immediately put his fleet on high alert, vowing that they would not be caught off-guard again. They would never suffer a repeat of the embarrassment that followed the *David*'s attack on the *New Ironsides*.

"I have reliable information that the Rebels have two Torpedo Boats ready for service, which may be expected on the first night when the weather is suitable for their movement," Dahlgren wrote in his orders to the South Atlantic Blockading Squadron. "One of these is the *David* which attacked the *Ironsides* in October, the other is similar to it.

"There is also one of another kind, which is nearly submerged, and can be entirely so; it is intended to go under the bottoms of vessels and there operate.

"This is believed by my informant to be sure of well working, though from bad management it has hitherto met with accidents, and was lying off Mount Pleasant two nights since."

Dahlgren ordered all his tugs and picket boats to be on the lookout, and told the ironclad commanders to keep moving. He would no longer allow his blockaders to anchor

U.S. Navy Rear Adm. John A. Dahlgren, the commander of the South Atlantic Blockading Squadron, learned in January of 1864 that the Confederates had a boat capable of traveling underneath the water—which only supported the report of troops in New Orleans, which had recently discovered the scuttled Pioneer. *Dahlgren immediately put his fleet on alert and took precautions to prevent his ships from being destroyed. His orders would save more than 100 lives, but could not prevent the loss of one of his ships. Courtesy National Archives.*

in the deepest part of the channel because he did not want this torpedo boat to have room to sail beneath them. To some of his captains, it must have seemed that Dahlgren was over-reacting. But the admiral was simply not going to take any chances.

Dahlgren's caution would save more than 100 lives in the coming months. But three days after he issued his warning to the fleet, at least part of his intelligence was already outdated.

On January 10, George Dixon and William Alexander rowed a borrowed skiff to Sullivan's Island and greeted the sentries at Battery Marshall with orders from Beauregard's office. This, the general had decided, would be the *Hunley*'s new base of operations, and the letter Dixon carried informed the officers there that they had no say in the matter. Beauregard had spoken, and he asked the base commander to give Dixon whatever he needed.

Battery Marshall was the perfect location for the submarine. The sprawling earth and sand fort sat beachfront on the northern tip of Sullivan's Island, overlooking the treacherous inlet that separated Sullivan's from Long Island. It also had a perfect view of the northernmost ships in the South Atlantic Blockading Squadron. Several navy vessels were anchored just a few miles away, most watching for blockade runners trying to reach the safe confines of Charleston Harbor. One ship in particular caught Dixon's eye immediately: the USS *Wabash*. The ship he most wanted to sink was just offshore, within easy sight of the parapet. So close, yet so far away.

The former Breach Battery had been renamed Battery Marshall by Beauregard's office nearly two years earlier. The fort protected Charleston's northern flank from invasion and guarded Breach Inlet as well as the creek behind the island. The battery, with nearly a dozen guns, also provided some cover for blockade runners that attempted to elude the U.S. Navy by skirting the north beaches. It was a respectable complement to Fort Moultrie on the southern end of the island, but Battery Marshall had a mixed record of success.

Eight months earlier the fort's troops had watched helplessly as navy ships ran the *Stonewall Jackson* aground on Long Island, blasting the blockade runner to bits as it foundered in the breakers. Although Sullivan's Island was home to hundreds of Confederate troops, there was only so much a land fort with a modest complement of guns could do against a fleet of navy warships. Dixon believed the *Hunley*, armed with a single torpedo, could do more.

The battery's dock, where Dixon would moor the submarine, was within a couple of hundred yards of Breach Inlet. From there, the *Hunley* could slip into the water between the two islands and let the

Battery Marshall, the eventual home base of the Hunley, *had been set up to prevent an invasion of the island from the north and to provide covering fire for blockade runners attempting to reach the city. Most times the earthen fort could not fend off the attacks of the U.S. Navy, and blockade runners ended up wrecked on the beaches of Sullivan's and Long Island (the Isle of Palms today). Courtesy National Archives.*

ebb tide currents propel it into the ocean like a slingshot. Then it was simply a matter of traveling a few miles out to reach the fleet. This would shave several miles off the trip, finally making the *Hunley* a feasible attack weapon.

Dixon allowed himself a little optimism, probably because he desperately needed some good news. For nearly a month he had shown no more success with the submarine than his predecessors. Beauregard had been patient and even secured him another 30-day leave from Mobile, but the general expected action, sooner rather than later. Dixon was confident the sub would work; he just needed better conditions—and more time. The Twenty-first Alabama would expect him back soon and he knew the chances that Mobile commanders would approve another leave were slim. Moving the submarine to Sullivan's Island had certainly improved his circumstances, but nothing could stop the clock from ticking.

The troops at Battery Marshall welcomed the *Hunley* graciously, no doubt happy for the distraction. Over the course of the war, these men had seen many strange things but the fish-boat had to rank at the top of that list. From the moment the submarine docked at Battery Marshall, there was rarely a moment when there weren't a few men standing around to gawk at it. They were also eager to help with anything Dixon needed.

Suddenly, the *Hunley* had a shore crew.

By mid-January, the crew of the *Hunley* fell into a daily routine. They left their Mount Pleasant boardinghouse at 1 P.M., took a small boat they had requisitioned across the inlet to Sullivan's Island, and then walked along the beach to Battery Marshall. The route left them exposed to occasional enemy fire but it afforded them a clear view of the blockade, and the sand made for an easy walk. In all, it was a five-mile journey that limbered them up for long hours crammed inside the *Hunley*'s unforgiving crew compartment.

Every day Dixon's men took the sub out for two hours before the sun went down. They practiced diving, surfacing and various maneuvers in the deep creek behind Sullivan's Island. The boat responded well, performing just as James McClintock had envisioned. Before long they had logged more hours aboard the *Hunley* than any other crew. They were growing more confident each week, more comfortable with the fickle nature of the fish-boat. After a solid workout, Dixon allowed the men to rest while he and Alexander walked to the beach to scout potential targets.

"Dixon and I would then spread out on the beach with a compass between us and get the bearings of the nearest Federal vessel as she took her position for the night," Alexander recalled.

When night came, the men at Battery Marshall would help Dixon fasten a torpedo to the sub's spar—it was far too dangerous to leave the explosives in place when docked. Once that was finished, Dixon would lower the spar and order his men to load up. Their departure time depended on the tide. Some nights they left just after dark, other times closer to midnight. There was simply no way for the *Hunley* to escape the pull of Breach Inlet on an incoming tide, at least not without exhausting his crew before they cleared the breakers.

In smooth water the *Hunley* could make about four knots; in rough seas, Alexander recalled, it was much slower. They found that the dive fins and momentum had minimal effect on adjusting the submarine's depth. The only sure way to descend, or ascend, was by using the ballast tanks. Dixon and Alexander were learning more about the sub's performance every trip, but had little occasion to make use of this knowledge. During the winter of 1864 the weather scarcely cooperated. Most nights were long journeys of frustration, the blockade remaining just out of reach. But they kept trying.

Eventually, Dixon knew, everything would fall into place.

"Through January and February 1864 the wind held contrary making it difficult with our limited power to make much headway," Alexander later said. "During this time we went out an average of four nights a week, but on account of the weather and considering the physical condition of the men to propel the boat back again, often, after going out six or seven miles, we would have to return. This we always found a task, and many times it taxed our utmost exertion to keep from drifting out to sea, daylight often breaking while we were yet in range ... We often had all we could do to get back to shore."

Every trip offshore was a risk. Dixon had to time the *Hunley*'s trips to the tides and the limitations of his crew's endurance. And he soon discovered that he had to be even more careful than he already was. Confederate spies had alerted Beauregard to Dahlgren's recent orders for his fleet—anchor in shallow water, hang chains from the sides of all ships—and Dixon had to assume that somehow the Yankees had learned about the submarine. Alexander later claimed, in fact, that the move to Sullivan's Island was prompted by the fleet's pre-emptive orders. It became clear to Dixon that the *Hunley* could no longer simply sail into the middle of the blockade. They no longer had total surprise on their side. The sub would have to pick off ships on the outskirts of the blockade.

The Yankees' new precautions were worrisome, but they gave Dixon all the excuse he needed to ignore Beauregard's orders not to dive in the *Hunley*. Sailing underwater, he knew, was the only way to avoid detection from Union sailors on high alert. Most nights, the *Hunley* spent long hours beneath the waves, sailing blind, inching toward the blockade.

"We found that we had to come to the surface occasionally, slightly lifting the after hatchway, and letting in a little air," Alexander said. "Sometimes, when we rose for air, we could hear the men in the Federal picket boats talking and singing."

Throughout January, Dixon's preferred target remained the *Wabash*. It may have been the mercenary in him. Aside from the *New Ironsides*, the *Wabash* carried the highest bounty of any navy ship. The people of Charleston considered the frigate particularly trouble-some as it had intercepted several blockade runners trying to deliver supplies to the city. The *Wabash* may not have been the best ship in the South Atlantic Blockading Squadron, but it was one of the most successful—and rich Charleston businessmen had offered $100,000 to anyone who could sink it. Even after such a reward was split with the sub's owners, the crew would earn life-changing money. Dixon wouldn't turn down the cash but, in truth, he simply wanted to sink a ship—any ship. But if he had a choice, the *Wabash* was an attractive target.

Thus far, that had proved more difficult than he imagined.

Most mornings the crew returned to the dock at Battery Marshall exhausted, frustrated and facing a long walk back to the boarding-house. They would take the torpedo off the spar, arrange for some of the fort's men to guard the sub and then walk back to Mount Pleasant to cook breakfast before falling into fitful sleep. Within hours, they would be awake and ready to do it all over again.

The *Hunley* had been equipped with two snorkel tubes and an elaborate bellows system to draw air into the crew compartment. McClintock had believed this system would work fine, but Dixon and Alexander found it inadequate. The bellows never drew enough air and the snorkels were only a few feet long, which did not allow the *Hunley* to submerge deep enough to avoid detection, even in the murky water off Charleston. It was a design flaw that Dixon chose to simply work around. The crew rarely, if ever, raised the snorkels. They chose to simply surface and open the hatches for their fresh air.

The closer the *Hunley* got to the fleet, the more dangerous it was to surface. Dixon realized that if anyone spotted the submarine it neutralized their only advantage: surprise. Once they were far enough offshore, the *Hunley* needed to stay submerged as long as possible. But Dixon was not sure how much time he had—no one had ever calculated how long the air in the sub would last once the hatches were closed. And he needed to know. It was literally a matter of life and death.

Years later, Alexander said that he and Dixon had an unpleasant understanding. Neither of them wanted to endure the slow and agonizing death that came with suffocation. They agreed that if the sub ever became stuck underwater, or anything prevented them from surfacing, they would open the seacocks and flood the *Hunley*'s interior. It would be best for the crew, they decided. "If this were carried out their sufferings were soon ended," Alexander said. But Dixon had no intention of committing suicide. Not if he could help it.

One afternoon Dixon and Alexander agreed to test the crew's endurance, to see exactly how much time they had if they were trapped underwater. They went out for their regular training in the creek behind Battery Marshall that day, diving and resurfacing several times over the course of an hour. Some of the men from the fort stood along the banks to watch, as they often did. Finally Dixon checked the time on his pocket watch, ordered the ballast tanks opened and put the *Hunley* into a deep dive. Within a minute, the sub settled into the pluff mud on the creek's bottom.

The interior of the *Hunley* was silent. The eight men sat there staring at the white walls of the sub's interior, the scant light from Dixon's candle casting shadows on their faces. They had agreed beforehand that if anyone needed air, felt a shortness of breath, they could simply yell "up" and the experiment was over. The crew considered it a challenge, a test of their worthiness. Each of them had privately promised themselves that they would not be the first to break. None of them wanted to be the weakest.

After 25 minutes the candle went out. Dixon could not re-light it—there was not enough air left in the crew compartment to feed even a small fire. For weeks he had looked for a light that would illuminate the sub's dark interior without consuming too much air, but so far he had found nothing. The candle would have to do. He finally gave up trying to light the wick and relaxed as best he could on his small bench. The time passed in silence, broken occasionally by Dixon calling out to Alexander, "How is it?"

It was stifling, suffocating. They sat there for what felt like hours.

All of them had grown accustomed to the dark and cramped interior, but sitting there in total blackness was unnerving. Most likely their thoughts eventually turned to the men who had died in those very seats. No one said anything for a long time, however, conserving what little air they had. Finally, Alexander claimed, all eight men cried out "Up" in unison. And then they went to work, expelling the water from the ballast tanks, desperate to float the *Hunley* as quickly as possible.

"We started the pumps," Alexander recalled. "Dixon's worked all right, but I soon realized that mine was not throwing. From experience I guessed the cause of the failure, took off the cap of the pump, lifted the valve, and drew out some seaweed that had choked it."

Alexander had the benefit of experience, as well as an intimate knowledge of the sub's inner workings. Working blind, he was able to take the pump apart, find the problem and reassemble the fittings in little more than a minute. He moved quickly but, by the time he finished, the *Hunley*'s bow was rising much faster than the stern. It threw the men decidedly off balance.

"During the time it took to do this the boat was considerably by the stern," Alexander recalled. "Thick darkness prevailed. All hands had already endured what they thought was the utmost limit. Some of the crew almost lost control of themselves. It was a terrible few minutes, better imagined than described."

In fact, that day the men thought they would die aboard the *Hunley*.

Although it felt like much longer, it took only a few minutes for the sub to surface. Dixon and Alexander reached into the conning towers and rushed to throw open the hatches. Fresh air washed over the crew and, after sucking in oxygen hungrily for a moment, they noticed that in their absence the world had changed. Darkness had settled on the island and only a single soldier remained onshore. He stood vigil over the creek, watching the spot where the fish-boat had dived. Dixon quickly lit a match and checked his watch. They had been down for two hours and thirty-five minutes.

The man onshore did not see the submarine until Alexander called out to him, asking him to take the line and pull them to the dock. Soon the sub was secured and the crew slowly crawled out of the *Hunley*. The soldier told Dixon and Alexander that they had been given up for lost, that a messenger had already left for Charleston to inform General Beauregard that the fish-boat had gone to the bottom once again.

Dixon allowed his men to rest the following day while he and Alexander crossed the harbor to meet with Beauregard. They wanted to assure the general that the boat and crew were fine. Beauregard's staff was surprised to see them, but skeptical that the boat had remained underwater for nearly three hours. Dixon and Alexander offered Beauregard a demonstration, which he declined. It must have seemed that Dixon had cheated death, or at least knew what he was doing. This gave Beauregard even more confidence in the lieutenant, if not the submarine. He issued new orders for Dixon to attack the blockade at his discretion.

If only the weather would cooperate. For the rest of January the seas were rough and a heavy fog settled over the water nearly every night. Conditions were so bad that it was simply impossible for the *Hunley* to go out. The men grew restless and bored. Wicks took a week's leave to participate in a raid in his home state. The man leading the covert operation had invited him in part because of how well he knew the North Carolina terrain.

With little else to do, Dixon settled into the Mount Pleasant boardinghouse to plot and wait out the weather. On January 31, he and Alexander went into Charleston to ask the harbor pilots for an update on the weather. The pilots reported that these unfavorable conditions would probably hold for several weeks. It was not what they wanted to hear.

Dixon was frustrated, a black mood settling over him like the harbor fog. Beauregard's office had put in for another extension of his leave but they had not yet heard back from Mobile. He was running out of time. That afternoon, he wrote to his friend Henry Willey in Mobile. Dixon had sent Willey a letter several weeks earlier and had not received a reply, but he needed to vent his frustrations. In the letter, Dixon came off as alternately defensive and pitiful, defiant and resolved. He was a man nursing serious internal conflicts.

"I suppose that you think strange that I have not done any thing here yet, but if I could tell you all of the circumstances that have occurred since I came here you would not think strange of my not having done any execution yet," Dixon wrote. "But there is one thing very evident and that is to catch the Atlantic Ocean smooth during the winter months is considerable of an undertaking and one that I never wish to undertake again. Especially when all parties interested at sitting at home and wondering and criticizing all of my actions and saying why don't he do something. If I have not done anything 'God Knows' it is not because I have not worked hard enough to do some thing. And I shall keep trying until I do some thing."

Dixon spent much of his letter grousing about his circumstances in Charleston: the poor quality of the food, the shelling of Sumter that rattled the windows in his boardinghouse so badly "you would imagine that they would break." He conceded the Union fleet knew he was coming, "and of course they have taken all precautions that is possible for Yankee ingenuity to invent."

But Dixon was resolute and, despite all these problems, he remained confident. He was pleased with his crew, he told Willey, and the government had been kind to him. Eventually, Dixon wrote, he was certain the night would come when he would surprise the Yankees completely.

"I hope to Flank them yet."

The weather remained poor through the first week of February, as the harbor pilots had predicted, and the *Hunley* sat untouched at the Battery Marshall dock. The Mobile command granted Dixon another leave, but the officers of the Twenty-first Alabama would not allow William Alexander to remain in Charleston another day. They claimed he was needed to build some new guns for the city's defenses—there was a definite shortage of engineers in Alabama. Perhaps the Mobile commanders knew they could not fight Beauregard over Dixon, but wanted some small victory to soothe their damaged egos.

Dixon and Alexander took the news hard. They were not only friends but partners in this submarine project, and Alexander may have understood the boat even better than Dixon. After all, he had supervised its construction. Alexander could not bear to face the crew with this news and would leave town without saying goodbye. He took his leave of Dixon at the train station that evening and settled in for the long ride across the Southern countryside. The two men would never see each other again.

Alexander's departure left Dixon with an even deeper malaise. He was alone, felt the odds were stacked against him and had to wonder if the damned weather would ever let up. That same night he wrote another letter—his second in a week—to his commander in the Twenty-first Alabama. In the note, he assured Capt. John Cothran that he would return to Mobile eventually, but first he had work to finish in Charleston. It seemed he was trying to convince himself more than Cothran.

"You stated my presence was very much needed on your little island. I have no doubt it is, but when I will get there is far more than I am able to tell at present, for beyond a doubt I am fastened to Charleston and its approaches until I am able to blow up some of the Yankee ships," Dixon wrote.

Dixon said that he doubted General Maury could convince Beauregard to send him back, that this project had come too far to give up now. Although he said "a more uncomfortable place could not be found in the Confederacy," he was committed to Charleston. In truth, Dixon was only committed to the *Hunley*.

"I do not want you and all the company to think that because

I am absent from them that mine is any pleasant duty or that I am absent from them because I believe there is any post of honor or fame where there is any danger, I think it must be at Charleston.

"Charleston and its defenders will occupy the most conspicuous place in the history of the war, and it shall be as much glory as I shall wish if I can inscribe myself as one of its defenders," Dixon wrote.

The next day, Dixon resolved to get back to work. With Beauregard's blessing, he recruited a replacement for Alexander from the German artillery. J. F. Carlsen was exactly the sort of man he needed. Carlsen had served aboard the fearsome privateer, the *Jefferson Davis*, and fought in the battle of Port Royal. There, he had proven himself fearless—charging into enemy fire to replant his company's flag. He will work, Dixon thought.

Dixon appointed Carlsen to a seat in the middle of the submarine and made Ridgaway his new first officer. The Marylander had proven his mettle, and Dixon was certain he would be an able replacement, at least as good as he had on this crew. In truth, there was no replacing Alexander.

With Wicks returned from North Carolina, Dixon had a full crew and a submarine in perfect working order. All he had to do was wait out the bad weather. As he sat on the boardinghouse porch overlooking Charleston Harbor, perhaps he even reached for the comforting, heavy weight of the gold coin in his left pocket. It had saved him before, and he could use its luck again now with the weather. Everything else was in place. The crew was ready. The *Hunley* was ready.

Dixon was ready.

CHAPTER 15

1999–2000 North Charleston

Warren Lasch reached for the gold coin.

He found it quickly, exactly where it had been a moment before, and relaxed. It was not easy to find a Civil War–era $20 gold piece in 1999—there had been several frantic calls to antique coin dealers—and Lasch had worried about losing it ever since. The *Hunley* was about to make its national debut, and Lasch was ready. So long as he had the coin.

On George Street, it was 1864 all over again. People in period dress lined the sidewalks outside the Sottile Theatre, reenactors guarded the entrance and a woman in a hoopskirt played "Dixie" on the violin. This spectacle was atypical even for Charleston, a town that stood on ceremony. And this was certainly an occasion that called for some ceremony. In an hour, about 600 guests would crowd into the theater to see the world premiere of the Turner Network Television movie about a long-lost Confederate submarine.

The movie would launch the *Hunley* on a national stage, and Lasch intended to get as much mileage out of it as possible. Now, he thought, everyone would know the story of the sub. And hopefully they would all want to help pay for its recovery. All he needed was the media to take an interest, and that was all but assured the moment a horse-drawn carriage pulled up in front of the Sottile carrying Ted Turner and Jane Fonda.

"I thought it was just a great story—a very sad story obviously—but about the courage of the crews and everything and I thought 'Gee I'd love to see a movie about the *Hunley*,'" Turner told the Associated Press.

The ever-quotable Turner did not disappoint on this night, and the reporters lapped up every word. Between the appearance of the media mogul, his famous wife and Armand Assante—who starred as George Dixon—Lasch hoped this would create the buzz the *Hunley* needed. But he would leave nothing to chance and wanted to ensure all the attention landed where he needed it—on his fund-raising campaign. So he came up with a plan to draw attention to the charity.

Armand Assante starred as Lt. George Dixon in the TNT movie The Hunley, *and the actor attended the film's premiere in Charleston. Friends of the* Hunley *Chairman Warren Lasch, right, considered the film the sub's coming out party and a chance to raise awareness—and money—for the* Hunley's *recovery. U.S. Navy Rear Adm. (retired) Bill Schachte is at the far left in this photograph. Courtesy Warren Lasch.*

Turner had already agreed to serve as an honorary board member on Friends of the *Hunley*, so Lasch decided to show his thanks by giving him a gold coin just like Dixon had carried. Lasch bought the coin—it wouldn't be appropriate for the charity to buy it, he'd thought—and would present it to him in a ceremony just before the premiere. It was a gesture—an expensive gesture—of appreciation from the Friends. Turner accepted the gift good-naturedly, but proved to be his usual cranky self. He could not resist a wisecrack.

"Gold ain't what it used to be, but it's better than a kick in the butt," he said.

It was not exactly the reaction Lasch expected, but he was pleased with the way the evening had turned out. The crowd loved the movie, Glenn McConnell's scene with Donald Sutherland remained in the final cut, and as the party moved downtown to Hibernian Hall, Lasch and Schachte mingled with Assante. For a moment, Lasch and McConnell could forget the pressures weighing on them, the pending recovery proposal due from Oceaneering, and their desperate quest to raise the money needed to bring the *Hunley* home.

The gold coin Lasch had given Turner only reminded McConnell of the dangerous game they were playing. Priceless treasures— possibly even Dixon's coin—were sitting unguarded just a few miles away. State archaeologist Jonathan Leader had warned Lasch and McConnell that the longer the *Hunley* sat unprotected, the more they had to worry about the threat of looters. McConnell had hinted to reporters that the sub was now covered by a steel cage, but that was simply a ruse—much like Cussler's fib about the water's depth at the wreck site. Once again, the only protection for the sub was subterfuge.

In truth, there was only a single camera atop the Sullivan's Island Lighthouse that monitored the *Hunley* wreck site. But unless the coast guard was monitoring the feed at exactly the right moment, the sub could be looted, cut up and sold in pieces on the black market without anyone knowing. The *Hunley* was a sitting duck, and thanks to Turner's movie it was about to get a lot more famous. The thought sent chills through both Lasch and McConnell. But on this evening, they would try to ignore those fears.

It was June 14, 1999—one of the last relaxing evenings Lasch or McConnell would have for more than a year.

In the four years following NUMA's discovery of the *Hunley*, the efforts to raise and recover the sub had plodded along at a politician's pace. There had been one delay after another as McConnell and Lasch worked to find the engineering plan, staff and the money they needed to pull off one of the most complicated archaeological recoveries in history. Although they did not realize it at the time, the summer of 1999 marked a turning point. The project was hurtling toward the finish line faster than either one of them expected.

For most of the next year, the *Hunley* would not be out of the news. There would be another development every week, often followed by another problem. The *Hunley* was becoming a bigger phenomenon than either McConnell or Lasch could have guessed, and they would struggle to put out constant fires and keep the sub on course for a recovery date that was suddenly just around the corner.

It all started with the movie premiere.

Two weeks after Randy Burbage watched the cinematic demise of the *Hunley*'s final crew, he found himself staring at the bones of its first. Buried beneath the floor of the Booster Club lounge in Johnson Hagood Stadium, Burbage uncovered the grave of a sailor he was certain had died aboard the sub in August 1863. The scientists would not immediately confirm the identity of the remains, but Burbage knew he was right. The hacksaw marks on the man's bones were a dead giveaway.

The South Carolina Institute of Archaeology and Anthropology began its search for the *Hunley*'s first crew in the third week of June 1999. The scientists had been granted permission to tear up the stadium's floor in advance of a planned renovation, and Jonathan Leader estimated there were as many as a dozen Confederate graves beneath the lounge. Using a team of volunteers, scientists and members of Burbage's Sons of Confederate Veterans camp, they busted through the concrete and spent nearly a week sifting through the soft earth below, every day finding more evidence of forgotten graves.

Finally, on June 26, they found a man whose arms and legs had been cut off and carefully reassembled in a coffin.

There was little doubt, even among the scientists, that they had found the sub's lost crew. When the *Hunley* sank off Fort Johnson in 1863, divers took nearly a week to recover it. In that time, saltwater bloated the men's bodies to twice their normal size. Workers had to cut the men into pieces just to get them through the sub's narrow hatches. Records indicated the dismembered bodies had to be buried in oversized coffins.

"You have the head around the chest bone and the knees up around the head," Leader told reporters. "What it shows to us is a pattern of dismemberment."

For Burbage, this marked the end of a 16-year quest. He had first learned of the Seaman's Burial Ground in 1983, found the first of those lost graves a decade later, but had never been able to locate the men who perished in the *Hunley*'s first accident. It had become his life's work, literally. He had grown up studying Southern history, spent years coordinating local reenactments. Staring into the ground at a man whose history he knew so well, Burbage was overcome with emotion. Burbage and his SCV members formed a circle around the grave and quietly sang "Dixie" as the scientists carefully uncovered more of the mangled bones.

The next day, scientists would find a second crewman buried beneath the first. Over the course of several weeks, they found more than two dozen graves—including four of the five men who died aboard the sub. Their remains told a sad story: most of the *Hunley* crewmen were around 20, but one may have been as young as 13. In one of the graves, a left arm was found lying across the body's ribcage. Leader said the men had been buried in a hurry, stacked atop one another, most likely to prevent spies from learning the actual cause of the men's deaths.

The fifth man who died aboard the *Hunley* was found months later beneath the stadium parking lot. For years, the fifth sailor to go down with the submarine had remained lost to history. When Burbage finally found the name, it suggested another dimension to an already complicated story. Absolum Williams was most likely black and, no matter how he died, in 1863 he would not have been buried alongside his shipmates in the Seaman's Burial Ground. He had been laid to rest in a different part of the long-forgotten cemetery.

Burbage would not allow that to happen again. Soon, Absolum Williams would be buried with his crewmates—where he belonged.

There was never any doubt the first crew of the *Hunley* would be buried in Magnolia Cemetery alongside Horace Hunley and its second crew. Randy Burbage would make all the arrangements, and it would keep the submarine in the news in the months before the recovery. McConnell and Lasch were grateful Burbage handled the funeral, for at the moment they had a bigger problem: where to put the *Hunley* once they had it.

McConnell and Lasch had spent nearly six months trying to find a home for the *Hunley*. When the city and county refused to pay for an addition to the Charleston Museum, it nearly derailed the entire project. Lasch and McConnell knew they'd be lucky to raise the money to recover the sub; building a laboratory to house it was beyond their fund-raising ability. It would take years, and the *Hunley* did not have that kind of time. They needed a Plan B.

Lasch had a process for solving his most difficult business problems, and it always served him well. He would go to bed with a dilemma on his mind and in the morning a solution would just come to him. It was as if his mind sorted through all the options while he slept, spitting out an answer when he woke. He didn't dare question this unorthodox process; he only knew that it worked.

This time he did not even need an entire night. Early in the summer of 1999, Lasch awoke in the middle of the night with the answer. It was so simple, so apparent, that Lasch could not believe he hadn't thought of it before: Building 255. The idea gave him chills.

He had found the building on the old Charleston Naval Base years earlier while scouting locations for BMW. The building was cavernous, nearly a shell, and brand new. It had been built to house ship parts just before the federal government shut down the base, so its floor was rated to hold 80 tons. It was close to the docks, and practically a fortress. It was perfect.

Lasch had suggested Building 255 to the TNT producers in 1998, and the film crew eventually used it to house sets for some interior shots. Since then, the building had sat dormant. Lasch realized it offered just about everything the project needed. McConnell loved the idea. The base was controlled by the state Redevelopment Authority (RDA), with a lot of influence from North Charleston's city government—and the senator had strong ties to both. As soon as Lasch suggested the building, McConnell reported to the *Hunley* Commission that he had begun talks with the RDA and North Charleston. He was certain they could get permission to use the building.

The only question was: could they get the building ready for the *Hunley* in time.

~

So many details.

The *Hunley* consumed most of Lasch's summer. With recommendations from Neyland, he began to put together a list of all the equipment needed to convert Building 255 into a state-of-the-art laboratory capable of housing a nineteenth-century artifact. Now he had to find a staff to do the actual work. Neyland knew plenty of scientists and offered a list of people to interview, but it wasn't that simple. Leader clashed with him on some of the selections. Neyland, in the state archaeologist's view, was too focused on personnel from his alma mater, Texas A&M. The fights grew vicious, and Lasch had to play referee far too often.

Lasch and McConnell would make the final hires. Eventually they chose a Danish archaeologist with ties to Texas A&M as their chief archaeologist. Maria Jacobsen had worked with Neyland on several projects and had excavated some of the world's oldest shipwrecks. Her no-nonsense style and experience appealed to Lasch immediately. But Lasch would not go along with Neyland's suggestion for a lead conservator. He sided with Leader, hiring a Frenchman named Paul Mardikian. Lasch believed Mardikian had more fire, more passion for the project, and his resume was extensive—he had conserved other Civil War–era objects as well as the first artifacts recovered from the *Titanic*. Lasch believed the *Hunley* project would benefit from the comparison. Hiring Mardikian brought expertise and that Lasch "sizzle" to the project.

They would start with a small team. Jacobsen hired a few other archaeologists to help with the excavation, including Harry Pecorelli—the NUMA diver who had first touched the sub on the 1995 expedition. Mardikian would begin his work alone, but within years he would need an even larger staff than Jacobsen. No one could have guessed what they would find inside the *Hunley*.

Jacobsen and Mardikian were aboard in time to see the first animation video from Oceaneering. The short video illustrated just how the company intended to raise the *Hunley* from the ocean floor. Lasch would agree with scientists from around the world that Leonard Whitlock had devised an ingenious, nearly flawless plan. Whitlock had followed the directive of Lasch and McConnell literally—failure was not an option—and come up with a blueprint for recovery that put all other proposals to shame. Although it was a complicated operation, Oceaneering had recently bought animation equipment that illustrated the idea so simply that even the engineering-challenged could understand it.

First, two 18-foot-wide hollow suction piles would be planted in the ocean floor at either end of the submarine. These huge steel barrels would be set down in the sand and the water pumped out of them.

As the water was sucked out, the piles would sink into the muck, providing a sturdy and stable foundation. A 55-foot truss that looked like the superstructure of a highway bridge would then be set over the submarine, its ends supported by the piles. It looked very much like the cage McConnell had told reporters already protected the *Hunley*.

Then the sub would be harnessed to the truss with a series of straps, each about a foot wide. Divers would bolt a strap to one side of the truss and then burrow under the hull, lapping the heavy canvas strap beneath it and then securing it to the other side of the steel cage. This allowed workers to capture and support the sub while only excavating a small amount of sand from beneath it at any time. Whitlock did not know how fragile the *Hunley* might be and would not take the chance of leaving it unsupported for even a minute.

The *Hunley* was listing to starboard at a 45-degree angle, and no one wanted to risk turning it. This might put undue stress on the hull or shift the location of artifacts inside it. And Whitlock knew the location of artifacts told scientists nearly as much as the objects themselves. To keep the sub in exactly the same position it had sat for more than a century, he designed bags that would be attached to one side of each strap. Divers would inject these bags with a polyurethane substance that came out of the can like shaving cream, but hardened in less than a minute. The foam, developed by a subsidiary of Dow Chemical, would set up underwater and, inside the bag, conform to the shape of the sub's hull. The idea was to cushion the *Hunley* and hold it firmly in place.

Once all the straps were slung, the entire truss would be lifted out of the water by a simple crane—a process that would take barely more than a minute. The sub could be placed on a barge and towed into Charleston Harbor, its truss welded to the deck for stability. The animation made it look all too easy.

Once the *Hunley* Commission members saw the Oceaneering video, they abandoned plans to raise the *Hunley* in the spring of 2001, which had come up as a fallback deadline. They hired Oceaneering immediately and set the lift date for July 17, 2000—barely six months away. They had pushed the "Go" button. Lasch was excited—this is what he had wanted—but for the next several months he harbored a nagging fear. Animated video was one thing; a flawless operation was another. Lasch knew everything had to go perfectly. There could not be one slip.

The navy and the state agreed to lease Building 255 to the Friends of the *Hunley* for $1. This solved several problems, but the building needed to be outfitted within six months to be ready when the *Hunley* arrived. That task fell to Lasch. For most of the winter of 2000, Lasch was at the building once or twice a week, supervising construction of the laboratory. The equipment his scientists needed was expensive, so Lasch solicited donations. Several companies surprised him by simply giving him equipment. Fuji even sent an X-ray and imaging machine.

The lab needed a tank large enough to hold the submarine and its lift truss. The sub would be kept under cold water most of the time to slow down corrosion, so the tank needed intricate plumbing that allowed water to be pumped in and out regularly, and piping strong enough to hold the caustic chemicals that would eventually be used to preserve the iron hull. The tank Lasch had built looked like a shipping container or a train car, and was just about as big.

The construction project was a huge drain of time, and deadlines were routinely missed. The lab had to have two cranes powerful enough to lift the sub and its truss—and those had to be installed or the *Hunley* couldn't be lifted into the tank. But that winter one of the construction crews had fallen woefully behind. The contractor blamed a steel shortage and said he could not get beams strong enough to support such heavy-duty cranes. Lasch pressed, but the man would not budge. Finally, Lasch played his hole card.

"Tell me how to spell your name," he told the contractor.

When the man asked why, Lasch said "Because when the *Post and Courier* asks why the project has been delayed, I'm going to tell them it's your fault."

The steel was delivered the next week.

Lasch wanted the conservation center finished by April to give the scientists a month to test all the equipment and ensure the lab was ready for the *Hunley*'s arrival. He would not scramble to find equipment, or call in the contractors, after the submarine was already in the building. He had enough problems. Already his scientists were giving him a hard time over the public relations firm the Friends had hired.

The scientists preferred to work in relative peace. They did not want to work under the glare of a media spotlight, forced to make instant analysis on a daily basis. But Lasch knew that was not only bad for publicity, it was wrong for any project that took government money. The team complained, but Lasch refused to budge—they would tell everything they knew, he said, within reason. At one point, Neyland became frustrated by the divide and asked McConnell exactly who he reported to: the senator or Lasch.

"Whatever Warren says goes," McConnell told him.

The scientists feared their work would be compromised by the constant interruptions the media team wanted. This whole operation was turning into a circus, they believed, and finally the scientists complained in writing. Lasch responded with an even harsher note, letting the scientists know who was in charge and what they could do if they didn't like it. "I do not react well to insubordination," Lasch wrote. "I do not react well to threats."

Basically, get with the program—or resign.

In truth, the scientists had little room to gripe. Throughout the spring, Lasch continued his weekly visits to the navy base, and soon Building 255 began to look like a real working laboratory. By the time the submarine arrived, the conservation center would be one of the most advanced underwater archaeology facilities in the country. Lasch didn't have to bow to any threats from staff—any scientist worth his degree would kill to work on the project.

On March 25, 2000, Randy Burbage dressed in his Richmond grays and led a solemn procession through the streets of Charleston. Starting at The Battery on that Saturday morning, hundreds of reenactors set out on a five-mile march to bury the first crew of the *H. L. Hunley*. Each of the caskets was draped in a Second National Flag of the Confederacy and pulled by its own horse-drawn caisson.

The procession moved slowly up East Bay Street toward Magnolia Cemetery, where the five men who died in the submarine's first sinking would be laid to rest beside Horace Hunley and the second crew to perish in the peripatetic coffin. The route was lined with men and women in period costumes, as well as a healthy number of tourists. In all, more than 2,500 attended the funeral—a small taste of the tourism boon Charleston could expect from *Hunley* traffic. Burbage considered this ceremony a dress rehearsal for the funeral that would come in a few years, when George Dixon and the *Hunley*'s final crew would be laid to rest in the same plot.

The delicate operation to bring Dixon and his crew home for that funeral began less than two months later.

In May, divers returned to the *Hunley* wreck site for the first time since 1996. Neyland brought in Harry Pecorelli and several National Park Service divers to prepare the site for Oceaneering's intricate recovery plan. Ralph Wilbanks—who was in France, searching the waters off Normandy Beach for World War II artifacts—planned to join them later in the summer. Most of the men and women involved had dived on the *Hunley* site during the assessment survey four years earlier. This suited Lasch just fine. He didn't want newbies coming onboard; too much was at stake.

The divers were relieved to find the site had not been disturbed; the sub was intact. Despite all the warnings, it appeared no vandals had stumbled onto the site. It was an often overlooked stroke of luck. The *Hunley* was in the exact same shape as they'd left it, still buried under five feet of sand. And all of that had to be cleared away before the recovery could begin. It would be tedious work.

Using vacuum hoses, they cleared an area 40 feet wide and 130 feet long—eventually moving about 20,000 cubic feet of sand. As they worked, the hull of the submarine slowly came into view. For the first time scientists could see exactly how sleek, how elegant the lines of McClintock's submarine actually were. The submarine looked so advanced, so hydrodynamic, that Pecorelli had to question the old accounts that claimed the *Hunley* had been built from a converted boiler. He thought the sub was straight out of Jules Verne's *20,000 Leagues Under the Sea.*

The plan called for setting the suction piles at either end of the submarine to serve as a platform for the lift truss. But before the piles could be sunk into the seabed, divers had to determine if the submarine's spar was still attached. The truss design did not take the spar into account, and Whitlock worried that setting the piles too close to the bow might chop it off—if the sub's torpedo delivery system was even still attached. The trouble was no one knew exactly where the spar was mounted. The earlier expeditions had not excavated the bow, and no one knew exactly what they might find.

The *Hunley*'s method of attack was one of its greatest mysteries. Historians weren't sure whether the sub's armament was a contact mine or triggered by a lanyard. There were even conflicting accounts of where it was mounted. Most believed the spar had sat atop the bow, in part because Conrad Wise Chapman's painting showed a wooden bowsprit of some kind lashed there. But if the spar had been made of wood, the scientists knew there was a good chance it had rotted away years before.

The engineers on the TNT movie had guessed the spar was mounted at the bottom of the bow. This was necessary, they explained, for the crew to have any leverage to adjust its angle—and historical accounts suggested Dixon could change the spar's position. The scientists were skeptical of this explanation, however, and assumed that if the spar existed they would find it atop the *Hunley*'s bow. But when the sand was removed, all they found was a hole that had probably held the sub's bowline.

The bow was a surprise in itself. The sub tapered forward until it was barely an inch wide but divers found that it had no straight edge. Instead, the nose of the sub curved inward from the top like an icebreaker ship. What was the purpose of this flourish? The bow swooped back out at its bottom until it was even with the top. And there, at the lower tip of the bow, divers found the base of a metal pole attached to a yoke.

It was the spar.

The spar extended away from the submarine for 17 feet. The first two feet were solid, but the rest was hollow—most likely to make the pole lighter. It took days to dig the metal spar out of the muck, the trench collapsing nearly as fast as divers could dig. Once they reached the end, Neyland realized it was far too long to be recovered with the submarine.

The suction piles had to be set close enough together for the lift truss to rest on them, and Oceaneering had not taken into account nearly 20 additional feet of submarine. It was a flaw in the 1996 survey, not Whitlock's plan. No one had considered the idea that the sub's weapon system was intact—and none of the plans included options for saving it. Even if the lift truss would accommodate the spar, it wouldn't fit into the 55-foot tank back at the conservation center. There was no choice. It had to be removed.

This created an ethical dilemma for the archaeologists. The first rule of excavation was to do no harm. Cutting off the spar would destroy a piece of history and could compromise the study of the submarine. Lasch noted that, if nothing else, it would be a public relations disaster. They had come too far to adjust the recovery plan, however. The spar had to go.

Some of the scientists suggested simply cutting the spar off, but Mardikian offered a better solution: "Just unbolt it." Divers had found that the yoke was mounted to the *Hunley* with a single bolt and, after some measuring, decided it required a six-point, two-inch wrench. This was not exactly standard issue in modern toolkits. Scientists searched local hardware stores, and Oceaneering even tried to make a wrench, but nothing worked. Finally, one of Lasch's employees at Charleston International Ports offered the team a deep-well socket that fit perfectly.

On Sunday, June 4, they put the socket on the nut and it spun off on its thread. That nut became the first piece of the *Hunley* recovered.

The bolt itself proved more difficult. The divers tried to knock the bolt out using a hammer and a brass punch, but it wouldn't budge. Neyland finally concluded it must have bent on impact with the *Housatonic* (they would later learn the entire spar was slightly warped from the collision). If the bolt was bent, the divers could not wiggle it out of the hole. They believed it had to be cut, although Mardikian later said he could have saved it. Regardless, when the bolt was cut, the spar came free of the sub.

Once the spar was detached from the *Hunley*, scientists lowered an I-beam to hoist it out of the water. But when divers tried to move the spar into its makeshift lift truss, it broke in two pieces—one 13 feet long, the other four feet. The hollow iron pole had rusted more heavily than the rest of the submarine. In one spot the spar had deteriorated to the point that there was only a sliver of metal holding the two pieces together, and it could not withstand the trauma of being moved.

After all the planning, all the trouble they had gone through to make sure they did minimal damage to the submarine, this bit of bad luck terrified Neyland and Jacobsen. They feared the wrath of Lasch and the media, believed they would be blamed for damaging a unique piece of American history. It was the sort of thing that gave scientists nightmares. They knew the story of the *Cairo* all too well.

The scientists wanted to keep the spar under wraps, literally, and away from reporters after they delivered it to Building 255. But Lasch knew the spar recovery was big news—just the sort of story he needed to boost the Friends' fund-raising efforts. It was, to date, the biggest *Hunley* news of the year. He would not let them hide the first piece of the sub to reach the lab.

Lasch scheduled a press conference to show off the catch, but

Jacobsen would not cooperate. When reporters and TV crews showed up, they found themselves waiting in the brutal Lowcountry sun on the outside of a locked laboratory door. Jacobsen wouldn't let them in. She was insistent that no one could see the broken spar. Eventually, someone had to call Lasch.

Lasch had decided to skip the media circus and was at his office on South Adgers in downtown Charleston—a townhouse that was just steps away from the remnants of the dock where Horace Hunley had last sailed his sub. When Lasch heard that Jacobsen had the press corps stuck out in the heat, he was livid. The archaeologist was threatening to turn their best story of the year into the worst. He called his archaeologist on her cell phone.

"Maria, if you don't open that door right now, you're fired," Lasch said. "Do you understand?"

She argued for a moment, but could not withstand the wrath of Lasch—"The Lascher," as McConnell had taken to calling him. He berated his archaeologist for several minutes, explaining the necessity of publicity to the project, and outlining her role in getting that news coverage. When he asked a second time if she understood what he had said, Jacobsen meekly responded with a short "Yes."

"Let me hear you say it," Lasch said. He wasn't playing. Jacobsen repeated his orders, and then opened the door.

Despite their time in the heat, reporters were excited to see an actual piece of the *Hunley*, and it would show in their stories. Neyland had the damage to the spar wrapped in protective cloth and explained that the spar was in two pieces, conveniently ignoring the fact that it had been found still in one—albeit fragile—piece. Few reporters paid any attention to that detail; they devoted most of their copy to McConnell's enthusiastic reaction.

"It sends chills up you to touch part of the *Hunley*," the senator said. "It's phenomenal we found it, much less to get it back in this shape. This is a historic moment. It's been 136 years since this touched South Carolina soil."

The journalists provided Lasch with his publicity, and none of them questioned the condition of the spar. The news made national headlines, the stories overwhelmingly positive. If an iron pipe commanded this much publicity, Lasch thought, the recovery of an entire Civil War–era submarine could be one of the biggest news events of the year. It seemed the project was blessed, but Lasch feared it was too good to be true.

And it was.

There was a 3 percent chance the *Hunley* could be crushed during recovery.

Warren Lasch did not take this news well. The scientists and engineers had tried to explain it in their own versions of techno-speak, but the Friends of the *Hunley* chairman was not comforted by statistics and probability. Three percent was three percentage points too many. There could be no chance of failure. But despite the team's best effort, there was still a small chance something could go wrong. And worst of all, no one told him until one month before the scheduled recovery day.

Detyens Shipyard had donated a floating crane to lift the submarine, a gesture that would save the project hundreds of thousands of dollars. The trouble, engineers pointed out, was that the crane was mounted on a barge that floated at the mercy of the Atlantic waves. Depending on conditions, the barge might dip and rise as much as six feet in a matter of seconds. But the crane could only lift the submarine 14 feet in one minute—less than one foot per second.

It all came down to math. If the crane began to lift the sub while it was at the crest of a six-foot swell, for instance, the *Hunley* might only be three feet above the ocean floor by the time the barge slipped into a trough between waves. The sub would then drop those six feet, or more, slamming it into the ocean with the same force as if it had been dropped on the ground from a height of ten feet.

If that happened, the *Hunley* would crack open like an egg, dumping its contents into the unforgiving sea and breaking into a dozen pieces. The mental image of that scene gave Lasch nightmares. It was a disaster that, until moments before, had been unthinkable. Remember the *Cairo*, Lasch thought.

Leonard Whitlock delivered this unfortunate scenario with a bit of trepidation. In April, he had quit Oceaneering to work directly for Friends of the *Hunley*. Whitlock had worried that he might be reassigned to some other project, and seeing the submarine safely home meant more to him than any job. Now he was in a position to answer directly to Lasch, to serve as an intermediary between the Friends and Oceaneering. And his concern over the floating crane barge convinced Lasch that hiring Whitlock had been a good investment. He asked the engineer if the tides could be taken into account. Whitlock assured him they could, but still there was no guarantee.

"What are the chances this happens?" Lasch asked.

"Three percent," Whitlock repeated.

"That's not good enough."

And that was the final word. They were going to need a bigger barge.

Lasch, Neyland and Whitlock scrambled to find a new crane barge while dive crews continued their work on site, although they could do little until the suction piles and lift truss were delivered. One company in New Jersey claimed to have a barge that would do the job, but it was only a slightly larger version of the Detyens crane. Lasch passed. He eventually talked to a woman in Louisiana, but the Cajun would not budge off her price. At least that's what Lasch thought he heard; her accent complicated negotiations.

There were several barges out there, but none of them appreciably better than the one Detyens had provided for free. There was only one way to take the tides out of the equation, and that was to use a stationary crane. Whitlock explained the vessel they needed. A jack-up crane had legs that could be deployed to the ocean floor. Once the legs were set, the barge could hoist itself up on the legs, rising above the water like an oil platform. It was the only way to be sure.

But such a vessel did not come cheap, and they were not easy to find.

Somehow Whitlock found one within a week. Titan Maritime Industries, a Fort Lauderdale company, owned a huge barge called the *Karlissa* that they had just cut in two. The halves now worked separately. The *Karlissa B* got the barge's crane in the split, and it was strong enough to lift a 33-ton submarine. A quick check with the owners and he discovered the barge was currently on a job in the Dominican Republic.

Whitlock wanted to fly down and check it out, but an international flight was out of the question at the moment. A week earlier, his car had been broken into on the streets of Charleston, the thieves making off with his laptop, his notes—and his passport. It couldn't have come at a worse possible time. Whitlock had to see the barge before hiring Titan. Finally, McConnell made a few calls and Whitlock was shuttled aboard a plane to Washington. There, Sen. Strom Thurmond's staff escorted Whitlock to a private office where members of Congress had their passports handled.

Within 30 minutes, Whitlock was legal to fly to the Caribbean.

The *Karlissa B* was perfect.

After inspecting the barge in the Dominican Republic, Whitlock quickly negotiated a deal with Titan officials. They promised the barge could be in South Carolina within weeks, which wasn't quite good enough. Hurricane season had begun on June 1, and even though storms usually did not reach South Carolina before August, no one wanted to take a chance. Whitlock knew Lasch would not be happy with anything that dropped the probability of success below 100 percent. And a hurricane was certainly an unwelcome, and unpredictable, variable.

But hurricane or no, the *Karlissa B* almost didn't make it at all. The New Jersey company that Lasch had contacted earlier filed a complaint with the U.S. government soon after the deal was struck. Although Titan Maritime was an American company, the *Karlissa B* operated under the flag of Belize for business reasons. And American law—the Jones Act—prohibited foreign-flagged ships from doing salvage work in U.S. waters. There was no way the crane barge could legally lift the *Hunley*.

Whitlock knew there was little chance of finding another crane barge as perfect for the job as the *Karlissa B*, and he dreaded telling Lasch the bad news. But he wouldn't have to—the growing prestige of the *Hunley* project ensured that. Titan officials were so eager to lift the sub they offered to have the barge re-flagged, a considerable expense—but they could afford it. The discounted rate for the *Karlissa B* they offered to Friends of the *Hunley* was $750,000. Lasch took the deal. But the *Karlissa* still had to sail from the Caribbean and navigate the tricky waters of Washington bureaucracy.

If it wasn't one thing, Lasch thought, it was twenty.

The crane barge fiasco slowed the recovery project to a crawl. It soon became apparent that the July 17 lift date would pass before the *Karlissa B* reached South Carolina. But U.S. Maritime Administration agents rushed the re-flagging paperwork for Titan, declaring it a case of "maritime peril." Lasch was relieved to see there were *Hunley* fans in the federal government. The clock was ticking, but the barge was en route. For the moment, it seemed everything would fall into place.

The *Karlissa B* arrived on July 21 and went to work immediately. First the two suction piles were set in place at either end of the *Hunley*, and they worked exactly as promised. Once the platform was in place, the lift truss was lowered into the ocean. It set down on the piles perfectly. The crane barge operator, Jenkins Montgomery, made it look easy.

By Friday, July 28, divers had attached four of the 32 lift straps that would cradle the *Hunley* beneath the truss. At the same time, they were patching three holes found in the submarine—a long, narrow opening on the starboard stern; another nearly the size of a pie plate about 10 feet from the bow on the starboard side; and the conning tower breach. The divers would make sure nothing fell out of the *Hunley* before it reached the lab.

The dive crews worked 24 hours a day for the rest of July. Visibility in the water was nearly nonexistent, so it mattered little if they worked in the daylight. Besides, they had to make up for lost time. Divers worked in short shifts, taking turns attaching the lift straps to the truss and threading them under the sub, tunneling as they went. It was slow work.

Their work was made slower by the amount of time they spent untangling themselves from the lift truss. The divers were using oxygen lines fed to them from the *Karlissa B*, which allowed them to stay down longer than if they were using tanks. But these lines trailed behind them, tracing their every move through the bridge-like structure of the truss. Ralph Wilbanks—who arrived in time to help with the strapping—sometimes felt like a rat in a maze, winding his way in and out of the truss several times just to get free. Still, the work was finally moving at a good clip. By the end of July, more than 10 straps were in place. It appeared the last one would be slung by August 5.

As they worked, the divers began to find other pieces of the *Hunley*. The aft cutwater had been recovered in late June, two weeks after the spar was removed. During the strapping, workers found the snorkel tubes and even the rudder. Every find was mapped, tagged and taken to the lab. It appeared most of the pieces had simply rusted and fallen off, except for the rudder. It was found late in the expedition, buried directly beneath the sub's hull. This led Neyland to believe it may have come loose from the *Hunley* before it crashed.

Eventually, the team brought up nearly every piece of the sub. McConnell and Lasch thought it was unbelievable luck. If Oceaneering's plan worked, they would recover a complete warship—practically a first. With the delays behind them, it appeared everything was working in their favor, finally. McConnell and Lasch allowed themselves to relax a bit.

And then Bob Neyland stopped by Adger's Wharf.

Neyland was concerned. It was mid-July and he explained that the project was well past its window of safety. They were now too late into the hurricane season, and too many things could go wrong. A storm could come. Even a glancing blow could wreak havoc on the recovery. The lift would have to wait until the next dive season.

"Well, when is that?" Lasch asked.

"Uh, next spring," Neyland said.

Lasch exploded. The project could not afford the expense of waiting eight months, he said. They could not afford to let the crane barge go or leave the *Hunley* exposed in its lift truss for the better part of a year. The "Go" button had been pushed, Lasch said, and there was no turning back. But Neyland would not budge.

Lasch thought Neyland was being hopelessly bureaucratic, and his by-the-book attitude did not take into consideration the costs, the work completed or any consequences of a delay. Not even the wrath of the Lascher could move Neyland, however. Finally, Lasch got on the phone with William Dudley at the Naval Historical Center and threatened to fire Neyland if Dudley did not explain the error of his ways.

Dudley quickly agreed with Lasch and Neyland was forced to back down. There would be no more arguments, no more excuses—and no more delays. The *Hunley* was coming home, hell or high water. And the high water was coming. On August 3, a tropical wave formed off the western coast of Africa, heading toward America.

Soon, it would become known as Hurricane Alberto.

For two months, there had been one problem after another. The project that had started so smoothly felt in danger of flying apart every week. But if nothing else went wrong, there was still a chance the *Hunley* could come up without a hitch. McConnell and Lasch would not dally and wait for more problems to arise. They decided that August 8, a Tuesday, would be the lift date. The strapping would be completed days earlier, but they did not want to raise the *Hunley* on a weekend, especially not at the height of boating season. There would be more traffic on the water then, more opportunities for trouble. A few days would not matter much anyway, they reasoned.

Besides, the weather reports suggested there was no way Alberto could reach the Carolina coast that quickly.

There was only one more thing McConnell had to do. The *Hunley* would not return to Charleston and settle into a new home with a bureaucratic name like Building 255. The first week of August, Lasch was summoned to the navy base on the pretense of some minor business. When he arrived, he found himself at the center of a ceremony. McConnell was christening Building 255—discovered by Lasch six years earlier—as the new Warren Lasch Conservation Center.

The senator explained that this honor was meant to immortalize the Friends of the *Hunley* chairman for getting the project to the finish line. Somehow, they had managed to keep the whole dedication secret, no easy feat for a project that barely made a move without Lasch's approval. Scientists, divers, reporters and Lasch's wife, Donna, turned out to give him a standing ovation. It took a moment for the honor to sink in, but Lasch finally realized how much the gesture meant: his name would forever be linked to the *Hunley*.

For once, Lasch was speechless.

On August 6, Ralph Wilbanks stood on the deck of the *Karlissa B* as Harry Pecorelli helped him climb into an old-fashioned canvas diving suit complete with a navy Mark V helmet. Wilbanks wanted to visit the *Hunley* once more in the spot where he'd found it, and he had decided to take this last trip in nineteenth-century diving gear to honor Angus Smith and David Broadfoot, the men who had raised the sub the first two times it sank. It was a nod to history, a symbolic gesture.

The night before, some National Geographic Society officials had asked Wilbanks if he would wait to make the dive until a film crew arrived. The cable network had negotiated a deal with Lasch for exclusive access to produce a documentary about the recovery, and they knew the sight of a man in old-fashioned diving gear would make great video. But Wilbanks politely turned them down.

"I'm not doing this for you," Wilbanks said. "I'm doing it for me."

When he reached the quiet ocean floor in his 200-pound dive suit, Wilbanks took a slow lap around the huge lift truss, occasionally reaching out to touch the *Hunley*. All of this had come from a simple discovery on a day when he had set out to investigate another site. Because Wilbanks was a scrupulously honest man, and had not wanted to cheat Clive Cussler out of any money, he had kept looking. And it had changed the history of this little submarine.

It was a good feeling, Wilbanks thought, as he took one last look at the *Hunley* resting at the bottom of the ocean. He had played a large role in bringing the lost Confederate submarine home. Now, there was nothing left to be done. The team was ready, the *Karlissa B* was ready, the sub was ready.

In two days, the *H. L. Hunley* would finally sail for home.

Two days before the Hunley *was recovered from the Atlantic Ocean, Ralph Wilbanks took one last dive on the sub wearing a Mark V diving helmet and canvas diving suit in honor of Angus Smith and David Broadfoot, the men who raised the* Hunley *the first two times it sank. Here, Warren Lasch poses with Wilbanks and his diving suit on the* Karlissa B *crane barge. Courtesy Ralph Wilbanks.*

The Hunley *finally surfaced at 8:39* A.M. *on August 8, 2000. The recovery was almost scrubbed due to high waves, but the tide died down just enough to be able to lift the sub safely. Courtesy Barbara Voulgaris.*

Glenn McConnell and Warren Lasch were amazed at the parade of boats that followed the Hunley *barge into the harbor on August 8, 2000. As impressive as this armada was, Lasch was most touched when he saw traffic stop on the Cooper River bridges so motorists could get a better look at the passing Confederate submarine. Courtesy of Warren Lasch.*

Once the Hunley *cleared the water, the job was only h[...] done. Setting it down on the recovery barge would pro[...] nearly even more dangerous than pulling it up from the A[...] lantic floor. Courtesy Barbara Voulgaris.*

Riding the billy pew to get on the deck of the Karlissa B *was the most harrowing part of the trip to the* Hunley *recovery site. Here Warren Lasch and Glenn McConnell are lowered from the* Karlissa *to the recovery barge where they would touch the submarine for the first time. Courtesy of Warren Lasch.*

he Hunley's sleek, hydrodynamic design was a surprise to most people when it surfaced on August 2000. It bore little resemblance to most historical sketches and the squat model sitting outside e Charleston Museum. Courtesy Barbara Voulgaris.

Once the Hunley cleared the water, the next trick was to set it down n the recovery barge. All four legs of the truss had to touch the deck t once or the submarine could be twisted enough to break it in ieces. Courtesy Barbara Voulgaris.

Glenn McConnell was amazed by the complex machinery of the submarine, the details that were not recorded by history. Here he inspects the Hunley *propeller on the recovery barge as Warren Lasch talks with Bob Neyland. Courtesy Friends of the* Hunley.

Scientists set up a rudimentary sprinkler system by poking holes in a garden hose. They had to keep the Hunley *wet on its ride to the conservation center to stem the corrosion that began as soon as it was exposed to the air. Conservators had wanted to cover the sub with wet burlap sacks, but Lasch vetoed the idea. People wanted to see the* Hunley *as it passed through the harbor, he correctly noted. Courtesy Friends of the* Hunley.

An honor guard of Confederate and Union reenactors escorted the Hunley from its recovery barge to the Warren Lasch Conservation Center, just one of several ceremonies for the fallen crew on recovery day. Courtesy Cramer Gallimore cgphoto.com.

Horace Hunley was the only member of the second crew to get a full headstone in 1863. Following the discovery of the first crew's graves in 1999, every Hunley sailor was buried in Magnolia Cemetery. All of them got new headstones, except Hunley. His is the original.

After years of lying in its recovery truss at a 45-degree angle, scientists at the Warren Lasch Conservation Center finally set the Hunley *upright in 2011. Areas of the sub hidden beneath the lift straps were visible for the first time since its recovery. Courtesy Friends of the* Hunley.

The grapefruit-sized hole in the forward conning tower was probably the Hunley's first hull breach. Before it was damaged, the port side of the conning tower held a view port similar to the one seen to the left in this photograph. Courtesy Friends of the Hunley.

The captain's station in the Hunley was crowded with the controls and axle for the dive planes, as well as the joystick-type rudder. Here, conservator Philippe de Vivies works in Dixon's station just after the initial excavation of the sub, illustrating just how little room the crew had to maneuver. Courtesy Friends of the Hunley.

Before chemical conservation began, scientists kept the Hunley *submerged in cold water to cut down on corrosion. Note that in addition to the four topside hull plates removed for the initial excavation, the aft hatch has been removed. Conservators had to remove several pieces of the sub to rescue rubber and other materials that would not survive in the caustic chemicals used to preserve the iron hull. Courtesy Friends of the* Hunley.

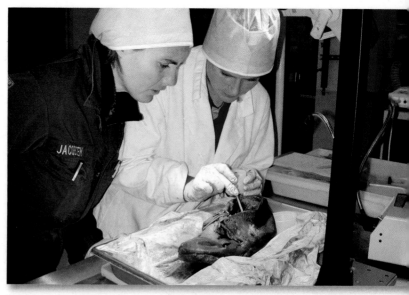

Senior archaeologist Maria Jacobsen inspects a shoe under restoration by Hunley conservators. Scientists recovered all the crew's clothing, but most of the cloth was deteriorated to the point of being unrecognizable. The shoes, even those of poor quality, survived much better during more than a century in seawater. Courtesy Friends of the Hunley.

The Hunley crew compartment is a mere 42 inches wide, leaving little room for movement. From this vantage, just below where the snorkel box was mounted, the hand cranks and bench dominate the interior. In the back the round flywheel, which allowed the men to "crank" the submarine, is visible behind the concreted aft ballast pump. Courtesy Friends of the Hunley.

Scientists found the interior of the Hunley cramped and confining. They could not work inside the crew compartment for long without a break. Eventually, they had to pump air into the sub to help them work. Courtesy Friends of the Hunley.

The Hunley's *rudder, found beneath the sub's keel during the recovery, was so encrusted with shell and hardened sand—concretion—that it was nearly unrecognizable. Courtesy Friends of the* Hunley.

After conservation, the rudder—this is its original color—was found to still have some of its hardware attached. The hinges at the bottom, only one of which remains, apparently connected to the propeller shroud. Courtesy Friends of the Hunley.

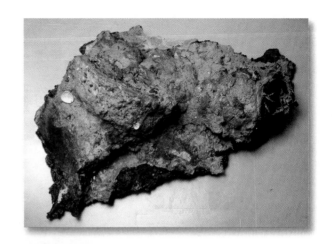

Inside the Hunley, *dozens of artifacts were found so heavily encased in concretion that scientists had to use X-rays to determine exactly what they had. Over several months, conservators chipped away at the concretion and eventually restored the oil can—probably used to keep the interior gears oiled—to near-pristine condition. Courtesy Friends of the* Hunley.

While restoring the Hunley's *spar, senior conservator Paul Mardikian made a discovery that changed the sub's story considerably. Remnants of the torpedo's copper casing were still attached to the end of the spar. Most historical accounts said the sub planted a torpedo with a barbed hook into the side of its prey and then backed away, detonating the charge with a lanyard. In fact, the* Hunley *attacked with a contact mine that exploded as soon as it touched the side of a ship. In this detail shot (spar tip), you can see the nut and bolt that held the torpedo in place, leaving no question the torpedo was supposed to remain on the spar. Courtesy Friends of the* Hunley.

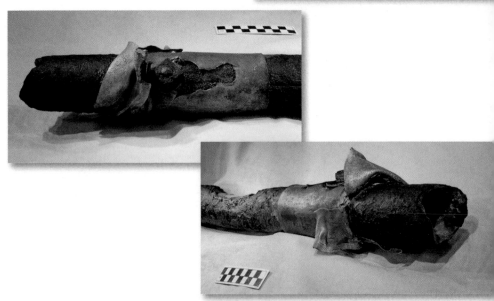

The explosion of 135 pounds of gunpowder destroyed the torpedo, save for some of its outer casing which was blown backward in the blast. Courtesy Friends of the Hunley.

Clive Cussler thought his association with the Hunley *was over after he found it, but he has remained close to the project. When he is in Charleston, Cussler always stops by the Warren Lasch Conservation Center to see what new artifacts have been restored. Here, Paul Mardikian shows Cussler and Lasch one artifact still in the early stages of preservation. Courtesy Friends of the* Hunley.

The majestic arch of the Hunley's *bow is not how the submarine looked in 1864; the sub was buil with a bow that was flat and straight. Underwater currents sanded down the bow to its curren shape and also did significant damage to the starboard side of the submarine. Courtesy Friends o the* Hunley.

Clive Cussler poses a [Chapman painting next t the Hunley *propeller in Jul 2013. This was Cussler' first chance to inspect th submarine after it was re moved from its lift truss Courtesy Kellen Correia.*

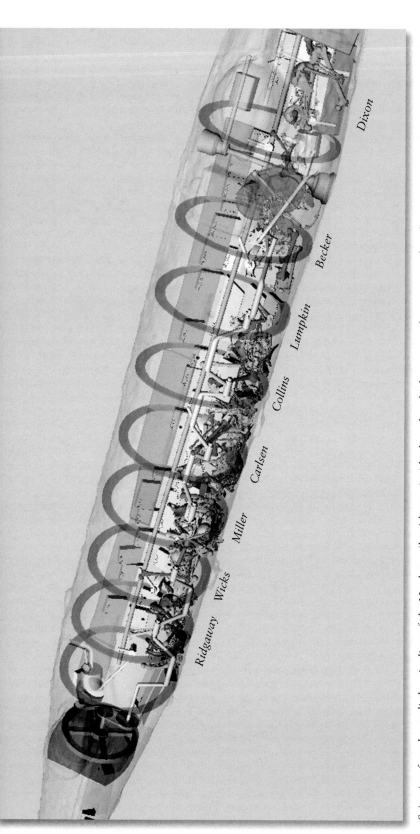

Scientists found very little mingling of the Hunley sailors' bones inside the sub, which suggests the men stayed at their posts up until the moment of their deaths. Archaeologists recorded the location of every bone using a three-dimensional plotting program. This color-coded illustration shows where the remains of each crew member were found in the sub. Note that some of Arnold Becker's bones were atop the Hunley's bellows, a feature that was never mentioned in any historical account of the sub. Left to right Joseph Ridgaway, James Wicks, Miller, J. F. Carlsen, Frank Collins, C. Lumpkin, Arnold Becker, George E. Dixon. Courtesy Friends of the Hunley.

Friends of the Hunley *hired forensic artist Sharon Long and physical anthropologist Doug Owsley of the Smithsonian Institution to re-create the faces of the* Hunley *crewmen. The method they used was similar to the one law enforcement uses when working with unidentified skeletal remains. Using the crew members' skulls, these reconstructions represent the best approximation of what the crew looked like— there are no known photos of any of the men. The hair styles are all educated guesses, based on the fashion of the 1860s. Courtesy Friends of the* Hunley.

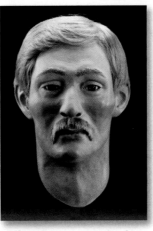

George Dixon *was either born in the Midwest or spent a lot of time there. Genealogist Linda Abrams has tracked Dixon to Cincinnati, where he lived in the years before the war, working the steamboat circuit. But his origins remain a mystery.*

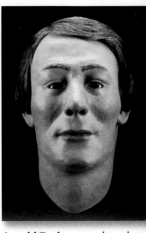

Arnold Becker *may have been a teenager and was likely a recent arrival from Europe. He was working on a New Orleans steamboat when Southern military leaders converted it to a warship. Becker, along with most of the crew, joined the Confederacy.*

Lumpkin *Scientists know little about the man who appears on duty rosters as "Lumpkin," with perhaps the first initial C. He was a middle-aged man, recently arrived in the United States from Europe, at the time the war broke out.*

James A. Wicks *was perhaps the oldest man on the* Hunley *and is the one with the clearest history. A native of North Carolina, he had served in the U.S. Navy for a decade when the war broke out. Aboard a U.S. ship during the Battle of Hampton Roads, Wicks switched sides and was soon sent to Charleston.*

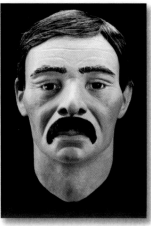

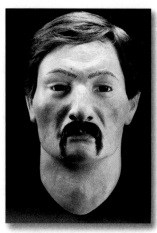

Miller *is one of the more mysterious members of the Hunley crew. A middle-aged man of European descent, there is some scant evidence to suggest he joined the crew in the weeks before the sub disappeared as one of two replacements for William Alexander. That is contradicted, however, by Alexander's postwar writing in which he indicates that he knew Miller.*

Joseph Ridgaway *hailed from the Eastern Shore of Maryland and was one of the more experienced sailors on the* Hunley *crew. When William Alexander was recalled to Mobile, Dixon promoted Ridgaway to first officer.*

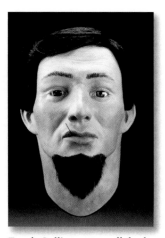

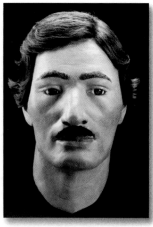

Frank Collins *was a tall, lanky native of Virginia with little sailing experience. But for some reason, Dixon hired him to serve aboard the* Hunley's *final crew.*

J. F. Carlsen *was the final member of the* Hunley *crew. A member of the German artillery, Carlsen was chosen to replace William Alexander, after Alexander was forced to return to Alabama. Carlsen had served aboard the Confederate raider* Jefferson Davis *early in the war.*

This heavily encrusted pocket knife was found on the floor of the Hunley late in the initial excavation of the crew compartment. Scientists eventually recovered and conserved two pocket knives from the sub. It's unclear which crew member carried this knife. Based on the location where it was found, only Dixon can be ruled out. Courtesy Friends of the Hunley.

Scientists found several used matchsticks littering the floor of the Hunley, where they would have been used to light the sub's candles and perhaps the lantern's wick. The work of Hunley conservators has been so exact that today these matches look as if they were struck just yesterday, not 150 years ago. Courtesy Friends of the Hunley.

George Dixon's famous lantern, source of the popular—and controversial—blue light legend, was found near the captain's station, encased in a thick cocoon of concretion. After it was conserved, scientists discovered that it was a fairly common lantern used in mid-nineteenth century and had a bull's eye lens that could direct a beam of light a great distance. Courtesy Friends of the Hunley.

Senior archaeologist Maria Jacobsen was attempting to remove George Dixon's remains from the Hunley *on May 23, 2001, when she found his legendary gold coin. Scientists had been skeptical they would find the $20 piece, which was mentioned in letters by members of the Twenty-first Alabama. The coin was one of—if not the— greatest find of the excavation. Courtesy Friends of the* Hunley.

George Dixon carried this coin in his pants pocket during the Battle of Shiloh, April 6, 1862, and it saved his life. Early in the fighting, a bullet struck the coin at Lady Liberty's hair bun, warping it but sparing Dixon's life. The impact pushed the coin into the meat of his leg and actually made a trench in his femur. Dixon would walk with a limp for the rest of his life. Courtesy Friends of the Hunley.

Although George Dixon's lucky coin was legend before the Hunley was recovered, there was no historical mention of the inscription he had engraved on the coin. As a memento of the battle, Dixon had the coin inscribed "Shiloh/April 6th 1862/My life Preserver/G.E.D." When Maria Jacobsen found the coin on May 23, 2001, this previously unknown inscription gave her chills. Courtesy Friends of the Hunley.

Archaeologists found this Union dog tag, which originally belonged to Ezra Chamberlin of the Seventh Connecticut Volunteers, stuck to the back of Joseph Ridgaway's skull. The discovery led to any number of conspiracy theories, including a popular—and often repeated—story that perhaps a Yankee had been forced to crew aboard the sub. The facts, while circumstantial, tell a different story. Chamberlin was reported killed in the battle of Morris Island in July 1863. The crew of the CSS Indian Chief, aboard which Ridgaway served, often pulled picket duty on Morris Island that summer. Mostly likely he or one of his shipmates simply found the ID tag on the island. But why would he wear it around his neck? It remains a mystery. Courtesy Friends of the Hunley.

Archaeologists found at least three canteens aboard the Hunley, each stored beneath the crew bench. The crew had to carry as much drinking water as they could, as the sub would sometimes be at sea for up to 12 hours. The canteens were cheap, paper thin and conservators had little to preserve. The canteen corks, found in the bottom of the sub, were also conserved. Courtesy Friends of the Hunley.

Several of the men aboard the Hunley *smoked pipes (it appears Frank Collins did not smoke, but often held a sewing needle in his teeth). Many crew members' teeth showed evidence of smoking, and one had even worn a space in his teeth from holding a pipe stem in his mouth for so long. These two pipes were found in the bottom of the submarine. The men did not smoke aboard the* Hunley—*it would have fouled the air. Instead, they carried the pipes so they would not lose them and could smoke as soon as they got out of the sub. Courtesy Friends of the* Hunley.

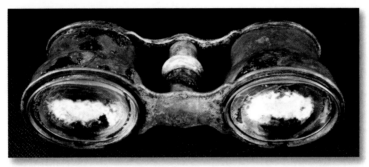

These binoculars were found in George Dixon's pocket after the initial excavation of the Hunley *in 2001. He would have used these to get his bearings and observe any activity on the decks of potential targets. As with most things on the* Hunley, *these binoculars were small, as space was at a premium inside the sub. Courtesy Friends of the* Hunley.

Several pieces of jewelry were found in George Dixon's pockets during the examination of his remains. Scientists suspect this ring and brooch were likely currency or perhaps items he won in card games. Regardless, they were valuable, and Hunley *crew members often carried their valuables to keep them from being lost or stolen. Courtesy Friends of the* Hunley.

Scientists found eight pairs of shoes aboard the Hunley *and, because they were all made of leather, they survived 136 years in saltwater much better than the crew's clothing. However, there was a definite social hierarchy evident in the shoes. Dixon's, and perhaps Ridgaway's, were of much higher quality than the footwear worn by the other sailors. Courtesy Friends of the* Hunley.

Several Union Navy buttons were found aboard the Hunley, *including at least two rubber buttons that said "U.S.N." on the front and "Goodyear" on the back. Those buttons almost undoubtedly came from a peacoat worn by James Wicks, a U.S. Navy veteran. These buttons, depicting an anchor, were also found aboard the sub and could have come from Wicks's clothing or any other sailors'. Buttons—like everything during the war—were at a premium, and men would collect them wherever they could. This cameo-style button was found among the remains of Frank Collins months after the initial excavation ended. It's unclear if this button was a part of his clothes or just something he carried in his pocket. It was found close to his cervical vertebrae. Courtesy Friends of the* Hunley.

George Dixon was found wearing suspenders of English origin. Despite their fragile state, it is clear that the sub captain wore much finer clothes than any of his crew. This clasp is about all that remains of those suspenders. Courtesy Friends of the Hunley.

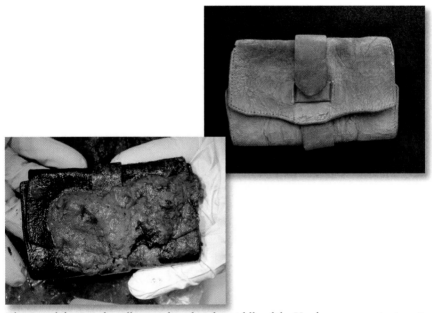

This 3-inch by 5-inch wallet was found in the middle of the Hunley crew compartment. There were no identifying papers in the wallet, and scientists have not identified which sailor carried it. Courtesy Friends of the Hunley.

Archaeologist Maria Jacobsen shows Warren Lasch and Glenn McConnell the pocket watch carried by George Dixon as it undergoes conservation. McConnell in particular was hopeful that the watch would reveal some clue to the Hunley's *final moments. Courtesy Friends of the* Hunley.

George Dixon's watch has proven one of the most tantalizing pieces of evidence found onboard the Hunley. The 18-karat gold watch, with an ornate chain and fob, stopped at 8:23. But so far no one has been able to say conclusively whether the watch simply wound down or quit as a result of the concussion of the torpedo blast that sank the USS Housatonic. That attack occurred around 8:45, and some have said Dixon's watch could have been running slow and the shock waves from the blast broke the watch. Scientists are skeptical. Courtesy Friends of the Hunley.

In August 2014, conservators began removing the hardened shell of sand and shell—concretion, as the scientists call it—that has covered the Hunley for more than a century. Here, conservator Liisa Nasanen chips away at concretion on the lower port side of the sub. The scientists began their work on the wrought iron section of the main hull, avoiding the cast iron end pieces and conning towers until they learn more about removing the concretion. Courtesy Friends of the Hunley.

This is the actual surface of the Hunley, exposed for the first time in more than a century. The photograph also provides a good perspective on the thickness of the concretion that covers the hull. Although the sub has soaked in caustic chemicals for several months, it is still difficult to remove the substance, which is as hard as concrete. It was left on the sub for years to protect the hull until the Hunley was ready for conservation, and it appears to have worked. The surface of the submarine looks nearly as good as it likely did in 1864. Courtesy Friends of the Hunley.

Conservator Johanna Rivera-Diaz holds a thick piece of concretion removed from the Hunley's hull as Senior Conservator Paul Mardikian looks on. In some places, the concretion on the sub's hull was only a quarter-inch thick while in other spots there can be as much as two inches worth of accumulated sand, shell, and sediment. Courtesy Friends of the Hunley.

Scientists first removed concretion from the Hunley's wrought-iron hull plates and also tried to work along seams between those two plates. Paul Mardikian explained that the wrought iron was less delicate than the cast iron parts of the sub and allowed conservators to get more experience with their tools before moving on to the more fragile parts of the submarine. Courtesy Friends of the Hunley.

This is one of the first photographs ever taken of the Hunley's *actual hull. For more than 14 years, scientists left the sub encased in a thick layer of sand and shell to help preserve the iron underneath. Conservators began to deconcrete the wrought iron main hull in August 2014. By the year's end, they had exposed 70 percent of the sub's surface. Note the bow is still covered in concretion, as conservators waited until the wrought iron was uncovered to explore the "forensic hot spots" of the sub's cast iron features. Courtesy Friends of the* Hunley.

Conservator Virginie Ternisien chips away at some of the last remaining concreted areas of the Hunley's *hull. This photograph, shot from the same angle as Conrad Wise Chapman's famous portrait of the sub, shows just how accurate that 1863 painting is. Chapman's painting has proven to be the most detailed, accurate contemporary record of the submarine. Courtesy Friends of the* Hunley.

The final crew of the Hunley *was laid to rest in April 2004, buried in an order reflecting their posts in the submarine. The coffins were laid side-by-side in a single grave and then covered with a concrete lid to prevent looting. The crew is buried in the same Magnolia Cemetery plot as the victims of the* Hunley's *first two sinkings.*

About 10,000 people from all over the country traveled to Charleston for the burial of the Hunley's *final crew. The eight caskets were carried on separate caissons from Charleston's Battery to Magnolia Cemetery, about a six-mile march. Hundreds of Union and Confederate reenactors escorted the casket, as well as women dressed in traditional nineteenth-century mourning garb.*

CHAPTER 16

February 17, 1864 Off Charleston

The ocean was cold that night.

After weeks of miserable weather that kept the Atlantic churned into a violent froth, the South Carolina winter had finally settled into a more typical pattern. The temperature had dropped into the 30s before sunset and would continue to fall overnight. The wind was light out of the northwest, the sea was calm and there were few clouds in the sky. A waxing moon cast a faint light on the swells, but for the moment there was nothing to see—nothing but endless miles of black water.

Charleston was dark, the shoreline little more than a silhouette against a midnight blue sky. The city had been quiet of late, as if the fight had gone out of her. A week earlier, the Confederates had bombarded Morris Island but little had come of it. It seemed both sides were just going through the motions, waiting for some change in their circumstances—or the end of the war. Both sides realized it was coming.

The South Atlantic Blockading Squadron was so confident there would be no activity on this evening that most of the ships had already staked out their positions and anchored for the night. It had been ages since the Confederates had attempted a naval assault, and anymore

Fort Sumter, which was taken by the Confederates in the opening battle of the Civil War, remained Charleston's best line of defense in 1864—even though much of the fort had been reduced to rubble. Some sailors from the USS Housatonic *participated in a disastrous raid on the fort in September 1863, but most managed to escape and were aboard the ship when it met the* Hunley *in battle on February 17, 1864. Courtesy National Archives.*

few blockade runners even approached the city. There was not much business to be had there these days. Everyone who could leave the city had done so months before. Charleston was all but a lost cause.

The USS *Housatonic* swung at anchor on the northern flank of the blockade, its usual post. The ship's deck was nearly as quiet as the sea, the sails on its two towering masts furled so tight that the slight breeze could not ruffle them. Nine men were milling about topsides, settling in to what they expected would be a long shift. The watch had changed at 8 P.M. and the sailors were still adjusting to the cold. The salt air had a definite bite to it on this evening.

Six of the nine men were lookouts, as per regulations, but they had nothing to look at but the other blockaders rocking in the distance. The two sailors on bow watch may have been able to see the dark mass of Fort Sumter nearly six miles away. They knew, at least, that it was still there. The fort was not simply the city's first line of defense; these days Sumter was practically its *only* defense. Decimated as it was, Fort Sumter still had enough firepower to keep the U.S. Navy out of Charleston.

Life aboard the *Housatonic* was, frankly, about as dull as it got in the South Atlantic Blockading Squadron. The 205-foot sloop of war was—as its designation suggested—built for fighting, but she had scarcely seen any action. The *Housatonic*, named for a river in Connecticut, had arrived off the coast of Charleston in late September 1862, took its place in the blockade and was promptly ignored.

The ship had not participated in the regular shelling of Sumter, although its crew was part of a disastrous amphibious assault on the fort five months earlier. In September, boats from the *Housatonic* and several other blockade ships had attempted to land on the rocks outside Sumter's walls. Dahlgren planned to take the fort in hand-to-hand combat and assumed 500 sailors would be more than enough to take the "corporal's guard" at Sumter. But General Beauregard had learned of the attack, and he was ready.

The entire Charleston Battalion had been sent to Fort Sumter and they struck as soon as the first boats reached the rocks. The gunboat *Chicora* suddenly appeared from the inland side of the fort and fired on the approaching barges. The Union sailors were surprised and quickly overwhelmed. Most escaped, but the Confederates took about 100 as prisoners. It had been a humiliating defeat for Dahlgren. The *Housatonic* sent dozens of men in four boats—including C. H. Craven and F. J. Higginson—but the crew suffered no casualties and all managed to escape. The *Housatonic* ultimately played only a small role in the attack, but it was about as much excitement as anyone on the ship had seen in more than a year.

The *Housatonic*'s primary role in the squadron was to intercept blockade runners. The regular approach to Charleston was from the south, and that's where most of the Union Navy patrolled. But blockade runners often tried to sneak into the city by sailing north around the fleet and then skirting the shore of Sullivan's Island until they reached the protective covering fire of Forts Moultrie and Sumter. The *Housatonic* routinely anchored within sight of Breach Inlet, the channel between Sullivan's and Long Island, to keep watch over that route.

In the past year, the *Housatonic* had stopped a number of these blockade runners—one of which was attempting to carry cotton and turpentine into Charleston. Perhaps the crew's greatest victory was its role in the attack on the *Georgiana* in March 1863. The iron-hulled ship was sailing for Charleston on the northern route when the squadron spied it and gave chase. Eventually, the *Housatonic* and other ships forced the *Georgiana* aground at Long Island. But that had been nearly a year ago. By the winter of 1864 that sort of action was rare, and most nights on the ship were just plain boring.

By February of 1864, the USS Housatonic *had been part of the blockade of Charleston for nearly a year-and-a-half, but had seen little action. Mostly the* Housatonic *guarded against blockade runners trying to reach the harbor along the northern route. The 205-foot sloop of war was infinitely larger—and carried more firepower—than the 40-foot* Hunley. *But the* Housatonic's *big guns would do no good against the fish-boat's sneak attack. Courtesy of the U.S. Naval History and Heritage Command.*

The *Housatonic* carried a crew of 155 sailors, and most of them were below deck, sleeping or passing the time as best they could. Capt. Charles Pickering was in his cabin near the stern, talking with the ship's doctor and working on some charts. Ensign C. H. Craven was in his room listening to the banter of the men above him on deck. J. W. Holickan, the ship's third assistant engineer, had just gone on duty in the engine room.

Holickan's primary job on this evening was to keep the engine's fire stoked and the steam pressure at 25 pounds, as per Admiral Dahlgren's orders. This seemed like a waste of fuel to the engineer, given the *Housatonic*'s chronic inaction. But orders were orders and he would not question them. The admiral's instructions had stood for more than a month now, and the crew of the *Housatonic* had followed them to the letter.

Given their slight role in the blockade of Charleston, it would have been understandable if the crew of the *Housatonic* had grown complacent. But the sailors carried out their duties competently one night after another, no matter how little action they saw. They realized that, in war, inattention to detail could get men killed. That attitude would pay off for the crew of the USS *Housatonic*, because on this night there was something out there.

And it was coming for them.

George Dixon had waited months for this moment.

In the two weeks since William Alexander had returned to Mobile, Dixon hadn't taken the *Hunley* into the ocean once. The weather had not allowed it. The sub had been away from the Battery Marshall dock only a few times for training in the creek behind Sullivan's Island, both to keep his men sharp and give his newest crew member—J. F. Carlsen—some familiarity with its operation. A few nights earlier, Charles Stanton claimed, he had seen the *Hunley* in the harbor. It pulled up alongside the ironclad *Chicora* and Dixon passed a few words with the crew. He told Stanton he was going to sink the *Housatonic*.

Dixon didn't consider that a boast, simply a fact. He knew that he could do this—that his boat could do this—but so far he hadn't the chance to back up those words. And he was running out of time. His leave would be up in two weeks and he realized that this time Mobile command was not inclined to grant him another extension— no matter how much Beauregard might insist. But Dixon knew taking the *Hunley* offshore in the violent conditions that had plagued the coast all month would be worse than a waste of time—it would be suicide. So he had waited. When the weather finally broke overnight, he would wait no longer. It was time. There was more moonlight on the water than he would have liked, but George Dixon had long ago given up on perfect conditions.

He had decided to target the *Housatonic* weeks earlier. He initially wanted to attack the *Wabash*—take out one of the Union's more formidable ships first. But the *Wabash* was out of reach and the *Housatonic*, sitting alone at the northernmost point in the blockade, would have to suffice. Dixon had kept his eye on the ship for weeks and realized that, even if it was not the most attractive target, it likely would be the easiest.

That afternoon he had walked to the beach to get a bearing on the ship. It hadn't moved—it rarely did. Dixon estimated the *Housatonic* was about four miles out, although the ship's crew later claimed they had anchored less than three miles from the island. The *Hunley* could reach the *Housatonic* in about two hours by riding the outgoing tide, Dixon calculated. The wind was at his back, and that would help as well. The only hitch in his plan was the return.

If they left at 7 P.M. and attacked two hours later, that would leave them with about two hours to wait before the tide turned to carry the *Hunley* back to shore. There wasn't anything he could do about that. The attack was the important part of the plan; they had to show that the fish-boat could sink a blockade ship. Dixon would worry about the voyage home after he had accomplished his primary mission.

Dixon and his men had taken the *Hunley* out into the creek behind Sullivan's Island earlier that afternoon. The final test had not gone well. He returned to the dock frustrated, complaining that something was not working right. It was the spar, he believed. Dixon needed to make some adjustments—in reality, he needed Alexander—before setting out. He would leave nothing to chance. Not on this night. Finally, he walked up to the fort and asked a couple of men to give him a hand.

One of those men, D. W. McLaurin, would remember that afternoon for the rest of his life.

"Lt. Dixon landed and requested that two of my regiment, the Twenty-third South Carolina Volunteers, go aboard and help them to adjust the machinery, as it was not working satisfactorily," McLaurin wrote years later. "Another man and I went aboard and helped propel the boat for some time while the lieutenant and others adjusted the machinery and rods that held the torpedo, and got them working satisfactorily."

Once Dixon declared the *Hunley* ready, the night could not come fast enough. He watched as the sun set over the marsh, over Charleston, checking his watch time and again. Darkness would fall just before the tide turned, and he would set out as soon as both were on his side. Around 6 P.M., after he had slipped the torpedo onto the sub's spar, Dixon briefed Lt. Col. O. M. Dantzler.

The Battery Marshall commander listened to Dixon's plan politely, but likely did not take him too seriously. Dixon had set out to sink a blockade ship a dozen times at least, and Dantzler had no reason to believe the results would be any different this time. But he did agree to honor Dixon's final request. He wanted Dantzler's men ready to guide the *Hunley* back into the inlet.

Dixon told Dantzler that if they survived the attack, he would shine two blue lights toward Sullivan's. When the troops on watch spotted them, Dixon wanted them to light a signal fire on the beach.

He might have been able to steer for land in the darkness, but Dixon knew that trying to sail into Breach Inlet blind would be nearly impossible. Dantzler assured him that his men would be on high alert.

Just after 6:30, Dixon ordered his men to load up. They knew the drill well. The first men to board stowed several canteens beneath the crew bench, then checked to make sure they were carrying enough provisions. Matches were a necessity, both for the lantern and the candle they used to see and monitor their oxygen supply. It would be cold aboard the sub, but most of the men knew they would soon be bathed in sweat from the hard labor of turning the propeller. Only Wicks carried a heavy jacket, his U.S. Navy peacoat. He used the plush coat as a cushion. The hard bench was hell on his chronically aching back.

Dixon was the last to board. As he wiggled into the hatch he asked the men onshore to cast off the lines. The Battery Marshall troops always saw the submarine off, and gave it a push for momentum. As the boat slid away from the dock, Dixon disappeared into the conning tower, shutting the hatch behind him. The *Hunley* was underway.

At first the crew fell into the familiar routine. They had spent two months learning the submarine and had gone offshore countless times. The repetition was sometimes monotonous, but this night did not feel like any other. After weeks of inaction, Dixon was more determined than ever. Perhaps the crew sensed this. They said little once he closed the hatch, both to conserve air and because they understood there was nothing to say. Maybe they all realized that on this night they would attack, no matter what the consequences.

The submarine turned into Breach Inlet, where the current propelled it out past the breakers. The men at Battery Marshall watched the boat cut through the water slowly, gracefully. The waves washed over the conning towers and the sub disappeared, only to emerge a moment later beyond the surf. It continued to churn through the swells and, minutes later, disappeared into the blackness. The men watched until they could no longer spot any trace of the fish-boat on the dark water.

They would never see the *Hunley* again.

Robert Flemming was the first man to see it.

The black landsman had the starboard bow watch that night, a post he covered often. In the past year Flemming had learned these waters as well as anyone aboard the *Housatonic*. In all likelihood, he could have mapped the South Carolina coast from memory. Sometimes it must have felt as if he did nothing but watch the endless march of Atlantic swells.

He stood on the *Housatonic*'s cathead, scanning the dark ocean for hours at a time, disregarding the usual flotsam and jetsam that littered the waters off Charleston. This evening Flemming could see the lights of the blockade ships in the distance and watched the scant moonlight dance on the water. Occasionally he passed a few words with C. P. Slade, the sailor who had the portside bow watch. But mostly, Flemming stood in complete silence.

About a half hour into his shift, Flemming saw something on the water. It was less than 500 feet away and approaching from the land. The object appeared to be about 22 feet long, he would later recall, with only its ends visible. Water seemed to wash over its middle, but parts of it stood out of the water nearly two feet high. Flemming could not tell how wide the object was, because he was looking at it broadside. He called out to the officer of the forecastle.

"There is something coming that looks like a log," Flemming told him. "It looks very suspicious."

Lewis A. Comthwait did not share Flemming's immediate concern. He walked to the gunnels, glanced across the water and studied the object for a second. He was not impressed and promptly dismissed his lookout's concern. There was never anything of consequence on the water anymore, and he did not see why this night would be any different. Comthwait declared the object nothing more than floating debris—a common sight in the war zone.

"It's a log," he said.

"Queer-looking log," Flemming replied.

Flemming did not fear arguing with a superior officer; he knew what he had seen. Flemming pointed out that the "log" was not floating with the tide but moving across it. But Comthwait would not listen, assuring his lookout that he had spotted a log. Flemming did not accept this answer and decided to ask Slade for his opinion. By the time Slade joined the other two men, the object was only 300 feet from the ship.

At first, it looked like a log to Slade as well. But then he noticed that it was moving fast and appeared to be headed directly toward the *Housatonic*'s aft pivot gun post. This was not natural, he knew, and Slade began to have second thoughts about his initial impression. Flemming told him there was "a torpedo coming." He was sure of it. And Slade began to believe he was right.

The crew of the *Housatonic*, like all sailors in the South Atlantic Blockading Squadron, had heard the stories of the Confederate's alleged secret weapon. In January, Dahlgren had alerted the fleet that the rebels had built a boat capable of traveling nearly or completely under the water. The *Housatonic* was anchored in 24 feet of water to prevent these boats from passing under its keel. It was the reason the engineers kept the ship's engine idling, ready to move at a moment's notice. The men who stood watch had been warned specifically to look out for these craft, and Flemming had taken those orders seriously. Now he thought he had spotted one of these torpedo boats, and no one believed him. He decided to act on his own.

"If no one is going to report this, I will cut the buoy adrift myself and get ready for slipping," Flemming said, loud enough for most of the men on deck to hear him.

The lookout's insistence forced Comthwait to take another look, this time with his binoculars. And upon further review he saw something that was entirely at odds with his first impression. This "log" had two lumps on its topside, each the size of a man's head, with water rippling around them as it cut through the swells. It was,

Comthwait realized, moving under its own power. Flemming was right.

Without another word, Comthwait turned and ran aft to find the officer of the deck. As he stepped off the cathead, he heard Flemming ask Henry S. Gifford whether they should fire at the object. The second captain of the forecastle noted that their orders were to shoot anything that moved. Within seconds, a shot rang out in the dark.

By the time Lewis Comthwait decided he should alert his superiors, nearly everyone on the deck of the *Housatonic* had spotted the mysterious object. George Kelly, a cooper, had seen something that he thought looked like a "capsized boat, around 25 feet long, about three points on the starboard bow and 75 yards distant, moving astern nearly parallel with the keel." Thomas H. Kelly, the gunner manning the aft pivot gun, said that he saw something "about 30 feet long with a hub on each end as large as a mess kettle." Even John H. Crosby, the man whom Comthwait was running to alert, had seen what he thought was "a porpoise coming up to the surface to blow."

Crosby, however, recognized his mistake more quickly than Comthwait had. He asked a quartermaster for his opinion of the object, but did not need to wait for a reply. He knew this thing was no dolphin—it was something far more sinister. And it was no more than 100 yards away, closing in on the starboard flank. He cried out to the captain below deck, told him that something was coming for the ship, and it was moving "very fast."

The *Housatonic* was under attack.

Capt. Charles Pickering was sitting at the table in his cabin when he heard the commotion on deck. He had been overhauling a book of charts and talking to the ship's doctor, William T. Plant, when he heard the confused sounds and the stir of excitement. Crosby then called out to him, said that something was coming in fast. Pickering assumed it was a blockade runner. Perhaps, he thought, the night would not pass so quietly after all.

When he heard Crosby barking orders, Pickering sprang from the table to see what was happening. In his rush, he grabbed the doctor's hat by mistake and had to turn around to get his own. By the time he reached the deck, Crosby had taken control of the situation. He was ordering everyone to quarters and preparing the *Housatonic* to beat a fast retreat.

"Slip the anchor chain and fire up the engine," Crosby yelled.

When Crosby noticed Pickering on deck, he reported to him that a torpedo boat had been spotted, that it was headed for them and closing fast. Pickering repeated the order to slip the chain and called out for the engine room to prepare to go astern, just as Dahlgren had instructed him to do. At that moment Charles Muzzey, the captain's clerk, appeared at Pickering's side. He was holding the captain's double-barreled gun, which was filled with buckshot.

Without pausing to think, Pickering took the gun from Muzzey and jumped onto the ship's horse block. There, the captain got his first—and only—look at the *H. L. Hunley*.

"It was shaped like a large whale boat, about two feet, more or less, under water," Pickering would later recall. "Its position was at right angles to the ship, bows on, and the bows within two or three feet of the ship's side, about abreast of the mizzen mast, and I supposed it was then finding the torpedo on."

Pickering took aim with his gun, picked out "two projections or knobs about one third of the way from the bows," and fired.

His shots joined a cacophony of gunfire from the *Housatonic*'s deck. The officers and several of the lookouts were shooting at the object in concert from various points along the starboard railing. C. P. Slade had left his post at bow watch to fire on the torpedo. Lt. F. J. Higginson had taken a sidearm from another landsman, but when he took aim at the strange craft the gun misfired. Ensign C. H. Craven, who had responded to the call to quarters, arrived on deck and got off three rounds at the "water logged plank." He had to lean over the rail to fire his final shot because the strange craft was almost alongside the ship.

Most of the men were aiming their fire at the submarine's two conning towers, the twin lumps they would remember so vividly. Some of them may have also shot at the "glimmer of light" coming from the top of the thing, which Higginson correctly assumed was the torpedo boat's deadlights. At least some of their shots hit the craft, but Pickering quickly realized it had no effect. The thing just kept coming.

By the time the *Housatonic* crew recognized the danger, the torpedo boat was too close to train any of the ship's cannons on it; they could not get an angle on the boat—some of the crew had tried. Pickering concluded that their only chance was to outrun it. He repeated the order he'd given just moments before, this time making sure his crew understood the urgency of the situation.

"Go astern faster."

The torpedo boat was aiming for the *Housatonic*'s starboard flank, just aft of the mizzenmast, and it was almost there. The engineers had been ready and had kicked the ship's engine into gear within seconds of hearing the order. But the ship was sluggish to start, and Crosby realized they would not get clear in time. At this point, the torpedo boat was moving faster than the *Housatonic*. Crosby ordered some of the sailors to try and clear the lifeboats. He told everyone else to move forward, to get as far away from the impact as possible.

The second after Pickering called out to the engine room, he heard Crosby's command. He turned toward the cathead, toward safety, but then thought better of it. He was the captain, and his place was on the command deck. He should be there, no matter what the situation. Pickering turned to run toward the bridge, but when he took a step the deck was no longer there.

John H. Crosby would later say that it "sounded like a collision with another vessel," which is exactly what it was.

The explosion came just seconds after the engineers had locked the engine into reverse. The *Housatonic* had barely started to move when Crosby was knocked off his feet. It was as if the ship had suddenly run aground, he thought. There was no smoke that he noticed, no flame, no sharp report, no column of water thrown into the air, Crosby later said. There was only a great pressure, and then the *Housatonic* simply blew up.

The *H. L. Hunley* struck the USS *Housatonic* in its rear starboard quarter, just below the graceful curve of hull that arched toward the stern. When the mine at the end of its 17-foot spar slammed into the wooden hull, 135 pounds of gunpowder ignited instantly. The force was directed upward, forcing the *Housatonic* to lurch violently to port—recoiling as if it had been shot. The blast would blow a hole 10 feet wide into the ship. Seawater poured into the hull just as quickly as its contents spilled out.

The ship creaked and moaned, as if it knew it had been dealt a fatal wound, and then sank back into place. Within seconds water washed over the deck. The *Housatonic* was going down fast.

The force of the blast had knocked most of the *Housatonic* sailors off their feet, and some were even blown into the ocean. Craven had been attempting to train a big gun on the torpedo boat and was thrown into the topsail sheet bits. He soon felt water around his feet and noticed that the deck was almost completely awash. He looked over the side and saw furniture from the ship's wardroom floating in the ocean. The hole in the ship's hull was so large that a sofa floated out broadside.

"I supposed the whole starboard side of the ship abaft of the mizzenmast was blown off," Craven would later recall.

There were dozens of men in the ocean around the sinking wreck, others tangled in the ship's spider-web rigging, and Craven saw at least two bodies of men he was certain had been killed by the blast. Amidst the chaos, Crosby managed to keep his head and told the crew to clear away all the lifeboats. There were men in the water, and he knew it would be a race to get them before hypothermia set in.

Lt. F. J. Higginson had been knocked down near the mizzenmast, but recovered quickly. He tried to wrestle one of the portside life boats free of its rigging, but the boat was soon swamped and he was thrown into the water. Adrift in the cold black Atlantic, Higginson found an oar and clung to it as he tried to swim back to the sinking *Housatonic*. Before he reached the hulk, some shipmates in a small gig pulled him out of the water.

Higginson directed the men to pick up any sailors they found treading water around the wreck. He noticed that no alarm had been given and decided they needed more help than they could get from a single lifeboat. He grabbed an oar and directed the other men to help him row. They were going to make for the USS *Canandaigua*, at anchor nearly two miles away.

John Crosby had jumped from the sinking *Housatonic* into another dinghy, but the boat was swamped in the wake thrown by the sinking ship. He pulled himself back onto the deck, where he quickly found four crewmen who had not been injured in the blast. Together they crawled to the starboard side of the *Housatonic* to clear another lifeboat. Most of the tackle used to lower the boats had been damaged, but they eventually managed to free one boat and launch it. But one boat would not be enough.

Crosby took command of the gig and within a minute was picking sailors out of the water. As he worked, Crosby heard the captain call out to him. Pickering had climbed into the mizzenmast rigging and, although he did not realize it, had been seriously injured—probably by flying debris, as he had been closest to the blast. He remembered deck planking flying up into his face during the explosion, but that was all he could recall. The captain was disoriented, not entirely sure of himself. At first he told Crosby to come get him, but then stopped himself.

"No, pick up all the men and officers you can find in the water who are in danger," Pickering said. "Pull for the *Canandaigua*."

Crosby rescued a few more men and then went back for Pickering.

Together they set out for the *Canandaigua* and intercepted it already en route. Higginson had reached the ship ten minutes earlier, at 9:20, and alerted the captain to the *Housatonic*'s emergency. It had taken the huge warship only a couple of minutes to get underway. The ship picked up Crosby and Pickering and, at 9:35 P.M., arrived alongside the wreck of the *Housatonic*.

The *Canandaigua* launched all its boats and, with Crosby's help, pulled all the cold and wet *Housatonic* sailors from the water in less than an hour. The ship's crew kept watch for the torpedo boat during the rescue efforts, but it seemed to have disappeared. Craven had last seen it the second before the explosion, and reported that it appeared to be backing away at that time. The little boat could have been nearby, and perhaps even on the surface, but the crew of the sinking warship was too preoccupied with saving themselves. No one thought to worry about the rebel ram's whereabouts.

The *Hunley* had simply vanished.

The *Housatonic* had been anchored in relatively shallow water, so most of its rigging remained above the water after it settled on the ocean floor. The boat was listing heavily to port, and some of the lines were just a few feet above the swells, but many of the survivors had climbed into the thick ropes to await their rescue. In the chaos of the night, there was no way to get an accurate head count. It would be more than a day before they could sort out their losses. When they did, they realized that they had been relatively lucky. Out of a crew of 155, the *Housatonic* lost five men that night, including Muzzey, the captain's clerk, Ensign E. L. Hasiltine, John Williams, John Walsh and Theodore Parker, a black sailor. The rest managed to survive an explosion that sank a 205-foot warship in less than five minutes.

About 45 minutes after the attack, Robert F. Flemming was still hanging in the *Housatonic* rigging awaiting rescue. The first man to spot the *Hunley* that night was cold and disoriented, but he clung to old habits: he kept a look out. He saw the *Canandaigua* approaching when it was about 800 feet away, apparently making good time. They would be rescued, Flemming had realized.

And then Flemming saw something else, something that was strangely familiar. Later, he would testify that as the rescue ship approached, "I saw a blue light on the water just ahead of the *Canandaigua*, and on the starboard quarters of the *Housatonic*."

If anyone else noticed the strange torpedo boat lurking nearby after the attack they never mentioned it. As far as most of the *Housatonic*'s crew was concerned, the ram had simply disappeared at the moment of the explosion—perhaps it was even lost in the attack. But Flemming never changed his story and maintained for the rest of his life that he had seen a "blue light."

For years, historians would speculate that Flemming—the first Union sailor to spot the *H. L. Hunley* on February 17, 1864—was also the last man to see it for more than a century.

CHAPTER 17

August 8, 2000 Off Charleston

The little boat rounded the Charleston Harbor jetties just after 4 A.M., gliding over roiling black water, steering for the blue light.

Warren Lasch and Glenn McConnell stood together on the boat's deck, watching silently as they drew closer to the light. It had been mounted on the *Karlissa B*'s deck the night before in homage to the signal that George Dixon had allegedly flashed after the *H. L. Hunley*'s attack on the *Housatonic*. Standing 20 feet above the waves, the blue light had been visible from Sullivan's Island all night.

The blue light was a controversial element of the *Hunley* mythology. Some believed the story was apocryphal, a legend based solely on the testimony of a Union sailor who was probably suffering from hypothermia (it apparently mattered little that the Confederates reported seeing it as well). But for McConnell and Lasch, the blue light had come to symbolize the recovery—a signal of mission accomplished. And now that signal, that goal, was so close that they could actually see it.

It was recovery day.

McConnell had been waiting more than five years for this moment. Now, with the sub scheduled to surface in just a few hours, he worried that something would go wrong. It was a primal fear, tempered only by the senator's overwhelming excitement. He had made it his life's mission to bring the *Hunley* home, and for the past several years it had seemed as if nothing else mattered as much. McConnell had devoted himself to the cause no matter how much bad publicity, political fallout or inattention to personal business he had to endure. All of that had taken a toll.

For most of the past year, McConnell had been fighting a serious infection that stubbornly refused to subside. It left him weak, hospitalized, and constantly worried. He pressed on because he believed the *Hunley*'s recovery was more important than his own health, and there was simply too much to do. At one point he had said a silent prayer, "Don't let me go and leave all of this on Warren."

"And," McConnell had added, "don't let me go before I see it."

It had been three years since McConnell had conscripted Lasch to his cause, and he realized the man standing next to him was more responsible for this day than anyone else. Lasch brought to the project the business experience and leadership it needed. He handled the planning and preparations. Recruiting Lasch, McConnell thought, had been the key decision that had led them to this moment. Now it all came down to two minutes—the amount of time it would take for the *Karlissa B*'s crane to lift the *Hunley* off the bottom of the ocean and set it on the barge that would carry it home.

As the boat approached the *Karlissa B*, McConnell checked his watch. He had made it; in just about four hours, he would see the *Hunley*. Finally.

That is, if nothing went wrong.

～

Warren Lasch approached the day like a moon shot. To pull this off, a thousand things had to go right in sequence. If any one of those steps failed, he knew the entire recovery was in jeopardy. For weeks, Lasch had been haunted by a vision of the *Hunley* popping out of the water and immediately breaking open, its contents spilling into the sea. Leonard Whitlock had assured him that would not happen—

it was as close to a 100 percent guarantee as humanly possible.

But Lasch could not help it, he was as nervous as he'd ever been. Overconfidence was a liability, he believed, one he could not afford. A priceless, historical treasure was completely in their hands. And if something went wrong, Lasch and McConnell had only half-jokingly agreed, they would jump off the crane barge and swim for England.

Onboard the *Karlissa B*, Lasch was relieved to see the Oceaneering crew already at work. Whitlock and Steve Wright, the Oceaneering project manager, had scheduled the day down to the minute. They had even taken a page out of NASA's playbook, planning to go over everything one final time to declare it "go" or "no go" before proceeding with the lift. They had organized everything perfectly, building in redundancies to cut down on any chance of a problem. The only thing they had not accounted for in all those months of planning was the sea.

Four-foot swells had not been part of the plan.

The Atlantic had been uncharacteristically restless for several days. The water off Charleston was usually dead calm throughout the late summer, as if the oppressive Lowcountry heat could lull even the ocean into lethargy. This was a troublesome variable that was decidedly beyond their ability to fix. There had been one setback after another on the road to this day and it seemed Mother Nature intended to make sure the recovery team sweated until the last second.

Nothing, Lasch thought, is ever easy.

Lasch paid Whitlock to worry about such things, and this week he was earning his check. As dawn broke on the horizon, Whitlock had been up for 48 hours straight, and he vowed to not sleep until he saw the *Hunley* home. But the tide presented a serious obstacle. Although the seas would have no effect on the fixed-leg *Karlissa B*, they would leave the recovery barge bobbing up and down like a fishing line float. It was worrisome, but Whitlock did not consider it a deal-breaker—that is, until he and Wright talked to the crane operator. And then it seemed the *Hunley* might not come home this day after all.

Jenkins Montgomery, the man hired to operate the crane that would actually lift the sub, delivered the bad news. Montgomery was a Lowcountry native and knew the local waters well, but he understood offshore recovery even better. And he realized four-foot swells lapping at the crane barge's jack-up legs were potentially a huge problem. They could have dramatic effects on the sub and its lift truss. In three-foot seas, the 30-ton package of submarine and lift truss would likely come out of the ocean swinging at the end of the lift cable—and Montgomery knew he would not be able to control it. Setting it down gently on the recovery barge would be impossible.

"I can lift it, but you won't like what you get," Montgomery told them.

The thought of a 58,000-pound pendulum swinging into the deck of the *Karlissa B* was just about the worst thing either Whitlock or Wright could imagine. It was all too close to Lasch's vision of total failure. But neither man wanted to pull the plug at the last minute. A delay would cost money and bring negative publicity. Already, a small armada of boats had gathered in the ocean around the *Karlissa B*. Thousands of people were waiting within sight of the recovery. The only thing worse than sending them home disappointed, Whitlock thought, would be having an audience of 2,000 people witness the *Hunley* slam into the crane barge before tumbling back into the sea.

Eventually, Whitlock and Wright decided that conditions were not bad enough to abort—not yet. If the ocean followed normal patterns, the swells would subside shortly after daybreak. The weather report for the day looked good, even better than they had hoped. Perhaps the ocean would calm down by mid-morning. Montgomery agreed they were on the cusp. He assured them that if conditions improved slightly, everything would be just fine.

If not, there was going to be trouble.

Whitlock ordered the last dive crew into the water just after 6 A.M. The team would double-check the straps cradling the *Hunley*, connect the crane cable to the lift truss and vacuum the sea around the sub one final time. Sand was in constant motion on the ocean floor and if the sub was partially reburied, it could create suction when the crane began the lift. That would put tremendous stress on the 137-year-old iron hull, perhaps even a dangerous amount. And Whitlock wanted to make sure that wasn't an issue. He believed he was already carrying more than enough stress for both himself and the *Hunley*.

Ralph Wilbanks was not among the divers making that final inspection. He had been the bridge for the project—both between the discovery and recovery, and the archaeologists and divers. But he would not be on the barge for the lift, and that's exactly how he wanted it. He had found the sub and had helped prepare it for recovery. His job was done. While the divers were still in the water, Wilbanks motored up to watch the *Hunley* break the surface from the finest seat in the house—the helm of *Divercity*.

Wilbanks had worked every day of the recovery up to that point, a fact that Bob Neyland had pointed out to him the week before. Even for a contract worker, that was too many hours in the water. Neyland had told him, "We need to schedule you some time off." Wilbanks said that was fine; he would take August 8.

"But that's lift day," Neyland said.

"Yeah, I know."

"Don't you want to be here?"

"Oh, I will be," Wilbanks said. He had pointed to a spot just a few yards away from the *Karlissa B.* "I'll be right there aboard *Divercity*."

Neyland said, however, he could not do that. The area around the crane barge was a restricted area—no boats allowed.

"Who's going to stop me?" Wilbanks asked. He listed the agencies patrolling the water—the coast guard, the state Department of Natural Resources—and pointed out that men from both came by every day. And routinely they waved and yelled, "Hey, Ralph!"

No, Wilbanks said, no one would stop him.

Neyland said nothing more, but later asked Harry Pecorelli to intervene. Pecorelli, who had been part of Wilbanks' NUMA team on the day the *Hunley* was found, was now in charge of security for the project. When Neyland told Pecorelli to do something, the young archaeologist said nothing. Pecorelli simply took out his cell, dialed Wilbanks' number, and handed the phone to Neyland.

"I don't tell Ralph anything," Pecorelli said.

The *Divercity* took its place across from the *Karlissa B* just after sunrise. Wilbanks had a boat full of guests, including his wife, Frances, and Wes Hall, as well as Clive Cussler's full entourage—his wife, Barbara; his son, Dirk; and his *Sea Hunters* coauthor, Craig Dirgo. His Authorship was not onboard, however. He had agreed to hold court on the press boat, providing color and quips for the reporters covering the story. As the mimosas flowed, Wilbanks joked that Clive was missing the party.

Wilbanks was both pleased and amazed by the spectacle unfolding around him. A tour boat was anchored near the *Karlissa B*, providing a front-row seat for VIPs, their friends and other spectators. Hundreds of small boats were gathering around the site, and Wilbanks could see more approaching from land—some of them flying Confederate flags. Among this motley armada, he could pick out johnboats, cabin cruisers and fishing boats. There was even one guy in a kayak. It was pure craziness, and Wilbanks was almost giddy with excitement.

Even the landlocked would be able to watch the lift. Besides the National Geographic film crew documenting the recovery, CNN and the local television stations were broadcasting live from the fleet. It was officially a national news event. Five years earlier, when they'd found the *Hunley*, Wilbanks had told Hall and Pecorelli that the discovery would bring the circus to town. Now it's here, Wilbanks thought—just as he'd always expected.

By 7 A.M., the recovery was officially behind schedule.

The seas had abated somewhat and the tour boat and recovery

barge provided a bit of a seawall, but it still wasn't as calm as Montgomery would like. Although his job included all the heavy lifting—literally—in some ways it was the easiest one on the *Karlissa B*. From his perch, he would take the signal from Wright and begin spooling in industrial cable as if he was reeling in a fish. A big fish.

The lift truss would rise more slowly than an elevator, but it would still only take two minutes to clear the water. If the sub and its truss came out of the water gently, it might take another couple of minutes to set it down on the barge. His biggest concern, other than the seas, was to make sure all four legs of the truss set down on the recovery barge deck at once. If the ocean cooperated, his job would be a piece of cake.

Montgomery spotted Lasch wandering around on deck and decided to mess with him. The tension onboard the *Karlissa B* was thick and Jenks—as Montgomery's friends called him—thought he would lighten the mood. When he saw Lasch headed toward him, he began shaking the coffee cup in his hand like a man suffering from withdrawals. Lasch had a look of panic on his face.

"Are you OK?"

"I'm just a little shaky," Montgomery said. "I seem to be dropping things this morning."

Later, Lasch would find this hilarious, but at that moment he was not in a joking mood. Not when the *Hunley* recovery was at the mercy of an unforgiving sea.

Whitlock had warned him that the recovery might have to be scrubbed, and Lasch was terrified by the possibility. He could not calculate all the problems a delay might cause. It made him sick to think of all the precautions they'd taken only to have the weather come in and screw up their plans at the last minute. There was nothing Lasch could do but wait, and the minutes were ticking by far too slowly.

When the next problem was brought to his attention, Lasch nearly blew a gasket. Some divers had not received passes to see the *Hunley* delivered to the conservation lab and were upset. It mattered little that there were more counterfeit tickets to the lab floating around than real ones. To the divers, it seemed ungrateful. Later, bureaucratic foul-up would be blamed, but for the moment Lasch was livid. Now was not the time to come to him with this sort of thing. He was afraid the entire recovery was in jeopardy, and it brought out the Lascher—as McConnell called it—in him.

Lasch would not relax until he saw the *Hunley* rise out of the water.

Shortly after 7:30, the divers returned to the *Karlissa B*. They reported that the straps were fine, the cables were snug and there was plenty of clearance beneath the sub. It was textbook perfect. The *Hunley* was completely suspended in its lift truss with water flowing under its keel for the first time since the nineteenth century. There was nothing left to be done except wait for the weather, just as Dixon had done more than a century before.

Wright reported all this to Lasch and Whitlock. Finally, Lasch thought, some good news. And the weather slowly seemed to be coming around. The swells were less than three feet; they'd died down by more than a foot in the past 90 minutes. They would give it a little more time, but Wright said this was about as good as it would get for the day.

This is it, Lasch thought. Years of preparation and fund-raising, fighting with contractors and scientists, long days plotting the recovery, it was all over. The lab was ready and now the engineers were ready. The *H. L. Hunley* was about to be introduced to the twenty-first century. Lasch thought about it a second, then gave Wright the thumbs-up. When you're ready, Lasch told him, you go.

"Get yourself to the barge," he told Wright.

It was time.

Engineers have little use for sentimentality.

There was no pause for ceremony before the lift began, no special words spoken, no announcement to the fleet of boats lingering a quarter-mile away from the *Karlissa B*. At 8:38, Steve Wright decided it was now or never. Stray swells were rolling in that were larger than they had been earlier, and he knew the sea had flattened as much as it would for the day. The longer he waited, the more likely the prospects that they would have to abort the recovery. He called Montgomery on the radio and told him to go.

Raise the *Hunley*.

Inside the crane's control booth, Montgomery pulled back on a lever and the cable started to spool. Lasch and McConnell watched the water in front of the crane barge, but it was impossible to see any movement. With 10 feet to go, Montgomery paused to give divers a chance for one last look. They scanned the truss to make sure nothing had come loose, that no errant lines had become tangled. They gave Montgomery a thumbs-up and he hit the lever once again.

Less than 30 seconds later the gray outline of the lift truss appeared in the cloudy water, growing clearer as it rose. Five seconds after Lasch and McConnell caught sight of the truss, the forward conning tower of the *H. L. Hunley* broke the surface.

The first glimpse of the sub was a brief one. As soon as the hull rose above the water a swell washed over it, briefly covering it again. Finally, a long few seconds later, the entire truss was hanging in the air, nearly at eye level. Horns sounded and the thunder of applause echoed over the ocean. The *Hunley* had left the Atlantic for the last time.

It was beautiful.

Nothing could prepare McConnell and Lasch for their first look at the treasure they had chased for so long. Lying in its rescue sling, the *Hunley* looked small, fragile and old. It was covered in a hard coating of sand and shells the same color as a wet Lowcountry beach. But it also looked far sleeker than historical accounts suggested, more advanced than anyone could have imagined. The scientists had described the advanced hydrodynamic shape of the sub to them before, but nothing prepared Lasch and McConnell for the actual sight of the long-lost submarine. It was slender and tapered at the ends, its knife-like bow menacing, even while suspended in the air like a rescued whale.

McConnell and Lasch took one look at the *Hunley* and hugged.

"We did it!" Lasch screamed.

McConnell was almost too stricken with emotion to speak. He remembered a promise he had made to this crew years earlier on the floor of the South Carolina Senate. Yes, they had done it.

"Those fellas will not spend another night in the Atlantic Ocean," McConnell whispered.

The two men most responsible for the *Hunley*'s recovery stood on the deck of the *Karlissa B*, staring at the submarine and listening to the cheers of people in boats a quarter-mile away. They accepted congratulations from the people around them, but barely noticed. It seemed as if the world had slowed down, and they could not allow themselves to relax. The *Hunley* was not out of danger yet.

In some ways, lifting the sub had been the easy part. The most crucial moment came next, as Montgomery swung the truss over the top of the recovery barge waiting to take the *Hunley* home. All four legs of the truss had to set down on the barge's deck simultaneously or else it could put enough stress on the submarine to crack it open. Montgomery had been timing the sea, and calculated he had a 28-second window between swells. It would be the only time the deck of the barge was level.

Montgomery lined up the truss with Wright and Neyland directing him from the barge. He began to lower the *Hunley* as engineers pulled the entire rig with guide lines. When the legs of the truss were less than five feet from the deck, a swell hit the barge broadside, causing it to buck violently and nearly knocking the people onboard off their feet.

Montgomery waited a few more seconds and the deck seemed to stabilize. If he hesitated too long, or gave the men time to regain their footing, he knew another swell would come rolling in and the entire chain of events would repeat itself. Carefully, Montgomery pushed the lever forward. Slowly, gently, the truss set down on the deck. Another cheer went up and Montgomery reminded himself that he needed to breathe.

The *Hunley* was safe.

The atmosphere on the press boat was not nearly as tense or solemn as it was on the *Karlissa B.*

Clive Cussler proved to be a good sport and a capable babysitter for the media. He had taken control of the boat as if he were an emcee, telling stories and jokes that kept the reporters and cameramen from getting bored during the long morning at sea. He had graciously answered every one of their questions—twice—and sat for a couple of formal interviews. The author even told a reporter from the Mobile newspaper that he would be happy to search for the *American Diver* in the city's bay if Alabama would give him a permit.

"You people won't let me go down and find the *Pioneer II*," Cussler said with a grin. "If you did, we'd find it for you."

Cussler was in an expansive mood, as excited as Wilbanks. In some ways this recovery was NUMA's crowning achievement. The good work of his team had led to this moment, and he was happy to share his thoughts with reporters. But when the lift began, Cussler stopped talking and grabbed a pair of binoculars. Nothing would distract him from his first look at the *Hunley.*

While most cameras were trained on the spot in the water where the sub would appear, others were focused on Cussler, simply to record his reaction. He would not let them down, and even offered a play-by-play that some television stations used as a voiceover for their recovery footage. The former ad man never said whether he'd done that on purpose.

"Look at that! Look at that, it's just hanging there—hurrah," Cussler said when the *Hunley* broke the water. "After all this time, to see it happen, and with all this going on it's there."

Clive Cussler watched the recovery of NUMA's greatest find from the press boat on August 8, 2000, regaling reporters with stories as they waited for the Hunley *to surface. Here Cussler is interviewed by Kellen Butler, who would go on to become Kellen Correia, president of Friends of the* Hunley.

Then he stopped. For once in his life, the words wouldn't come. His emotions had caught up with him, and it was overwhelming. All of this, he thought, began with a little expedition 20 years earlier. All of this had sprung from his imagination, just as his books did. Ultimately, NUMA deserved credit for saving the *Hunley* and Cussler was proud. But as he watched the sub land safely on the recovery barge, he could hardly speak.

"It's one of the great pieces of American history," he finally offered.

Cussler recovered quickly and tossed off a few more quips for the reporters, but he was finished babysitting. He wanted to see the sub up close, and he wanted to celebrate. As he offered a few parting thoughts, Cussler climbed onto the press boat's gunnels and looked at the reporters with a mischievous gleam in his eye.

"Well, I have to go now," he said. "NUMA's job is over."

The 69-year-old author then jumped into the Atlantic Ocean, leaving the reporters standing gape-jawed on the deck.

Ralph Wilbanks fortuitously had been watching the press boat and saw his friend go into the water. Earlier that morning Cussler had told him to be ready, that they would rendezvous at some point. But he never let Wilbanks in on the plan. Cussler trusted Wilbanks would know what to do when the time came—and he did. When he saw Cussler dog-paddling away from the press boat, Wilbanks threw the *Divercity* into gear and raced to intercept him.

Within minutes, Cussler was aboard, reunited with his family and enjoying a mimosa. The *Hunley* was safe, and NUMA had fulfilled its mission. Now, he said, the party could begin. It was time to celebrate—and get a better look at that submarine.

The rest was easy.

It took about two hours to get the *Hunley* ready to move. Workers had to secure the lift truss to the barge's deck so that it wouldn't slide in the swells that persisted throughout the day. Then they had to wait for the tugboat to get there to tow the barge on the 15-mile trip through the jetties, across the harbor and up the Cooper River to the navy base. And they had to set up a sprinkler system on the truss.

The plan originally called for scientists to drape the sub in wet burlap blankets to keep it wet. Paul Mardikian warned them against letting the *Hunley* dry out. For the past century, the cold saltwater had slowed the oxidation process, hindering it from completely rusting out the hull. Once the sub was allowed to dry that process would work fast, making up for lost time. But Lasch had nixed the burlap blanket idea immediately. People would want to see the submarine as it came into the harbor, and he did not want to let them down.

He had no idea. Although the boats slowly began to disperse after the raising, many hung around to follow the barge in. And soon Lasch got reports that people were lining the beach at Sullivan's Island and standing on the parapets at Forts Sumter and Moultrie. The Battery was lined with people, as well as Charleston's waterfront park. And hundreds had paid to stand on the flight deck of the USS *Yorktown* to watch the *Hunley* sail into the harbor. In all, there were about 20,000 people waiting for the sub to return home, 136 years after it left.

Lasch, McConnell and the scientists would spend the next three hours waving at people as if they were in a one-float parade. The barge was surrounded by boats, some of which were driven by people dressed in period costumes. Cannons were fired from The Battery, the Maritime Center and the *Yorktown* to commemorate the day. It looked as if the entire city had turned out, and the recovery team could not believe it.

"She's coming home," Pecorelli said. "A little bit late, but she's coming home."

Leonard Whitlock missed much of the excitement. More than two days of straight work leading up to the moment had taken its toll. He had done his job and it had worn him out. For most of the ride, Whitlock was parked in a lounge chair on the deck, right next to the *Hunley*, fast asleep.

Just before the barge set out on the trip through the harbor, Lasch took all the money he had in his pocket and gave it to someone to go for pizza. The pies were delivered just about the time the procession passed Castle Pinckney in the middle of the harbor. The crew ate furiously, laughing and joking in the euphoria that came with success. Lasch didn't bother taking a slice—he was too busy enjoying the ride and the sight of all these people for whom the *Hunley* meant so much. But even after hours of waving at onlookers, he was not prepared for what came next.

As the barge approached the Cooper River bridges, the twin spans that connected Charleston to Mount Pleasant, Lasch noticed that traffic had stopped. People were actually getting out of their cars and leaning over the bridges' railings to watch the *Hunley* pass.

Some of them were even saluting.

Just before 2 P.M., the barge carrying the *Hunley* arrived at the navy base's Pier Juliet. When it docked, welders went aboard to cut the overhanging ends off the lift truss—the parts that had set down on the suction piles—so that it would fit into the conservation lab tank. For two hours the welders toiled while a color guard of Confederate reenactors prepared to escort the sub from the dock to the lab. In that time, several people walked out to the dock for a closer look at the sub. One of them was Randy Burbage, the *Hunley* Commission member who had just buried the sub's first crew.

As he stood staring at the first submarine to sink an enemy ship in battle, tears welled up in his eyes. He was looking at an antique machine that had been cutting-edge technology when it last departed Charleston. This boat had sailed at a time when the Civil War was tearing the country apart. Burbage had spent a lifetime studying those years, and now he was face-to-face with an important chapter in that history. But his thoughts were with the men entombed inside the *Hunley*.

"I'm looking forward to getting these men an honorable, proper burial," he said. "We'll reunite them with the other two crews."

It took another feat of engineering to get the *Hunley* from the back door of the lab and into the tank that would serve as its new home. Using the crane that carried it from the dock, as well as the two mounted in the ceiling of the Warren Lasch Conservation Center, the truss was inched into place with an audience of 300 watching. Finally, 13 hours after McConnell and Lasch had started the day, they had the *H. L. Hunley* safe and secure in the lab. The people who watched the final step of the journey broke into thunderous applause as the sub was set down in its tank. Leonard Whitlock—refreshed from his nap—had finished his job. His plan had worked flawlessly.

Once most of the people had filed out of the lab, McConnell presided over a quiet ceremony at the rim of the tank. It was in part a thank-you for all the people who had worked to get the sub there, as well as a memorial for the men who had been on eternal patrol since the waning days of the Civil War. Running purely on adrenaline, McConnell was able to add emotional heft to an already poignant day.

"If these men could stand here today, they would tell you thank you for bringing them home," McConnell said.

Warren Lasch celebrated by lighting a cigar and enjoying a long smoke with Neyland and *Hunley* Commission attorney John Hazzard. Nearby, as McConnell's ceremony ended, one reenactor played "Taps" on a bugle. Lasch was tired, but he was in a great mood—and with good reason. He had done it.

The recovery of the *Hunley* was a feat unparalleled in the history of underwater archaeology. Under the guidance of Lasch and McConnell, a team of scientists and engineers had salvaged an intact Civil War wreck—literally a time capsule from the nineteenth century. They had done all this under budget, on time and without a single injury. And now the sub would be excavated and restored in a laboratory that was the envy of the scientific world.

It had been a textbook operation and set a new standard for maritime recovery. For years the project would be honored with one safety award after another. Not bad for a couple of guys who had never done anything like it before. Lasch felt he had waited a long time for that cigar, and he had earned it.

What Lasch did not know that evening was that his job was not finished, and the problems were far from over.

CHAPTER 18

1864 Aboard the USS *Wabash*

The federals put on quite a show that evening.

Throughout the night of February 17, the troops on Sullivan's Island watched the "frantic signaling" between the Union blockade ships off Charleston. These rapid-fire flashes of light were passed back and forth for hours—bursts that were clear enough to see, but obscure enough to remain indecipherable. The men at Battery Marshall knew the enemy's patterns well and realized that this much communication was out of the ordinary. Unless a blockade runner approached the coast, the Union fleet usually lay dormant after dark.

But on this night something was afoot, and it had caused the Yankees an inordinate amount of stress.

Col. D. W. McLaurin, the man who had helped Dixon adjust the fish-boat's machinery just hours earlier, was one of the soldiers stationed on the beach that evening. At the time, he did not even entertain the idea that all this drama might have been caused by the torpedo boat he called the "Little Devil." McLaurin and his men simply feared the lights would interfere with their orders for the evening: to watch for George Dixon's signal.

Eventually, the troops believed they spotted the two blue lights that Dixon had told Dantzler he would show if he needed a fire to guide the *Hunley* home. The men were grateful for the task. The night was particularly cold and the fire made their shift infinitely more palatable. Usually the soldiers simply had to endure the weather. Battery Marshall was on strict blackout orders; Dantzler did not want to give the Yankees anything to shoot at. The blazing signal, large enough to be seen for miles, put out a generous amount of heat—and light. But the Union would not fire one round in the direction of Sullivan's Island that night.

They were otherwise occupied.

The evening watch ended with no further sign of the torpedo boat and the men finally wandered off to bed. They did not consider the *Hunley*'s failure to return an unusual occurrence—the sub often stayed out until sunrise. Perhaps they thought it strange that Dixon had signaled for the fire and then did not return immediately, but it was not so curious that they mentioned it to anyone.

When the overnight watchmen took over, they assumed the boat had already returned and included it in their daily report. Dixon and his crew rarely lingered at Battery Marshall after returning from a long trip. They usually just slipped the torpedo, gathered their belongings and set out for Mount Pleasant. Most of the time, they were far too tired to venture into the fort and make conversation. It wasn't unusual for them to pass through without seeing any troops from the fort.

No one bothered to check the dock that next morning. And later that day the entire fort was preoccupied by a mild dusting of snow—a rare occurrence in Charleston. After a cursory look at the strange precipitation, most of the men remained huddled in their quarters when not on duty. For the other troops, the weather was such a distraction that it would be nearly two days later before anyone noticed the *Hunley*'s absence or thought to mention this news to Lieutenant Colonel Dantzler.

The Battery Marshall commander finally realized the *Hunley* was missing on February 19. Dantzler interviewed the men who had been on watch that evening, and they claimed to have spotted Dixon's signal. None of these men thought it odd that they had not personally seen the torpedo boat and, despite its reputation, none of them assumed it had sunk. The troops stationed at Battery Marshall had watched Dixon and his crew return in the boat so many times over the past six weeks they had come to have some measure of faith in the "Little Devil."

But Dantzler was alarmed. He knew that Dixon had been missing far too long and immediately sent word to headquarters in Mount Pleasant.

"I have the honor to report that the torpedo boat stationed at this post went out on the night of the 17th instant (Wednesday) and has not yet returned," Dantzler wrote. "The signals agreed upon to be given in case the boat wished a light to be exposed at this post as a guide for its return were observed and answered. An earlier report would have been made of this matter, but the Officer of the Day for yesterday was under the impression that the boat had returned, and so informed me."

Brig. Gen. Roswell S. Ripley—commander of the First Military District—forwarded the word to Beauregard and noted that unless it had sailed into harbor, the torpedo boat was most likely lost or captured. Ripley, an Ohio native who had lived in Charleston for more than a decade, held Dixon in high regard. He never considered the possibility that Dixon and his crew might have defected—a real problem for the Confederacy in 1864.

"I fear that it is more likely that she has gone down judging from past experience of this machine," Ripley wrote.

It never occurred to Ripley or any of the other Confederates that the *Hunley* might have succeeded in sinking a blockade ship before its disappearance. No one had connected the submarine's absence with the signaling between the Union fleet that night. But the following day Dantzler spotted the listing smokestack and rigging of the *Housatonic*, as well as a tug boat and barge attending to it. He reported this to Ripley, who told Beauregard, "it may be that she was blown up by the torpedo boat."

Beauregard was disheartened by the loss of Dixon. In some ways he blamed himself for having allowed the lieutenant to take the fish-boat back out. But Dixon had seemed so confident and, for most of the winter, the boat had performed exactly as promised. It had even returned the day the men at Battery Marshall reported it lost behind Sullivan's Island, and that had given Beauregard a small amount of confidence.

For a while the general held some brief hope that Dixon and his boat might yet turn up. That was clear when he sent out orders to his staff with a qualifier that no one else believed necessary: "As soon as its fate shall have been ascertained, pay a proper tribute to the gallantry and patriotism of its crew and officers."

When Beauregard heard reports of a sunken blockade ship from Ripley, he reported the news to Richmond immediately in a telegram that credited the *Hunley* with the attack. At that point he did not know this for certain—and wouldn't for another week. Perhaps it was a political claim, or wishful thinking. More likely, the general simply wanted it to be true.

"A gunboat sunken off Battery Marshall. Supposed to have been done by Mobile torpedo boat under Lieutenant George E. Dixon, Company E, Twenty-first Alabama Volunteers, which went out for that purpose, and which I regret to say has not been heard of since."

It was a long week.

The same day Beauregard reported the sinking of the unidentified blockade ship, the Union began a weekend bombardment of the city that would not end until 112 shells had been fired. Two errant shots would hit Fort Sumter, but most of the firepower was aimed squarely at downtown Charleston. That Monday the *Mercury* would report that a sunken blockader lay in Maffitt's Channel and repeated rumors that another Yankee ship had gone down as well.

In Mobile, William Alexander received a letter from George Dixon that had been written on February 17. In it, Dixon reported that he would try to sink a ship that night. Alexander was worried about his friend, particularly when no follow-up letter came. He soon wired Charleston for information. He feared the *Hunley* had simply lost the battle with the tide and was carried out to sea. Thomas Jordan, Beauregard's chief of staff, sent a note back explaining the situation, but it was not nearly enough information for Alexander. He was desperate and sent a telegram to Charleston nearly every day for a week.

Jordan replied to each one, often repeating the same mantra: "No news of the torpedo boat."

The news that Alexander and Charleston had been waiting to hear came at the end of the following week. On February 26, sailors from the *Indian Chief* captured a Union picket boat that had drifted into the harbor near Fort Sumter. The receiving ship crew had been watching the Yankees for days as they tried to slip past the harbor defenses and they finally intercepted a launch carrying six sailors. The Union men gave up without a fight.

These captured navy sailors talked at length about the torpedo boat attack on the *Housatonic*, as it was the most excitement the blockade had seen in months. These men just assumed the Confederates knew all about the battle; they didn't realize that the *Hunley* had not returned. The *Housatonic* had been attacked with little warning, they said, and sank within minutes. Five members of its crew had been lost. The surviving crewmen claimed gunfire did not deter the strange boat, and this news had caused much distress throughout the fleet. The navy had spent a nervous week worried that the South's new secret weapon would strike again.

The Confederates played it cool and did not reveal that this was the first confirmation they had received of the attack. And they allowed the Yankee sailors to believe the *Hunley* had returned. The military leaked the news of the attack to the local papers over the weekend. On Monday, February 29, both the *Daily Courier* and the *Mercury* lauded the great success of the torpedo boat and its fearless crew.

"The glorious success of our little torpedo-boat, under the command of Lieutenant Dixon, of Mobile, has raised the hopes of our people, and the most sanguine expectations are now entertained of our being able to raise the siege in a way little dreamed of by the enemy," the *Courier* reported.

The *Mercury*, as usual, was even more blatant in its subterfuge: "We are glad to be able to assure our readers that the boat and crew are now safe," editor Robert Barnwell Rhett Jr. wrote. Well into spring, the *Mercury* would report new details of the attack every week, often reprinting various accounts from Northern papers. Rhett never admitted that the *Hunley* had simply vanished after its glorious attack on the *Housatonic*.

All this propaganda led to several rumors around Charleston that maintained the *Hunley* had survived and was still stalking the blockade. Some claimed that the sub had gone to Georgetown, nearly 50 miles up the coast. Anyone with any knowledge of the sub would have known that such a journey was impossible, but that did not stop Charleston residents—desperate for any good news—from hoping. One local woman wrote to her sister that she was frustrated because "we can't get at the truth of the fish-boat story."

"Some say she has never returned—while the Generals believes she came ashore safe somewhere near Georgetown," Susan Middleton wrote on March 4. "She is said to have sunk two vessels besides the *Housatonic*—one a transport loaded with troops—this time she did not dive but attacked the enemy on the surface of the water—they seeing her all the time and firing grape and canister without any effect. Torpedoes have been sent to Georgetown to start another expedition."

These rumors spread throughout the South quickly. The day after Middleton penned her letter, Henry Leovy received "vague dispatches" that claimed the *Hunley* had sank the *Housatonic* off

Charleston. Leovy—Horace Hunley's friend and the executor of his will—immediately wrote to General Beauregard for more information. He said, "I am exceedingly anxious to learn whether Lieut. Dixon accomplished his gallant act with our boat or not and whether he had escaped. It will be a source of infinite pride to me to learn this, even in the least manner."

Leovy may have been fishing for information that might lead to a windfall for Hunley's estate. Based on the promises of Charleston shipping companies, the sinking of the *Housatonic* should have been worth $50,000 to the sub's owners. But no one would ever collect that reward money, and Beauregard could offer few details to help. It is not clear whether the general even replied to Leovy. Most likely, Beauregard would not have dared to put the truth of the matter into writing for fear that it might be intercepted by the Union.

Beauregard did not want the Yankees to find out that, in truth, no one knew where the *Hunley* was.

~

The loss of the *Housatonic* was confirmation of Rear Adm. John A. Dahlgren's worst fears. He felt it was a personal defeat, and he was humiliated. Dahlgren had taken the word of Confederate deserters, believed their tale of underwater boats when others would have dismissed such an unlikely story as fantasy. He had issued detailed orders to his fleet on how to avoid attacks. Still this had happened, and Dahlgren felt helpless.

He had fought hard for this command—anything to get him out of the navy's Bureau of Ordnance, which he'd run for 20 years—and now he had to explain to the Secretary of the Navy how one of his ships had been sunk by a tiny boat while he was in Florida assisting his fleet near the St. John's River. Gideon Welles would not take the news well.

Dahlgren returned to Charleston to find the crew of the *Housatonic* living like refugees on the decks of the *Canandaigua* and *Wabash* while the rest of the fleet tried to salvage their wrecked sloop.

It would do no good. The *Housatonic*, Dahlgren's engineers reported, was a total loss. When the admiral reported this news to Welles on February 19, he defensively included a copy of the orders he'd issued to his fleet in January—as if he needed to prove that he had taken the threat seriously.

Dahlgren predicted the entire blockade would soon be "infested with these cheap, convenient and formidable defenses, and we must guard at every point." The admiral had already put in a requisition for several floating torpedo mines to shore up the fleet's defense, and now suggested the navy offer a reward of "not less than $20,000 or $30,000" for the capture or destruction of any "David."

"They are worth more than that to us," Dahlgren noted.

His greatest scheme, however, was to fight fire with fire. Dahlgren was a talented engineer, responsible for some of the greatest weapons employed by the U.S. Navy. The attack on the *Housatonic* inspired him to propose an entirely new fleet of warships. He asked Welles to have the navy build a "number" of torpedo boats for use in and around Charleston. Dahlgren offered detailed descriptions of what he wanted: "length about 40 feet, diameter amidships 5 or 6 feet, tapering to a point at each end; small engine and propeller, an opening of about 15 feet above with a hatch coaming, to float not more than 18 inches above the water."

He was basically describing a *David*, and even included a sketch for the secretary. Based on the report of *Housatonic* sailors, Dahlgren believed it was a *David* that sank the *Housatonic*; he did not realize it was the more advanced weapon the deserters had warned him about. But in truth, Dahlgren feared he no longer had any idea what manner of strange craft was stalking his ships.

As soon as he dispatched his note to the secretary, Dahlgren issued new orders to the fleet. The ships were to keep moving throughout the night; those on the inside of the blockade should take positions on the outside at night, and remain on patrol when not moving. He told his commanders to exercise the "utmost vigilance—nothing less will serve."

"The success of this undertaking will, no doubt, lead to similar attempts along the whole line of the blockade," Dahlgren wrote.

Already, Dahlgren had received a report from Capt. J. F. Green of the *Canandaigua*, who had ordered his crew to inspect the *Housatonic* wreckage. The news was not good—the ship's spar deck was 15 feet underwater and "appears to have been entirely blown off." Although Green believed some of the *Housatonic*'s guns could be salvaged, the ship could not. Whatever had attacked the blockader, it had been deadly effective. The thoughts of a small boat inflicting so much damage on his fleet made Dahlgren shiver. He immediately ordered a full inquiry into the incident, to see what—if anything—his men had done wrong. Dahlgren wanted to know if he could have done something to prevent the loss of one of his ships.

But mostly, he wanted to find out if there was anything he could do to save the rest of the fleet.

~

The hearing convened on the deck of the USS *Wabash* at 11 A.M. on February 26—the same day the Confederates got confirmation that the *Hunley* had sank the *Housatonic*. Dahlgren had appointed the captains of the *Canandaigua*, the *Wabash* and the USS *Flag* to serve as his Naval Court of Inquiry. For more than a week they would hear testimony from the *Housatonic*'s survivors—and the sailors had quite a story to tell. The war along the South Carolina coast became little more than background noise as they relived the night they became victims of the first successful submarine attack in history.

Eventually, 18 men would take the stand and their stories largely corroborated one another's. They painted a scene of military men acting swiftly and as professionally as possible in a moment of confusion and horror. The court would find little contradiction in these accounts, no evidence the men were trying to cover up any mistakes. For the most part, the court simply let them tell their stories. Most of these sailors were greeted by the same opening question from Marine Corps Judge Advocate James B. Young: "Please state all you know of the recent disaster that befell the *Housatonic*."

John Crosby, who had been the acting master on deck that night, was the first called to testify. For more than three hours Crosby recounted everything he could remember from the incident—and he remembered nearly every detail.

"I took the deck at 8 P.M. on the night of February 17 ..." he began.

The *Housatonic*'s crew was eager to talk. For more than a week, they had suffered through the winter—and the lingering effects of the attack—on the decks of the *Canandaigua* and the *Wabash*. They were cold, homeless and simply wanted to get this all over with. Crosby had written two letters to his wife in that time, and they chronicled the trauma of the attack far more emotionally than his testimony suggested.

Crosby lamented that he had lost his only picture of his dear Irene, and he needed her to save money so that he could buy a new suit. His only surviving possessions were the clothes on his back, although he noted that many of his men had escaped only wearing shirts. But mostly he wanted to tell her about the events that would haunt him for years. He was overcome with guilt and could not forget the "pitiful sounds" of the men he had plucked from the cold ocean that night.

"I cannot describe to you the sceen [sic], it was awfull to behold ... Be a good girl and don't worrie about me. I have lost all your pictures. Send me one ... Telegraph to Father and Mother that I am safe & OK," Crosby wrote.

Crosby mentioned none of this to Young. His answers were delivered with the professional detachment the court expected of a naval officer. He described the moment he first saw the strange object in the water. He had asked the quartermaster if it was "nothing but a tide ripple" before realizing that it was in fact a manmade craft—and that it was moving toward the ship very fast. He had given orders to slip the anchor chain and "back the engine." He had called for the captain.

"Describe particularly its apparent dimension, shape and appearance when you saw it on going forward to see if the cable had been slipped," Young asked.

"It looked to me about 25 or 30 feet long, and between 3 and 4 feet wide, like a whale boat upset, and there was a raised appearance about the center of it, which made a ripple in the water," Crosby recalled.

Although the *Housatonic* crew could not reach a consensus on the exact time of the attack, they would agree on most of the actions they took that night. But the men offered wildly different descriptions of the boat that had attacked them. Almost none of them recognized it as an iron warship. J. W. Congdon claimed the boat "resembled a very old water logged piece of timber." C. P. Slade said it looked like "an old log about 24 feet long, only the two ends visible, the middle being underwater." And Lt. F. J. Higginson recalled it having the appearance of a "plank, sharp at both ends." But Higginson conceded that he realized it was no plank when he noticed "a glimmer of light through the top of it."

All of the men swore that by the time they spotted the torpedo boat it was much too close to aim cannons at it—the deck guns were not designed to shoot anything on the water less than a dozen yards away. Several men had shot at the object with side arms or rifles, but none of them saw any evidence their gunfire did any harm to the boat. Ensign Charles Craven, who testified over the first two days of the inquiry, described his attempts to shoot the attacking boat. Craven said he had been in his room when he heard the captain firing at the object, and he ran to the deck to join him.

"I fired two shots at her with my revolver as she was standing towards the ship as soon as I saw her, and a third shot where she was almost under the counter, having to lean over the port to fire it," Craven said. "I then went to my division, which is the second, and consists of four broadside 32 powder guns in the waist, and tried with the captain of the No. 6 gun to train it on the object, as she was backing from the ship, and about 40 or 50 feet off then. I had nearly succeeded, and was about to pull the lock string when the explosion took place."

Craven's testimony would influence *Hunley* mythology for nearly

150 years. His impression that the sub was backing away from the *Housatonic* when the explosion occurred supported the recollections of William Alexander. Forty years later, Alexander would claim the sub used a barbed hook to plant its torpedo into the side of its prey, and then—when the boat was a safe distance away—pulled a lanyard to detonate the explosion. This became accepted fact, supported by Craven's testimony.

But every other man who testified in the inquiry insisted that the explosion happened the moment that the *Hunley* rammed the *Housatonic*.

"The explosion started me off my feet," Crosby recalled, "as if the ship had struck hard on the bottom. I saw fragments of the wreck going up in the air. I saw no column of water thrown up, no smoke and no flame. There was no sharp report, but it sounded like a collision with another vessel."

Some of the other sailors would report seeing a thick, dark smoke in the seconds following impact. But for the most part, they agreed that there had been no tremendous flash or brilliant light from the explosion. All they remembered was feeling tremendous pressure. The little torpedo boat had simply rammed the ship, and within five minutes, the *Housatonic* sank.

"The ship was shaken violently and caused to sink immediately, settling by the stern, keeling over to port as she sank," Higginson recalled. "Many articles about the deck floated off and drifted astern when she sank. I heard a report, not very loud, a low stunning crash, a smothered sound."

The court interviewed nearly all of the men on watch that night, as well as the officers of the deck, and found most of them open and honest. The only hint of subterfuge or revisionist history came during Lewis Comthwait's self-serving account. He recalled a man on bow watch pointing out the object to him, but conveniently omitted the disagreement he'd had with Robert Flemming—an exchange that had wasted nearly a minute.

"The lookout on the starboard cathead reported something adrift on the water, about two points on the starboard bow, and about 100 yards distant. I then made it out with my glasses and it looked to me like a log with two lumps as large as XV inch shell bones on it, about ten feet apart. There was a break of the water forward and aft and between these two lumps," Comthwait claimed. "As soon as I saw it I ran aft and reported it to the officer of the deck."

Flemming, the man who initially alerted him to the object, told the court about Comthwait's hesitation and 2nd Asst. Engineer C. F. Mayer Jr. backed him up. Comthwait had refused to believe the object was dangerous and argued with Flemming. This had delayed the ship's reaction time by precious seconds. But the court made little of this discovery. As soon as they had interviewed the *Housatonic*'s engineers, they realized that another minute would not have made much difference.

J. W. Holickan, the 3rd Asst. Engineer, had been on duty in the engine room at the time of the attack. He testified that his orders for the evening had been to keep "heavy banked fires and 25 lbs. of steam from 6 P.M. to 6 A.M.; to keep everything ready for getting underway at a moment's warning, and to have the engine ready for backing." This followed Dahlgren's orders to the fleet exactly, and Holickan said he kept the steam pressure up a little higher because that was better than having too little.

But it didn't matter.

"I heard the gong beat for Quarters, and gave orders to have everything ready for starting the engine," Holickan said. "Immediately three bells were struck and I gave orders to open the stop valves and back the engine. The engine had made about ten or twenty revolutions, at the rate of about thirty per minute, before I heard the crashing of timber."

The *Housatonic* had barely begun to move when the *Hunley* struck.

On March 5, the court moved to the deck of the *Canandaigua* to take testimony from Capt. Charles Pickering. His injuries from the attack were extensive enough that his doctor would not allow him to leave the ship to attend the hearing on the *Wabash*. The crew had testified that Pickering acted properly on the night of the attack, and he in turn backed up his officers and crew. His orders were promptly obeyed, the captain said, and "Nothing was omitted that could have been done."

Pickering, nursing serious injury and overwhelming regret, said there simply had not been enough time to save the *Housatonic*.

"If I had had two minutes to work in, I could probably have saved the ship and sunk the torpedo craft," Pickering said.

After that the inquiry was effectively over. Dr. Plant reported that five men had been killed, and two—including the captain—"painfully but not dangerously injured." It was clear the men of the *Housatonic* had not panicked, that they had followed their orders and did all that could have been done under the circumstances. The court took only a day to reach a verdict. In his report, Young stated there was little dispute about the incident, and the findings were clear:

First: That the U.S. Steamer *Housatonic* was blown up and sunk by a Rebel torpedo craft on the night of February 17th, Last at about 9 o'clock P.M., while lying at anchor in 24 feet of water off Charleston S.C. bearing E.S.E. and distant from Fort Sumter about 5½ miles. The weather at the time of the occurrence was clear, the night bright and moonlight, wind moderate from the Northward and Westward sea smooth and tide half ebb, the ship's head about W.N.W.

Second: That between 8:45 and 9 o'clock P.M. on said night an object in the water was discovered almost simultaneously by the Officer of the Deck and the lookout stationed at the Starboard cathead, on the starboard bow of the ship about 75 or 100 yards distant, having the appearance of a log. That on further and closer observation it presented a suspicious appearance, moved apparently with a speed of 3 or 4 knots in the direction of the Starboard Quarters of the ship, exhibiting two protuberances above, and making a slight ripple in the water.

Third: That the strange object approached the ship with a rapidity precluding a gun of the battery being brought to bear upon it, and finally came in contact with the ship on her starboard Quarter.

Fourth: That about one and a half minutes after the first discovery of the strange object the crew were called to Quarters, the cable slipped, and the engine backed.

Fifth: That an explosion occurred about three minutes after the first discovery of the object which blew up the after part of the ship, causing her to sink immediately after to the bottom, with her spar deck submerged.

Sixth: That several shots from small arms were fired at the object while it was alongside or near the ship before the explosion occurred.

Seventh: That the watch on deck, ship and ship's Battery were in all respects prepared for a sudden offensive or defensive movement. That lookouts were properly stationed, and vigilance observed and that Officers and crew promptly assembled at Quarters.

Eighth: That order was preserved on board and orders promptly obeyed by Officers and crew up to the time of the sinking of the ship.

The report completely exonerated the crew of the USS *Housatonic*. There was nothing, the court concluded, that the sailors could have done to stop the Confederate torpedo boat or save their ship. Young and the three blockade captains declared that no further proceedings were necessary. The loss of the *Housatonic* was simply a tragedy that should be expected as part of the normal course of war.

The U.S. Navy was not interested in rehashing the first attack by the Confederate torpedo boat. At that moment, they were much more concerned with the next one—and when it might come.

Dahlgren would not let his guard down again. For the rest of the year his fleet remained on high alert, constantly in motion and with a wary eye on the horizon. The watch crew on every ship was ordered to keep a look out for anything strange on the water. They were not to discount anything, especially any object that might at first glance appear to be a log or an old plank.

The Confederates did their best to keep up the ruse. That spring, Beauregard dispatched the *David* on two separate attacks. In March, the little boat rammed the USS *Memphis* twice in the North Edisto River, but its torpedo failed to explode on both tries. The *David* then attempted to sink the *Wabash* at sea, barely a month after the court of inquiry proceedings had concluded on its deck. The *Wabash* crew spotted the semi-submersible as it approached and avoided being hit. But they were not able to capture or sink the infernal little torpedo boat, which they may have mistaken for the *Hunley*.

As the days passed and there were no further signs of the fish-boats, the blockade began to relax. Dahlgren never got his own fleet of submarines, but he would not need them. By then, he had probably learned what the Confederates had known for months.

The *Hunley* was lost.

Part Four

Beneath the Sand

CHAPTER 19

1865–1980 Charleston

The Confederates raised a new flag over Fort Sumter on the morning of February 17, 1865—the first anniversary of the *H. L. Hunley*'s disappearance.

Most people in Charleston likely did not realize the significance of the date, and many probably did not even remember the lost fish-boat, for at that moment they had far more pressing concerns on their minds: the Stainless Banner hoisted above the parapet that day would be the last to fly at Sumter. When the flag was lowered in the evening, the men who had held the fort for nearly four years slipped out under the cover of darkness and boarded boats for the mainland. Fort Moultrie and Castle Pinckney kept their colors flying overnight in hopes of buying time for the retreating troops.

The Confederate military was abandoning Charleston.

It had been a miserable winter. Charleston was on strict rations, crime was rampant and the siege continued with thunderous regularity. For two months, the city's remaining residents had been following news of Sherman's march to the sea with a mix of awe and terror. They feared the unmerciful general would turn his attention to Charleston after capturing Savannah at Christmas. In truth, the Union did not need Sherman in Charleston—there were more than enough troops en route to take the city without his help.

On February 10, Union barges had landed nearly 4,000 soldiers on James Island, while more regiments decamped at Bull's Bay, 20 miles north of the city. They cut the telegraph lines into Charleston and blocked the roads. The Confederates were outnumbered and weary. There were just too many damned Yankees. General Beauregard, who had since moved on to another command, sent orders to Charleston instructing all troops to retreat.

It would take days for the Confederates to make the necessary preparations. Beauregard gave them a long list of tasks to complete before they abandoned the city, the most important of which was to "burn all papers before you leave." The Union might take Charleston but they would find little of use left behind by the Confederates.

While the Southerners prepared to abandon the city on February 17, Sherman marched into Columbia 100 miles to the north. By nightfall South Carolina's capital city would be captured and ablaze. But the fires there were almost matched by those that spread across Charleston that night. In a single evening the Confederates did more damage to the city than the siege ever had. Fire ravaged the peninsula as the Southerners burned cotton, rice and ammunition—anything that might be of value to invading troops. It would be the worst night in Charleston's long and storied history.

The Confederates ignited powder magazines, blew up their batteries and finally set charges to sink the city's three ironclads. The *Charleston* and *Chicora* went quietly, but locals later swore that as the *Palmetto State* burned to the waterline the distinct image of a palmetto tree formed in the smoke rising from its hull. The legend would endure for more than a century. It was the only thing resembling hope Charleston would see for a long time.

The next morning Union blockade ships sailed into the harbor and landed at the Cooper River docks. Navy lookouts had suspected something was up for days, having spied Confederates moving equipment that had not been touched for years. Just after sunrise they realized the forts at the harbor mouth were abandoned, and the blockade fleet steamed into the city. When the first Union officers stepped ashore, a city alderman met them with a letter from the mayor, surrendering Charleston and asking for their help extinguishing the fires that still burned across the peninsula. There was no one else left to do it.

Less than two months later Gen. Robert E. Lee laid down his sword at Appomattox Court House, Virginia, ending the War Between the States. As Lee and Gen. Ulysses S. Grant went through the war's ceremonial end at the McLean House, Confederate and Union troops played baseball on the lawn—the first step in a long and painful road to reconciliation and reconstruction.

More than 620,000 men—and perhaps as many as 800,000—had died as a result of the American Civil War, making it the bloodiest conflict in the country's history. Few families were left unscathed by the war, and some would never learn the fate of their husbands, sons or brothers. In the midst of this devastation, the loss of eight men aboard a strange iron boat barely rated a footnote.

Even if Charleston had momentarily forgotten the *Hunley*, the Union Navy had not. Adm. John Dahlgren, still obsessed with the loss of the *Housatonic*, sent Lt. W. L. Churchill to the waters off Sullivan's Island to examine the ship's wreckage three months before Charleston surrendered. Dahlgren wanted to know if the ship could be salvaged but, perhaps more importantly, he wanted to know if the torpedo boat was down there alongside it. Months had passed without an attack, and the admiral suspected the Confederates' secret weapon had been lost.

Churchill examined several blockade runners wrecked in the waters off the South Carolina coast and declared them all beyond saving. The *Housatonic*, he reported, was a worm-eaten mess. The ship was sitting mostly upright, buried in about five feet of sand as best he could tell. Churchill battled rough weather for the entire expedition and claimed he could not find the *Housatonic*'s magazine. What he did find told Dahlgren all he needed to know.

"The cabin is completely demolished as is also all the bulkheads aft of the mainmast," Churchill reported. "The coal is scattered about her lower decks in heaps as well as muskets, small arms and quantities of rubbish. The propeller is in an upright position—the shaft appears to be broken. The rudder-post and the rudder have been partly blown away. The upper parts of both are in their proper position while the lower parts have been forced aft."

The *Hunley* had done a thorough job of destroying the only blockade ship it ever engaged—there was nothing left to salvage from the wreck of the *Housatonic*. Had the fish-boat survived, it possibly could have repeated this trick over and over, even with Dahlgren's extra precautions. The admiral realized this, which is why he wanted confirmation that the torpedo boat had sunk as well. But Churchill's report left Dahlgren unsettled, his questions unanswered.

"I have also caused the bottom to be dragged to an area of 500 yards around the wreck, finding nothing of the torpedo boat. On the 24th the drag ropes caught something heavy. On sending a diver down to examine it, it proved to be a quantity of rubbish."

Churchill never specified, however, whether his search for the torpedo boat extended 500 yards in every direction.

On February 15, 1868, just two days before the fourth anniversary of the *Hunley*'s disappearance, its ancestor resurfaced. *The New Orleans Picayune* announced the public sale of a two-ton "torpedo boat" built during the war. The boat was lying near the New Basin Canal, where Union troops had discovered it in December 1863. The auction was scheduled for noon that day in front of the Custom House—where Horace Hunley had once toiled, dreaming of greatness.

"It was built as an experiment, and was never fully perfect," the paper reported, "and is only valuable now for the machinery and iron which is in and about it."

That afternoon, the *Pioneer* was sold for scrap iron. The only submarine ever officially recognized during the Civil War brought $43.

A decade later, in July 1878, another strange boat was found on a canal near Lake Pontchartrain. It lay in the weeds on the banks of the Bayou St. John until 1895, when it was moved to the nearby Spanish Fort. The craft was made of iron, 20 feet long, with a small propeller and odd fins on its side. For nearly a century, most people would assume the tiny craft was the long-lost first effort of James McClintock. But by the time it was discovered, the real *Pioneer* had been destroyed by scrappers.

In 1942, the mysterious submarine was acquired by the Louisiana State Museum and eventually went on display in New Orleans' Jackson Square. Some believe the vessel was a prototype built during the war by the Tredegar Iron Works, back in the day when New Orleans was on the cutting-edge of maritime technology. Others claimed a planter built the boat, and two slaves drowned attempting to sail it. There is no proof of either story. The origin of the tiny sub remains a mystery.

In 1870, the Army Corps of Engineers commissioned a study of the approaches to Charleston Harbor. The plan was to locate and clear obstructions left over from the war, and there were plenty of them—enough to keep surveyors busy for months.

Early in the fighting, the Union Navy sank a number of junk ships in the channel to hinder the movement of blockade runners. They were old whaling ships, stripped of their rigging and ballasted with heavy New England rock. Charleston residents derisively called these ships "the Stone Fleet." Half a dozen years after the war's end, those ships still blocked the harbor entrance, along with a number of Union wrecks including the ironclads *Weehawken*, *Patapsco* and *Keokuk*. Almost every approach to the city was littered with the reminders of war.

These wrecks interfered with Charleston commerce, such as it was. The city had not recovered from the war; it would take most of a century to return to its prominence as a leading East Coast port. But all this war debris was not helping the city reestablish its maritime industry. Over the course of several months, the Corps of

Engineers found several troublesome hulks in the channel, none causing more problems than the *Housatonic*. The survey report claimed the warship and its attacker were found four miles west of the *Weehawken*. Although the report gave no details of the *Hunley*'s condition—if that's indeed what they found—the engineers said the *Housatonic*'s entire stern had been blown off. Someone, the engineers claimed, had tried to salvage parts of it. But much of the ship remained in the channel.

"It is a dangerous wreck lying in deep water in the track of northerly bound vessels, and should be removed," the report stated.

Six months after the Army Corps of Engineers report, Charleston newspapers ran stories that alleged the *Hunley* had been discovered by the engineers. These short notices recounted the battle, the speed with which the *Housatonic* was dispatched, and noted that the torpedo boat had been lost with it, "disappeared forever from mortal view."

"Whether she went down with her enemy or whether she drifted out to sea to bury her gallant dead, was never known, and their fate was left till the great day when the sea shall give up her dead," the *Daily Republican* reported. "But within a few weeks past, divers in submarine armor have visited the wreck of the *Housatonic*, and they have found the little torpedo vessel lying by her huge victim, and within are the bones of the most devoted and daring men that ever went to war."

A few days later, the *Charleston Daily Courier* also reported the discovery of the *Hunley* with "Nine skeletons at the wheel."

Neither of these stories offered sources for their claims, and if the Army Corps of Engineers believed the *Hunley* was lying next to the *Housatonic*, they obviously had made a mistake. But these claims, the first of many, served to keep the legend of the fish-boat alive a few more years. By then, the age of the submarine was slowly arriving. The same year French author Jules Verne published *20,000 Leagues Under the Sea*, military leaders began to show interest in building warships much like the one Captain Nemo sailed around the globe.

The British Navy, at the time still clinging to its reputation as the best fleet in the world, sought advice from the one man who knew quite a bit about building craft that sailed beneath the waves. In October 1872, James McClintock secretly met with British Navy officials on the *Royal Alfred* just off Halifax, Nova Scotia. The British were interested in McClintock's plans for a new submarine and he was searching for a new country. He felt that his own had left him behind.

Onboard the *Royal Alfred*, McClintock presented papers that outlined his work on three underwater craft built during the American Civil War. He said the most successful of these, the *Hunley*, had been lost in a storm a few hours after sinking the *Housatonic*. He never said where he got this information and may have made up the story to downplay the fact that his crowning engineering feat had not survived its first battle.

His drawings of the *Hunley* were simplistic, and it seemed McClintock confused design elements from his earlier boats. He may have forgotten some of the details, but he had not lost interest in building submarines. After all, the *Hunley* had been his greatest achievement. But as usual, McClintock's ambition was tempered by his meager finances. Ultimately he offered to build the Royal Navy a submarine that could carry a crew of three—for a "fair remuneration" and the chance to become a British subject.

The navy officers eventually invited McClintock to London to discuss a business arrangement in greater depth, but he would never get the chance. McClintock claimed to be broke and asked the navy to pay his travel expenses. But the British refused and quietly dropped the idea. Within years, the British Navy began work on their own submarines, perhaps inspired by drawings and technical details of the world's first successful attack sub.

McClintock would never get a chance to surpass his work on the *Hunley*. He reportedly died in 1879 while a submarine mine he was testing in Boston Harbor exploded. It was the one time he was not cautious enough. At the time, McClintock was only 50 years old and nearly penniless. In his lifetime, he never received recognition as the father of the modern submarine.

More than a year after his purported death, a man professing to be James McClintock showed up at the British consul offices in Philadelphia. He claimed to have a background in submarines and marine warfare and was willing to sell his technology. This man, who some speculate could have been a later associate of McClintock, eventually delivered several faulty devices to the British—and collected more than $1,000—before he simply disappeared.

In 1872, the year the real McClintock met with British Navy officials off Halifax, Benjamin Maillefert was hired by the Army Corps of Engineers to remove some of the wrecks identified in their study of Charleston Harbor. It was a major operation that would take months. Maillefert's divers used explosives to destroy and scatter several wrecks, including the *Weehawken* and *Housatonic*, in an attempt to clear the channel to a depth of 20 feet. When he finished his work, Maillefert said the wooden gun-boat *Housatonic* was cleared to a depth of 20-and-a-half feet, but claimed "(t)he torpedo boat, sunk at the same time and place, could not be found." However, he may have stumbled across the *Hunley* and not realized it.

In the winter of 1872–73, Maillefert ran afoul of local divers who claimed they had the rights to salvage Confederate wrecks. One of these men was Angus Smith, who had raised the *Hunley* the first two times it sank. Smith later said the two clashed over the torpedo boat, but nothing came of it when Maillefert declared it could not be found.

A few years later, however, Smith told Beauregard that he had in fact located the *Hunley*. At the time the general was writing his memoirs and sent Smith a note inquiring about some small detail of their work together in Charleston during the war. Smith responded promptly, answering Beauregard's question, and then noted that he had seen the fish-boat.

"I went to work to save the torpedo boat, and I got on top of her, and found out the cause of her sinking," Smith wrote to Beauregard in 1876. "The boat is outside or alongside the *Housatonic*. She can be lifted any time our people wish. Maillefert is busted and out of the way. I have no more to say than that she can be saved, and in my opinion she is as good as the day she was sunk."

Smith's account, which was overlooked by researchers for more than a century, is perhaps the only confirmed sighting of the *Hunley* between 1864 and the day NUMA discovered it in 1995. Angus Smith was an impeccable witness: he had spent weeks diving on the submarine the first two times it sank and knew exactly what it looked like. But the most intriguing part of the letter, which lends the most credibility to his claim, is that he said the *Hunley* was "outside" the *Housatonic*—which meant it was farther out to sea.

For more than a century, no one could find the *Hunley* because they assumed it had been lost on the way back to shore, somewhere between the wreck of its victim and Sullivan's Island. Until Clive Cussler arrived in Charleston, no one had thought to look for the sub beyond the wreck of the *Housatonic*.

Smith returned to the waters off Sullivan's Island a few years later with his son, James. The master showman P. T. Barnum had allegedly offered $100,000 to anyone who would recover the fish-boat for his traveling show of oddities, and Smith believed this would be easy money. The hint of such a reward attracted an untold number of treasure hunters, but none of them had the same advantages as Smith. But he could not relocate the *Hunley*. Smith and his son eventually searched five acres of the ocean floor, but they found no sign of the fish-boat. The *Hunley*, it seemed, had vanished.

By that time, 15 years after its sinking, the torpedo boat may have been completely buried beneath the Atlantic sand. If it wasn't, it soon would be.

In 1879, the same year P. T. Barnum put a bounty on the *Hunley*, the federal government began work on an ambitious public works project outside Charleston Harbor. Engineers began building two stone jetties, each four miles long, to protect the channel leading into the harbor. These rocks walls would prevent silting and save the Army Corps of Engineers millions in recurring dredging costs. As the nineteenth century came to a close, ships were growing larger, with deeper drafts, and they needed more clearance to reach the harbor—a problem that would continue into the twenty-first century.

Construction of these jetties would take more than a decade and, when finished, they changed the geography of the South Carolina coast. The jetties stopped the natural flow of more than two billion cubic feet of sand each year. Along the Atlantic coast, sand naturally flows from north to south. The sand that erodes from one beach helps replenish another one farther down the coast. But the jetties disrupted nature's natural course. South of the new channel into Charleston Harbor, Morris Island would nearly disappear into the sea. Within decades, all traces of Battery Wagner were gone. Even the island's lighthouse would eventually stand in a shallow inlet, waves lapping at its base.

To the north of the jetties sand began to build up, allowing Sullivan's Island to accrete. The ocean just off the island became much shallower. The *Housatonic* wreck would continue to be a hazard to navigation and in 1901 the *News and Courier* carried an account of divers inspecting its wreckage in anticipation of moving, or dynamiting, it once more. But for the most part the stratigraphy of the Atlantic seabed was changing, forever covering—and protecting—the lost fish-boat in a heavy blanket of sand. Most likely, nature saved the *Hunley* from the treasure hunters who would soon be searching for it.

In the final years of the nineteenth century—and three decades after John Dahlgren had first suggested it—John P. Holland and Simon Lake worked separately to build the first submarines for the U.S. Navy.

Lake, who came to be called "the father of the modern submarine," befriended Charles Hasker—one of the few surviving men with any recollection or knowledge of the *H. L. Hunley*. Even in middle age, Hasker had a serviceable memory and provided Lake with a sketch of the boat. The engineer was skeptical; he did not believe the submarine's entire crew had sat along one side of the boat. He argued that such a configuration would have thrown the sub off keel. Lake did not understand, and Hasker did not realize, that the sub was heavily ballasted and the propeller cranks forced the men to hunch over. Essentially, the crew sat with their body weight almost exactly in the center of the boat.

Still, Lake incorporated several McClintock ideas into his boat and eventually even published one of Hasker's sketches in a magazine article he had written about his own submarine. In appreciation for all his help, Lake even gave the one-time *Hunley* crewman a ride on the *Argonaut*. It was Hasker's most uneventful submarine voyage.

The launch of submarines built by Lake and Holland just after the turn of the century rekindled memories of the *Hunley*—most of them wildly inaccurate tales about a shaky boat that sank six times and killed upwards of fifty men. Most of the people who remembered the fish-boat actually knew little about it; just rumors repeated during the war and in the years after it ended. Only one man alive truly remembered the *Hunley*, and he was offended by the wild stories that he felt desecrated the memory of his friend George Dixon.

In 1902, William Alexander was an old man still living in Mobile. For decades, he had said little of his experiences with the *Hunley* in Mobile and Charleston—those were old times best forgotten, to Alexander's thinking. He occasionally responded to letters seeking information about the submarine, including several from Charleston resident and Confederate veteran Augustine Smythe. His short notes to Smythe, Alexander finally decided, were not enough. In 1902, he wrote a long reminiscence of his association with the *Hunley* for a New Orleans newspaper.

Alexander's "The True Stories of the Confederate Submarine

This sepia-wash drawing by R. G. Skerrett was done in 1902, around the time William Alexander revived the legend of the fish-boat. The drawing is obviously based on Conrad Wise Chapman's painting and sketches of the Hunley. *Courtesy of the U.S. Naval History and Heritage Command.*

Boats" proved so popular that it was reprinted in newspapers around the country. Soon the old man found himself asked to speak to various groups about his experiences, which he did happily. Alexander was the only survivor of the first attack submarine's final crew and his memories ensured the *Hunley* would not be forgotten.

Addressing members of the Iberville Historical Society in Louisiana in 1903, Alexander criticized a *Harper's Weekly* article that had recently declared the era of "Submarine navigation has arrived."

"The trouble with it, however, is the implied date of its arrival. All of these operations had been successfully accomplished by the *Hunley,*" Alexander told the group. "If so then it would not seem to indicate but absolutely demonstrate that submarine navigation arrived with the *Hunley* forty years ago."

Official military records tell scant little about the operations of the *Hunley* in that winter before its attack on the *Housatonic*. It was not technically a Confederate project, so it operated in a vacuum—kept secret from the public and largely out of the purview of military leaders. Only Alexander knew exactly what transpired in December and January of 1863–64, when the sub was preparing for its historic mission. He realized that if he did not tell the story, no one else ever would.

Alexander recalled his work with Dixon to refurbish the submarine after it sank with Horace Hunley at the helm; their efforts to recruit a new crew; the long walk from that Mount Pleasant boarding house to Battery Marshall; the time they nearly died in the creek behind Sullivan's Island. But mostly, Alexander remembered the day he was called back to Mobile, the last day he saw George Dixon.

The rest he knew only from Dixon himself.

"I received from Dixon two notes shortly after reaching Mobile," Alexander wrote, "one stating that the wind still held in the same quarter, etc., and the other telling the regrets of the crew at my leaving and their feeling toward me; also that he expected to get men from the artillery to take my place. These notes together with my passes, etc, are before me as I write. What mingled reminiscences they bring!"

Alexander recalled amazing details about the *Hunley* but age had left his memory faulty and he inadvertently added to the mountains of misinformation about the submarine. The engineer claimed the fish-boat carried a crew of nine. He said the sub's spar was made of pine, the hull simply a boiler cut into two pieces. In some cases, he may have been remembering the *American Diver*, which he also helped build. And Alexander's sketches of the *Hunley*, the boat he was most familiar with, contained several glaring errors.

But Alexander had done something far more important than leave behind a schematic of the torpedo boat. He had preserved its history.

Harper's Weekly had been right about one thing: by the dawn of the twentieth century, the era of the submarine had arrived—this time for good. Lake eventually lost the contract to his competitor and the U.S. Navy launched the USS *Holland* in 1900. But it would be another 14 years before anyone repeated the *Hunley*'s amazing feat. On September 5, 1914, the German *U-21* torpedoed the British cruiser

Pathfinder in the Firth of Forth. The blast killed 256 men and sank the *Pathfinder* in seconds. It had taken more than 50 years to repeat what George Dixon and his crew had accomplished in the waning days of the Civil War.

Less than a year later another German U-boat, the *U-20*, torpedoed the Cunard Line's RMS *Lusitania* on May 7, 1915. The attack drew the United States into World War I, and the navy quickly needed more ships. Soon Simon Lake had another chance to build submarines. His design would incorporate many features of the *Hunley* based solely on the descriptions Charles Hasker had provided. McClintock had truly been generations ahead of other engineers. By the time the United States was drawn into the Second World War, the navy had a fleet of about 250 submarines.

It seemed only fitting that Charleston would one day become a base for some of those submarines. In the 1940s, the navy decided to divert several of its subs to the Charleston Naval Shipyard for refits, and the federal government opened the Charleston Naval Weapons Station— home of two submarine squadrons and a tender. By the middle of the twentieth century, the sight of conning towers slicing through Charleston Harbor became a familiar sight to local residents. The subs departed the city on a course that took them within a mile of their lost ancestor.

In 1957, Charleston resident and World War II veteran Robert Bentham Simons took note of this coincidence and suggested the navy use its fleet to search for the fish-boat. The *Hunley* was at the time enjoying a mild resurgence in popularity, due in part to F. van Wyck's novel *Our Valiant Few*, which fictitiously recounted the story of the sub, George Dixon and Horace Hunley. Simons knew the U.S. Atlantic Mine Force staged drills just offshore and he asked base officials to use their minesweepers to try and locate the *Hunley*.

Simons had studied the harbor and the location of the *Housatonic*'s wreckage, and he developed several theories as to where the *Hunley* might rest. He turned over his notes and his maps to the navy. Eventually, the minesweeper *Adroit*'s sonar picked up one promising anomaly on the ocean floor. Simons was ecstatic—the target was in a location where he had concluded the *Hunley* might be. In June 1957, the Charleston papers reported "Salvage of Sub *Hunley* has 50-50 Chance For Success." The article mentioned the navy's promising target and quoted experts already planning to recover the sub—if its hull was stable enough.

But the navy, in the midst of a cold war, had little time to devote to such a non-strategic endeavor. Two months later, the *Hunley* project was suspended. Navy officials promised Simons to get back to the area "at some future, indefinite date," as "time and official assignments allowed." But the navy never returned to check out the anomaly detected by the *Adroit*. A year later, however, when the first nuclear-powered submarine—the *Nautilus*—sailed under the North Pole, it carried a binder to honor the trailblazing *Hunley*. The notebook held all known documents relating to the Confederate submarine.

Three years after the *Nautilus*' historic voyage, the U.S. Navy honored Horace Hunley by naming the first Tender in its Polaris Submarine Fleet after him. The USS *Hunley* was launched in 1961 and commissioned the following year. It sailed the world assisting navy subs until 1995, when it was decommissioned. When the government finally sold the ship for scrap in 2007, it was bought by a recycling company in, of all places, Louisiana.

Hunley had come home.

For the next two decades, treasure hunters and amateur divers occasionally wandered into Charleston waters to look for the lost submarine. Many of them had nefarious designs on salvaging the submarine for personal profit—or at the very least cutting off pieces to sell as souvenirs. But as the centennial of the war came and went, the Confederate submarine was nearly as lost to history as these modern-day pirates. The only memorial to the *Hunley* came when a group of technical college students built a model of the submarine based on William Alexander's faulty drawings.

The model was given a small display area in the basement of a downtown Charleston bank and soon forgotten by all but the most ardent Civil War aficionados—even though the war was suddenly more popular than it had ever been. Shelby Foote's three-volume epic of the War Between the States offered only passing reference to the most advanced naval attack of the nineteenth century, relying on that 1870 news report that claimed the little sub had been found alongside its victim.

But by then, most people around Charleston knew better. It seemed nearly everyone had given up any hope that the lost Confederate submarine would ever be found. No one even bothered to seriously look for the *H. L. Hunley* anymore. It had become just another Civil War legend, another sad story of a lost cause.

And then, in 1980, an adventure novelist named Clive Cussler arrived in Charleston.

The rest is history.

This model of the Hunley *was built by technical college students in the 1960s, based on William Alexander's sketches of the submarine. The model is a very accurate depiction of Alexander's drawings, but bears only passing family resemblance to the real thing. For years, the model was housed in a small museum in the basement of a downtown Charleston bank. Today, the model sits in front of the Charleston Museum. Courtesy Ralph Wilbanks.*

CHAPTER 20

2001–2014
North Charleston

The sub's interior was claustrophobic, the smell overpowering and a want of air made it nearly impossible to breathe.

Maria Jacobsen almost choked. On her first venture inside the *H. L. Hunley*, the crew compartment was still mostly filled with sediment, rotting marine life and the stench of sulfur. This was all bad enough, but the sub was also just so *confining*. She felt trapped, and could not take it for long before she had to get out, get some fresh air. Jacobsen—the first person to enter the *Hunley* in more than a century—suddenly had a much better appreciation for the conditions George Dixon and his crew endured.

But before the archaeologist crawled out of the *Hunley*, she found the remains of one of those men.

It was March 21, 2001, and the excavation of the submarine had been underway for nearly two months. After scientists spent the fall of 2000 mapping and studying the sub's exterior, Bob Neyland determined the only way to get inside was to remove some of the *Hunley*'s hull plates. Conservator Paul Mardikian had assured the team he could open the hatches easily, but they were far too small to accommodate the delicate work of excavation. The archaeologists simply needed more room.

The central hull compartment of the *Hunley*, they had learned, was made of eight semicircular wrought iron plates topsides, another eight on the bottom (the conning towers and other pieces, by contrast, were cast iron). The hull plates, each one about 33 inches wide, connected to a central strip of iron that ran down both flanks (the "expansion strake," Alexander had called it). The forward conning tower sat on the first of the topside plates, the aft hatch on the eighth. After days of calculation, Neyland and his team decided it would not harm the hull's structural integrity to take off a few of those plates.

On February 16, scientists removed the first of three hull plates from the sub. They eventually took off the third, fifth and seventh top-side hull plates by drilling out their rivets, prying them off and lifting them by crane. Beneath those hull plates they found the sub packed to the ceiling with a gray-black mud that had the consistency of fudge. This sediment would be difficult to sift, the work slow. For weeks the dig turned up almost nothing—an animal bone in the aft ballast tank, a medicine bottle, a few buttons. Two of the buttons, found on the crew's bench, had come off the uniform of an artilleryman. The other button was rubber, from a U.S. Navy overcoat. Jacobsen assumed it had belonged to James Wicks, the old salt of the crew.

The early days of the excavation were disheartening, but Jacobsen realized most of the sub's contents probably had settled to the bottom of the crew compartment. They would find nothing in the high mud. Finally, they decided someone must climb into the sub to expand the reach of the dig. Jacobsen was the logical choice. She was the senior archaeologist, and she was the smallest.

Despite her discomfort inside the sub, Jacobsen was optimistic. The mud had left the *Hunley*'s interior nearly devoid of oxygen and that was a promising sign; less oxygen meant the artifacts they found would be better preserved. Jacobsen did not expect to find anything on her first trip inside, however. So she was surprised that, while digging just under the snorkel box, she found something. Jacobsen concentrated on the area, scooping away one spoonful of mud at a time, until she recognized what she had.

It was a human rib cage.

Jacobsen had excavated grave sites around the world, so bones did not bother her. But she was not ready for this. Not so soon. She had found the remains of a *Hunley* crew member, and it broke her heart when she realized these were the remains of someone who was barely more than a boy. He couldn't have been older than 19 or 20 when he died a mysterious death at the bottom of the Atlantic Ocean. But already this young man had a herniated disk in his spine; he had worked himself ragged, most likely aboard the submarine. And it had gotten him killed. Jacobsen, normally a stoic scientist, was overcome with emotion. It was just so sad.

The second crewman was uncovered six days later; the next on March 30. On April 2, the scientists reached the first officer, Joseph Ridgaway, in the back of the sub. By the middle of April, the archaeologists had located seven crewmen (and briefly thought they had eight). The only man unaccounted for was Dixon. Along with these human remains the scientists found canteens, pocket knives, hats. The most startling discoveries were still weeks away.

By early May, the archaeologists determined there were only seven stations on the propeller crank, a revelation that caused them to question all *Hunley* history. Together with the captain, that added up to eight men on the crew. The bench extended forward beyond the first crank station, but the purpose of that space wasn't clear. Another man could have fit inside, they decided. But everything they found suggested there were only eight men onboard the night the *Hunley* disappeared.

It was odd. Most accounts of the submarine, including William Alexander's extensive writings, insisted the *Hunley* carried a crew of nine. Even documents produced contemporary to the *Hunley* suggested it took nine men to operate the sub. But the record of casualties did not reflect this. In the first sinking, five men died, and three were listed as survivors. When the sub sank the second time, with Horace

Hunley at the helm, there had been eight men aboard. Why did most people insist the sub carried nine men? It was just another question the *Hunley* would not answer. The only plausible explanation was that the crew had always included alternates.

No matter how many men they found onboard, Jacobsen's favorite would always be the kid she found first. She didn't realize it at the time, but Jacobsen had discovered the remains of Arnold Becker, the young immigrant and riverboat engineer whom Dixon had recruited off the *Indian Chief* in December 1863. Given Becker's place at the first crank station, she figured Dixon must have liked him, too.

After Jacobsen expanded the dig, new discoveries came nearly every day. The scientists found tattered shoes, remnants of clothing and what looked like human hair. And nearly a month after Becker's remains were discovered, archaeologists found the first skull at the bottom of the submarine. They ultimately found seven skulls, all in a remarkable state of preservation—they still held the sailors' brains. It was an astonishing find and suggested that the sub's interior had not been exposed to large marine life for very long—if at all. Scientists tried to downplay the discovery to avoid sensationalism. Luckily, they soon found something else that kept everyone distracted.

Stuck to the back of one of the sailor's skulls they found the I.D. tag of a Union soldier.

The round copper medallion was about the size of a half-dollar, the sort of thing soldiers bought themselves and wore onto the battlefield for the helpful but morbid purpose of allowing their remains to be identified. This medallion had George Washington in profile on one side, and a name on the other: Ezra Chamberlin. He had been a member of Company K, Seventh Regiment of Connecticut Volunteers—a man who was a long way from home. This raised the obvious question: Had a Connecticut Yankee been aboard the *Hunley*?

It was perhaps the most controversial find of the dig. The dog tag sparked several conspiracy theories around Charleston, and the media picked up several of the stories. Some believed Chamberlin must have defected; others assumed he was a prisoner of war, forced to sail on the *Hunley*. A few suspected the man wearing the medallion had, in fact, killed Chamberlin in battle. It made for good speculation, but there was little evidence to support any of those theories.

Union records suggested Chamberlin had been lost during the first attempt to take Battery Wagner on Morris Island in July 1863 (the second attempt was the subject of the movie *Glory*, which told the tale of a regiment of free black soldiers, the Fifty-fourth Massachusetts). But it was not that simple. Pension records indicated that the government refused to pay benefits to Chamberlin's family because they had no official record of his death. Had he been taken prisoner instead?

The most likely explanation, which would come months later, was far less romantic. Scientists eventually concluded the man wearing the medallion was Joseph Ridgaway, Dixon's first officer on that final mission. Ridgaway had come from the *Indian Chief*, which supplied troops for picket duty on Morris Island in the summer of 1863. Most likely, Ridgaway had found Chamberlin's I.D. on the island, or got it from someone who had. It wasn't the sexiest story, but it made the most sense.

Other mysteries would not be put to rest so easily.

The medallion only intensified what had become something of a gold rush mentality on the excavation. Every day brought a new discovery. Some of these items solved lingering mysteries while others raised frustrating new questions. It added to the excitement of the dig and, soon, even McConnell and Lasch occasionally joined in. They were no less immune to artifact fever than the scientists.

One day, Lasch was siphoning through mud taken from the crew compartment. He found the work slow and tedious, but interesting. Chamberlin's story had fascinated him, and he wondered what other information the sub might hold. As he dug, Lasch finally hit something. His heart raced as he pulled it from the mud and wiped it off.

He was holding a piece of Confederate money. Could this be Dixon's coin?

Lasch alerted the scientists and Neyland immediately jumped into action. "Which bucket did this come out of?" He started quizzing the scientists, trying to determine exactly where this Southern currency had been found.

Lasch ran back to the bucket and furiously started digging again. This could be big, he thought. But within minutes, it struck him that no one else was nearly as excited as he was. When he looked up, the scientists were all laughing at him.

He'd been had.

Lasch took the gag in good humor—nothing could dampen his spirits in the spring of 2001. He had assumed that the *Hunley* would make a big splash in the media on recovery day and that would pretty much be it. Lasch realized there would be a few headlines when the crew was recovered, but he had expected it would be difficult to maintain the public's interest in the sub. He was wrong. It seemed the world was hanging on every development of the excavation.

In the weeks following the recovery, McConnell had been bombarded with requests to see the *Hunley*. The plan was to build a museum for the submarine, but that was years down the road. No one wanted to wait that long. McConnell was particularly struck when one elderly lady told him she wouldn't be around by the time the sub went into a museum. He realized an entire generation might miss out on the *Hunley* if he didn't do something.

Against the scientists' wishes, Lasch and McConnell decided to open the lab for tours. The conservation center had not been designed to accommodate the public, and it would cost money to upgrade access, but the demand was overwhelming. Lasch realized revenue from tours would help the Friends of the *Hunley* and also provide a good gauge for how well a museum might do. In the fall of 2000 they started tours on a limited basis, and they regularly sold out. Demand was high, but McConnell and Lasch agreed with the scientists that, for safety and security, the lab remain closed during the excavation.

In the meantime, the Friends of the *Hunley* set up Internet cameras so their members could watch the excavation. Almost immediately the charity sold thousands of new memberships. For many people the *Hunley* became a live soap opera, playing out on their computers every day. McConnell and Lasch would insist, however, that the cameras were turned off when the crew was removed from the submarine. There would be no images of remains released, out of respect for the crew.

The drama was nearly over by May.

The archaeologists had excavated every corner of the sub they could reach, and the work had slowed to a crawl, even by the scientists' measured standards. The areas left to excavate were so impossibly small that only one or two people could actually dig at once. Neyland decided they would have to remove a fourth hull plate, No. 2—the one with the snorkel box on it. This would give them better access to the forward reaches of the crew compartment and the captain's station. They still had not found Dixon.

The area beneath the forward conning tower provided archaeologists with their clearest picture yet of how the sub operated. They found the dive plane control lever, the forward ballast pump and finally were able to remove the object that Becker had been lying on. It was a bellows, and it had apparently been attached to the snorkels to draw in air. No historical account mentioned this feature. Perhaps, they thought, it was a late addition—an attempt to make use of the snorkels, which Alexander claimed never worked. The bellows occupied the space at the forward end of the crew bench. Could the addition of the bellows have forced Dixon to sail with one less hand?

Soon after the bellows was removed, the archaeologists found a large round object encased in concretion—a mix of sand and shell that had hardened like concrete. Using a portable X-ray, they examined the mass, and the image was unmistakable: Dixon's lamp. Was it the famous blue light? Pictures of the X-ray showing the lamp returned the *Hunley* to the front pages but the answer to that question would not come until much later. The scientists could not stop the excavation to chisel the lamp out of its protective shell.

On May 17 the scientists finally uncovered George Dixon. He was within reach of the lamp, slumped beneath the forward conning tower in a pose that suggested he had simply gone to sleep. There was no mistake, this was their man. His suit was much finer than the clothes worn by the rest of the crew; his teeth were perfect save for one cavity that had been filled with gold; and he appeared to be in good health. Dixon was carrying a pocket watch and binoculars. His pockets were filled with jewelry and other trinkets.

The archaeological evidence supported most of the stories about Dixon. Everything they found suggested he was wealthy, unlike most Confederate soldiers. His clothing came from London, his watch and binoculars were high quality. It only raised more questions about the elusive captain, about whom they knew scant little. Why, the scientists wondered, would a man of such a high station in life devote himself so fully to a temperamental and untested technology?

Jacobsen would handle the removal of Dixon personally. On May 23, she was working late, desperately trying to finish the initial excavation. The only thing left to do was take Dixon out of the sub, and they had decided to do this in a series of what the scientists called "block lifts." Rather than try to pull his remains and artifacts out of the mud, they slid a support tray underneath small areas and took them out at one time; they would excavate the blocks of mud later.

Around 9:30 that evening Jacobsen was preparing to slide a baking sheet–sized tray under Dixon's torso. Before she did that, she stuck her hand into the muck to make sure the tray was not going to tear any of Dixon's clothing. She was bent over at an odd angle, up to her elbow in the mud, when suddenly she froze. Her face went as gray as the mud she was working in.

"I think I've got it," she said. "I'll bet you $100 this is it."

When Jacobsen pulled her hand out of the muck, she ran water over it. As the mud fell away, she saw a glint of brilliant color. Jacobsen was holding a heavy, round gold piece—and it was warped. She had found George Dixon's gold coin.

The gold coin was perhaps the *Hunley*'s greatest story. Legend held that Dixon's sweetheart gave him the $20 gold piece when he marched off to war, and some Mobile historians believed her name was Queen Bennett. There was no documentation, no records to back up that assertion, but the discovery proved the coin was not merely lore. In several letters, members of the Twenty-first Alabama had recounted the story of how the coin had saved Dixon's life at Shiloh. A bullet had hit the coin, taking the brunt of the shot. The bullet warped the coin and drove it deep into Dixon's leg.

If not for the coin he likely would have bled to death on the battlefield. Many people, and possibly Dixon, believed he had been spared for a higher purpose. For some, the coin took on almost mystical qualities. And now Jacobsen held that piece of history in her hand. It was a stroke of luck, not only for the project—but for history. It said that sometimes legends are true.

The coin was in remarkable condition. The ball had hit the coin at Lady Liberty's hair bun, and the gold had recoiled around it. In some places, the coin was buffed smooth, and the scientists concluded this was from Dixon constantly rubbing it. Later, they would find a long trench in Dixon's femur where the bullet had driven the coin into his leg. The coin fit into the trench perfectly. There was no doubt Dixon was in constant pain and likely walked with a limp on those long hikes from Mount Pleasant to Sullivan's Island.

There was never any doubt as to what Jacobsen had found. And if there had been nothing else, the gold coin's discovery would have been the find of the excavation. But when she turned the coin over, Jacobsen found the biggest revelation of the *Hunley* dig: a message from Dixon himself. He'd had the coin engraved with a long inscription that was both a confirmation of the legend and a testament of its importance to him. The inscription read:

Shiloh
April 6th, 1862
My life preserver
G.E.D.

Before the excavation, scientists had downplayed the chance that they would find the coin. It was a small artifact and it had been lost for more than a century. Anything could have happened to the coin in that time—it could have fallen out of his pocket, been washed out of the submarine by ocean currents. The story could have been merely apocryphal, the coin a souvenir that Dixon didn't even keep. But it was real, and the project now had its greatest artifact. As a historical record, it was nearly perfect—it left no doubt that they had found George Dixon. But as a relic, it was much more; it was priceless.

Lasch got the call late that night and was so excited he could barely sleep. The next morning, he called the *Post and Courier* at 7:30—press releases be damned. He had to tell this story. By the time the paper announced the discovery on the Internet, the coin was under armed guard. McConnell would take no chances. He said it was perhaps the greatest Civil War artifact of all time and, for the moment, no one could argue that was much of an exaggeration.

Paranoia set in after the discovery was announced. McConnell and Lasch realized they could not simply keep Dixon's coin at the lab—it needed to be somewhere far safer. After a long debate, they decided to store the coin in a safe deposit box in the vault of a downtown Charleston bank. They moved the coin regularly for security purposes, and when they did it was carried by an entire motorcade. Only a few people knew which car the coin was in. Neither McConnell nor Lasch thought this was overkill. They were haunted by the idea that someone would steal their prize artifact. They believed it was worth more on the black market than any piece of the submarine.

Eventually, the Friends of the *Hunley* would negotiate with the U.S. Mint to manufacture replicas of the coin. These replicas could not be exact—that would be counterfeiting—but they would be close enough. They would become the best-selling item in the charity's gift shop. For $10, anyone could carry a coin like the one Dixon had rubbed for luck in the final two years of his life. It was perfect advertising for the *Hunley* project.

With the discovery of Dixon's coin, the initial dig inside the *Hunley* came to a close. Unexplored corners of the submarine would be excavated in the coming years, and scientists slowly learned far more about its inner-workings. They discovered that the hand cranks powered a series of reduction gears that made the sub more efficient. The propeller had not turned at a 1:1 ratio with the cranks, an important point Alexander never mentioned in his writings. Eventually Mardikian found that the ballast tank pumps could work in tandem, sending water from one tank to another or, most importantly, expel water from the crew compartment. The *Hunley* was far more advanced than anyone ever imagined.

There were other things that would remain mysteries for years. Archaeologists found a rudimentary battery in the sub's forward ballast tank with some wires attached, and speculated it had something to do with the torpedo. They realized the *Hunley* was equipped with heavy iron covers for the deadlight ports, but there were none on the conning tower ports. They learned the hatches could not be locked when the men had their heads in the conning towers. Was it a design flaw or did it serve another purpose? It was nearly impossible to determine what McClintock had been thinking.

These finds offer a number of tantalizing clues that may reveal what was happening onboard the *Hunley* the night it sank. For instance, the bilge pumps were not set to remove water from the crew compartment. That could suggest there was no water inside the sub when the men died, although that's far from certain. As Jacobsen noted, the bilge pumps probably could not have moved a large amount of water, at least not quickly enough to save a drowning crew.

The forward hatch to the submarine was found unlatched, which could lead some to believe the crew was trying to escape. But in fact Dixon could not get his head into the conning tower to see out of the forward port without removing the locking mechanism, and the hatch was heavy enough to keep it sealed even underwater. Besides, the aft hatch was securely locked. The fact that the forward hatch was unlatched is proof of nothing in itself.

In addition, the submarine's deadlight covers were all closed, which meant that in the crew's final moments the submarine was in "blackout mode." This is curious because one *Housatonic* crew member mentioned seeing light coming from the top of the sub—he even called them deadlights. So at some point after the attack, the crew closed the covers. There are only two reasons they would have done that. They could have been trying to hide their presence from ships coming to the *Housatonic*'s aid, which is a reasonable assumption. But the deadlight covers served another important function: they sealed the ports. If one or more of the glass deadlights were leaking, the crew would have certainly closed the hatches to keep water out, particularly if the *Hunley* was submerged.

None of these discoveries, however, answered the question that loomed largest over the *Hunley*: why did it sink? For more than a decade after that initial excavation, scientists would continue to study the submarine, analyze their notes and unearth small details about the submarine. Still they found no smoking gun, no single answer to that nagging question. As McConnell often told reporters, many of whom had become obsessed with the answer, the *Hunley* does not give up her secrets easily.

In the years following the *Hunley*'s disappearance, most people speculated that the sub went down with the *Housatonic*. Some would even claim the submarine was sucked into the hole it blew into the side of the great warship—a theory floated by some Confederates immediately after the sinking. William Alexander half-heartedly endorsed that theory and repeated it often in later years. If not that, Alexander conversely believed that, given its relative lack of power, the *Hunley* may have been pulled out to sea by the tides. These theories were created in a vacuum, without any facts to back them up. There was little way of knowing what had happened to the submarine because they could not examine it. It was simply lost.

When NUMA discovered the *Hunley* in 1995, some people believed they had not only found the sub but the cause of its sinking. The most famous image of the sub taken by Wilbanks, Hall and Pecorelli showed a fist-sized hole in its forward conning tower. Several people speculated that small arms fire from the crew of the *Housatonic* had shattered the brittle cast iron, and the hole allowed enough water inside the crew compartment to sink the submarine.

Years after the initial excavation, Jacobsen found those missing pieces of the conning tower. The cast iron shards were buried in the mud at the bottom of the crew compartment, a placement that confirmed the hole was made before the submarine filled with sediment. This evidence supported the single-bullet theory. But it did not prove the damage occurred on the night of February 17, 1864. The tower could have been punctured by an anchor years after the *Hunley* sank.

An analysis of the *Hunley*'s hull has determined that the largest hole on the sub—a breach roughly three-foot by two-foot in the starboard stern—was likely caused by scouring. On the ocean floor, the *Hunley* sat listing to starboard at about a 45-degree angle. In the decades before it was buried, a steady ocean current blasted sand through the narrow gap between the hull and seabed. Over the years the starboard side of the hull was essentially sanded down until finally the hull was breached in two places—the starboard stern hole and another, pie-sized hole in the forward ballast tank. This scouring is evident on the O-rings around the starboard conning tower ports and is responsible for the concave, icebreaker shape of the *Hunley*'s bow. The sub's bow was straight when it sank; the current chipped away at it over the years.

If scouring is responsible for the hole in the sub's stern, it may have been years after the sinking before the *Hunley* filled with sediment.

But patterns in the mud found inside the submarine suggest that some of the first sediment in the sub poured in through that hole in the forward conning tower. Given the location where Jacobsen found those shards, it was most likely the first hole in the hull—otherwise the pieces of the conning tower would have been higher in the stratigraphy. The question that remains is: When did those breaches occur?

There are several clues that the *Hunley*'s interior remained sealed and at least partially dry for a long time after it sank. During the initial excavation, Paul Mardikian found stalactites on the sub's ceiling. Stalactites are simply calcium icicles formed by dripping water. This water could have been condensation or a pinprick leak in one of the sub's deadlights. The important point is that stalactites do not form underwater. Archaeologists say these stalactites could have formed in an air bubble inside the submarine while the rest of the compartment filled with water. But at least part of the *Hunley*'s interior was dry for a long time after it sank.

The presence of those stalactites has led some people to believe the crew simply ran out of air after the attack and suffocated or succumbed to anoxia—a lack of oxygen to the brain. When the *Hunley* sank the *Housatonic*, it was just about halfway through an ebb tide off the coast of South Carolina. Fighting the tide would have been nearly impossible for the submarine, and Dixon knew this. The crew likely could not have generated the power to go against the ocean flow. At the same time, the outgoing tide would continue to pull the *Hunley* farther out to sea, making the journey home even longer.

An anchor was found near the wreck site and some people believe it may have come from the *Hunley*, that Dixon used it to keep the sub from drifting out to sea. But it is just as likely that Dixon set the submarine down on the ocean floor to wait for the tide to turn. That would have prevented them from drifting farther away from Sullivan's Island and given his crew some much needed rest. It would have also hidden their presence from the blockade ships. Dixon knew from earlier tests that the *Hunley* held enough air to remain submerged for more than two hours, and that was almost exactly how long he had to wait for favorable tides. Was the *Hunley* parked on the ocean floor while the crew of the *Canandaigua* was just overhead, working feverishly to save the *Housatonic* survivors?

In January 1864, the crew managed to stay submerged for two and a half hours, and Dixon concluded that was the limit of their endurance. But that day the crew had not exerted themselves beforehand nearly as much as they did in the moments leading up to the attack. The men may have expended their oxygen faster after the trauma of the attack, and they may have run out of air much more quickly. If that happened, the *Hunley* sailors may have simply ran out of air while waiting for the tide to turn, and then died peacefully in their sleep.

There are, however, other reasons the sub may have gone to the bottom after the attack. Clive Cussler believes the answer lies in the testimony of the *Housatonic* crew taken during the Naval Court of Inquiry. Robert Flemming, the first man to spot the *Hunley*, said he saw a "blue light" on the water shortly after the ship sank. The light was directly in the path of the USS *Canandaigua*. Cussler notes that the large warship may have collided with the *Hunley* and not even realized it.

There is evidence to support this theory, even beyond Flemming's testimony. First, the fact that the deadlights were closed could suggest that the sub was still on the surface. Also, the *Hunley* was notoriously slow to turn, most accounts suggest, and if it was close to the *Canandaigua* it would have had a hard time avoiding impact. In fact, with no ports facing aft, the crew would not have seen it coming. Also, half of the shroud around the sub's propeller is missing, but the part that remains is damaged by three nearly uniform triangular cuts. These cuts resemble propeller strikes, as if another ship ran over the sub. It is nearly impossible that any ship's prop hit the shroud after it had set down on the ocean floor, particularly since the cuts are on the starboard side of the shroud—the side that was pointed toward the sea floor.

There is another intriguing piece of evidence that supports the *Canandaigua* collision theory. The *Hunley*'s rudder was found underneath the hull, which suggests it may have fallen off just before the sub sank. Could it have been sliced off by the same propeller that clipped the sub's shroud? If so, it creates a logical scenario. Without any way to steer the sub, Dixon may have set down on the bottom to consider his options for repair, or prevent the *Hunley* from drifting farther out to sea. And then, the crew simply ran out of air.

As Cussler notes, Flemming's testimony was taken shortly after the attack—when it was fresh in his mind. The bow watch man was a trained lookout, and his insistence that he saw a blue light on the water so soon after the attack—a light that perfectly matches the description Confederates gave of the light—cannot simply be dismissed as coincidence.

In 2012, conservator Paul Mardikian made a discovery that completely changed the narrative of the *Hunley*'s attack on the *Housatonic*. Nearly every historical account claimed that the sub attacked by ramming a torpedo with a barbed hook into the side of its prey. Then the sub would back away and detonate its charge with a rope trigger. One *Housatonic* crewman testified that the sub was between 50 and 80 feet away from the ship when the blast occurred, and because that fit with *Hunley* mythology—and Alexander's description of the sub's attack plan—his account was accepted as fact. But more than a dozen other *Housatonic* sailors claimed the blast came as soon as the *Hunley* rammed their ship. Those reports were discounted for nearly 150 years.

While removing concretion from the spar, Mardikian found remnants of the *Hunley*'s copper torpedo. The copper skin, the outer shell of the torpedo, had been blown backward, as if from an explosion. The torpedo was still attached to the sub when it detonated, and that was no accident. Mardikian found a bolt that had fastened the copper, and presumably the rest of the torpedo, to the spar. That one piece of evidence changed the entire story.

The *Hunley* attacked exactly like a *David*—that is, as a ram. This should not have been a surprise, since the spar was a design element of the *David* added to the *Hunley* only two months before its attack on the *Housatonic*. Still, the discovery raised questions about the effect the blast may have had on the sub and its crew. While the *David* and its crew were not injured by the blast in any of its attacks, the *David* was an open cockpit boat that sat atop the water, albeit with a low profile. Such an explosion may have had an entirely different effect on a submarine that was all but submerged. When 135 pounds

Clive Cussler and Warren Lasch's association with the Hunley *forged a friendship between the two men, and they still visit the submarine regularly to this day. Here, Cussler and Lasch are on the mezzanine overlooking the* Hunley *at its North Charleston conservation lab, which is named after Lasch.*

of gunpowder (alleged twice as much as the *David* used) ignited in the *Housatonic*'s flank, the *Hunley* was less than 20 feet from the explosion. Could the blast have buckled the sub's hull plate, allowing water inside? Could the percussion from the explosion have been enough to leave the crew unconscious, concussed or disoriented enough that they could not make their escape? The answer may be recorded in the *Hunley*'s hull.

Since the *Hunley* was recovered, it has remained encased in the hard coat of sand and shell that built up on its hull over a century on the ocean floor. Scientists did not remove the concretion after recovering the sub because it provided stability and protected the 150-year-old iron beneath it. But it has come at a cost: no one has seen the sub's actual skin. If the sub was damaged in the attack on the

Housatonic, or in a collision with the *Canandaigua*, the evidence will be on the exterior hull.

In August 2014, conservators began the arduous task of removing that shell of concretion in preparation for the sub's long chemical bath. The *Hunley* will have to soak in chemicals for years to remove all the salt that seeped into the hull over 137 years in the Atlantic. And the concretion must be removed before that can begin. When that outer shell is removed, which will take between eight months and a year, scientists will learn if there is additional damage to the *Hunley*. So far, all they know for sure is that the impact with the blockader was severe enough that the 17-foot iron spar was warped in the collision.

The only other damage associated with the collision so far may turn out to be the smoking gun that has eluded scientists for a decade. Years after the initial excavation, Mardikian examined the sub's seacocks to determine whether they were open prior to its sinking. That information could reveal whether the *Hunley* was attempting to surface or submerge in its final moments. But Mardikian could not figure out the settings.

There are two seacocks on the sub, one for each ballast tank. Basically, the seacocks are holes in the hull—each little more than an inch and a half wide. Inside the sub, brass pipes connect these holes to the ballast tanks. A valve attached to the opening can be turned to admit water or plug the hole. The forward seacock is on the port side of the hull, roughly across from where Dixon sat. The pipe comes out of the hole and then turns at a 90-degree angle, then feeds into the ballast tank wall.

Mardikian was outside the sub, looking through the forward seacock port, trying to determine the valve's position, when he noticed it. The brass pipe was not aligned with the hole—it had broken off and was offset considerably. That was not the sort of damage that would occur because of corrosion; brass is nearly immune to deterioration caused by seawater or age. It doesn't rust. Mardikian is certain the damage was caused by some sort of trauma.

The *Hunley*'s impact with the *Housatonic* could have snapped the pipe. Or, Mardikian believes, Dixon could have been thrown against the pipe during the collision, causing it to break. One thing is for sure: when that pipe broke away from the seacock inlet, gallons of water poured inside the *Hunley*. The water that would have come through a hole that size below the hull's waterline could have caused the submarine to sink within minutes. And there would have been no way to stop it.

Archaeologists are skeptical and will not endorse any theory until the entire hull is examined. If the hull plates buckled, that damage would have admitted as much or more water into the sub's crew compartment. But that evidence has yet to be found, and Mardikian is certain of one thing: the damage to the seacock occurred on the night of the attack. There is simply no other time it could have happened. And that damage alone would have been enough to doom the *Hunley* crew.

If Mardikian is right—and he understands the *Hunley*'s machinery better than anyone—he may have finally solved a mystery that has lingered for 150 years.

Any one of these clues, or a combination of them, might ultimately prove to be the reason the *Hunley* never returned home. If the hull plates buckled as a result of the explosion, or the seacock pipe broke on impact, either would have been enough to sink the sub. If both occurred, it would have been devastating—there would have been more water inside the crew compartment than Dixon's men could have bailed out with the small ballast tank pumps. And if they were injured in the explosion, another possibility, they may not have even had the chance to try.

It could be years before anyone definitively answers these questions. Removing the concretion, years of chemical conservation and a final study of the submarine could take another decade. More theories may arise as the hull is examined more closely, or evidence could be found to rule out one or more of the scenarios. But it is curious that few of these theories offer outright contradictions to the others. There may not be one simple explanation for why the *Hunley* sank; it could be that several factors added up to an unavoidable catastrophe.

Cussler maintains that the testimony of Robert Flemming suggests whatever happened, it was not instantaneous. Flemming saw something on the water that night, long after the attack, and Cussler believes it was the *Hunley*. If that's the case, Dixon and his men survived the battle with the *Housatonic* and had every intention of returning to Sullivan's Island. After all, they signaled for the troops to guide them home. Perhaps at that moment they were trying to repair the submarine, or bailing water furiously, but believed they would ultimately prevail.

It is a notion that appeals to Cussler's sense of story, and it fits perfectly with the mythology of the world's first attack submarine. There could be no better coda to the Civil War legend than to conclude that, in the end, the crew of the *Hunley* died fighting.

Last Rites

Eight caissons rolled through the city that morning, each one carrying a simple pine coffin. The coffins had been draped in flags that were completely white except for a small red and blue canton of stars and bars. It was the flag that had flown over Charleston when these men died, the last flag they ever knew.

They would be buried under it.

The caissons were pulled by horses and escorted by a color guard, police officers and hundreds of men and women in period costume. The men were dressed as Confederate and Union soldiers and sailors, the women wore long black veils. The entire procession moved silently, save for the clopping of the horses walking on paved streets.

The march began at The Battery, within sight of Fort Sumter and overlooking the harbor where 140 years earlier a strange iron fish-boat had sailed in preparation for its historic mission. Thousands of people crowded along The Battery seawall this morning—the same place their ancestors had gathered to watch the beginning of the American Civil War—just to catch a glimpse of history. On this day, April 17, 2004, these people would witness some of the last remaining unfinished business from the great conflict.

Nearly 10,000 people had lined East Bay Street to watch the

procession pass. Some of them waved and cheered, a few flew flags. Others simply saluted. On the porch of one of Charleston's great mansions, a group of women sang a soft a cappella version of "Dixie." For many of these onlookers this was a curiosity, a spectacle broadcast around the world. But the men and women marching alongside the caissons were respectfully silent. They knew that beyond the costumes, beyond the parade, this was a much more solemn event.

It was a funeral.

For more than two hours the procession moved slowly under a blistering Lowcountry sun. The route followed East Bay Street nearly five miles to Magnolia Cemetery, a nineteenth-century graveyard where the city's elite elected to spend eternity under a canopy of live oaks dripping with Spanish moss. There, George Dixon and his crew would be laid to rest alongside Horace Hunley, the other 12 men who had died aboard the world's first attack sub and thousands of other casualties from the country's deadliest conflict.

Sen. Glenn McConnell led the procession astride a horse. He would set the pace, just as he always had. McConnell had made a promise nearly a decade earlier to see these men returned home, to see that they were given a proper burial. And everything he had done since then had led directly to this morning. When he was interviewed on national television moments before the march began, he explained that this was the final act in a long, epic saga.

"We are here to honor their bravery, their courage and their sacrifice," McConnell said. "We are here to give them the burial that fate denied them."

⁓

The crew of the *H. L. Hunley* made history. They were the world's first submariners, the nineteenth-century equivalent of astronauts. It took something beyond daring, beyond courage, to climb inside an untested machine that had killed the better part of two crews. It took the right stuff. They succeeded where so many others had failed, pushing the limits of industrial age technology. Their feat was so far ahead of its time that it would not be repeated for more than 50 years. As William Dudley, director of the Naval Historical Center noted before the funeral march began, "The men of the *Hunley* are the fathers of submarines."

For years, however, their contribution to naval warfare was forgotten. Soon after they disappeared, their names were lost in a sea of anonymity. The world moved on. The crew of the *Hunley* lingered in obscurity at the bottom of the Atlantic for more than a century, their fate unknown, their story one without a conclusion.

It took a writer to give them their ending.

As the funeral procession passed through the gates of Magnolia Cemetery, Clive Cussler watched the scene with the awe of a child. It had been 24 years since he set out on a quest to find the lost Confederate submarine. Four expeditions, hundreds of thousands of dollars, and years of his life had been dedicated to preserving maritime history. And he had saved one of the most important chapters of that history. Now Cussler was reaping the rewards of his dedication. He had traveled across the country to see an ending that he, more than anyone, had scripted.

Not even a funeral that continued for nearly two hours could foul Cussler's mood. At one point the proceedings gave way to a Masonic burial ceremony for Dixon. As the ritual went on, and on, Cussler turned to Ralph Wilbanks seated behind him and offered a mischievous smirk.

"My God, Ralph, what have we done?"

On the podium above Cussler's front-row seat, Warren Lasch looked over the words he would deliver in eulogy to the crew. The two men had struck up a friendship over the submarine, one that would endure for the rest of their lives. Although neither was a Southerner, the Confederate submarine had brought them together and they were closer than brothers. Lasch had done everything he could to ensure Cussler's contribution to *Hunley* history was not forgotten; Cussler had immortalized Lasch as a villain in his 2001 Dirk Pitt novel, *Valhalla Rising*.

For Lasch, the funeral was a solemn, emotional, inspirational moment. Seven years earlier he had never heard of the *Hunley*, and now he was forever tied to its history. Lasch had brought these men home. He had directed what became the model of maritime recovery. Under his leadership, a group of scientists and engineers had saved the only intact Civil War shipwreck ever found. The project had come in on time, under budget and without a single injury. Lasch was proud of all those achievements, but his greatest accomplishment wasn't the business model or the charity—it was his role in preserving a unique piece of history.

"The *Hunley* is a tribute to the innovative spirit and bravery of the men who were in the greatest military conflict our nation has endured. The *Hunley* belongs to all of us. All Americans have a responsibility to preserve our nation's history," Lasch said in his eulogy. "The achievement we honor today transcends geographical lines. It unites North and South, East and West. And it spans the vast oceans that separate nations. The *Hunley* project is about discovery. It's about learning what history can teach us. This project shows us what science, innovation, technology and the human spirit can make possible."

"It is about courage."

Perhaps more than anyone else, Lasch drew the parallels between the men who built and sailed the sub with those who found and saved it. He called his team of twentieth-century adventurers the "fourth crew," a name that would stick among those most closely associated with the submarine. These people were now a large part of the *H. L. Hunley*'s long and storied history and as they assembled, for perhaps the last time, Lasch honored them with words that Dixon wrote about his own crew just weeks before inscribing their names in maritime history: "I have got a splendid crew of men. The best I think I ever seen."

"They were indeed a splendid crew," Lasch concluded. "May God bless their souls as we lay them to rest today."

The *Hunley*'s final crew was buried in the shade of live oaks near the banks of the Cooper River, the very water where Horace Hunley had died. One common grave had been dug for all eight coffins, and the men were laid to rest in the same order that they sat inside their submarine. Descendants of some of the crew accepted the flags off their coffin, but most of the men did not have living relatives—at least not any that could be found. As a bugler played a mournful rendition of "Taps," Lasch accepted the flag from Arnold Becker's coffin. Then he turned and threw a single rose into the grave.

As he stepped away, Lasch wept uncontrollably. The magnitude of the past few years, and all that his crew had accomplished, had finally sunk in. These men were here because of him. Lasch would never forget that feeling.

McConnell and Lasch had given the *Hunley* crew a proper burial, just as they had promised years earlier. It had taken nearly a decade after Cussler found them, but they had accomplished their mission. The fish-boat sailors were no longer on eternal patrol, anonymous souls lost in a sea of history. Their legacy had been cemented, and there was no doubt that none of them would be forgotten ever again.

Finally, the men of the *Hunley* had come home.

The funeral for George Dixon and his men was the culmination of the "fourth crew's" work. Their study of the *Hunley* and the conservation of its artifacts would continue for more than a decade, and in that time they would learn far more about the world's first attack submarine than anyone ever anticipated. But on that day, they felt as if they had come to the end of a long journey.

The *Hunley* recovery and conservation would become one of the most influential projects in underwater archaeology. The team that raised parts of the USS *Monitor* would take its cues from the work of the *Hunley* team, and the men who discovered the Confederate raider *Alabama* would bring its cannons to the Warren Lasch Conservation Center for treatment. There simply was no place better equipped to save such precious artifacts.

In the fall of 2000, the Warren Lasch Conservation Center opened for weekend tours. The scientists had won the battle to keep people out during the week, so the Friends group was limited to Saturdays and half-days on Sunday. The first tours sold out in a day and the *Hunley* remained such a popular draw that by 2004, the lab would see more than 40,000 visitors in a year. By comparison, The Mariners Museum in Newport News, Virginia—home to the USS *Monitor*—drew 55,000 a week, but it was open seven days.

The success of the *Hunley* tours reassured Lasch and McConnell that the submarine deserved its own museum. In 2002, the *Hunley* Commission's museum siting committee accepted proposals from Charleston, North Charleston and the town of Mount Pleasant. All of them wanted to host the *Hunley*, all of them claimed a share of the submarine's legacy. It had sailed from Charleston in 1863; the crew had refurbished the submarine and stayed at a Mount Pleasant boardinghouse in the winter of 1863–64; North Charleston was home of the Warren Lasch Conservation Center.

Charleston Mayor Joe Riley offered $5 million and a plan to build a museum for the sub at the foot of Calhoun Street, the spot where the sub had likely launched in the summer of 1863. Mount Pleasant offered up to $7 million to build a separate facility for the sub at Patriot's Point, home of the World War II–era aircraft carrier USS *Yorktown*. These two proposals were considered front-runners in the competition—until North Charleston made its offer.

North Charleston Mayor Keith Summey had hired Ralph Applebaum, the famous architect behind the Holocaust Museum in Washington, to design a *Hunley* museum. The city also offered to raise $11 million toward building the facility, which would sit on the banks of the Cooper River. For a year after those proposals came in, everyone asked Warren Lasch the same question: Where is the *Hunley* going? His answer never varied:

"To court," Lasch said.

Eventually, the *Hunley* Commission accepted North Charleston's proposal. The museum plans remain on hold until the submarine's conservation is complete. And that could be as much as a decade away. The work is far from over.

In 2007, Clemson University took charge of the *Hunley* project and the Warren Lasch Conservation Center. Professors from the college had been brought in to help with conservation of the most fragile materials found inside the submarine in the early days of the excavation, and their work led to several technological breakthroughs. Along with Paul Mardikian, the Clemson Restoration Institute would develop a subcritical process for preserving metals far faster than conventional methods allowed.

The Institute would become a technological research center and a huge economic engine that helped the state of South Carolina in a new war between the states—the fight for jobs. Clemson established a graduate education center and planned a materials research center for the complex. Eventually, the university built a large wind turbine testing facility across from the lab. The center was cast as an environmentally safe project to create energy and lessen the world's dependence on fossil fuels. This plant was renowned for its work, and gave the state of South Carolina an economic benefit far beyond what it had invested in a little lost Confederate submarine.

Although the project was a success by any measure, the three men most responsible for bringing the *Hunley* home—Cussler, Lasch and McConnell—would all pay a personal price for their efforts. For years, McConnell would fight the erroneous perception that his pet project had cost taxpayers millions more than it actually had. In 2006, a Columbia newspaper published a misleading story that left the impression that $90 million in government money had been "funneled" to the *Hunley*.

In fact, only $9 million in state and federal dollars had been used to recover and preserve the submarine. The article conveniently ignored the fact that the sub was, in fact, owned by the federal government—which justified the use of some taxpayer money. The story inflated talk of a $50 million museum, although there had never been any question that such money likely would have to be raised privately. McConnell could disprove all of the charges, but the paper never corrected the record. The perception of *Hunley* pork would linger for years.

Lasch was hounded for years by men claiming to be government watchdogs looking out for taxpayer money. The Friends of the *Hunley* was bombarded by Freedom of Information Act requests that seemed more like harassment than actual inquiries about the project. These men, some of whom had ties to Lasch's business competitors, repeatedly claimed he had profited from his association with the *Hunley*.

One man found a bill for dry cleaning in the Friends' records and assumed Lasch was doing his laundry on the charity's dime. It was a cleaning bill for the scientists' jumpsuits. Another time, the same man called the *Post and Courier* to complain that Lasch was buying pet supplies with charity money. Mardikian had bought the aquarium heater to conserve a small artifact. The Friends questioned this harassment, and even fought it in court, but the charity never closed its books. Lasch was intent on keeping the project completely transparent.

And some men would keep looking to find some way to tear it all down.

A few years after the *Hunley* was recovered, Clive Cussler became embroiled in a lawsuit against a man who insisted the author had jumped his claim. This man had posted libelous statements about Cussler on the Internet, including the ludicrous claim that the author had made as much as $300 million off the *Hunley*. Cussler's lawyers prepared a lawsuit against these people but after several years of delay brought on by a litany of excuses—and unpaid lawyer bills—from the defendant, the author walked away. It was clear to all but the most conspiracy-minded people who had actually saved the *Hunley*.

Had the case gone to trial, it would have revealed some interesting details about the men trying to discredit Cussler. The author's lawyers had found one man who testified that the self-proclaimed "archaeologist" at odds with Cussler had, in fact, never found the *Hunley*. The witness knew this because he had gone with the treasure hunter on an expedition in the mid-70s to find the sub. They carried underwater blowtorches, planning to chop the sub up into pieces and sell them on the black market.

Fortunately, they did not find it.

~

To this day, unfinished business lingers. Ralph Wilbanks and Dirk Cussler—now a novelist in his own right—have continued NUMA's search for lost pieces of history. In the years after the *Hunley* recovery, they found a target in Mobile Bay that they believe is the *American Diver*. But if it is James McClintock and Horace Hunley's second submarine, it is probably lost to history. Alabama salvage laws are stringent, and Wilbanks says the sub is probably buried too deep in the muck to make recovery a financially feasible possibility. But Wilbanks has a good feeling about it—he believes he located the *American Diver*. It's hard to bet against him.

~

Warren Lasch stepped down as Friends of the *Hunley* chairman a few months after the crew's funeral. The submarine had been his life for nearly eight years, and he had decided that all good things must come to an end. The project was in the hands of the scientists and, other than speeding them along, there was little he could do. He would remain associated with the project for years, however. Everyone who visited Lasch and his wife, Donna, could count on at least one trip to see the *Hunley*.

In later years, Lasch often thought back to the day after the funeral. It was the event that put everything in perspective, reminded him why he had done all that he did. Everyone had stayed downtown after the burial for a party at a hotel overlooking the harbor. The next morning, Lasch drove Cussler to the airport. Arizona was calling, and the author had books to write.

As they drove out of Charleston on Interstate 26, Cussler spotted a line of motorcycles backed up at an exit ramp off the eastbound lane. The line extended nearly a mile up the interstate. Cussler, a man with an eye for motorized toys, was fascinated.

"I wonder where they are all going?" he said.

Lasch looked over at his friend and smiled. "That's the exit for Magnolia Cemetery," he explained. The bikers were in line to pay their respects to the *Hunley* crew, to ride by their graves.

Cussler was astonished. He had done this. All it had taken was a single mention of a lost submarine in a history book and he'd been hooked. There was research in a dozen archives, weeks of scanning the ocean with a magnetometer, more cigars than he could recall. Now, a generation later, Cussler and Lasch had ensured the *Hunley* would never again be a footnote to history, would never again be forgotten. William Alexander would have thanked them.

To this day, Clive Cussler, Glenn McConnell and Warren Lasch have not made a dime off the *Hunley*. One found it and saved it from treasure hunters, the other two made sure it was recovered safely. They are still occasionally criticized for their role in the project, but the days of Cussler book-burnings have long since passed. As the author once said, if that's the price of saving the *Hunley*, it's worth it.

In 2011, National Geographic premiered its third documentary on the submarine in a decade. Its first show had been controversial for several minor errors pointed out by the Friends of the *Hunley*. In 2001 Lasch traveled to National Geographic headquarters to get the documentary fixed, only to find himself seated across a table from nearly two-dozen lawyers and television officials. He had said, "You're going to need more guys." Lasch was able to smooth out differences with the network, enough so that they would make two more specials.

The third of these documentaries featured interviews with scientists, historians and McConnell. The program was an update, a meditation on the *Hunley*'s disappearance, a retrospective. The show was a huge success and still runs regularly on cable television. The documentary tells the entire story of the *H. L. Hunley* with two glaring omissions.

Neither Cussler nor Lasch are mentioned.

Afterword

On the 150th anniversary of the battle between the *H. L. Hunley* and the USS *Housatonic*, I joined hundreds of other people on the beach at Breach Inlet—where the Confederate submarine set out on its long journey into history. It was an unforgiving evening, not quite as cold as February 17, 1864, although the wind may have been a bit brisker. Some of the reenactors even committed the relative sacrilege of wearing modern coats over their gray uniforms. But this was a matter of survival, one that *Hunley* captain George Dixon and his crew likely would have understood.

I have spent several anniversaries at Breach Inlet—as well as the night of August 7, 2000, when I watched the blue light signaling from the deck of the *Karlissa B* (the crane barge that would raise the *Hunley* the following day). Each year, the faithful gather on Sullivan's Island for a short service honoring the men who died in the world's first successful submarine attack. It is always a moving ceremony, but this time was perhaps the most meaningful for me. One year to the day earlier I had begun writing this book and finished the day before the 150th anniversary. This is my second trip into the *Hunley* (the other, *Raising the Hunley*, was coauthored with my friend Schuyler Kropf). Finally, after more than 16 years of following this story, I felt

I had finally gotten inside Dixon's head. Standing alone on the beach, looking out at the uninviting sea, I felt a fraction of the trepidation he must have felt. In 1864 most people thought what Dixon planned to do was—at least subconsciously—suicide. But he knew it could work.

When the sun dropped over the marsh, it got dark fast and I was reliving those final moments before Dixon and his men climbed into a fragile iron boat that had already killed 13 men. It took an incredible amount of bravery. They put their lives at risk, either for a cause they believed in or the promise of reward money. They made history that night. They never returned.

February 17, 2014, was cloudy, and the sea showed a mild chop, but Dixon probably would have risked it all over again. It was so dark no one could have seen an iron boat that rode barely two feet out of the water. Standing on the Sullivan's Island beach, it struck me how frightening it must have been to sail out on that endless black ocean, steering a tiny boat toward what amounted to little more than a few specks of deck lights nearly four miles offshore. This was a dangerous, daring mission—something that is lost on many people today. Getting into the *Hunley* on a sunny day and sailing into the creek behind Sullivan's Island was scary enough. It took what we call "the right stuff" to take that boat into the ocean. And yet they did it.

I felt just as close to this history after spending a few days at Clive Cussler's home in Arizona. When I sat down to interview him in his writing studio, I was distracted by the paintings of all the ships the National Underwater and Marine Agency (NUMA) has found since he started searching 35 years ago. Cussler hunts shipwrecks for exactly the right reason—the adventure of it. It's astounding what his nonprofit National Underwater and Marine Agency (named for the employer of his literary hero, Dirk Pitt) has accomplished over the years, and yet Cussler is modest about it to a fault. Although he has an amazing story—much of which has never been told—Cussler was more interested in seeing Warren Lasch and Ralph Wilbanks get their due for all their work on finding and recovering the *Hunley*.

I wrote this book because Clive and Warren—both friends of mine—wanted the inside story told, and I was honored they asked me to tell it. The behind-the-scenes story of the discovery and recovery of the submarine is in many ways just as compelling as the sub's history. I could think of no better way to illustrate that than by chronicling the adventures side by side, highlighting the similarities between the two quests.

In the years since *Raising the Hunley* was published, many new details and accounts of the *Hunley*, its crew and its history have surfaced. Within two years of *Raising*, in fact, the entire story had changed. I have always wanted another shot at the *Hunley* and now, 14 years after the submarine was recovered, there is a much richer story to tell. This book is the result of my nearly 20-year association— and fascination—with the *Hunley*. Unless there is some stunning new discovery down the road, I think this is as complete a picture as we will ever have of what happened to the men who built and sailed— and saved—the world's first successful attack submarine.

And it is a pretty compelling picture.

Brian Hicks
Charleston, South Carolina
July 21, 2014

Notes

Tracking the *Hunley*'s circuitous route through history is a long and sometimes frustrating endeavor. There are no surviving plans of the submarine and few firsthand accounts written by the men most intimately involved with its construction and operation. These were men of action, not record-keeping.

Because the *Hunley* was a private vessel, there is little about it in the military records of the Confederate States of America. There are some vague references and short accounts of the various accidents, but very little information about the six months it was in operation around Charleston. Most of what we know comes from William Alexander, who was charged with building the sub from James Mc-Clintock's plans, and McClintock himself.

The *Hunley* designer wrote a couple of largely technical descriptions of his boat in the years following the Civil War, and then only because he was trying to find work as an engineer. He offered some short vignettes about the operation of all three subs, but was not around for the most significant events in the career of his greatest creation. Its final fate remained a mystery to McClintock.

Alexander waited until the dawn of the submarine age to recount his time on the first such vessel. By that time, his memory was spotty and there were few people still alive to corroborate or enhance his accounts. Still, he is the only reason we know where the crew of the *Hunley* bunked, what their days were like, and the adventures they lived through in the days leading up to their one great mission. He only survived to preserve this history because he was called back to Mobile two weeks before the *Hunley* attacked the *Housatonic*. Had Alexander been granted another 30-day leave of absence, we would not know nearly as much as we do.

Confederate Gen. P. G. T. Beauregard and various other Southern soldiers and sailors provided fairly helpful reminiscences of the *Hunley*'s time in Charleston. Other than that, we are left with a few scant letters and testimonials published in the pages of the now-defunct (obviously) *Confederate Veteran* magazine.

George Dixon wrote several letters during his months in Charleston, but only two survive. Luckily, he writes freely about his thoughts, his frustrations and his plans for the *Hunley*—and the blockade. Those two letters tell us nothing about the sub captain's background, but they offer a revealing glimpse into his mindset in those dark days of the Civil War. His letters are invaluable to this narrative.

In truth, there has been more bad information than good written about the *Hunley*. In the late nineteenth century and early part of the twentieth century, several men tried to pen histories of the submarine—and most of those only added to its over-the-top mythology. The *Hunley* did not sink six times, it did not kill 45 men—and George Dixon did not survive. Most of these accounts repeat the erroneous fact that the sub carried a crew of nine men. It is obvious most of these stories borrowed heavily from each other, as most official records make it clear the *Hunley* carried only eight men.

The following notes provide a map of where I obtained the information to write this book. I was able to interview nearly all the principal characters in the twentieth-century chapters and, in some cases, was even present for important scenes. The nineteenth-century chapters were, of course, more difficult. One of the tricks to writing narrative history is compiling all the accounts, however contradictory, and then using your knowledge of the subject, common sense and a little luck to determine what rings true. This is the route of that journey.

Prologue *February 17, 1864—Sullivan's Island*

17 *This could be*: William Alexander, "The True Stories of the Confederate Submarine Boats," *New Orleans Picayune*, June 29, 1902.

18 *That became evident*: "President Davis in Charleston," *Charleston Daily Courier*, November 3, 1863.

18 *Still, Dixon had*: Many of George Dixon's thoughts in this chapter, including the "why don't he do something" quote, come from his letter to Henry Willey, January 31, 1864, reprinted in *Post and Courier*, April 11, 2004.

18 *Capt. John Cothran*: As quoted by Julia Hartwell in "An Alabama Hero," *Montgomery Advertiser,* March 11, 1900.

19 *You stated that*: Letter of George Dixon to John Cothran, February 5, 1864, copy in the Eustace Williams Collection, Mobile Public Library.

19 *His crew had*: Alexander, "True Stories." Alexander wrote that he and Dixon took the *Hunley* offshore an average of four nights a week through most of January 1864.

20 *I have got*: Dixon letter to Willey, January 31, 1864.

20 *Before the war*: Brian Hicks, "*Hunley*'s captain fiercely determined to succeed," *Post and Courier*, April 11, 2004. This profile of George Dixon, which included what little we know of his background, was written using information provided by *Hunley* genealogist Linda Abrams and archaeologist Maria Jacobsen. Abrams pored through mountains of public documents to find such gems as Dixon's engineer's license, the address of his Cincinnati apartment and even the name of one of the riverboats he worked on.

20 *He was shot*: John Kent Folmar, ed., *From That Terrible Field: Civil War Letters of James M. Williams, Twenty-first Alabama Infantry Volunteers* (Tuscaloosa: University of Alabama Press, 1981), 53.

22 *Dixon had told*: Dixon letter to Cothran, February 5, 1864.

22 *He had spent*: D. W. McLaurin, "South Carolina Confederate Twins," *Confederate Veteran*, vol. 33 (1925), 328. McLaurin, who was stationed at Battery Marshall in the winter of 1864, wrote about his work on the "Little Devil" with perhaps greater detail than any other contemporary save for Alexander. His short account of February 17, 1864, is striking for what detail it does provide—the relative time of departure, the action of the troops onshore awaiting the sub's signal, as well as the maintenance he

helped Dixon with earlier in the day.

23   *Dixon had explained*: J. N. Cardozo, *Reminiscences of Charleston*
(Charleston: Joseph Walker, 1866), 124–5; and report of O. M. Dantzler,
February 19, 1864, reprinted in *Official Records of the Union and
Confederate Navies in the War of the Rebellion* [*ORN* hereafter], series 1,
vol. 15 (Washington, D.C.: Government Printing Office, 1921), 335.

23   *Originally, Dixon and*: William Alexander, "The Heroes of the *Hunley*,"
Munsey's Magazine, August 1903, 748.

23   *The Fleet offshore*: Dixon letter to Willey, January 31, 1864.

Chapter 1 *1980—Sullivan's Island*

32   *The two women*: Clive Cussler and Craig Dirgo, *The Sea Hunters*
(New York: Simon and Schuster, 1996), 201–202.

34   *Cussler was born*: Interview with Cussler, January 2013. Additional
information comes from Wayne Valero, *The Adventure Writing of
Clive Cussler* (Kearney, NE: Morris Publishing, 2007).

36   *The team gathered*: Cussler, *The Sea Hunters*, 20–25.

39   *The H. L. Hunley*: Cussler interview, January 2013.

42   *The team took*: Cussler, *The Sea Hunters*, 200. Additional information on
the 1980 expedition comes from the photographic archives of Bill Shea.

42   *Cussler had been*: Cussler interview, January 2013.

43   *The Institute of*: Interview with Ralph Wilbanks, June 2013.

45   *Cussler was always*: Ibid.

45   *A week into*: Fred Rigsbee, "Divers May Have Located *Housatonic*,"
Charleston Evening Post, July 18, 1980.

48   *On Sunday, July*: Wilbanks interview.

50   *The search for*: Fred Rigsbee, "*Hunley* Search to Resume at Later Date,"
Charleston Evening Post, July 21, 1980.

Chapter 2 *1861—New Orleans*

51   *It looked very*: This account of the 1861 Battle of the Head of Passes is taken
from the reports of Capt. Henry French, commander of the USS *Preble*,
Lt. Francis Winslow of the USS *Water Witch*, and D. L. Winslow, acting
master of the USS *Richmond*, all found in the *ORN*, series 1, vol. 16, 712–17.

53   *The CSS Manassas*: Craig L. Symond, *The Civil War at Sea* (New York:
Oxford University Press, 2012), 31.

55   *The South did*: For a more detailed account of the rise of privateers,
see William Morrison Robinson, *The Confederate Privateers* (Columbia:
University of South Carolina Press, 1994).

56   *The same month*: Charles L. Dufour, *The Night the War Was Lost* (Lincoln:
University of Nebraska Press/Bison Books, 1994), 107.

56 *Hunley, 37, was*: The background of Horace Lawson Hunley comes from Ruth H. Duncan, *The Captain and Submarine CSS H. L. Hunley* (Memphis: S.C. Toof & Company, 1965), 13–20. Duncan, a Tennessee genealogist, tracked down much of what little information is known about Hunley and his family.

58 *His work at*: Tom Chaffin, *The H. L. Hunley: The Secret Hope of the Confederacy* (New York: Hill and Wang, 2008), 21.

58 *Horace Hunley did*: Horace Lawson Hunley, Memorandum Book, record group 140, folder 12, Louisiana Historical Society. I looked at Hunley's ledger in January 2001, and the staff at the historical society said there wasn't much in it. In fact, a child had gotten hold of the book at some point and drawn on many pages of the ledger. Upon closer inspection, however, you could still read Hunley's musings about octagonal towers and the like.

59 *When I hear*: Letter of Volumnia Hunley Barrow to her husband, Robert Ruffin Barrow, March 13, 1862, as reprinted in Duncan, *The Captain and Submarine*, 44–45.

59 *In early June*: Ibid, 57.

59 *On arriving off*: Letter of Horace Hunley to Francis Hatch, July 9, 1861, reprinted in Duncan, *The Captain and Submarine*, 59.

60 *The Rev. Franklin*: The full text of Smith's letter is in Mark K. Ragan, *The Hunley* (Orangeburg: Sandlapper Publishing, 2005), 6–7.

61 *James McClintock proved*: McClintock's background is culled from a number of sources, including Mrs. Edwin J. Palmer, "Horace Lawson Hunley," *The United Daughters of the Confederacy Magazine*, May 1962, 14.

62 *That summer, Leovy's*: James Kloeppel, *Danger Beneath the Waves* (Orangeburg: Sandlapper Publishing, 1992), 6.

63 *McClintock started with*: This account of the *Pioneer*'s construction is taken largely from a James McClintock letter to Matthew F. Maury, 1868, copies of which are on file in the Friends of the *Hunley* archives and in the Eustace Williams Collection, Mobile Public Library.

63 *The first tests*: When Union troops later found the *Pioneer*, their report—which included a drawing of the sub—passed along a rumor that two slaves died in it during trials. There is no proof of this—it was merely stated as fact in a letter by J. H. Shock to the Assistant Secretary of the Navy G. W. Fox. The letter survives on microfilm at the National Archives. Additional descriptions of the trials, attributed to McClintock, are included in G. W. Baird, "Submarine Torpedo Boats," *Journal of American Societies of Naval Engineers* 14 (1902), 845.

64 *Hunley friend John*: John K. Scott handled the paperwork and provided a brief description of the *Pioneer* in his application for a letter of marque, which allowed the sub to operate as a licensed privateer. Scott is identified as

the ship's captain in correspondences in the *ORN*, series 2, vol. 1, 399–400.

64 *McClintock himself would*: Captain Peter Hore, Royal Navy (Retired), "A Secret Journey to Halifax," *Naval History*, June 2002, 32–36. McClintock's visit with the British Navy, in an attempt to sell them a submarine, is recounted in this fascinating magazine article.

64 *Later, McClintock claimed*: Baird, "Submarine Torpedo Boats," 845.

66 *Three weeks after*: ORN, series 2, vol. 1, 399.

66 *The CSS Manassas*: Naval History Division, *Civil War Naval Chronology 1861–1865* (Washington, D.C.: Department of the Navy, 1971), II–54.

67 *When it became*: McClintock letter to Maury, 1868.

67 *The Pioneer would*: Shock letter to Fox. A copy of his drawing is in the Friends of the *Hunley* archives.

Chapter 3 *1981—Charleston*

70 *Just the sight*: Interview with Cussler, March 2013.

70 *As a teenager*: An old friend of Cussler's converted some of their 1940s films to DVD and I watched them one afternoon with the author at his home. Not only were they hilarious, the car chases looked about as good as anything Hollywood produced in those days.

72 *The owners gave*: Valero, *The Adventure Writing of Clive Cussler*, 27.

73 *Using fixed points*: The particulars of the Motorola Mini-Ranger workings are explained in "Search for the Confederate Submarine *H. L. Hunley* off Charleston Harbor, South Carolina," a booklet put together by Cussler, Wilbanks and Wes Hall and submitted to the U.S. Naval Historical Center in August 1995.

73 *Eventually the crew*: Some of the specifics of the 1981 expedition are taken from Cussler, *The Sea Hunters*, 207. Additional information is taken from the photographic archives of Bill Shea.

74 *Before they dropped*: Interview with Wilbanks, June 2013. Wilbanks swears he likes gin, but only the rotgut brands.

76 *He was standing*: Cussler interview, March 2013.

78 *One day, a*: The television crew's adventures aboard the *Sweet Sue* were recounted by Wilbanks in a June 2013 interview.

79 *When the Confederates*: The details of Charleston's fall are taken from two sources: Milby Burton, *The Siege of Charleston* (Columbia: University of South Carolina Press, 1970), 316–25; and Arthur M. Wilcox and Warren Ripley, *The Civil War at Charleston* (Charleston: Evening Post Publishing, 1966), 76–77.

81 *The dreams of*: No matter what else they've forgotten, Cussler and Wilbanks remember every detail of their brief encounter with the *Hunley* in 1981. Both say they are glad they didn't find it then; without modern conservation

techniques, it probably would have rotted by now.

83   *Let's face it*: Fred Rigsbee, "*Hunley* Eludes Searchers," *Charleston Evening Post*, June 26, 1981.

83   *We don't know*: Edward C. Fennell, "Search Ends for Confederate Sub *Hunley*," *News and Courier*, June 27, 1981.

83   *I'm a writer*: Rigsbee, "*Hunley* Eludes Searchers."

Chapter 4   1862—Mobile

87   *Shortly after arriving*: William Alexander, "Heroes of the *Hunley*," 746.

87   *These men, if*: McClintock letter to Maury, 1868.

89   *Together, Thomas Park*: Jack O'Brien Jr. "Where Was the *Hunley* Built?" *Gulf South Historical Review*, vol. 21, no. 1, Fall 2005, 29–48. O'Brien did considerable research into the old machine shop and offers a detailed look at its business during the war.

89   *Alexander was an*: Alexander outlined his background in engineering during a speech to the Iberville Historical Society on December 15, 1903, a copy of which resides in the Eustace Williams Collection at the Mobile Public Library.

89   *Alexander was intrigued*: Alexander believed Horace Hunley deserved as much recognition as McClintock for being the spark to the project. He said as much in a letter to Charles Stewart dated November 11, 1902, on file in the Friends of the *Hunley* archives.

90   *McClintock later said*: Hore, "A Secret Journey to Halifax," 34; and McClintock letter to Maury, 1868.

91   *The aspiring architect*: Horace Hunley's offer to design a protective wall around the city is outlined in a letter on file at the Mobile Historic Preservation Society and is paraphrased in Chaffin, *The H. L. Hunley*, 79.

92   *My poor Brother*: Duncan, *The Captain and Submarine*, 43.

92   *One of the*: Dixon's immediate fascination with the submarine project was recalled by Alexander in "Heroes of the *Hunley*," 747–48.

92   *Dixon may have*: Dixon's background and his work on the steamboat *Flirt* were provided by *Hunley* genealogist Linda Abrams.

92   *Friends would later*: The description of Dixon as an "attractive presence" was attributed to his friend Capt. John Cothran, in Hartwell, "An Alabama Hero."

93   *When the regiment*: The story of how George Dixon came into possession of his gold coin is literally Civil War legend. The popular tale is that the coin was a gift from Queen Bennett, a Mobile girl who was allegedly Dixon's sweetheart. To date, there is no documentary evidence of that relationship (some researchers are skeptical given the vast age difference between Bennett and Dixon). There is a legend circulated in the *Hunley* project's inner circle that Bennett's daughters had letters between Dixon and Bennett that they

published in a newspaper after her death. But so far those letters remain lost to history. Mobile historian Caldwell Delaney said in 1990 that he once had a clipping that named Dixon's love—the article claimed they were engaged—but lost it.

Stories in two Mobile newspapers recount the story without naming the sweetheart: "George E. Dixon's Submarine. Details of How Brave Man Lost His Life—Sons of Mobile Honor Him," from *Mobile Daily Item*, April 26, 1910, and "First Submarine to Sink a Warship Was Mobile Product" from the *Mobile Item*, date unknown. These articles tell almost the same story, and it seems the latter may be copied from the first. There is no sourcing for the claim that a woman gave Dixon his coin. Letters from members of the Twenty-first Alabama mention the coin that saved Dixon's life, but none of them note its origin.

93 *An errant bullet*: Folmar, *From That Terrible Field*, 53.

93 *George Dixon, shot*: Ibid.

94 *Shiloh, April 6th*: There is no historical record of the inscription on Dixon's coin. The *Hunley* conservation team was amazed to find it when archaeologist Maria Jacobsen recovered the coin in May 2001.

94 *McClintock gave up*: McClintock letter to Maury, 1868.

95 *To obtain room*: Ibid.

95 *A Confederate deserter*: One of the few official accounts of the *American Diver* in action comes from James Carr, who deserted the CSS *Selma* and told Union Navy officials about the submarine. His report is in the *ORN*, series 1, vol. 19, 626–29.

96 *Once the crew*: Ibid.

96 *One night the*: Alexander, "True Stories."

96 *Confederate Admiral Franklin*: Franklin Buchanan complained at least twice about the *American Diver* to Confederate Secretary of the Navy Stephen Mallory. Those letters are preserved in his letter book on file at the University of North Carolina Library. This letter is reprinted in Ragan, *The* Hunley, 25–26.

97 *Since then other*: Ibid.

98 *The boat cannot*: Ibid.

98 *In March, as*: The account of E. C. Singer's partnership with Hunley and McClintock was first told by Horace N. Hill, "Texan Gave World First Successful Submarine Torpedo," *San Antonio Express*, July 30, 1916. This account also includes additional information from Duncan, *The Captain and Submarine*, 63–64.

Chapter 5 1984—At Sea

101 *The NUMA team*: Interview with Clive Cussler. Additional information

on the *Leopoldville* is from Cussler, *The Sea Hunters*, 309–24.

104 *A few months*: Cussler writes more about his Mississippi River expedition in *The Sea Hunters*, 144–49.

106 *In July he*: Cussler's 1982 search for the *Cumberland* and the *Florida* is recounted in *The Sea Hunters*, 112–17.

114 *Cussler announced the*: Margot Hornblower, "Historic Sea Hunt: Cussler Finds Troopship and *Lusitania* Sub," *Washington Post*, July 26, 1984.

114 *It is still*: Ibid.

115 *I am not*: Ibid.

115 *But the French*: Thirty years later, Cussler is still a little sore he didn't get the chance to find the CSS *Alabama*. And he still remembers that call from the CIA very well.

116 *Some men play*: Hornblower, "Historic Sea Hunt."

Chapter 6   1863—Mobile

119 *Spy just returned*: Letter of U.S. Secretary of the Navy Gideon Welles to all commanders of the East and West Gulf Squadrons, March 9, 1863, *ORN*, series 1 vol. 17, 382–83.

120 *A group of*: Arthur W. Bergeron, *Confederate Mobile* (Baton Rouge: Louisiana State University Press, 2000), 120–21.

121 *The third boat*: McClintock to Maury, 1868.

122 *The reason for*: Ibid.

122 *Instead of attaching*: While some descriptions of the *Hunley* come from McClintock and Alexander, the only two men who wrote extensively—and with knowledge—of her construction, much of the material in this chapter is from personal observation. I have had the opportunity to study the *Hunley* at length over the years, and much of my understanding of its inner workings comes from conversations with conservator Paul Mardikian and archaeologist Maria Jacobsen, the two senior members of the staff at the Warren Lasch Conservation Center. Paul and Maria, along with the rest of the conservation team, understand how the submarine worked better than anyone save for McClintock and Alexander. And Alexander's memory, as you will see, was faulty by the time he wrote about his exploits with the *Hunley*, nearly 40 years after the fact.

124 *In the first draft*: Even Alexander claimed the *Hunley* was a converted boiler, "True Stories." It's much more likely he was recalling the construction of the *American Diver*. Studying her today, it's clear the *Hunley* is not a converted boiler.

125 *The USS Alligator*: The account of the Union submarine is taken from several sources, including Kevin J. Weddle, *Lincoln's Tragic Admiral: The Life of Samuel Francis Du Pont* (Charlottesville: University of

Virginia Press, 2005), 103–5.

126 *William Alexander began*: Alexander, "Heroes of the *Hunley*," 746.

126 *The pieces of*: The dimension of the hull plates is provided by the Friends of the *Hunley*, from research by scientists at the Lasch Conservation Center.

128 *By the time*: O'Brien, "Where Was the *Hunley* Built?" 33–35.

129 *In early May*: Hunley's movements are chronicled in a letter he wrote to Henry Leovy, May 4, 1863, a copy of which is on file at the Friends of the *Hunley* archive. Parts of the note are also found in Duncan, *The Captain and Submarine*, 62–63.

129 *I have some*: Ibid.

129 *One of these*: Ibid. The mention of a "Dixon" is unexplained in the letter.

130 *By late July*: Hunley letter dated July 27, 1863, from Rome, Georgia (either to Leovy or his friend Gardner Smith), Duncan, *The Captain and Submarine*, 63. Also, there is a letter from Leovy confirming Hunley's travel in the Friends of the *Hunley* archives.

131 *The bench was*: These descriptions of the *Hunley* are from the author's own observations and explanations provided by the staff of the Lasch Conservation Center.

132 *Alexander had his*: Alexander, in "True Stories," mentions the ballast tank walls and notes "unfortunately these were left open on the top." In his 1902 letter to Charles Stewart, Alexander writes "There were no watertight compartments. Would to God there had been!—here was the fatal error in the boat."

132 *The H. L. Hunley*: O'Brien, "Where was the *Hunley* Built?" collects most of the old accounts of the submarine's launch.

133 *Other than its*: McClintock to Maury, 1868.

134 *The first officer*: This long explanation from Alexander in "True Stories" is the only real account of what the crew did aboard the *Hunley*.

134 *The boat and*: McClintock to Maury, 1868.

135 *On Friday, July*: Dabney Maury, "How the Confederacy Changed Naval Warfare," *Southern Historical Society Papers*, vol. 22, 1894.

136 *So far as*: Letter of James E. Slaughter to Gen. P. G. T. Beauregard, July 31, 1863. The letter, in the National Archives, is reprinted in Ragan, *The* Hunley, 38.

137 *If it can*: Franklin Buchanan letter to John Tucker, August 1, 1863. Ibid.

138 *Please expedite transportation*: Letter of Gen. P. G. T. Beauregard to quartermasters and railroad agents between Mobile and Charleston, *The War of Rebellion: A Compilation of the Official Records of the Union and Confederate Armies* [*ORA*, hereafter] (Washington: Government Printing Office, 1880) series 1, vol. 28 (II), 265.

138 *It would take*: The account of the *Hunley* being loaded onto a train and

shipped to Charleston comes from a letter written by George Washington Gift to Ellen Shackelford on August 8, 1863. Gift wrote that he operated the crane that lifted the *Hunley* out of the Mobile River. The letter is among his papers on file at the University of North Carolina's Southern Historical Collection. A copy is in the Friends of the *Hunley* archives.

Chapter 7 1994—*Off Sullivan's*

143 *The Divercity cut*: Interview with Wilbanks, June 2013, with additional information from Cussler, *The Sea Hunters*, 212–17.

144 *Idiots, Wilbanks thought*: Ibid.

145 *Or perhaps Cussler's*: Interview with Cussler, March 2013.

145 *In 1878, a*: A longer account of the search for the lost locomotive appears in Cussler, *The Sea Hunters*, 236–44.

146 *Cussler had phoned*: Interview with Cussler, January 2013.

146 *NUMA advance man*: Cussler, *The Sea Hunters*, 212–13.

147 *Even before the*: Tony Bartelme and Schuyler Kropf, "Bad blood, thin egos may torpedo salvage," *Post and Courier*, August 27, 1995. My colleagues (both former coauthors of mine, incidentally) did a good job with a long yarn about the disaster that was the 1994 *Hunley* expedition.

148 *It took NUMA*: Interview with Wilbanks.

149 *So Cussler was*: Cussler interview, January 2013.

150 *Cussler, Wilbanks and*: Interview with Wilbanks.

150 *Cussler had given*: Ibid.

151 *It soon became*: Bartelme and Kropf, "Bad blood, thin egos."

152 *In fiction, you*: Interview with Cussler, January 2013.

153 *The ocean was*: Interview with Harry Pecorelli in 2001.

153 *The greatest drama*: Ibid, and interview with Wilbanks, June 2013.

154 *Newell was excited*: Bartelme and Kropf, "Bad blood, thin egos."

155 *In September, Wilbanks*: Interview with Wilbanks.

155 *In the story*: Lynne Langley, "Divers may have located *Hunley*," *Post and Courier*, January 28, 1995.

156 *Around friends, Newell*: Bartelme and Kropf, "Bad blood, thin egos."

156 *Ralph Wilbanks took*: Interview with Wilbanks.

Chapter 8 1863—*James Island*

159 *The train carrying*: William E. Beard, "The Log of The C.S. Submarine," U.S. Naval Institute *Proceedings*, vol. 42, no. 5, September–October 1916. Beauregard's own correspondences suggest the submarine arrived on August 12.

159 *On August 11*: Note on file at the National Archives. Reprinted in Ragan, *The* Hunley, 45.

159   *Just two days*: "Latest from Morris Island," *Charleston Mercury*,
      July 21, 1863.
160   *On August 4*: "From Morris Island—Capture of a Yankee Boat and Crew,"
      Charleston Mercury, August 6, 1863.
160   *Beauregard had become*: "More Negro Labor Wanted Immediately for the
      Defence of Charleston," *Charleston Mercury*, August 3, 1863.
161   *The Charleston import*: ORA, series 1, vol. 28 (II), 285.
161   *From its shape*: [P.] G. T. Beauregard, "Torpedo Service in the Harbor and
      Water Defences of Charleston," *Southern Historical Society Papers*,
      vol. 5, no. 4, April 1878.
161   *He sent his*: Letter of Beauregard to Hutson Lee, August 12, 1863, on file
      at the National Archives and reprinted in Ragan, *The* Hunley, 48.
162   *Soon, letters from*: Letter of Eweretta Middleton to Harriott Middleton,
      August 17, 1863, South Carolina Historical Society; quoted from a copy
      on file in the Friends of the *Hunley* archives.
162   *It was tested*: Ibid.
162   *McClintock's first priority*: There is no record of who served aboard the
      Hunley when it first arrived in Charleston. As subsequent notes show,
      various correspondence suggest Gus Whitney was "in charge" of the boat,
      but it was McClintock who would draw the ire of the Confederate
      commanders, which likely means that he was, in fact, running the
      submarine. There's also no indication of who comprised the rest of the crew.
      The obituary of Mobile resident Jeremiah Donivan ("Man Who Served in
      Three Wars Dies in Mobile," *Mobile Register*, November 19, 1928) claims
      he was the last surviving man to serve aboard the "first submarine ever built
      in this country." Of course, it also claims the unnamed sub was built in
      Selma. It's possible that Donivan sailed aboard the *Hunley* on its test runs
      in Mobile, or even followed McClintock and Whitney to Charleston—but
      there's no proof of it.
163   *One Confederate officer*: Colonel Charles H. Olmstead, "Reminiscences
      of Service in Charleston Harbor in 1863," *Southern Historical Society
      Papers*, vol. 11, 1883.
163   *You doubtless remember*: Letter of Theodore Honour to Beckie Honour,
      August 30, 1863, on file at the South Caroliniana Library at the University
      of South Carolina, copy on file in the Friends of the *Hunley* archives.
163   *McClintock resented the*: McClintock to Maury, 1868. Although he
      never said it explicitly, McClintock was clearly complaining about the
      Charleston Confederates.
164   *I have been*: Letter of Horace Hunley to James McClintock, August 15, 1863,
      quoted from a copy in the Eustace Williams Collection, Mobile Public
      Library. The full text is also available in Duncan, *The Captain and*

Submarine, 65–66.

164 *On August 21*: "The Day of Prayer," *Charleston Mercury*, August 21, 1863.

165 *Just before 11*: This account of the beginning of the Siege of Charleston is compiled from various newspaper articles in *Charleston Mercury*, August 24, 1863, including "Gen. Gillmore's Demand for the Evacuation of Morris Island and Fort Sumter—Gen. Beauregard's Reply, Etc." and "Progress and Events of the Siege."

166 *The next night*: Report of Col. T. L. Clingman, *ORA*, series 1, vol. 28 (Part I), 671.

167 *The torpedo boat*: Clingman to Capt. F. W. Nance, August 23, 1863, Ibid, 670.

167 *He reported to*: A second note from Clingman dated August 23, 1863, Ibid, 670.

167 *Whitney, already suffering*: Ibid.

168 *Payne was as*: C. L. Stanton, "Submarines and Torpedo Boats," *Confederate Veteran*, vol. 22, 1914, 398–99.

168 *It did not*: The names of Payne's crew (often called the "first" crew) come from a brief notice in the *Charleston Daily Courier*, August 31, 1863. The name of the final crewman, Absolum Williams, was found years later by *Hunley* Commission Vice Chairman Randy Burbage.

169 *The Confederates had*: Ragan, *The* Hunley, 64.

169 *They practiced in*: Stanton, "Submarines and Torpedo Boats," 398.

169 *On Saturday afternoon*: Ibid.

170 *Payne had gone*: Ibid.

170 *Hasker, a native*: W. B. Fort, "First Submarine in the Confederate Navy," *Confederate Veteran*, vol. 26, no. 10, 1918, 459–60.

171 *Later, no one*: Both Stanton and Hasker say the wake of the passing *Etiwan* swamped the *Hunley*, sending water into its open hatches. But the official report by Col. Charles Olmstead, found in the *ORA*, series 1, vol. 28 (Part I), 551, states that the sub "became entangled in some way with ropes, was drawn on its side, filled and went down."

171 *Payne jumped free*: Stanton, "Submarines and Torpedo Boats," 398.

171 *As the Hunley*: Fort, "First Submarine in the Confederate Navy," 459.

171 *I had to*: Ibid.

172 *One Confederate private*: Letter of Theodore Honour to Beckie Honour, August 30, 1863, Friends of the *Hunley* archives.

172 *They were all*: Letter of Augustine Smythe to a relative, August 30, 1863, Augustine Smythe Papers, South Carolina Historical Society.

172 *It seems a*: Letter to Harriott Middleton, dated September 2–3, 1863, Middleton Papers, South Carolina Historical Society, copy in the Friends of the *Hunley* archives.

173 *On Saturday last*: *Charleston Daily Courier*, August 31, 1863. That same day, the *Charleston Mercury* ran exactly three sentences on the *Hunley* sinking under the brief headline "Lamentable Accident."

173 *Over the years*: There are far too many inaccurate accounts of *Hunley* sinkings to list them all, but the most egregious has to be Augustine Smythe's 1907 account, "Torpedo and Submarine Attacks on the Federal Blockading Fleet Off Charleston During the War of Secession." Smythe's article, published in 1907 in both "Charleston Mayor Rhett's Annual Review" and the University of Virginia magazine. Smythe, a native of Charleston who was stationed in the city, actually claimed that the sub sank two days after the incident at Fort Johnson. "Remarkable as it may seem, the same accident occurred a few nights later at Fort Sumter, Payne and two others being the only ones to escape," Smythe wrote. Did he not find that a little too coincidental? A man who corresponded often with William Alexander—and was actually stationed in the harbor during that time—should have known better. But some people apparently believe everything they hear, never bothering to discount for rumor, faulty memories—or a lack of common sense. Of course, Alexander also once wrote that the sub sank twice under the command of Payne.

174 *Beauregard knew that*: The account of the Confederate withdrawal from Morris Island comes from "The Siege—Finale of the Contest for Battery Wagner—Unprecedented Bombardment—Evacuation of Morris Island by Our Forces, Etc." *Charleston Mercury*, September 7, 1863.

175 *Beauregard sent orders*: Beauregard correspondence on file at the National Archives. The general's orders are reprinted in Ragan, *The* Hunley, 77.

175 *Eventually, a Confederate*: Edmund Ruffin (William Kauffman Scarborough, ed.) *The Diary of Edmund Ruffin, Volume III: A Dream Shattered, June 1863–June 1865* (Baton Rouge: Louisiana State University Press, 1989), 177.

176 *Sir—I am*: Letter of Horace Hunley to General Beauregard, September 19, 1863, Eustace Williams Collection, Mobile Public Library.

177 *Three days after*: Orders from Thomas Jordan, Beauregard's chief of staff, September 22, 1863, reprinted in Duncan, *The Captain and Submarine*, 69–70.

177 *Hunley immediately sent*: Alexander, "True Stories."

177 *He would not*: Alexander, "True Stories," and Dixon's service records, copies of which are available in the Eustace Williams Collection, Mobile Public Library.

Chapter 9 1995—Isle of Palms

179 *Clive Cussler's phone*: Interview with Cussler, January 2013.

181 *The previous 24*: Interview with Wilbanks, June 2013.

181 *As it turned*: Interview with Harry Pecorelli, 2001.

182   *The trip offshore*: Interview with Wilbanks.

182   *Pecorelli may have*: Ibid.

183   *Hall found their*: This account of the May 3, 1995, expedition is taken largely from new interviews with Ralph Wilbanks. Additional information is taken from Wilbanks' "The Search for the *Hunley*," which is one chapter in Dr. Peter McClean Miller, *Diving With Legends* (privately published, e-book edition, 2011), 283–94.

185   *This is exactly*: Interview with Wilbanks.

185   *This time Pecorelli*: Wilbanks, "The Search for the *Hunley*."

188   *It's the Hunley*: Interview with Wilbanks.

188   *Slipping into his*: Ibid.

189   *Pecorelli was a*: Interview with Pecorelli.

189   *Back at the*: Interview with Wilbanks, September 2013.

190   *That's wrong, that's*: Ibid.

190   *Wilbanks called Cussler*: Interviews with Cussler and Wilbanks.

191   *We must have*: Cussler, *The Sea Hunters*, 216.

192   *On Sunday, May*: Interview with Wilbanks.

193   *Today, May 3*: The famous note left inside the *Hunley* resides in the files of the *Hunley* Commission. The state considers it an artifact, a piece of maritime history. Wilbanks believes it is a souvenir that belongs to him and Cussler, and he's been trying to get it back ever since.

194   *There's absolutely no*: John Noble Wilford, "Confederate Submarine Is Discovered Off South Carolina," *New York Times*, May 11, 1995.

194   *The NUMA crew*: Interview with Wilbanks.

194   *Cussler was patient*: Interviews with Cussler and Wilbanks.

195   *More than a*: The reward that P. T. Barnum offered for the *Hunley* is legendary, but there is only one known mention of it. An April 27, 1915, letter from James Gadsden Holmes to Joseph Daniels, Secretary of the Navy, mentions that Angus Smith's son told him that Barnum's offer prompted Smith and his old partner, Broadfoot, to search for the *Hunley* in the 1870s. Smith and Broadfoot were the perfect divers to hunt for the old sub—they had raised it from Charleston Harbor after its first two sinkings.

195   *This is without*: Schuyler Kropf, "The *Hunley* Will Be Slow to Rise," *Post and Courier*, May 12, 1995.

196   *Why not just*: Interview with Cussler, March 2013.

196   *The young man*: Interview with Pecorelli.

196   *It's an icon*: Kropf, "The *Hunley* Will Be Slow to Rise."

197   *I didn't spend*: Ibid.

197   *From the moment*: Interview with Wilbanks.

198   *On the same*: Interview with Glenn McConnell.

199   *When the press*: Interview with Wilbanks, September 2013.

Chapter 10 *1863—Adger's Wharf*

201   *The Union sailors*: The account of the *David*'s attack on the *New Ironsides* comes from several sources, including a letter from *New Ironsides* Capt. S. C. Rowan to U.S. Rear Adm. John Dahlgren, October 6, 1863; Dahlgren's subsequent report to U.S. Secretary of the Navy Gideon Welles, October 7, 1863; and additional correspondence between Union and Confederate officials, all found in *ORN*, series 1, vol. 15, 10–21.

202   *The David had*: James H. Tomb, "Submarines and Torpedo Boats, C.S.N.," *Confederate Veteran* magazine, Vol. 22, 1914, 168–69.

203   *Several of these*: "David C. Ebaugh on the Building of The *David*," *South Carolina Historical Magazine*, January 1953.

203   *As the David*: Tomb, "Submarines and Torpedo Boats."

204   *News of the*: "The Siege—Attack on the Enemy's Fleet," *Charleston Mercury*, October 7, 1863.

205   *The men from*: Beauregard, "Torpedo Service in the Harbor and Water Defences of Charleston," and special requisition orders dated September 28, 1863, suggest the sub was being cleaned under the supervision of Horace Hunley. Eustace Williams Collection, Mobile Public Library.

205   *In those early*: Letter of Robert Ruffin Barrow to Horace Hunley, September 1863, Tulane Special Collections, Barrow Family Papers, Tulane University.

206   *This is the*: Ibid.

206   *The submarine was*: George Dixon's military records in the National Archives reflect the date his leave was granted. A copy is on file in the Friends of the *Hunley* archives.

207   *Later, Beauregard would*: Beauregard, "Torpedo Service in the Harbor and Defences of Charleston."

207   *When some young*: "Terrible Explosion and Loss of Life," *Charleston Mercury*, October 13, 1863.

208   *Years later Beauregard*: Beauregard, "Torpedo Service in the Harbor and Defences of Charleston."

209   *Beauregard cryptically said*: Ibid.

209   *A crowd gathered*: Alexander, "Heroes of the *Hunley*."

210   *Aboard the Indian*: Stanton, "Submarines and Torpedo Boats."

210   *I happened to*: Ibid.

211   *Inside the Hunley*: The account of what happened inside the *Hunley* during its second sinking is re-created using evidence found by George Dixon and William Alexander after the sub was recovered. Alexander describes the scene in "True Stories."

212   *The loss of*: Journal of Operations, Confederate headquarters, October 15, 1863, *ORN*, series 1, vol. 15, 692–93.

213   *As soon as*: Ibid.

213 *On Thursday morning*: "Melancholy Occurrence," *Charleston Daily Courier*, October 16, 1863.

214 *Nearly three weeks*: A letter from Gardner Smith to Hunley's sister, Volumnia, November 29, 1863, details some of the troubles Smith and Broadfoot had raising the submarine. Tulane Special Collections, Barrow Family Papers, Tulane University.

214 *The morbid ceremony*: Beauregard, "Torpedo Service in the Harbor and Defences of Charleston."

214 *When the boat*: Ibid.

215 *Slowly, the story*: Alexander, "True Stories." Alexander explains what the workers found on the *Hunley* after its recovery, which came just about the time he and Dixon arrived in Charleston. According to Alexander, they verified the findings. And they, more than anyone in Charleston, would have been able to determine the cause of the accident. The wrench on the floor of the submarine is a particularly telling piece of evidence. Although, in fairness, it could have fallen at any time during the recovery.

215 *The honor guard*: "Last Honors to a Devoted Patriot," *Charleston Mercury*, November 9, 1863.

216 *Possessed of an*: Ibid.

216 *At the grave*: Smith letter to Volumnia (Hunley) Barrow, November 29, 1863. When I read the original letter at Tulane in early 2001, Horace Hunley's lock of hair was still in the envelope.

216 *Leovy would carry*: Ibid.

217 *Beauregard had decided*: Beauregard, "Torpedo Service in the Harbor and Defences of Charleston," and Alexander "True Stories."

217 *Lieutenant Dixon*: I: Beauregard's telegram suggests that Dixon had sent one to the general first, but it has not survived. The telegram is in the National Archives, a copy of which is in the Friends of the *Hunley* archives.

Chapter 11 *1995–1997—Columbia*

219 *The South Carolina*: Interview with Glenn McConnell, 2013.

220 *A week earlier*: The Associated Press, "The War Between the States," July 27, 1995.

221 *I am fully*: Ibid.

221 *The Hunley Commission*: Sid Gaulden, "Save the Sub: *Hunley* group ready for action," *Post and Courier*, August 3, 1995.

222 *McConnell's argument was*: Interview with McConnell.

222 *During the Hunley*: Gaulden, "*Hunley* group ready for action."

223 *The author had*: Cussler interview, March 2013.

224 *I've been accused*: Clive Cussler, "Author says money, glory not searchers' aim," Letter to editor, *Post and Courier*, September 13, 1995.

224 *Wilbanks spoke for*: Interview with Wilbanks, September 2013, and John Heilprin, "Funds Ok'd in search for *Hunley*," *Post and Courier*, October 12, 1995.

224 *Cussler was incredulous*: Schuyler Kropf, "Diver asked to lead team to *Hunley* Site," *Post and Courier*, October 11, 1995.

225 *When Navy brass*: The story of Strom Thurmond's wily *Hunley* blackmail comes from McConnell, 2001 interview.

225 *The sooner differences*: "The *Hunley* waits another 45 minutes," *Post and Courier*, October 29, 1995.

226 *On November 9*: Interview with Cussler, March 2013.

226 *Cussler offered the*: The official coordinates are provided by the South Carolina Institute of Archaeology and Anthropology.

227 *Divercity rounded the*: Interview with Wilbanks, September 2013.

228 *Although Wilbanks led*: Information on the 1996 survey of the *Hunley* is taken from the National Park Service Submerged Cultural Resources Unit's H. L. Hunley *Site Assessment* (Santa Fe: National Park Service, 1998).

229 *Leonard Whitlock was*: Interview with Leonard Whitlock, 2013.

229 *The work was*: National Park Service, H. L. Hunley *Site Assessment*.

230 *The Park Service's*: Colette Baxley, "It's Official! Experts verify sunken wreck as Confederate sub *Hunley*," *Post and Courier*, May 18, 1996. This newspaper article, which I read on vacation in Charleston a year before I took a job with the *Post and Courier*, was my introduction to the *Hunley* story. I'd never heard of the submarine before and was immediately hooked. I carried the newspaper home and still have it. When the paper hired me, it was to replace Colette, who took an editing job.

230 *Over the years*: National Park Service, H. L. Hunley *Site Assessment*.

230 *Whitlock got the*: Interview with Whitlock.

231 *Local newspapers reported*: "Death on the Bottom of the Deep. Discovery of Buried Torpedo Boat off Charleston—Nine skeletons at the Wheel," *Charleston Daily Courier*, October 11, 1870.

231 *That summer, the*: John Heilprin, "*Hunley* credit to Cussler?" *Post and Courier*, February 28, 1997.

232 *For McConnell and*: Interview with McConnell.

234 *There was one*: Interview with Warren Lasch, 2013.

235 *In June 1997*: Ibid.

236 *If anyone could*: Interview with McConnell.

236 *Lasch met McConnell*: Interview with Lasch.

237 *Warren, that will*: This is one of the more famous quotes in modern *Hunley* lore, and both McConnell and Lasch now laugh about how ridiculous that statement turned out to be.

237 *Within three months*: Interview with Lasch.

Chapter 12 1863—Mount Pleasant

239 *The president's train*: "Arrival and Reception of President Davis," *Charleston Mercury*, November 3, 1863.

240 *As he attempted*: "President Davis in Charleston," *Charleston Daily Courier*, November 3, 1863.

241 *Davis kept busy*: "Movements of the President," *Charleston Mercury*, November 4, 1863 and "The President's Movements," *Mercury*, November 5, 1863.

241 *Dixon and William*: Alexander, "True Stories."

243 *Armed with this*: A note in the logbook of Confederate Headquarters makes mention of Dixon's written request to take command of the *Hunley*. The original is in the National Archives. A copy is on file in the Friends of the *Hunley* archives.

243 *Beauregard granted Dixon*: Although Alexander makes mention of his and Dixon's meeting with Beauregard in "True Stories," the best account is in a letter written by Francis D. Lee to the general on May 15, 1876. Lee's letter is held in a private collection, with a typescript in the Eustace Williams Collection, Mobile Public Library.

244 *Jordan supplied them*: "Special Requisition for Submarine Torpedo Boat H. L. Hunley," Confederate military records, a copy of which is in the Eustace Williams Collection, Mobile Public Library.

244 *The spot was*: This is based on the Conrad Wise Chapman painting of the *Hunley*, which has proven to be a most accurate depiction of the submarine and, presumably, its environs during its final refit.

245 *Dixon and Alexander*: Letter of William Alexander to Col. J. G. Holmes, September 7, 1898, the South Carolina Historical Society, a copy of which is on file in the Friends of the *Hunley* archives.

245 *Even secluded in*: Ibid.

246 *Conrad Wise Chapman*: Brian Hicks, "City's Siege, On Canvas," *Post and Courier*, April 8, 2011.

248 *At first, Beauregard*: Alexander, "True Stories."

248 *In early December*: Dixon's request for five men to serve as crew aboard the *Hunley* is recorded in Confederate Headquarters books on December 11, 1863. The original is in the National Archives with a copy on file in the Friends of the *Hunley* archives.

248 *If military leaders*: Alexander, "Heroes of the *Hunley*."

249 *Arnold Becker was*: Brian Hicks, "'Kid' on *Hunley* proved his mettle," *Post and Courier*, April 13, 2004. These profiles of the *Hunley* crew, published in the week leading up to their burial, were based in large part on research by genealogist Linda Abrams and archaeologist Maria Jacobsen.

250 *Joseph Ridgaway, a*: Brian Hicks, "First officer Ridgaway was an old salt

at 30," *Post and Courier*, April 14, 2004. Abrams and Jacobsen provided much of the research in this article.

250 *James Wicks was*: Brian Hicks, "Witness to naval history also helped to create it," *Post and Courier*, April 16, 2004. In addition to research from Abrams and Jacobsen, Mary Elizabeth McMahon—the great-great-granddaughter of Wicks—provided family information. Her sister-in-law, Hope Barker, also provided a wealth of research on the Wicks family.

251 *Frank Collins was*: Brian Hicks, "Possible quest for bounty earned place in history," *Post and Courier*, April 15, 2004. Again, this article was written based on research by Abrams and Jacobsen.

251 *The final sailor*: Brian Hicks, "Lumpkin as mysterious as boat he helped power," *Post and Courier*, April 14, 2004. Information provided by Abrams and Jacobsen.

252 *Dixon's crew would*: Alexander letter to Holmes, September 7, 1898; Dixon letter to Willey, January 31, 1864; and Alexander "True Stories."

252 *Dixon and Alexander*: Ibid.

253 *Those early cruises*: Alexander, "Heroes of the *Hunley*."

253 *First Lieut. Geo.*: Special Orders No. 271, Confederate Headquarters, December 14, 1863, *ORA*, series 1, vol. 28, part II, 553.

253 *The general had*: James H. Tomb, "Submarines and Torpedo Boats," 169.

254 *Dixon kept up*: Notes from J. H. Tomb, January 1864, *ORN*, series 1, vol. 15, 334–35.

254 *Years later, Alexander*: Alexander, "True Stories."

254 *When Tomb reported*: Tomb, "Submarines and Torpedo Boats," 169.

Chapter 13   *1998—Tower of Babble*

257 *Warren Lasch felt*: Interview with Lasch, April 2013.

258 *As Lasch fought*: David Maraniss, *When Pride Still Mattered: A Life of Vince Lombardi* (New York: Simon and Schuster, 1999), 366. Lasch gives out this autobiography of his hero often. He gave me a signed copy in 2005.

259 *Bob, how much*: Interview with Lasch, April 2013.

260 *Lasch worked for*: Interview with Lasch. His notes on this plan are in the Friends of the *Hunley* files.

261 *It looks like*: February 19, 1998, *Hunley* Commission meeting minutes, Friends of the *Hunley* files.

261 *One commissioner refused*: Mike Soraghan, "Panel votes to Raise *Hunley*," *Post and Courier*, February 29, 1998.

262 *Using what information*: Ibid, as well as Lasch notes, Friends of the *Hunley* files.

262 *The Charleston Museum*: Information taken from the museum's proposal to the *Hunley* Commission, "Proposal: A Permanent Home for

Conservation, Preservation and Exhibition of the Confederate Submarine *H. L. Hunley,*" The Charleston Museum, January 1998.

262 *In the spring*: Robert Behre, "*Hunley* filmmakers on best behavior," *Post and Courier,* March 31, 1998.

263 *The movie engineers*: One of the favorite behind-the-scenes stories involved the scientists making fun of the TNT movie crew's decision to mount the spar on the bottom of the *Hunley*'s bow. For once, the scientists—who often claimed Conrad Wise Chapman's painting was too fanciful to be accurate—actually used Chapman to argue against this detail. When the spar was found, Lasch, McConnell and everyone else had a good laugh at the scientists' expense. The movie guys don't get everything wrong—sometimes common sense is better than science.

263 *The production used*: Matt Owen, "*Hunley* will resurface at Lake Moultrie," *Post and Courier,* July 9, 1998.

264 *Throughout the summer*: One local man wrote several letters to the *Hunley* Commission about liberties TNT took with the *Hunley* story. McConnell patiently wrote back to him, arguing that the movie would get the story out to a wider audience. Those letters are in the Friends of the *Hunley* files.

264 *Lasch intended to*: Interview with Lasch.

265 *State archaeologist Jonathan*: Schuyler Kropf, "*Hunley*'s dead await search," *Post and Courier,* August 12, 1998.

265 *With a little*: Interview with Randy Burbage.

266 *Clive Cussler followed*: Interview with Cussler, March 2013.

267 *Lasch wanted to*: Interview with Lasch, April 2013.

268 *Every week, Lasch*: Various proposals were kept and catalogued by Lasch. They reside in the Friends of the *Hunley* files.

269 *The USS Cairo*: The story of the *Cairo* disaster is handled expertly, and firsthand, in Edwin C. Bearrs, *Hardluck Ironclad* (Baton Rouge: Louisiana State University Press, 1980).

269 *Whitlock read the*: Interview with Whitlock.

271 *But as 1999*: Interview with McConnell. Additional information from letters, *Hunley* Commission folder, Friends of the *Hunley* files.

273 *Months earlier, the*: Schuyler Kropf, "*Hunley* may rise again in 2001," *Post and Courier,* November 7, 1998.

273 *The Hunley Commission*: Rachel Graves, "*Hunley* expected to surface from the sea six months early," *Post and Courier,* November 19, 1999.

273 *The first setback*: Schuyler Kropf, "*Hunley* to be preserved at warehouse," *Post and Courier,* March 16, 1999.

274 *Museum officials were*: Interview with Lasch, April 2013.

Chapter 14 1864—Sullivan's Island

277 *The men crept*: The narrative of Belton's escape comes from the report

"Examination of __ Belton," January 7, 1864, *ORN*, series 1, vol. 15, 227–29.

279   *George Shipp deserted*: Examination of George Shipp, *ORN*, series 1, vol. 15, 229–33.

281   *I have reliable*: Order of Rear Admiral Dahlgren, January 7, 1864, *ORN*, vol. 1, vol. 15, 226–27.

282   *On January 10*: Letter of Thomas Jordan, Confederate military records, National Archives, reprinted in Ragan, *The* Hunley, 155.

282   *Battery Marshall was*: Some of the description of Sullivan's Island and Battery Marshall is taken from a letter of Augustine Smythe, November 20, 1863, on file in the Smythe papers at the South Carolina Historical Society.

284   *The troops at*: McLaurin, "South Carolina Confederate Twins."

284   *By mid-January*: Alexander, "True Stories."

285   *Dixon and I*: Ibid.

285   *Through January and*: Ibid.

286   *Confederate spies had*: Dixon letter to Willey, January 31, 1864. Dixon found out the Union knew about his sub just weeks after Belton and Shipp deserted Charleston and provided this intelligence to blockade captains.

286   *We found that*: Alexander, "Heroes of the *Hunley*."

287   *Most mornings the*: Ibid.

287   *Years later, Alexander*: The famous "suicide pact" of the *Hunley* crew, as it has come to be called, was mentioned by William Alexander in a speech to the Iberville Historical Society, December 15, 1903. A transcript of his remarks is in the Eustace Williams Collection, Mobile Public Library.

288   *One afternoon Dixon*: This long account of the *Hunley* crew's endurance test in January 1864 comes from William Alexander, with various details taken from "Heroes of the *Hunley*" and "True Stories."

289   *We started the pumps*: Alexander, "Heroes of the *Hunley*."

289   *During the time*: Alexander, "True Stories."

290   *The man onshore*: Ibid.

290   *Dixon allowed his*: Ibid.

290   *Wicks took a*: Hicks, "Witness to naval history also helped to create it."

290   *On January 31*: Alexander, "True Stories."

291   *That afternoon, he*: Dixon letter to Willey.

291   *I suppose that*: Ibid.

291   *The Mobile command*: Alexander, "True Stories."

292   *That same night*: Dixon letter to Cothran, February 5, 1864.

292   *I do not*: Ibid.

293   *J. F. Carlsen was*: Hicks, "Dead man's seat held no stranger to courage," *Post and Courier*, April 16, 2004. This article was written using information provided by Linda Abrams and Maria Jacobsen.

Chapter 15 *1999–2000—North Charleston*

295   *He found it*: Interview with Lasch.

295   *On George Street*: Bruce Smith, "Premiere of *The Hunley* brings stars to Charleston," The Associated Press, June 15, 1999.

296   *I thought it*: Ibid.

297   *State Archaeologist Jonathan*: Gaulden, "*Hunley* group ready for action."

298   *Two weeks after*: Schuyler Kropf, "2nd likely *Hunley* body found," *Post and Courier*, June 28, 1999; and interview with Randy Burbage.

299   *For Burbage, this*: Interview with Burbage.

299   *The next day*: Kropf, "2nd likely *Hunley* body found."

300   *Lasch had a*: Interview with Lasch.

301   *As soon as*: Schuyler Kropf, "*Hunley* to be preserved at warehouse," *Post and Courier*, March 16, 1999.

301   *The Hunley consumed*: Interview with Lasch; Friends of the *Hunley* files.

302   *Whitlock had followed*: Interview with Whitlock.

303   *Once the Hunley*: Bill Swindell, "Commission sets goal to raise *Hunley* July 17," *Post and Courier*, February 11, 2000.

304   *That task fell*: Interview with Lasch.

305   *The scientists preferred*: Spring 2000 letter from Neyland to Lasch, Friends of the *Hunley* file.

305   *The scientists feared*: Ibid.

305   *On March 25*: Interview with Burbage.

307   *Using vacuum hoses*: Interviews with Leonard Whitlock and Ralph Wilbanks.

307   *The plan called*: Interview with Whitlock.

308   *The suction piles*: Ibid.

308   *This created an*: Interview with Paul Mardikian.

309   *The scientists wanted*: Interview with Lasch.

310   *It sends chills*: Schuyler Kropf and Brian Hicks, "*Hunley*'s spar plucked from ocean bottom," *Post and Courier*, June 14, 2000.

311   *There was a*: The story of the crane-barge fiasco comes from a joint interview with Lasch and Whitlock, summer 2013.

313   *Whitlock wanted to*: Interview with Whitlock.

313   *The New Jersey*: Interview with Lasch.

314   *The Karlissa B*: Schuyler Kropf, "*Hunley* crane arrives," *Post and Courier*, July 22, 2000.

314   *By Friday, July*: Brian Hicks, "First four straps looped under *Hunley*," *Post and Courier*, July 29, 2000.

315   *The dive crews*: Interview with Wilbanks.

315   *Neyland was concerned*: Interview with Lasch.

317   *There was only*: Brian Hicks, "High-tech haven awaits vessel," *Post and Courier*, August 8, 2000.

317   *On August 6*: Interview with Wilbanks; and Brian Hicks, "*Hunley* diver salutes crew of previous sub recoveries," *Post and Courier*, August 7, 2000.

Chapter 16 *February 17, 1864—Off Charleston*

319   *After weeks of*: The description of the weather off Charleston that night is taken from the testimony of various sailors in the Proceedings of a Naval Court of Inquiry into the Sinking of the *Housatonic*, February 26–March 7, 1864.

319   *A week earlier*: "Siege Matters—Two Hundred and Twenty-First Day," *Charleston Mercury*, February 15, 1864.

320   *Nine men were*: The crew complement on deck is from John Crosby's testimony, Naval Court of Inquiry.

321   *In September, boats*: ORN, series 1, vol. 14, 616–19.

322   *In the past*: Report of Lt. Cmdr. John L. Davis of the USS *Wissahickon*, March 19, 1863, ORN, series 1, vol. 13, 773–74.

323   *The Housatonic carried*: The crew complement and duties of the *Housatonic* sailors on February 17, 1864 is taken from the Naval Court of Inquiry.

323   *A few nights*: Stanton, "Submarines and Torpedo Boats."

325   *Dixon and his*: McLaurin, "South Carolina Confederate Twins."

325   *Dixon told Dantzler*: Cardozo, *Reminiscences of Charleston*, 124.

327   *Robert Flemming was*: This account is taken entirely from the Naval Court of Inquiry into the *Housatonic*'s sinking. Nearly two dozen survivors of the attack recounted that night in a hearing that lasted nearly a week.

328   *If no one*: Flemming did not report saying this in his testimony. This quote was offered verbatim by George W. Kelly, a cooper on the ship, when he testified after Flemming.

330   *It was shaped*: This quote is taken from Captain Pickering's testimony. He was the last member of the *Housatonic* crew, other than the ship's doctor, to testify in the Naval Court of Inquiry.

331   *John H. Crosby*: Crosby was the first man to testify at the Naval Court of Inquiry. Some of these reflections are also taken from letters he wrote in the days after the attack, two of which are in private collections.

334   *It had taken*: Report of *Canandaigua* Capt. J. F. Green, February 18, 1864, ORN, series 1, vol. 15, 327–28.

335   *I saw a*: Flemming's blue light quote, which is in his testimony in the Naval Court of Inquiry, corresponds with the account of Cardoza about "two blue lights." It's a controversial statement, but is the best proof the *Hunley* survived the attack on the *Housatonic*. Some people argue that Flemming was mistaken, but he had already proven that he had a good eye.

Chapter 17 *August 8, 2000—Off Charleston*

337   *The little boat*: Interview with Lasch.

337   *McConnell had been*: Interview with McConnell.

338   *Warren Lasch approached*: Interview with Lasch.

339   *Whitlock and Steve*: Interview with Whitlock.

340   *I can lift*: Jenkins Montgomery was originally interviewed shortly after the *Hunley* recovery. His remarks are taken from Brian Hicks and Schuyler Kropf, *Raising the* Hunley (New York: Ballantine, 2002), 7.

340   *Eventually, Whitlock and*: Interview with Whitlock.

341   *Ralph Wilbanks was*: Interview with Wilbanks.

342   *The seas had*: Interview with Whitlock.

343   *Montgomery spotted Lasch*: Interview with Lasch.

344   *Shortly after 7:30*: Interviews with Whitlock and Lasch.

346   *We did it*: Schuyler Kropf, "*Hunley*'s historic return," *Post and Courier*, August 9, 2000.

346   *Those fellas will*: Ibid.

346   *Montgomery lined up*: Interview with Whitlock.

347   *You people won't*: Eddie Curran, "History resurfaces in South Carolina," *Mobile Register*, August 9, 2000.

347   *Cussler was in*: This section was compiled from interviews with Cussler and video footage from the *Hunley* press boat on lift day.

349   *Ralph Wilbanks fortuitously*: Interviews with Wilbanks and Cussler.

349   *The plan originally*: Interview with Lasch.

350   *She's coming home*: Interview with Pecorelli.

350   *Leonard Whitlock missed*: Interview with Whitlock.

350   *Just before the*: Interview with Lasch.

351   *I'm looking forward*: Interview with Burbage.

352   *If these men*: Kropf, "*Hunley*'s historic return."

352   *Warren Lasch celebrated*: Interview with Lasch.

Chapter 18 *1864—Aboard the USS* Wabash

353   *Throughout the night*: McLaurin, "South Carolina Confederate Twins."

354   *Dixon and his*: Alexander, "Heroes of the *Hunley*."

354   *And later that*: *Charleston Daily Courier*, February 19, 1864.

354   *The Battery Marshall*: Report of Lt. Col. O. M. Dantzler, February 19, 1864, ORN, series 1, vol. 15, 335.

355   *I have the*: Ibid.

355   *I fear that*: Letter of General Ripley to Beauregard, February 19, 1864, Eustace Williams Collection, Mobile Public Library.

356   *As soon as*: Note from Beauregard to Lt. John A. Wilson, February 20, 1864, ORN, series 1, vol. 15, 336.

356 *A gunboat sunken*: Telegram from Beauregard, February 21, 1864, *ORN*, series 1, vol. 15, 336.

356 *The same day*: "Siege Matters—Two Hundred and Twenty-Eighth Day," *Charleston Mercury*, February 22, 1864.

357 *In Mobile, William*: Alexander, "True Stories."

357 *Jordan replied to*: Ibid.

357 *On February 26*: "Siege Matters—Two Hundred and Thirty Fifth Day," *Charleston Mercury*, February 29, 1864.

358 *The glorious success*: *Charleston Daily Courier*, February 29, 1864.

358 *We are glad*: "Siege Matters," *Charleston Mercury*, February 29, 1864.

358 *All this propaganda*: Susan Middleton, letter, March 4, 1864, Middleton Family Papers, South Carolina Historical Society.

359 *Leovy—Horace Hunley's*: Letter of Henry Leovy to Beauregard, March 5, 1864, Eustace Williams Collection, Mobile Public Library.

360 *Dahlgren predicted the*: Report of Rear Admiral Dahlgren, February 19, 1864, *ORN*, series 1, vol. 15, 329–30.

361 *The success of*: Order of Dahlgren, February 19, 1864, *ORN*, series 1, vol. 15, 330–31.

361 *Already, Dahlgren had*: Report of *Canandaigua* Capt. J. F. Green, February 18, 1864, *ORN*, series 1, vol. 15, 327–28.

361 *The hearing convened*: All quotes, accounts and description of the attack are from Proceedings of a Naval Court of Inquiry into the Sinking of the *Housatonic*, February 26–March 7, 1864.

362 *Crosby lamented that*: Crosby wrote two letters to his wife, Irene, on February 18 and 19, 1864, and his personal account of the tragedy— and his loss—is from those letters. The letters are in a private collection, and the donor wishes to remain anonymous.

362 *I cannot describe*: Ibid, February 19 letter.

368 *In March, the*: Report of Capt. S. C. Rowan, March 6, 1864, *ORN*, series 1, vol. 15, 356.

368 *The David then*: Report of Capt. J. DeCamp, April 19, 1864, *ORN*, series 1, vol. 15, 405.

Chapter 19 *1865–1980—Charleston*

371 *The Confederates raised*: This account of Charleston's final moments in the Civil War is compiled from various sources, including Burton, *The Siege of Charleston*, 316–25; Wilcox and Ripley, *The Civil War at Charleston*, 76–77; and Brian Hicks, *City of Ruin: Charleston at War 1860–1865* (Charleston: Evening Post Publishing, 2012), 205–19.

373 *Churchill examined several*: Report of Lt. W. L. Churchill, November 27, 1864, *ORN*, series 1, vol. 15, 334.

374   *On February 15*: Kloeppel, *Danger Beneath the Waves*, 17.

375   *In 1942, the*: Greg Lambousy, the Louisiana State Museum curator of exhibits, offered a more detailed history of the nameless submarine in *Louisiana Life* magazine, Summer 2001.

375   *In 1870, the*: *Report of the Secretary of War, being part of the Messages and Documents communicated to the Two Houses of Congress at the beginning of the Second Session of the Forty-Second Congress*, Vol. II (Washington: Government Printing Office, 1871), 580–84.

376   *Whether she went*: "The Remarkable Career of a Remarkable Craft," *Charleston Daily Republican*, October 8, 1870. The full text of the article is reprinted in Ragan, *The* Hunley, 241.

376   *A few days*: "Death on the Bottom of the Deep," *Charleston Daily Courier*, October 11, 1870.

377   *The British Navy*: Hore, "A Secret Journey to Halifax."

378   *More than a*: Mike Dash, "The Amazing (If True) Story of The Submarine Mechanic Who Blew Himself Up Then Surfaced as a Secret Agent for Queen Victoria," Smithsonian.com, the website of Smithsonian Magazine, June 30, 2014.

378   *In 1872, the*: *Annual Report of the Chief Engineers to the Secretary of War for the Year 1873* (Washington: Government Printing Office, 1873), 727–28.

378   *A few years*: Angus Smith's letter to Beauregard is printed as an appendix entry in Alfred Roman, *The Military Operations of General Beauregard*, vol. 2 (New York: Harper and Brothers, 1884), 528. This letter is the most valid piece of evidence that the *Hunley* was found at least once before it sank into the ocean floor. Even Ralph Wilbanks is impressed by this letter.

379   *Smith returned to*: The only known account of P. T. Barnum's offer is in a letter from James Gadsden Holmes to Joseph Daniels, Secretary of the Navy, on April 27, 1815. Holmes says he got the story from Angus Smith's son, who claimed Angus and his old dive partner (presumably David Broadfoot) searched five acres of ocean for the sub in hopes of getting one last payday for retrieving the *Hunley*. Obviously this happened after 1876, when Smith told Beauregard he knew exactly where the sub was.

380   *The Housatonic wreck*: "Diving for the *Housatonic*," *Charleston News and Courier*, July 12, 1908.

381   *Lake, who came*: Simon Lake letter to Horatio L. Wait, February 6, 1899, in the Augustine Smythe Papers, South Carolina Historical Society.

381   *In 1902, William*: Alexander, "True Stories."

382   *The trouble with*: Alexander, speech to Iberville Historical Society, December 15, 1903.

383   *I received from*: Alexander, "True Stories."

384   *In 1957, Charleston*: Tom Perry, "Salvage of Sub *Hunley* has 50-50

Chance for Success," *News and Courier*, June 18, 1957.

385   *Two months later*: "Navy Still Plans Hunt for *Hunley*," *News and Courier*, August 28, 1957.

385   *The USS Hunley*: Duncan, *The Captain and Submarine*, 97.

Chapter 20 2001–2014—North Charleston

387   *Maria Jacobsen almost*: Interviews with Maria Jacobsen, 2001.

387   *After scientists spent*: Schuyler Kropf, "Scientists find way to open *Hunley* without cutting hull," *Post and Courier*, January 20, 2001.

388   *On February 16*: Brian Hicks, "First iron plate removed from *Hunley*," *Post and Courier*, February 17, 2001.

388   *Two of the*: Brian Hicks, "Type of button pinpointed," *Post and Courier*, March 17, 2001.

388   *Jacobsen concentrated on*: Brian Hicks and Schuyler Kropf, "Human remains found in *Hunley*," *Post and Courier*, March 22, 2001.

389   *But already this*: Schuyler Kropf, "Sailor found in *Hunley* had bad back," *Post and Courier*, March 24, 2001.

389   *By the middle*: Schuyler Kropf, "2 more crewmen uncovered on sub," *Post and Courier*, April 17, 2001.

389   *By early May*: Schuyler Kropf, "Number of sailors cranking revised," *Post and Courier*, May 5, 2001.

390   *They ultimately found*: Interview with Paul Mardikian; Brian Hicks, "Brain tissue found inside skulls of Confederate sub's crew," *Post and Courier*, May 10, 2001.

390   *Stuck to the*: Schuyler Kropf, "Union soldier's ID tag found in *Hunley*," *Post and Courier*, April 28, 2001.

391   *Some believed Chamberlin*: Brian Hicks, "Union private's tale adds to *Hunley* lore," *Post and Courier*, May 1, 2001.

391   *One day, Lasch*: Interview with Lasch.

392   *In the weeks*: Interview with McConnell.

393   *The area beneath*: Brian Hicks, "Excavators search for Lt. Dixon," *Post and Courier*, May 11, 2001.

393   *Soon after the*: Schuyler Kropf, "*Hunley* commander found: Researchers also discover lantern that might have been used as signal of successful attack," *Post and Courier*, May 21, 2001.

394   *Jacobsen would handle*: Interview with Jacobsen.

394   *Around 9:30 that*: Schuyler Kropf and Brian Hicks, "Dixon's coin found," *Post and Courier*, May 25, 2001.

395   *Later, they would*: Interview with Mardikian.

396   *Lasch got the*: Interview with Lasch. I was the lucky reporter who got the 7:30 A.M. call.

396 *Paranoia set in*: The story of the extreme security measures used to guard Dixon's coin was related, off the record at the time, by McConnell and Lasch.

397 *Unexplored corners of*: Interview with Mardikian.

398 *None of these*: These theories of the *Hunley*'s sinking are taken from years of interviews and conversations with Maria Jacobsen, Paul Mardikian, Glenn McConnell and Bob Neyland. Some of these theories have been discussed for years; others are revealed here for the first time.

399 *The sub's bow*: Interview with Jacobsen.

400 *There are several*: Interview with Mardikian.

400 *An anchor was*: Interview with Wilbanks.

401 *There are, however*: Interview with Cussler.

402 *In 2012, conservator*: Brian Hicks, "Discovery alters *Hunley* history," *Post and Courier*, January 28, 2013.

404 *The only other*: Interview with Mardikian. The broken seacock pipe was discovered by Mardikian years ago, but archaeologists will not concede this damage is the cause of the sinking until the entire sub is examined after the hull is de-concreted. Still, some people associated with the project believe it is perhaps the most important discovery on the *Hunley* to date.

Epilogue *Last Rites*

408 *We are here*: Brian Hicks, "Final Respects," *Post and Courier*, April 18, 2004.

409 *The men of*: Ibid.

409 *As the ritual*: Interview with Cussler.

410 *The Hunley is*: Warren Lasch eulogy, Friends of the *Hunley* files.

412 *In 2002, the*: Brian Hicks, "Cities Make Big Promises for *Hunley*," *Post and Courier*, March 9, 2002.

412 *To court, Lasch*: Interview with Lasch.

415 *To this day*: Interview with Wilbanks.

415 *As they drove*: Interview with Lasch.

416 *Its first show*: Ibid

Bibliography

Alexander, William. Letter to Charles Stewart. November 11, 1902. Friends of
the *Hunley* archives.

———. Letter to Col. J. G. Holmes. September 7, 1898. South Carolina
Historical Society.

———. Speech to the Iberville Historical Society, December 15, 1903.
Eustace Williams Collection, Mobile Public Library.

———. "The Heroes of the *Hunley*." *Munsey's Magazine*, August 1903, 748.

———. "The True Stories of the Confederate Submarine Boats." *New Orleans
Picayune*, June 29, 1902.

Associated Press. "The War Between the States." July 27, 1995.

Baird, G.W. "Submarine Torpedo Boats." *Journal of American Societies of
Naval Engineers* 14 (1902): 845.

Barrow, Robert Ruffin. Letter to Horace Hunley. September 1863. Tulane Special
Collections, Barrow Family Papers, Tulane University.

Barrow, Volumnia Hunley. Letter to her husband, Robert Ruffin Barrow.
March 13, 1862.

Bartelme, Tony, and Schuyler Kropf. "Bad blood, thin egos may torpedo salvage."
Post and Courier, August 27, 1995.

Baxley, Colette. "It's Official! Experts verify sunken wreck as Confederate
sub *Hunley*." *Post and Courier*, May 18, 1996.

Beard, William E. "The Log of The C.S. Submarine." *U.S. Naval Institute
Proceedings*, vol. 42, no. 5, Sept.–Oct. 1916.

Bearrs, Edwin C. *Hardluck Ironclad*. Baton Rouge: Louisiana State University
Press, 1980.

Beauregard, P. G. T. Letter to Hutson Lee. August 12, 1863, National Archives.

Beauregard, [P.] G. T. "Torpedo Service in the Harbor and Water Defences of Charleston." *Southern Historical Society Papers*, vol. 5, no. 4, April 1878.

Behre, Robert. "*Hunley* filmmakers on best behavior." *Post and Courier*. March 31, 1998.

Bergeron, Arthur W. *Confederate Mobile*. Baton Rouge: Louisiana State University Press, 2000, 120–21.

Buchanan, Franklin. Letter to John Tucker. August 1, 1863.

Buchanan, Franklin. Letter book on file at the University of North Carolina Library.

Burton, Milby. *The Siege of Charleston*. Columbia: University of South Carolina Press, 1970, 316–25.

Cardozo, J. N. *Reminiscences of Charleston*. Charleston: Joseph Walker, 1866, 124–5.

Chaffin, Tom. *The H. L. Hunley: The Secret Hope of the Confederacy*. New York: Hill and Wang, 2008, 21.

Charleston Daily Courier. February 19, 1864.

———. February 29, 1864.

———. "Death on the Bottom of the Deep. Discovery of Buried Torpedo Boat off Charleston—Nine skeletons at the Wheel." October 11, 1870.

———. "Melancholy Occurrence." October 16, 1863.

———. "President Davis in Charleston." November 3, 1863.

Charleston Daily Republican. "The Remarkable Career of a Remarkable Craft." October 8, 1870.

Charleston Mercury. "Arrival and Reception of President Davis." November 3, 1863.

———. "The Day of Prayer." August 21, 1863.

———. "From Morris Island—Capture of a Yankee Boat and Crew." August 6, 1863.

———. "Gen. Gillmore's Demand for the Evacuation of Morris Island and Fort Sumter—Gen. Beauregard's Reply, Etc." August 24, 1863.

———. "Last Honors to a Devoted Patriot." November 9, 1863.

———. "Latest from Morris Island." July 21, 1863.

———. "More Negro Labor Wanted Immediately for the Defence of Charleston." August 3, 1863.

———. "Movements of the President." November 4, 1863.

———. "The President's Movements." November 5, 1863.

———. "Progress and Events of the Siege." August 24, 1863.

———. "The Siege—Attack on the Enemy's Fleet." October 7, 1863.

———. "The Siege—Finale of the Contest for Battery Wagner—Unprecedented Bombardment—Evacuation of Morris Island by Our Forces, Etc." September 7, 1863.

——. "Siege Matters—Two Hundred and Twenty-Eighth Day." February 22, 1864.

——. "Siege Matters—Two Hundred and Twenty-First Day." February 15, 1864.

——. "Siege Matters—Two Hundred and Thirty Fifth Day." February 29, 1864.

——. "Terrible Explosion and Loss of Life." October 13, 1863.

Charleston News and Courier. "Diving for the Housatonic." July 12, 1908.

Curran, Eddie. "History resurfaces in South Carolina." *Mobile Register.*
    August 9, 2000.

Cussler, Clive. Letter to editor, *Post and Courier.* September 13, 1995.

Cussler, Clive, and Craig Dirgo. *The Sea Hunters.* New York: Simon and Schuster,
    1996.

Cussler, Clive, et al. "Search for the Confederate Submarine *H. L. Hunley* off
    Charleston Harbor, South Carolina." Booklet submitted to the U.S. Naval
    Historical Center, August 1995.

Dixon, George. Letter to Henry Willey. January 31, 1864.

——. Letter to John Cothran. February 5, 1864. Eustace Williams Collection,
    Mobile Public Library.

Dufour, Charles L. *The Night the War Was Lost.* Lincoln: University of Nebraska
    Press/Bison Books, 1994, 107.

Duncan, Ruth H. *The Captain and Submarine CSS* H. L. Hunley. Memphis:
    S.C. Toof & Company, 1965. 13–20.

Fennell, Edward C. "Search Ends for Confederate Sub *Hunley.*" *News and
    Courier,* June 27, 1981.

Folmar, John Kent, ed. *From That Terrible Field: Civil War Letters of James M.
    Williams, Twenty-first Alabama Infantry Volunteers.* Tuscaloosa: University
    of Alabama Press, 1981, 53.

Fort, W. B. "First Submarine in the Confederate Navy." *Confederate Veteran,*
    vol. 26, no. 10 (1918): 459–60.

Gaulden, Sid. "Save the Sub: *Hunley* group ready for action." *Post and Courier,*
    August 3, 1995.

Gift, George Washington. Letter to Ellen Shackelford. August 8, 1863. George
    Washington Gift Papers, University of North Carolina's Southern Historical
    Collection.

Graves, Rachel. "*Hunley* expected to surface from the sea six months early."
    Post and Courier, November 19, 1999.

Heilprin, John. "Funds Ok'd in search for *Hunley.*" *Post and Courier,* October 12,
    1995.

——. "*Hunley* credit to Cussler?" *Post and Courier,* February 28, 1997.

Hicks, Brian. "Brain tissue found inside skulls of Confederate sub's crew."
    Post and Courier, May 10, 2001.

——. "Cities Make Big Promises for *Hunley.*" *Post and Courier,* March 9, 2002.

——. *City of Ruin: Charleston at War 1860–1865.* Charleston: Evening Post

Publishing, 2012, 205–19.

———. "City's Siege, On Canvas." *Post and Courier*, April 8, 2011.

———. "Discovery alters *Hunley* history." *Post and Courier*, January 28, 2013.

———. "Excavators search for Lt. Dixon." *Post and Courier*, May 11, 2001.

———. "Final Respects." *Post and Courier*, April 18, 2004.

———. "First four straps looped under *Hunley*." *Post and Courier*, July 29, 2000.

———. "First iron plate removed from *Hunley*." *Post and Courier*, February 17, 2001.

———. "First officer Ridgaway was an old salt at 30." *Post and Courier*, April 14, 2004.

———. "High-tech haven awaits vessel." *Post and Courier*, August 8, 2000.

———. "*Hunley* diver salutes crew of previous sub recoveries." *Post and Courier*, August 7, 2000.

———. "*Hunley*'s captain fiercely determined to succeed." *Post and Courier*, April 11, 2004.

———. "'Kid' on *Hunley* proved his mettle." *Post and Courier*, April 13, 2004.

———. "Lumpkin as mysterious as boat he helped power." *Post and Courier*, April 14, 2004.

———. "Possible quest for bounty earned place in history." *Post and Courier*, April 15, 2004.

———. "Type of button pinpointed." *Post and Courier*, March 17, 2001.

———. "Union private's tale adds to *Hunley* lore." *Post and Courier*, May 1, 2001.

———. "Witness to naval history also helped to create it." *Post and Courier*, April 16, 2004.

Hicks, Brian, and Schuyler Kropf. "Human remains found in *Hunley*." *Post and Courier*, March 22, 2001.

Hill, Horace N. "Texan Gave World First Successful Submarine Torpedo." *San Antonio Express*, July 30, 1916.

Holmes, James Gadsden. Letter to Joseph Daniels, Secretary of the Navy. April 27, 1915.

Honour, Theodore. Letter to Beckie Honour. August 30, 1863. South Caroliniana Library at the University of South Carolina.

Hore, Captain Peter, Royal Navy (Retired). "A Secret Journey to Halifax." *Naval History*, June 2002, 32–36.

Hornblower, Margot. "Historic Sea Hunt: Cussler Finds Troopship and *Lusitania* Sub." *Washington Post*, July 26, 1984.

Hunley, Horace. Letter dated July 27, 1863, from Rome, Georgia (either to Leovy or his friend Gardner Smith).

———. Letter to Francis Hatch. July 9, 1861.

———. Letter to General Beauregard. September 19, 1863. Eustace Williams Collection, Mobile Public Library.

———. Letter to James McClintock. August 15, 1863. Eustace Williams Collection, Mobile Public Library.

Hunley, Horace Lawson. Memorandum Book, record group 140, folder 12, Louisiana Historical Society.

Kloeppel, James. *Danger Beneath the Waves*. Orangeburg: Sandlapper Publishing, 1992, 6.

Kropf, Schuyler. "Diver asked to lead team to *Hunley* Site." *Post and Courier.* October 11, 1995.

———. "*Hunley* commander found: Researchers also discover lantern that might have been used as signal of successful attack." *Post and Courier*, May 21, 2001.

———. "*Hunley* crane arrives." *Post and Courier*, July 22, 2000.

———. "*Hunley* may rise again in 2001." *Post and Courier*, November 7, 1998.

———. "*Hunley* to be preserved at warehouse." *Post and Courier*, March 16, 1999.

———. "*Hunley*'s dead await search." *Post and Courier*, August 12, 1998.

———. "*Hunley*'s historic return." *Post and Courier*, August 9, 2000.

———. "The *Hunley* Will Be Slow to Rise." *Post and Courier*, May 12, 1995.

———. "Number of sailors cranking revised." *Post and Courier*, May 5, 2001.

———. "Sailor found in *Hunley* had bad back." *Post and Courier*, March 24, 2001.

———. "Scientists find way to open *Hunley* without cutting hull." *Post and Courier*, January 20, 2001.

———. "2nd likely *Hunley* body found." *Post and Courier*, June 28, 1999.

———. "2 more crewmen uncovered on sub." *Post and Courier*, April 17, 2001.

———. "Union soldier's ID tag found in *Hunley*." *Post and Courier*, April 28, 2001.

Kropf, Schuyler, and Brian Hicks. "Dixon's coin found." *Post and Courier* May 25, 2001.

———. "*Hunley*'s spar plucked from ocean bottom." *Post and Courier*, June 14, 2000.

Lake, Simon. Letter to Horatio L. Wait. February 6, 1899. Augustine Smythe Papers, South Carolina Historical Society.

Langley, Lynne. "Divers may have located *Hunley*." *Post and Courier*. January 28, 1995.

Lee, Francis D. Letter to General Beauregard. May 15, 1876. Eustace Williams Collection, Mobile Public Library.

Leovy, Henry. Letter to Beauregard. March 5, 1864. Eustace Williams Collection, Mobile Public Library.

Maraniss, David. *When Pride Still Mattered: A Life of Vince Lombardi*. New York: Simon and Schuster, 1999, 366.

Maury, Dabney. "How the Confederacy Changed Naval Warfare." *Southern Historical Society Papers*, vol. 22, 1894.

McClintock, James. Letter to Matthew F. Maury. 1868. Eustace Williams

Collection, Mobile Alabama Public Library.

McLaurin, D. W. "South Carolina Confederate Twins." *Confederate Veteran*, vol. 33 (1925): 328.

Middleton, Eweretta. Letter to Harriott Middleton. August 17, 1863. South Carolina Historical Society.

Middleton, Harriott. Letter to her, dated September 2–3, 1863. Middleton Papers, South Carolina Historical Society.

Middleton, Susan. Letter. March 4, 1864. Middleton Family Papers, South Carolina Historical Society.

Mobile Daily Item. "George E. Dixon's Submarine. Details of How Brave Man Lost His Life—Sons of Mobile Honor Him." April 26, 1910.

Mobile Item. "First Submarine to Sink a Warship Was Mobile Product." date unknown.

Mobile Register. "Man Who Served in Three Wars Dies in Mobile." November 19, 1928.

Montgomery Advertiser. "An Alabama Hero." March 11, 1900.

National Park Service Submerged Cultural Resources Unit's H. L. Hunley *Site Assessment*. Santa Fe: National Park Service, 1998.

Naval History Division, *Civil War Naval Chronology 1861–1865*. Washington, D.C.: Department of the Navy, 1971. II–54.

News and Courier. "Navy Still Plans Hunt for *Hunley*." August 28, 1957.

Official Records of the Union and Confederate Navies in the War of the Rebellion. Washington, D.C.: Government Printing Office, 1921.

O'Brien, Jack Jr. "Where Was the *Hunley* Built?" *Gulf South Historical Review*, vol. 21, no. 1, (Fall 2005): 29–48.

Olmstead, Colonel Charles H. "Reminiscences of Service in Charleston Harbor in 1863." *Southern Historical Society Papers*, vol. 11, 1883.

Owen, Matt. "*Hunley* will resurface at Lake Moultrie." *Post and Courier*, July 9, 1998.

Palmer, Mrs. Edwin J. "Horace Lawson Hunley." *The United Daughters of the Confederacy Magazine*, May 1962. 14.

Perry, Tom. "Salvage of Sub *Hunley* has 50-50 Chance for Success." *News and Courier*, June 18, 1957.

Post and Courier. "The *Hunley* waits another 45 minutes." October 29, 1995.

Rigsbee, Fred. "Divers May Have Located Housatonic." *Charleston Evening Post*, July 18, 1980.

———. "*Hunley* Search to Resume at Later Date." *Charleston Evening Post*, July 21, 1980.

———. "*Hunley* Eludes Searchers," *Charleston Evening Post*, June 26, 1981.

Ripley, Gen. Roswell S. Letter to Beauregard. February 19, 1864. Eustace Williams Collection, Mobile Public Library.

Robinson, William Morrison. *The Confederate Privateers*. Columbia: University of South Carolina Press, 1994.

Roman, Alfred. *The Military Operations of General Beauregard*, vol. 2. New York: Harper and Brothers, 1884, 528.

Rowan, Capt. S. C. Letter to U.S. Rear Adm. John Dahlgren. October 6, 1863.

Ruffin, Edmund (William Kauffman Scarborough, ed.). *The Diary of Edmund Ruffin, Volume III: A Dream Shattered, June 1863–June 1865*. Baton Rouge: Louisiana State University Press, 1989, 177.

Slaughter, James E. Letter to Gen. P. G. T. Beauregard. July 31, 1863. National Archives.

Smith, Bruce. "Premiere of *The Hunley* brings stars to Charleston." The Associated Press. June 15, 1999.

Smith, Gardner. Letter to Hunley's sister, Volumnia. November 29, 1863. Tulane Special Collections, Barrow Family Papers, Tulane University.

Smythe, Augustine. Letter November 20, 1863. Smythe Papers, South Carolina Historical Society.

———. Letter to a relative. August 30, 1863. Augustine Smythe Papers, South Carolina Historical Society.

Soraghan, Mike. "Panel votes to Raise *Hunley*." *Post and Courier*. February 29, 1998.

South Carolina Historical Magazine. "David C. Ebaugh on the Building of *The David*." January 1953.

Stanton, C. L. "Submarines and Torpedo Boats." *Confederate Veteran*, vol. 22 (1914): 398–99.

Swindell, Bill. "Commission sets goal to raise *Hunley* July 17." *Post and Courier*, February 11, 2000.

Symond, Craig L. *The Civil War at Sea*. New York: Oxford University Press, 2012, 31.

Tomb, James H. "Submarines and Torpedo Boats, C.S.N." *Confederate Veteran* magazine, Vol. 22 (1914): 168–69.

Valero, Wayne. *The Adventure Writing of Clive Cussler*. Kearney, NE: Morris Publishing, 2007.

War of the Rebellion: A Compilation of the Official Records of the Union and Confederate Armies. Washington, D.C.: Government Printing Office, 1880.

Weddle, Kevin J. *Lincoln's Tragic Admiral: The Life of Samuel Francis Du Pont*. Charlottesville: University of Virginia Press, 2005, 103–5.

Wilcox, Arthur M., and Warren Ripley. *The Civil War at Charleston*. Charleston: Evening Post Publishing, 1966, 76–77.

Wilford, John Noble. "Confederate Submarine Is Discovered Off South Carolina." *New York Times*. May 11, 1995.

Acknowledgments

This book could not have been written without the encouragement and support of Warren Lasch. He has been the project's cheerleader from Day One, and if he can raise a Confederate submarine he can certainly get a cigar-addicted newspaper columnist motivated to write a book. The man is simply inspiring.

Warren and I have been close friends for years. Since he resigned as chairman of Friends of the *Hunley*, we've kept in touch the way people who go through life-changing events often do. For years we have met regularly to smoke Padrons and catch up, tell a few jokes and laugh about the old days. Invariably, the idea of a behind-the-scenes book about the *Hunley* project would come up. He has always believed there was a bigger story to tell. As usual, Warren was right.

Clive Cussler was another early supporter of this book, and he's just about the best friend a writer can have. I've known Clive for more than a decade and he has always been gracious with his time, willing to give me sage advice and encouragement. Clive not only sat for interviews during the year it took to write this book, he also edited the manuscript in its earliest form. His endorsement of the alternating timelines gave me the confidence to tell the story this way. Clive is simply a class act, and I am eternally grateful for all he's done.

I am proud to call Ralph Wilbanks my friend, and honored that he served as consultant on this project (although the title "consultant" would probably come as news to him). Not only did Ralph share his memories, he read the manuscript twice to offer suggestions and corrections. Any mistakes that remain are my own and slipped through despite Ralph's best efforts.

The folks at the Friends of the *Hunley* and *Hunley* Commission have been supportive of my work for years. Glenn McConnell was enthusiastic about telling the expanded history and behind-the-scenes story from the beginning, and I was proud to have his blessing. Frankly, McConnell deserves more credit than he receives not only for his work on the *Hunley*, but for all his public service. He is, as Horace Hunley would attest, a Great Man.

There are too many folks associated with the *Hunley* to list them all in this space, but special thanks are in order to Cindy Elenberger, Kellen Correia, Josephine Starnes, John Hazzard, Paul Mardikian, Ric Tapp, Nestor Gonzalez, Michael Scafuri, Maria Jacobsen, Darlene Russo and, of course, Raegan Quinn-Smith.

The folks at Spry Publishing have been great advocates for this book and a pleasure to work with. Lynne Johnson, Jeremy Sterling, Carol Bokas and Jim Edwards are true pros and deserve a lot of credit for bringing *Sea of Darkness* to life.

As always, I also appreciate the support of my friends and colleagues at the *Post and Courier*.

And, of course, none of this would be possible without the love, infinite understanding and support of my family.

APPENDIX

Hunley Recovery Personnel

Telling any story is a matter of choices, and a lot of details are left out to keep the story moving. These people—some of whom appear in the narrative, while others don't—deserve mention and credit for their work in recovering the *Hunley* on August 8, 2000.

Clint Allison
Christopher Amer
Ira Block
John Bredar
Dave Conlin
Mike Crago
Doug Dawson
William Dudley
Kenneth Edwards
William Gotis
Todd Groseclose
Carl Hanson
Marcus Harper

Eric Howard
Steve Howard
Stacy Hruby
Maria Jacobsen
David Linstrom
Oscar Lopez
Paul Mardikian
Bennie Martin
Shea McLean
Jenkins Montgomery
Bob Neyland
Claire Peachey
Harry Pecorelli III

Tom Posey
Mark Ragan
Drew Ruddy
Matt Russell
Michael Scafuri
Jon Sears
Brett Seymour
Bill South
James Spirek
David Whall
Ralph Wilbanks
Jennings Woods
Steve Wright

Index

Italic page numbers refer to illustrations.
pic refers to photograph section.

1984 European expedition, 109
1996 *Hunley* survey, 269
20,000 Leagues Under the Sea
  (Verne), 376

Adela, 59
Adger's Wharf, 209
Adroit, 385
Alabama, 102, 411
Alabama, French government and, 115
Alabama, claims to *H. L. Hunley*, 197
Alabama, search for, 110
Albright, Alan, 40
Alexander, William, 89–90, 94, 124,
  133–34, 177, 323
  arrival in Charleston, 241–43
  at Battery Marshall, 282
  H. L. Hunley
    recollections of, 381–83
    letter from George Dixon, 357
    recalled to duty, 292
    sketches of *H. L. Hunley*, 190, 228,
      263
    suicide pact with George E. Dixon,
      288
  "The True Stories of the Confederate
    Submarine Boats," 381–82
  third model, 126–29
Amer, Chris, 195, 261
American Civil War, 377, 407
  loss of lives in, 373
American Diver, 94–96, 120, 122, 124,
  126, 133, 205, 280, 347, 383, 415
  attempts to recover, 97–98
  design faults, 121
  design of, 94–95

flaws of, 94–95
sinking of, 96
Andrea Doria, 267
Applebaum, Ralph, 412
Appomattox Court House (Virginia),
  373
Aquatic Center Dive Shop, 71
Argonaut, 381
Ariel, 109
Arlington Cemetery, 114
Army Corps of Engineers, 44, 80, 375,
  376, 378
Army of Northern
  Virginia, 125
Arvor, 102
Arvor II, 38
Arvor III, 101, 109, 110
Assante, Armand, 263, 296, *296*
Associated Press, 296
Atlantic Ocean, 32
Atlantis Found (Cussler), 267

Bamberg, 60
Barnum, P. T., 195, 379
Barrow, Robert Ruffin, 58, 62, 91, 205–6
Barrow, Volumnia Hunley, 205, 216, 217
Baton Rouge, 104
Battery Marshall, 20, 151, 152, *283*,
  326, 353, 354
  H. L. Hunley base of operations, 282
Battery Marshall dock, 323
Battery Wagner, 48, 137, 159, *165*,
  380, 391
  evacuation of, 175
Battle of Baton Rouge, 104
Battle of Flamborough Head, 35
Battle of Hampton Roads, 251
Battle of Port Royal, 293
Battle of Shiloh, 93
Battle of the Bulge, 101

Bavarian Motor Transport, 234
Bayou St. John, 375
Beard, Henry, 206
Bearss, Edwin, 269
Beauregard, Gen. Pierre Gustave
    Toutant, 18, 25, 135, *136*, 163,
    168, 170, 176, *176*–77, 198, 207,
    208, 290, 359, 368
  defense of Fort Sumter, 321
  dependence on the *H. L. Hunley*,
    137–38, 159, 160, 207–8
  fate of the *H. L. Hunley*, 217, 378–79
  first view of the *H. L. Hunley*, 161
  funeral for Hunley, 215–17
  letter to evacuate, 165–66
  meeting with Jefferson Davis, 240–41
  orders to retreat, 372
  permission to relaunch the
    H. L. Hunley, 243–44, 248, 253,
    284, 286, 292, 293
  raising of the *H. L. Hunley*, 174–75,
    213–14
  remorse at the loss of *H. L. Hunley*,
    355–56
Becker, Arnold, *pic 16*, 249, 253, 390,
    411
Belton, E. C., 277, 280
  deserter's model of *H. L. Hunley*, 281
Bennett, Jefferson, 172
Bennett, Queen, 395
Berryman, Eric, 38
black troops (Fifty-fourth), 137
blockade runners, 282, 321–22
  in Charleston, 163
  in Mobile, Alabama, 86
  Norseman, 83
  Raccoon, 77, 83
  Rattle Snake, 83
  Ruby, 77, 83
  Stonewall Jackson, 76, 83, 283
  wreckages of, 75–77, 83, 373
blockade-running schemes, 59
BMW, 234
Bonhomme Richard, 33, 34, 36, 83,
    102, 105
  search for, 36–37, 145

Booster Club lounge, 298
Bosch, 273
Brazil, 107
Breach Battery, 282
Breach Inlet, 31, 73, 151, 282, 283,
    322, 326
Breck's Place (North Charleston), 190
British Navy, 377
Broadfoot, David, 175, 213–14, 317
Broad Street, 235, 263
Brockbank, Robert, 206
Brooklyn, 67
Browning, Bob, 80
Buchanan, Adm. Franklin, 96–97, 135,
    136–37
Building 255, 263, 301, 317
  conversion to museum, 304–5
Burbage, Randy, 221, 265, 298–300,
    305–6, 351
Burbage's Sons of Confederate Veterans
    camp, 299
Bureau of Ordnance, 359
burning rafts, 52
Bushnell, David, 60

Calhoun Street, 79, 214
Cane, Michael, 168, 173
Cannon, J. W., 204
Captain Nemo, 376
Carlsen, J. F., *pic 17*, 293, 323
Castle Pinckney, 350, 371
Catalina Island, 71
Challenger disaster, 269
Chamberlin, Ezra, 390–91
  dog tag of, *pic 21*
Chancellorsville, Virginia, battle at, 125
Chapman, Conrad Wise, 190, 246–47
Chapman, John Gadsby, 246
Charleston, 40–41
  attack on, 356
  destruction of, 240
  evacuation by Confederates, 79, 371
  Yankee attack on, 159–60
Charleston, Siege of, 166, 168
Charleston, 79, 372
Charleston Battalion, 321

Charleston Daily Courier 213
Charleston Harbor, 40, 79, 136, 166, 202, 263, 278, 282
  jetties in, 44, 222, 227, 337, 380
  study of, 375
Charleston Harbor jetties, 44, 222, 227, 337
Charleston International Ports, 309
Charleston Mercury, 137, 160, 164, 173, 239
Charleston Museum, 149, 190, 193, 228, 257
  proposal for the *H. L. Hunley*, 262
Charleston Naval Base, 234, 301
Charleston Naval Shipyard, 384
Charleston Naval Weapons Station, 384
Charleston Post, 194
Charleston Post and Courier, 155
Charleston's military operations, desertion from, 277–79
Cherbourg, 102, 110
Chicora, 79, 168, 249, 321, 323, 372
Churchill, Lt. W. L., 373
CIA, 114–15
cigar boat, 63, 123, 163
The Citadel, 47
The Citadel's football stadium, 265
Civil War, 31, 125, 197, 351, 352
  shipwrecks from, 42, 48
Civil War artifact, 396
Civil War ironclad, 49
Civil War reenactment, 108
Civil War shipwreck, 229
Civil War vessel, 197
Clemson Restoration Institute, 413
Clemson University, 413
Clingman, Gen. Thomas, *167*, 167
Clive Cussler Foundation, 38
CNN, 344
Coastal Carolina University, 232
Coastal Explorer, 33, 42, 47, 73
  damages to, 44
College of Charleston, 199
College of William and Mary, 108
Collins, Frank, *pic 17*, 251
Comthwait, Lewis A., 327–29, 365

Condon, Charlie, 221
Confederacy, war and, 54–56
Confederacy cause, 53–54
Confederate Army, 59
  ammunition manufacturing for, 62, 89
Confederate bounty, for destruction of enemy ships, 55–56
Confederate graves, 298–99
Confederate guerrilla warfare, 52
Confederate Heritage Trust, 265
Confederate ironclad, 53
Confederate Naval Jack, 236
Confederate Navy, 88, 251
Confederate raider, 106
Confederate raider *Alabama*, 102
Confederates, evacuation of Charleston, 79
Confederate sailors, graves of, 265
Confederate spies, 286
Confederate States of America, 55, 197
  fight for, 54–55
  recognition of the *Pioneer*, 66
Confederate States Ship, *H. L. Hunley* as, 168
Confederate wrecks, salvage rights to, 378
Congdon, J. W., 363
Congress, 97
Connecticut Yankee, 390
Connor, James R., 57
conscription act, 125
Cook, George, 95
Cooper River, 199, 213, 349, 412
Cooper River bridges, 350
Cooper River docks, 161, 372
Correia, Kellen, *348*
Cothran, Capt. John, 18, 292
Courier, 194
Cousteau, Jacques, 70
Craven, Ensign C. H., 323, 330, 332, 363–64
Crescent City, 66
Crosby, John H., 329, 330, 331–32, 333, 362–63, 364
CSS *Alabama*, 186
CSS *Arkansas*, 104, 105

CSS *David*, 202, 202
CSS *Manassas*, 53, 56, 64, 104, 202
  last battle of, 66–67
CSS *Tennessee*, 86
CSS *Texas*, 144
CSS *Virginia*, 65, 87, 97, 107, 108,
  126, 168, 250
CSS *Virginia* vs USS *Monitor*, 65
Cuba, 120
Cumberland, 97
Cunard Line's RMS *Lusitania*,
  torpedoing of, 384
Cussler, Barbara, 37, 342
Cussler, Clive, *pic 13*, *pic 14*, 41, 69,
    81–83, 102, 200, 342, *348*, *403*,
    409, 415–16
  arrival in Charleston, 33
  as author, 34, 35
  early life of, 34–35
  fear for safety of *H. L. Hunley*,
    194–97, 223
  French bureaucracy and, 110–14
  Friends of the *Hunley* Board, 267–68
  locating the *H. L. Hunley*
    news of, 190–91
  personal price, 414–15, 416
  request for interview, 78–79
  search for the *Bonhomme Richard*,
    37–39
  shipwreck hunter, 33, 117
  threats against, 223–24
  underwater explorations and, 70–71
  wreck hunting hobby, cost of, 116
Cussler, Clive vs. Wilbanks, Ralph,
  friendly bet, 74
Cussler, Dana, 37
Cussler, Dirk, 32–33, 37, 42, 73, 76,
  102, 111, 342
Cussler, Teri, 37
Cyclops (Cussler), 103

Dahlgren, Adm. John A., *28*, 281–82,
  321, 328, 359–61, 373–74
Daily Courier, 173
Daily Delta, New Orleans, 56
Dantzler, Lt. Col. O. M., 325–26,

353–55
Dark 'n' Stormy, 200
David, 253, 281
  reward for capturing, 360
da Vinci, Leonardo, 60
Davis, Confederate President Jefferson,
  164
  visit to Charleston, 239–41
Davis, Nicholas, 168, 173
Dawson, Sarah Morgan, 105
day of fasting and praying, in
  Charleston, 164
deck meat, 79
Deep Six (Cussler), 103, 108
Deep Submergence Rescue Vehicles, 270
Denmark, 109
Detyens Shipyard, 311
de Vivies, Philippe, *pic 7*
Dillingham, 252
Dirgo, Craig, 180, 342
Dirk Pitt (fictional character), 34, 38,
  69, 71, 103, 144, 179, 267
disunion, threat of, 53–54
Divercity, 143, 147, 148, 150, 153,
  181, 182, 183, 185, 187, 188, 190,
  196, 227, 341, 342, 349
Diversified Wilbanks, 147, 154
Diving for Treasure (Throckmorton), 36
Dixon, George E., *pic 16*, 18, 92–93,
    133, 177, 206, 253, 356, 358, 381
  arrival in Charleston, 241–43
  attempt to attack the
    USS *Housatonic*, 323–25
  at Battery Marshall, 282, 283–93
  binoculars of, *pic 23*
  body of, 394
  captain of *H. L. Hunley*, 207
  despair at inactivity, 290–93
  gold coin replicas, 396–97
  jewelry from, *pic 23*
  lantern, *pic 18*
  letter to William Alexander, 357
  permission to relaunch the
    H. L. Hunley, 217, 243–44
  pocket watch of, *pic 26*, *pic 27*
  story of the gold coin, 93–94, 293,

394–96
suicide pact with William Alexander,
288
Dixon's lantern, *pic 18*
Doyle, Frank, 168, 173
drowning boys, rescue of, 32–33
Dry Tortugas, 229
Dudley, William, 226, 260, 409
Duke University project, 229

East Bay Street, 408
East Carolina University, 73
East Gulf Blockading Squadron, 119
Ebaugh, David C., 203
Edgerton, Doc Harold, 42, 43, 44
Elizabeth River, 108
Emancipation Proclamation, 124
Engine 51, 145
English Channel, 101, 109
Enoch Train, description of, 53
Etiwan, 171
Evening Post, 45
expansion strake, 388

Farragut, Adm. David, 66, 67, 86
Fifth Avenue, 76
Fifty-fourth, black troops, 137
Fifty-fourth Massachusetts, 391
fire-rafts, 52
Firmey, Tim, 73, 80
First Military District, 355
Firth of Forth, 384
fish-boat, 63, 130, 172
painting by R. G. Skerrett, 382
fish torpedo boat, 161
Flamborough Head, 36, 39
Flamborough Head, Battle of, 35
Flemming, Robert, 327–28, 334–35,
365, 401, 402
Flett, Jimmy, 38, 102, 109, 110
Flirt, 92
Florida, 106
salvage rights to, 108
sinking of, 107
Folly Beach, 149
Fonda, Jane, 296

Foote, Shelby, 386
Fort Jackson, attack of, 66
Fort Johnson, 172, 279, 299
Fort Johnson docks, 170, 174
Fort Morgan, 96, 99
Fort Moultrie, 161, 278, *279*, 350, 371
Fort St. Philips, attack of, 66
Fort Sullivan, attempted capture of, 31
Fort Sumter, 49, 54, 59, 78, 151, 174,
240, 278, 320, 321, 350, 371, 407
attack on, 321, 356
Fort Sumter and Wagner, letter to
evacuate, 165
Fraser and Co., 169
Fredericksburg, 251
French, Capt. Henry, 51
French Navy, 61, 103, 110–11
denial of permit and, 102
Friends of the *Hunley*, 233, 258, 264,
297, 414
Front Levee Street, 61
Fuji, 304
Fulton, Robert, 60–61, 63

Gaines, 87
Gates, Rev. W. B., 215
General Polk, 249
General Services Administration, 225
claims to the *H. L. Hunley*, 222
Geometrics marine magnetometer, 183
George Street, 295
Georgiana, 322
German submarine (*U-20*), 109
German U-boats, search for, 109
Gettysburg (Pennsylvania), battle at,
125, 133
Gifford, Henry S., 329
Gift, Lt. George Washington, 138
Gillmore, Brig. Gen. Quincy, 165
Giordano, Al, 71
Glassell, Lt. William T., 203–4
Glory, 391
Government Yards, 62
Governor Moore, 104
Grant, Maj. Gen. Ulysses S., 93, 125,
373

Great Trauma of 1980, 41, 46
Green, Capt. J. F., 361
Green Bay Packers, 258
Gressette, Marion, 219–20
Gronquist, Wayne, 38, 42, 48, 102, 111
guerrilla warfare, Confederate, 52
Gulf Coast Blockading Squadron, 86, 96
gun boats, 104

Hall, Wes, 144, 147, *189*, 267
    search for *H. L. Hunley*, 181, 186–88
Hampton Roads, 48, 65, 87, 97, 106
Hampton Roads, Battle of, 251
Harper's Weekly, 382, 383
Hasiltine, Ensign E. L., 334
Hasker, Lt. Charles, 170, 173, 381
    account of escape from the
      H. L. Hunley, 171–72
Hatch, Francis, 59, 85, 91, 130
Hazzard, John, 233, 352
Head of Passes, 51
Heckle and Jeckle, 47
Hickman Field, 70
Higginson, Lt. F. J., 321, 330, 331,
    332–33, 363
H. L. Hunley, 19, 31, 42, 46, 151–53
    150th anniversary of, 417–18
    1981 expedition, 72–84
    absence noticed, 354–55
    arrival in Charleston, 161
    artifacts from, *pic 8*, *pic 11*, *pic 14*,
      pic 18, *pic 20*, *pic 21*, *pic 22*, *pic*
      23, *pic 24*, *pic 25*, *pic 26*, *pic 27*,
      396
    attack method, 403
    attack of the USS *Housatonic*,
      327–35, 417
    descriptions of, 361–67
    bow from, *pic 14*
    Canandaigua collision theory, 401–2,
      404
    canteens from, *pic 21*
    captain's station, *pic 7*
    claims on, 197–98, 199
    claims to, 219–23
    conservation of, *pic 8*

crew, 248–55
crew, burial of, *pic 32*, 175, 215–17,
    226, *266*, 266, 299–300, 305–6,
    351, 407–11
crew, final, *pic 15*, *pic 16–17*, *pic 32*,
    306, 351, 387, 389, 390
crew, first, 265–67, 298, 351
crew, second, 300
crew compartment, *pic 9*, 387
crew of, 168
demonstration of, 209–12
departure for Charleston, 137–38
design faults, 287
design of, 307–8, 397–98
disappearance of, 32
discoveries about the, 397–404
Dixon's gold coin, *pic 20*
Dixon's lantern, *pic 18*
fear for safety of, 194–97, 223,
    297–98
floating mine incident and, 254
General Services Administration
    claims to, 222
honor guard, *pic 5*
housing of, 273, 300–301
hull breach, *pic 7*
Internet views of recovery work, 393
journey to Charleston, 159
launch date, 132
lift day for, 344–48
locating, 187–88
location of, 226–27
model of, *386*, 386
mysteries of, 397–403
National Geographic documentaries
    on, 416
offer to purchase the, 169
official confirmation, 229–30
operation of, 134–35
painting of, 246, 247
permission to attack, 253
permission to relaunch, 217, 243–44
picture of, *pic 28*
preservation efforts and, *pic 28–30*
private vessel, 222
propeller from, *pic 14*

raising of, 174–75
raising of the *H. L. Hunley*, 213–14,
    307–9, 314–18
  cost of, 230, 232–33, 262
  discussions about, 261–62
  fears of, 269–70
  plans for, 268–73, 298, 302–4
recovery of, *pic 1*, *pic 2*, *pic 3*, *pic 4*
recovery of spar, 309–11
rehabilitation of, 244–46, 248, 382–83
replica of, 78
rudder of, *pic 10*
salvage rights to, 46, 222
search for, 32, 39–40, 69, 144, 145,
    146–48, 384–85, 385
search for, plans for new, 224–25
seizure of, 168
shoes from, *pic 24*
sinking of, 171–72, 210–12, 215, 242
  possible reasons for, 404–6
size of, 230
sketches of, 246–47
South Carolina claim to, 219–23
spoils of war, 197, 221
stalactites in, 400
stories about, 43, 173–74, 231, 337,
    358, 364, 376, 381, 390–91
surface of, *pic 31*
television movie about, 261, 262–64,
    295
testing of, 253–55, 284–85
test of submersion limits, 288–89
torpedo remnants, *pic 12*
tours of, 392, 411–12
upright image, *pic 6*
videotaping of, 192
William Alexander sketches, *127*,
    228, 263
HMS *Hawke*, 109
HMS *Pathfinder*, 101
Holickan, J. W., 323, 365
Holland, John P., 272, 380
Hollings, Sen. Fritz, 272
Holocaust Museum, 412
Horne Brothers Shipyard Dock, 107
Howard, Ensign C. W., 202

Hunley, Horace Lawson, *57*, 56–61, 68
  arms supplies and, 59
  arrival in Alabama, 85, 87
  concerns about the *H. L. Hunley*,
      163–64
  death of, 212
  failed Cuban trip, 59–60
  funeral for, 215–16
  grave of, 200, 300
  headstone of, *pic 5*
  last will, 128–29
  Pioneer's letter of marque and, 66
  request for return for *H. L. Hunley*,
      176
  submarine boats and, 62, 91, 98
  Vicksburg trip, 128
  views about the Confederacy, 59
Hunley, John, 57
Hunley, Louisa Lawson, 56
Hunley, Volumnia, 56, 58–59, 92
Hunley Commission, 220, 221, 225,
    258, 273
  credit for discovering the
      H. L. Hunley, 231–32
Hunley Commission's museum, 412
Hunley Museum, proposals for, 412
Hunley Project, 413
Hunley project, management structure
    for, 260–61, 264
Hunley's bow, *pic 14*
Hurricane Alberto, 316
Hurricane Hugo, 148, 183

Iberville Historical Society (Louisiana),
    382
Iceberg (Cussler), 35
Inca Gold (Cussler), 179
Indian Chief, 208, 210, 248, 278, 279,
    357
Institute of Archeology and
    Anthropology, 40, 43, 69
Intelligent Whale, 272–73
ironclad ships, 65
  building of, 119
  destruction of, 79–80, 372
  development of, 56

CSS *Manassas*, 104
in Mobile, Alabama, 86–87
Tennessee, 97
USS *Carondelet*, 106
wreckages of, 375
Isle of Palms, 31, 76

Jackson, Andrew, 57
Jacobsen, Maria, *pic 8*, *pic 19*, *pic 26*,
    302, 387, 388, 394
James Island, 170, 372
Jefferson Davis, 19, 293
John Fraser & Co., 161, 203
Johnson Hagood Stadium, 265, 298
John Street depot, 239, 242
Jones, John Paul, 34–35
Jones Act, 313
Jordan, Thomas, 243, 246, 357

K-129, 270
Karlissa B, *pic 2*, 313, 314, 338, 417
Kelly, George, 329
Kelly, John, 168, 173
Kelly, Thomas H., 329
Keltic Lord, 36, 37, 38
Kemprecos, Paul, 267
Keokuk, 49, 50, 74, 75, 375
Kiawah Island, 235
King Street hotel, 245
Kiowa Creek (Colorado), 145
Korean War, 35
Koski-Karell, Dan, 32–33, 42
Kozak, Garry, 145
Kropf, Schuyler, 417
Kurt Austin (fictional character), 267

La Fourche Parish, 56
Lake, Simon, 380–81, 383
    submarine designs of, 384
Lake Moultrie, 263
Lake Pontchartrain, 64, 87, 375
Lasch, Donna, 235, 317
Lasch, Warren, *pic 1*, *pic 2*, *pic 4*,
    pic 13, *pic 26*, 234–238, 257–59,
    296, 318, 337, 403, 409–10
chairmanship of the Friends of the

Hunley, 237
fund-raising efforts, 296
gold coin, 295
personal price, 414, 416
resignation of, 415–16
Leader, Jonathan, 222, 265, 297, 299
Lee, Francis D., 243–44
Lee, Gen. Robert E., 125, 133, 373
Leeds Foundry, 62
Leopoldville, 112, 114
location of, 113
war memorial, call for, 114
Leovy, Henry, 58, 62, 128, 216, 301,
    358–59
Pioneer's letter of marque and, 66
letter of marque, for *Pioneer*, 66
Lexington, 108–9
artifacts from, 109
Lincoln, Abraham, 124, 125
"Little Devil," 353, 355
L. Marion Gressette Building, 219
Lombardi, Vince, 258
Long Island, 76, 282, 283, 322
Long Island Sound, 109
Lookout Mountain, 179
looting claims, NUMA crew and, 108
Lorrence, 252
Louisiana, 104
Louisiana State Museum, 375
Lumpkin (*Hunley* crew member),
    pic 16, 251–52
Lusitania, 109
Lyons, Thomas, 89
ammunition manufacturing and, 89

MacDonald, John D., 35
Maffitt's Channel, 151, 154, 183, 194,
    196, 356
magnetometer targets, 48
Magnolia Cemetery, 199, 215, 226,
    265, 300, 306, 408, 415
burial ground (*Hunley* sailors), *pic 5*
Maillefert, Benjamin, 222, 378
Mallory, Stephen, 97–98
Manchester Island, 106
Mardikian, Paul, *pic 12*, *pic 13*, 302,

308, 349, 387, 400, 402, 404, 413
Mariners' Museum (Newport News), 108, 412
Maritime Center, 350
Marshall, John, 206
Marsh Battery, 166
Martin Luther King Jr. Day, 220
Maury, Gen. Dabney H., 87–89, 88, 135, 159
Maury, Matthew Fontaine, 87, 121
Mayer Jr., Asst. Engineer C. F., 365
McClintock, James, 61–65, 62, 67, 68
  American Diver, 98
  arrival in Alabama, 85, 87
  arrival in Charleston, 161
  bullet making venture, 61
  complaints against, 167
  death of, 377–78
  electromagnetic engine, visions of, 90, 121
  end of tenure as captain, 166
  fake, 378
  meeting with British, 377
  refusal to train crew, 169
  submarine design and, 90–91, 119–20, 121–24
  third model, 131–35
  training of crew, 162
McConnell, Glenn, *pic 1, pic 2, pic 4, pic 26,* 198–99, 219–22, 226, 232, 337–38, 408
  Civil War–themed gift shop, 236
  personal price, 413–14, 416
  raising of the *H. L. Hunley*
    fund-raising efforts, 271–72
  television movie about *H. L. Hunley*, 263, 264, 297
McConnell, Sam, 236
McConnell's Sons of Confederate Veterans (SCV) camp, 221
McHugh, Charles, 206
McLaurin, Col. D. W., 325, 353
McLean House, 373
The Mediterranean Caper (Cussler), 35, 71
Meeting Street, 199

Merrimack, 97, 108
  conversion to ironclad ship, 65
  metal preservation technique, 413
Middleton, Susan, 358
Midway or Wake Island, 71
Military Air Transport Service, 70
Miller (*Hunley* crew member), *pic 17, 252*
Minnesota, 65
Mississippi, 105
Mississippi River, wreckages of, 104
Mobile, Alabama, effect of war on economy, 120
Mobile Bay, 85, 95, 96
  need to monitor, 119
Mobile Grays, 20, 92
  Confederacy and, 93
Montgomery, Jenkins, 340, 343, 345–47
Morgan, 87
Morris Island, 48, 49, 74, 380, 391
  attack on, 159, 166, 319
  invasion of, 137, 240
Motorola, 69
  positioning equipment, 72–73
Motorola Mini-ranger, 150–51
Mount Pleasant, 74, 244, 255, 278, 280, 412
Mount Pleasant Holiday Inn, 146, 194
"murder" machine, 206
Murphy, Larry, 229, 230
Muzzey, Charles, 330, 334

Napoleon, 60–61
Nasanen, Liisa, *pic 28*
Nashville, 87
National Geographic, 342, 416
National Park Service, 306
National Park Service's Submerged Cultural Resources Unit (SCRU), 227, 268–69
National Underwater and Marine Agency (NUMA), 34, 38, 69, 101, 418. *See also* NUMA
Nautilus, 385
Nautilus submarine, 195
Naval Court of Inquiry, 361, 401

Naval Historical Center, 221, 225, 226, 227, 258, 409
Naylor, Carl, 147
New Basin Canal, 62, 64, 67, 374
Newell, Mark, 146, 151, 154, 183, 194
  claims of locating *H. L. Hunley*, 155–56
  relieved of duties, 198
New Ironsides, 161, 168, 203, 253, 281
New Orleans
  Confederacy cause and, 53–54
  fall of, 68
New Orleans' Jackson Square, 375
New Orleans Picayune, 374
New York Times, 103, 193–94
Neyland, Bob, *pic 4*, 226, 258–59, 301
  Hunley project and, 264
Night Probe! (Cussler), 69
Norfolk Naval Museum, 108
Normandy Beach, 306
Norseman, 83
North Carolina
  economic development of, 413
  H. L. Hunley Museum project proposal, 413
North Sea, 36, 109
North Sea expeditions, 42
nuclear submarine, French, testing of, 115
NUMA, 69, 101
  1994 expedition, 146–50. *See also* National Underwater and Marine Agency (NUMA)
  credit for discovering the *H. L. Hunley*, 231–32
  crew, 72, 102, 107
  French bureaucracy and, 110–14
  locating the *H. L. Hunley*, 191
NUMA expedition, fifth, 104
NUMA Files (Cussler), 267
Oceaneering International, 230–31, 268
Ohio River, 106
Our Valiant Few (van Wyck), 384
Owsley, Doug, *pic 16–17*

Pacific Vortex! (Cussler), 103

Palmetto State, 79, 172, 173, 372
Park, Thomas, 89
  ammunition manufacturing and, 89
Park, Thomas W., 177, 206, 210
Park and Lyons Machine Shop, 99
Parker, Theodore, 334
Parrott, Robert Parker, 207
Parrott gun, 166, 207
Passailaigue, Sen. Ernie, 199, 221, 231
Patapsco, 75, 375
Pathfinder, 109, 384
Patriot's Point, 412
Patterson, Joseph, 206
Payne, Lt. John, 168, 173, 175
  H. L. Hunley, command of, 168
  H. L. Hunley, relief of command of, 176–77
Pearl Harbor, 229, 262
Pearman and Grace bridges, 80
Pecorelli, Harry, 152–53, 181, *189*, *195*, *196*, 267, 302, 306, 317
  lift day and, 342
  locating the *H. L. Hunley*, 186–88
  search for *H. L. Hunley*, 185–86
peripatetic coffin, 206, 248, 306
Pickering, Capt. Charles, 323, 329–30, 331, 333–34
  testimony of, 366
Pier Juliet, 351
Pioneer, 63–68, 68, 374, 375
  design faults, 121
  improvement on, 90
  life-size model of, 273
  scuttling of, 67–68
  Union troops and, 68
Pioneer II, 92, 347
pipes, smoking, artifacts from the *H. L. Hunley*, *pic 22*
Pittsburg Landing (Tennessee), 93
Plant, William T., 329
Polaris Submarine Fleet, 385
Port Hudson, 105
Port Royal (South Carolina), 126
Port Royal, Battle of, 293
Post and Courier, 224
Potomac River, 126

Project Azorian, 270

Quagmire, Horace P., 71
Quinn, Rep. Rick, 221

Raccoon, 77, 83
Raise the Titanic!, 48
Raise the Titanic (Cussler), 34
Raising the Hunley (Cussler & Kropf),
  417
Rappahannock River, 251
Rattle Snake, 83
Reconstruction, 40
Redcoats, 31
Redevelopment Authority (RDA), 301
reporters, practical joke on, 78–79
Revolutionary War, 31, 57, 60
Rhett Jr., Robert Barnwell, 200, 239,
  358
Ridgaway, Joseph, pic 17, 250, 253,
  293, 389, 391
Riley, Joe, 412
Ripley, Brig. Gen. Roswell S., 355
RMS Lusitania, 384
Robinson, Neil, 234
Robinson, William, 168, 171
Rochelle, Capt. James Henry, 277
Royal Alfred, 377
Ruby, 77, 83
Ruffin, Edmund, 175

Sahara, 144
salvage rights, claims of, 46
Sand Island, 96
Sanford, Mark, 197
"Save the Hunley" fund, 233
Schachte, William, 221, 234, 259, 296
  raising of the H. L. Hunley
    fund-raising efforts, 271–72
Schob, Walt, 37, 41, 45, 73, 81, 146
schools, desegregation of, 219–20
SCIAA boat, diving equipment on, 72
Scott, John K., 64, 66
SCUBA diving, Clive Cussler and, 70
The Sea Dwellers (Cussler), 103
Sea Hunt, 143

The Sea Hunters (Cussler & Dirgo), 180
Seaman's Bethel Church, 128, 130
Seaman's Burial Ground, 174, 175,
  299, 300
Seaman's Protection Certificate, 250
secession
  reasons for, 54
  views against, 59
Second National Flag of the
  Confederacy, 306
Secretary of the Navy, 108, 359
Senate Armed Services Committee, 225
Senate Judiciary Committee, 220
Serpent (Cussler & Kemprecos), 267
Seventh Regiment of Connecticut
  Volunteers, 390
Shea, Bill, 32–33, 38, 42, 49, 73, 81,
  102, 109
  sea sickness and, 143
Shem Creek, 252
Sherman, 371–72
Shiloh, 20, 89
Shiloh, Battle of, 93
Shipp, George, 279, 280
Shock Wave (Cussler), 179, 223
Siege of Charleston, 166, 168
Simons, Robert Bentham, 384
Singer, Edgar C., 98–99, 120, 169
Singer, Isaac Merrit, 98
Slade, C. P., 327, 328, 330, 363
Slaughter, Gen. James, 135
slavery
  ending of in Confederate States, 124
  Southern economy and, 54
slaves, needed as help against attack, 160
Smith, Angus, 175, 213–14, 317, 378
  locating the H. L. Hunley, 378–79
Smith, Gardner, 216
Smith, James, 379
Smith, Rev. Franklin, 60
Smithsonian Institute, 221
  H. L. Hunley, claims to, 197
Smythe, Augustine, 172, 381
Sons of Confederate Veterans, 199, 224
Sons of Confederate Veterans camp,
  divers from, 147

South Atlantic Blockading Squadron,
   68, 75, *138*, 201, 255, 282, 287,
   319, 321, 328
   warnings about torpedo boats, 281–82
South Carolina
   claims on *H. L. Hunley*, 199
   secession of, 54
South Carolina coast, 31
South Carolina Confederate soldier
   remains, fight for, 199, 220
South Carolina Institute of Archaeology
   and Anthropology (SCIAA), 144,
   146, 198, 224, 227, 232, 258, 261,
   298
Southern Navy, lack of, 55
Southern ports, blockage of, 55
Spence, Floyd, 272
Sprague, Charles, 169, 170, 209
SS *Leopoldville*, 101–2, 103
Stanton, Lt. C. L., 170, 210, 323
State Ports Authority, 234
Steak Boat, 74, 81
stealth boats, 201–3, 253–54
Stem Creek, 278
St. John's River, 359
Stone Fleet, 80, 375
Stonewall Jackson, 76, 83, 283
Stono River, 174
St. Philip's Church, 149, 245
submarine boats, design of, 60
submarines
   early design, 60–61, 62–65, 374–75
   Pioneer, 63, 68
   testing of, 63–64
   financing for, 99
   fish-boat, 63
   Intelligent Whale, 272–73
   iron, 42
   modern, 381
   refitting of, 384
   second model, 90–91
      financing for, 91, 98
   third model, 99, 119–20
   for the U.S. Navy, 380–81
   Yankee test runs, 126
submarines, iron, 39

Submarine Warfare, 60
Sullivan's Island, 31, 74, 263, 278, 282,
   322, 350, 380
Summey, Keith, 412
Sutherland, Donald, 263, 297
Swamp Angel, 166, 207
Sweet Sue, 74

Tennessee, 87, 97
Ternisien, Virginie, *pic 29*
Texas A&M, 301
Theatre Street dock, 133
Thompson, Bill, 42
Thompson Gravel Pit, Old, 105
Throckmorton, Peter, 36, 38
Thurmond, Strom, 225, 272, 313
Timeout Boats, 32, 46
Titanic, 302
Titan Maritime Industries, 313
Toft, Bob, 73
Toler's Cove, 74
Tomb, J. H., 204, 210, 253
torpedo boat, deserter's model of, 281
"Tower of Babble" conference, 258
Town Creek, 278
Travis McGee, 35
Tredegar Iron Works, 375
Trenholm, 172
Turner, Ted, 260, 296–97
Turtle, 60
TWA Flight 800, wreckage of, 269
Twenty-first Alabama Infantry
   Regiment, 89, 93, 284, 292, 395
Twenty-first Alabama Volunteers, 356
Twenty-third South Carolina Volunteer,
   325

U-12, 109
U-20, 101, 114, 384
U-21, 101, 109, 110, 383
U-9, 109
U-Boats, 101, 109, 110, 114, 283, 384
Underwater Archaeological Joint
   Ventures, 107
underwater explosives, 99

Union Army, 93
Union blockade, attack of, 51–53
Union camp, remains of, 149
Union fleet
    attack of Fort Jackson, 66
    attack of Fort St. Philips, 66
Union Navy, 280
    defense against torpedo boats, 360–61
Union Navy buttons, *pic 24*
Union Navy frigate, 105
Union Navy's Gulf Coast Blockading
    Squadron, 67
Union Pier, 80
United States, entry into World War I,
    384
University of Wales, 37
U.S. Air Force, 35
U.S. Atlantic Mine Force, 384
U.S. Embassy, 111
U.S. General Services Administration,
    198
U.S. Maritime Administration, 314
U.S. Mint, 396
U.S. Navy, 55, 282, 321, 367
    H. L. Hunley, claims to, 197
    submarines for, 380–81
U.S. Navy fleet, attack of, 65
U.S. Navy's submarine rescue system,
    270
U.S. News and World Report, report of
    Civil War vessels found, 49
USS *Alligator*, submarine, early design
    of, 125–26
USS *Arizona*, 229, 262
USS *Cairo*, 269, 270, 309
USS *Canandaigua*, 333, 334, 359, 401
USS *Carondelet*, 106
USS *Congress*, 250
USS *Cumberland*, 106, 107
    salvage rights to, 108
U.S. Secretary of the Navy, 119
USS *Essex*, 104
USS *Holland*, 383
USS *Housatonic*, 42, 320, 322, 355
    attack of, 327–35
    crew, exoneration of, 367

crew of, 323, 359
findings of investigation, 366–68
investigation into sinking of, 361–68
job of, 75, 321–22
reward for sinking, 359
salvage rights to, 46, 222
sinking of, 39
Smith, Angus and, 379
wreckage of, 45, 184, 373–74, 376,
    378, 380
USS *Hunley*, 385
USS *Intrepid*, 114
USS *Memphis*, 368
USS *Mississippi*, 67
USS *Monitor*, 65, 97, 107, 187, 225,
    229, 269, 411
USS *Monitor* vs CSS *Virginia*, 65–66
USS *New Ironside*, 201
USS *Pensacola*, 67
USS *Preble*, 51, 52
USS *Richmond*, 51, 56
    attack of, 51–52
USS *Sumpter*, 126
USS *Wabash*, 161, 253, 282, 286–87,
    359, 361
USS *Yorktown*, 350

ValuJet crash, wreckage of, 269
Vanderbilt, Cornelius, 108
Vanderbilt Museum (Long Island), 109
van Wyck, F., 384
Varuna, 104
Verne, Jules, 376
Vicksburg (Mississippi), 86, 91, 104,
    125, 128
Vicksburg National Military Park, 269
Vielby Beach, 109
Vincennes, 52

Walsh, John, 334
War Between the States, 250, 261
    end of, 373
    relics, search for, 33
    toll of, 125
War Between the States (Foote), 386
Warren, Rodney, 81

Warren Lasch Conservation Center,
  pic 5, 317, 351, 411, 413
  tours of, 392, 411–12
Washington Light Infantry, 163
Washington Post, 114
Water Street, 133
Water Witch, 52
Watson, Baxter, 62, 124, 136
  arrival in Alabama, 85, 87
  arrival in Charleston, 137
  bullet making venture, 61
Watts, Gordon, 186, 225
Weehawken, 49, 50, 74, 75, 375
  wreckage of, 378
Welles, Gideon, 119, 359, 360
West, Wilson, 80
West Ashley, 236
Whitlock, Leonard, 229, 268, 312, 338,
  351
Whitney, B. A. "Gus," 99, 124, 128, 136
  arrival in Charleston, 137
  death of, 205
  duties on third model, 162
  request for leniency, 167–68
Wicks, James, *pic 16*, 250–51, 290,
  293, 326, 388
Wignall, Sidney, 36
Wilbanks, Frances, 151, 182, 190
Wilbanks, Ralph, 43, 45, 47, 72, 74,
  81–82, 143–44, 146–47, *189*, 267,
  306, *318*, 409, 415
  fear for safety of *H. L. Hunley*, 224
  lift day and, 341
  locating the *H. L. Hunley*, 187–88
  as practical joker, 78–79
  search for *H. L. Hunley*, 156–57,
  180–83
  visit to *H. L. Hunley* site, 227, 317–18
Willey, Henry, 291
Williams, Absolum, 168, 173, 300
Williams, John, 334
World War I, 37, 101, 384
World War II, 101, 102, 384, 412
World War II artifacts, 306
wreckages
  artifacts from, 108, 109, 269

Civil War, 229
  locating, 74–75
  preservation efforts and, 108
  salvage rights to, 108
  U-boat targets, 37
  U.S. Navy claims to, 108
Wright, Steve, 339, 344–45
W. R. King, 59

Yazoo River, 249, 269
Young, Judge Advocate James B.,
  361–62

Zodiac, 31, 42